Minerva's Night Out

Minerva's Night Out

Philosophy, Pop Culture,
and Moving Pictures

Noël Carroll

WILEY Blackwell

This edition first published 2013
© 2013 Blackwell Publishing Ltd

Blackwell Publishing was acquired by John Wiley & Sons, in February 2007. Blackwell's publishing program has been merged with Wiley's global Scientific, Technical, and Medical business to form Wiley-Blackwell.

Registered Office
John Wiley & Sons, Ltd, The Atrium, Southern Gate, Chichester, West Sussex, PO19 8SQ, UK

Editorial Offices
350 Main Street, Malden, MA 02148-5020, USA
9600 Garsington Road, Oxford, OX4 2DQ, UK
The Atrium, Southern Gate, Chichester, West Sussex, PO19 8SQ, UK

For details of our global editorial offices, for customer services, and for information about how to apply for permission to reuse the copyright material in this book please see our website at www.wiley.com/wiley-blackwell.

The right of Noël Carroll to be identified as the author of this work has been asserted in accordance with the UK Copyright, Designs and Patents Act 1988.

Library of Congress Cataloging-in-Publication Data
Carroll, Noël, 1947–
   Minerva's night out : philosophy, pop culture, and moving pictures / Noël Carroll.
      pages   cm
   Includes bibliographical references and index.
   ISBN 978-1-4051-9389-4 (pbk.) – ISBN 978-1-4051-9390-0 (hardback)
   1. Motion pictures–Philosophy.   I. Title.
   PN1995.C35575 2013
   791.4301–dc23
                                             2013018957
A catalogue record for this book is available from the British Library.

Cover image: Popcorn © Christopher Carder / istockphoto; Composition with cinema symbols © elapela / istockphoto; Abstract cinema background © PixelEmbargo / istockphoto; Superstar Background © Matthew Hertel / istockphoto; Hegel © Classic Image / Alamy
Cover design by Simon Levy, www.simonlevy.co.uk

Set in 10.5/13pt Sabon by SPi Publisher Services, Pondicherry, India
Printed in Malaysia by Ho Printing (M) Sdn Bhd

1   2013

To Kayla Carroll Downes
For the future

Contents

Acknowledgments

The author and publisher gratefully acknowledge the permission granted to reproduce the copyright material in this book:

Chapter 1. "The Ontology of Mass Art," *Journal of Aesthetics and Art Criticism* 55(2) (1997): 187–99.

Chapter 2. "Modernity and the Plasticity of Perception," *Journal of Aesthetics and Art Criticism* 59(1) (2001): 11–17.

Chapter 3. "On the Ties that Bind: Characters, the Emotions, and Popular Fictions," in William Irwin and Jorge Gracia (eds.), *Philosophy and the Interpretation of Popular Culture* (Lanham, MD: Rowman & Littlefield, 2007), pp. 89–116.

Chapter 4. "Character, Social Information, and the Challenge of Psychology," in Garry Hagberg (ed.), *Fictional Characters, Real Characters: The Search for Ethical Content in Literature* (Oxford: Oxford University Press, forthcoming).

Chapter 5. "Movies, the Moral Emotions, and Sympathy," *Midwest Studies in Philosophy* 34(1) (2010): 1–19.

Chapter 6. "The Problem with Movie Stars," in Scott Walden (ed.), *Photography and Philosophy* (Malden, MA: Wiley-Blackwell, 2008), pp. 248–64.

Chapter 7. "Narrative," in Paisley Livingston and Carl Plantinga (eds.), *The Routledge Companion to Philosophy and Film* (London: Routledge, 2009), pp. 207–16.

Chapter 8. "Narration," in Paisley Livingston and Carl Plantinga (eds.), *The Routledge Companion to Philosophy and Film* (London: Routledge, 2009), pp. 196–206.

Chapter 9. "Psychoanalysis and the Horror Film," in Steven Jay Schneider (ed.), *Horror Film and Psychoanalysis: Freud's Worst Nightmare* (Cambridge: Cambridge University Press, 2004), pp. 257–70.

Chapter 10. "Philosophical Insight, Emotion, and Popular Fiction: The Case of *Sunset Boulevard*," in Noël Carroll and John Gibson (eds.), *Narrative, Emotion, and Insight* (University Park, PA: Penn State University Press, 2011), pp. 45–68.

Chapter 11. "*Vertigo* and the Pathologies of Romantic Love," in David Baggett and William A. Drumin (eds.), *Hitchcock and Philosophy* (Chicago: Open Court, 2007), pp. 101–13.

Chapter 12. "What Mr. Creosote Knows about Laughter," in Gary L. Hardcastle and George A. Reisch (eds.), *Monty Python and Philosophy* (Chicago: Open Court, 2006), pp. 25–35.

Chapter 13. "*Memento* and the Phenomenology of Comprehending Motion Picture Narration," in Andrew Kania (ed.), *Memento* (London: Routledge, 2009), pp. 127–46.

Chapter 14 "Tales of Dread in *The Twilight Zone*: A Contribution to Narratology," in Noël Carroll and Lester Hunt (eds.), *Philosophy in "The Twilight Zone"* (Oxford: Wiley-Blackwell, 2009), pp. 26–38.

Chapter 15. "Sympathy for the Devil," in Richard Greene and Peter Vernezze (eds.), *The Sopranos and Philosophy* (Chicago: Open Court, 2004), pp. 121–36.

Chapter 16. "Consuming Passion: *Sex and the City*," *Revue internationale de philosophie* 64(254) (2010): 525–46.

Chapter 17. "*Art* and Friendship," *Philosophy and Literature* 26(1) (2002): 199–206.

Chapter 18. "Martin McDonagh's *The Pillowman*, or The Justification of Literature," *Philosophy and Literature* 35(1) (2011): 168–81.

Chapter 19. "The Fear of Fear Itself: The Philosophy of Halloween," in Richard Greene and K. Silem Mohammad (eds.), *Zombies, Vampires, and Philosophy* (Chicago: Open Court, 2010), pp. 223–35.

Chapter 20. "The Grotesque Today: Preliminary Notes toward a Taxonomy," in Frances S. Connelly (ed.), *Modern Art and the Grotesque* (Cambridge: Cambridge University Press, 2003), pp. 291–311.

Chapter 21. "Andy Kaufman and the Philosophy of Interpretation," in Michael Krausz (ed.), *Is There a Single Right Interpretation?* (University Park, PA: Penn State University Press, 2002), pp. 319–44.

Every effort has been made to trace copyright holders and to obtain their permission for the use of copyright material. The publisher apologizes for any errors or omissions in the above list and would be grateful if notified of any corrections that should be incorporated in future reprints or editions of this book.

Introduction

Philosophy and the Popular Arts

> As long as it is not frightfully bad, [a film] always provides me with food for thoughts and feelings.
>
> Ludwig Wittgenstein[1]

This volume represents a selection of my essays on philosophy and the popular arts – including philosophy of, in, and through various popular art forms. Motion pictures, my first love, have an especially prominent place in what follows. I have been particularly lucky that I became a philosopher at a moment when it became acceptable to engage with the popular arts theoretically. It would probably have been impossible for an analytic philosopher do so anytime before World War II and maybe even before the Vietnam War.

But for at least several decades now, within the precincts of anglophone philosophy, interests of various sorts in the popular arts have grown in every direction and at a fast pace as presently evidenced by whole book series devoted to philosophy and the popular arts, such as those published by Wiley-Blackwell and Open Court. Perhaps the phenomenon first gained a substantial foothold among English-speaking philosophers with respect to film, not merely art films, but mass market entries as well. Then popular music enlisted philosophical respect, followed by TV, and now the vista is wide open, countenancing everything from comics and talent shows to video games.

Speaking from the perspective of the United States, this seems to be a predictable outcome of certain demographic trends. The post-World War II baby boomers as a group – of which I am a card-carrying member – were probably more involved with the mass, popular arts than any other previous generation. Owing to things like television and portable radios, for example, we have had

Minerva's Night Out: Philosophy, Pop Culture, and Moving Pictures, First Edition. Noël Carroll.
© 2013 Blackwell Publishing Ltd. Published 2013 by Blackwell Publishing Ltd.

more access to mass art than the preceding generations and, in all likelihood, more leisure time to pursue it as well.

We have been immersed in mass art. If Homer, despite Plato's deprecations, was the educator of the Greeks, mass art was the educator of the Americans, or at least those of my generation (and those that followed). Thus, it should have come as no surprise that we took our *first*, so to say, common culture very seriously. Surely, that is one of the reasons that when we came of age we were so invested in expanding the study of what was effectively our lingua franca. And, of course, nothing that stood so squarely in the center of our culture could escape the notice of philosophy. Our students and then theirs have benefited our obsessions with mass entertainments which have permitted them to write dissertations on topics that would never have been admitted into academia before the Vietnam War.

Among the mass arts that commanded the attention of the baby boomers, the moving image was among the most powerful, perhaps because constant reruns on TV of classic and not so classic Hollywood films gave us access to the tradition in a way that had not been available to the preceding generation. Moreover, our will to take movies in earnest was, by the time we were entering adolescence, given the intellectual wherewithal to make our wishes come true by several important developments, including the emergence of European and Japanese art films, which demonstrated that some films were worth taking seriously artistically, while the French auteur theory gave us the rhetoric to argue that some Hollywood films were among those movies worth taking seriously.

Thus, we began treating cinema with respect – by, among other things, inaugurating academic film departments – and, once the moving image became not only a legitimate topic of inquiry but a substantial one, cinema began to invite philosophical inquiry, serving as a runway off which the owl Minerva could take flight. The philosophical scrutiny of other mass arts ensued in short order.

Within the context of Anglo-American philosophy, one of the crucial figures who opened up the popular arts to philosophical interrogation was Stanley Cavell. By his own account, his reading of Wittgenstein's *Philosophical Investigations* liberated him through "its demonstration or promise that I can think philosophically about anything I want or have to think about."[2] Not only did Wittgenstein encourage Cavell's embrace of ordinary language philosophy. From thence Cavell became the philosophical apostle of the ordinary, of which the ordinary experience of the popular arts, most notably film, was an ordinary part of the American experience. From his chair in the Harvard philosophy department, Cavell's publications, including *The World Viewed* and *Pursuits of Happiness*, announced to the generation of his students and beyond that the popular arts were now a suitable topic of philosophy.[3]

Philosophical interest in the popular arts can take a number of different forms. I have entitled this introduction "Philosophy and the Popular Arts." But in truth the conjunction *and* masks a series of different relations describable by the prepositions "against," "in," "of," and "through."

Arguably, most of the encounters between philosophy and the popular arts – from Plato to Adorno – were of the order of the "philosophy against popular art" variety. The popular arts were charged with perpetrating all sorts of social diseases from undermining the state by arousing the emotions to maintaining the regime of capitalist system by stupefying the minds of the masses. Of the essays in this volume, my "Consuming Passion" comes closest to this category, although, unlike Plato and Adorno, I am not chastising *all* popular art, but only a specimen thereof, namely *Sex in the City.*

Under the rubric of philosophy in popular art, I include philosophical interpretations of popular artworks that maintain that a given work either illustrates or otherwise articulates some pre-existing philosophical idea as one might argue Chaplin's *Modern Times* illustrates Marx's notion of the alienation of labor or *The Matrix* serves to motivate Cartesian skepticism. In this volume the essay "*Art* and Friendship" exemplifies this tendency by discovering Aristotle's view of the highest form of friendship in Yasmina Reza's play.

The philosophy *of* popular art is a much more straightforward animal. It takes the popular arts and its various forms – movies, TV, theater and so forth – as its object of study. It probes the nature of such things as mass art in terms of the relationship of audiences to the characters of popular fictions, the nature of popular narratives and various popular genres and the structures therein, as well as the problems and paradoxes raised by the popular arts, including ethical ones. I reckon that more essays of this sort populate this collection than essays of any of the other categories in the philosophy and popular arts neighborhood.

The second largest group of essays in this volume probably belong to the category of philosophy through popular art. Roughly, this category regards the popular arts, or at least certain particular examples of popular art as capable of doing philosophy – as not only framing philosophical questions and inviting audiences to grapple with them, but also sometimes joining in the philosophical debate and advancing considerations on behalf of the philosophical conclusions they endorse.

Of course, not all philosophers believe that it is possible for any popular artwork to do philosophy, properly so called. So, whether the category of philosophy through popular art has any members is itself a philosophical question. This controversy has been staged most vociferously with respect to motion pictures. Thus the essays in this volume about motion pictures, including popular films and avant-garde ones, return to this question often. A range of different arguments and counter-arguments are raised both in terms of what I call popular philosophy, but also in terms of the level of philosophy we bandy about in our seminar rooms.

Because there are examples of all the various sorts of relationships between philosophy and popular art in this volume, and especially because there are mixtures thereof in individual essays, I thought that a more perspicuous way of organizing the text would be in virtue of the media and genres in which philosophy and the popular arts come together, rather than in terms of relationships as recounted above.

Hence, I begin with a section on "The Philosophy of Mass Art." The reason that I have started with mass art rather than popular art is because most of the popular art discussed in this book – indeed, most of the popular art consumed nowadays – is mass art (understood as a subcategory of popular art).

As previously mentioned, motion pictures probably comprise the domain of mass art that has attracted the most philosophical attention. For that reason, the next section of the volume concerns "The Philosophy of Motion Pictures." Within the larger category of motion pictures, I include not only mass market movies, but popular TV. Consequently, the next two sections of this book are "Philosophy and Popular Film" and "Philosophy and Popular TV."

Perhaps needless to say, not all popular art is mass art. Broadway theater is popular, but it is not available at multiple reception sites in the way a movie is. Nevertheless, mainstream theater is a place where philosophy and popular art meet, as in the case of *Copenhagen*, not to mention many of the plays of Bertolt Brecht and Tom Stoppard. Thus I have included a section on relations between theater and philosophy in which I look at Yasmina Reza's *Art* and Martin McDonagh's *The Pillowman*.

The last section in this volume is entitled "Philosophy across Popular Culture" because it takes up topics that sometimes cross not only the distinction between mass artworks and singular artworks, like stand-up comic performances, but as well practices of popular culture, like Halloween, that are not reducible to popular art.

Undoubtedly, these section headings are not as exclusive as they might be. To some degree, the choice of placing one article here rather than there may be arbitrary. Nevertheless, all the articles belong together. They all celebrate the way in which art stimulates the sort of pleasures that are associated with philosophy where philosophy itself is fun. In short, Minerva's nights out turn out to be like Minerva's nights in at work at home – a matter of entertaining ideas.

Notes

1 Ludwig Wittgenstein, *Public and Private Occasions*, trans. James Klagge and Alfred Nordman (Lanham, MD: Rowman and Littlefield, 2003), p. 97. Also cited by Béla Szabados and Christina Stojanova in "Introduction," *Wittgenstein at the Movies: Cinematic Investigations* (Lanham, MD: Lexington Books, 2011), p. ix.

2 Stanley Cavell, "Introductory Note to "The *Investigations'* Everyday Aesthetics of Itself," in John Glbson and Wolfgang Huemer (eds.), *The Literary Wittgenstein* (London: Routledge, 2004), p. 181. Also cited by Andrew Kleven in "Notes on Stanley Cavell and Film Criticism," in Havi Carel and Greg Tuck (eds.), *New Takes in Film-Philosophy*, (New York: Palgrave Macmillan, 2011), p. 62.

3 I have heard an anecdote, which is probably apocryphal, that Sartre became attracted to phenomenology when he learned that it would enable him to philosophize about a cocktail. This desire to philosophize about ordinary, contemporary experience, as manifested by Sartre and Cavell, has become rampant among the last three generations of American philosophers.

Section I

The Philosophy of Mass Art

1

The Ontology of Mass Art

If by "technology," we mean that which augments our natural powers, notably those of production, then the question of the relation of art to technology is a perennial one. However, if we have in mind a narrower conception of technology, one that pertains to the routine, automatic, mass production of multiple instances of the same product – be they cars or shirts – then the question of the relation of art to technology is a pressing one for our century. For in our century, especially, traffic with artworks has become increasingly mediated by *technologies* in the narrower (mass production/distribution) sense of the term. A technology in the broad sense is a prosthetic device that amplifies our powers.[1] In this respect, the technologies that mark the industrial revolution are prostheses of prostheses, augmenting the scope of our already enhanced powers of production and distribution through the automatization of our first-order technical means. Call such technologies "mass technologies." The development of mass technologies has augured an era of mass art, artworks incarnated in multiple instances and disseminated widely across space and time.

Nowadays it is commonplace to remark that we live in an environment dominated by mass art – dominated, that is, by television, movies, popular music (both recorded and broadcast), best-selling "blockbuster" novels, photography, and the like. Undoubtedly, this condition is most pronounced in the industrialized world, where mass art, or, if you prefer, mass entertainment, is probably the most common form of aesthetic experience for the largest number of people.[2] But mass art has also penetrated the nonindustrial world as well, to such an extent that in many places something like a global mass

"The Ontology of Mass Art," *Journal of Aesthetics and Art Criticism* 55(2) (1997): 187–99.

culture is coming to co-exist, as what Todd Gitlin has called a second culture, alongside indigenous, traditional cultures. Indeed, in some cases, this second culture may have even begun to erode the first culture in certain Third World countries. In any case, it is becoming increasingly difficult to find people anywhere in the world today who have not had some exposure to mass art as a result of the technologies of mass distribution.

Nor is any slackening of the grip of mass art likely. Even now, dreams of coaxial cable-feeds running into every household keep media moguls enthralled, while Hollywood produces movies at a fevered pace, not simply to sell on the current market, but also in order to stockpile a larder sufficient to satisfy the gargantuan appetites of the home entertainment centers that have been predicted to evolve in the near future. Intellectual properties of all sorts are being produced and acquired at a delirious pitch in the expectation that the envisioned media technologies to come will require a simply colossal amount of product to transmit. Thus, if anything, we may anticipate more mass art everywhere than ever before.

However, despite the undeniable relevance of mass art to aesthetic experience in the world as we know it, mass art has received scant attention in recent philosophies of art, which philosophies appear more preoccupied with contemporary high art, or, to label it more accurately, with contemporary avant-garde art. Given this lacuna, the purpose of the present paper is to draw the attention of philosophers of art to questions concerning mass art, a phenomenon that is already in the forefront of everyone else's attention.

The particular question that I would like to address here concerns the ontology of mass art – the question of the way in which mass artworks exist. Or, to put the matter differently, I shall attempt to specify the ontological status of mass artworks. However, before discussing the ontological status of mass artworks, it will be useful to clarify that which I take to be mass art. So, in what follows, I will first attempt to define necessary and sufficient conditions for membership in the category of mass art. Next, I shall introduce a theory about the ontological status of mass art. And finally, I will consider certain objections to my theories.

I. The definition of mass art

Perhaps the very first question that arises about my account of mass art concerns my reason for calling the phenomenon under analysis "mass art" rather than, say, "popular art."[3] My motivation in this regard is quite simple. "Popular art" is an ahistorical term. If we think of popular art as the art of the lower classes, then probably every culture in which class divisions have taken effect has had some popular art. On the other hand, if we think of popular art as art that many people in a given culture enjoy, then, it is to be hoped, every culture has some popular art. But what is called "mass art" has not existed everywhere throughout human history. The kind of art – of which movies, photography, and rock and roll provide ready examples – that surfeits contemporary culture has a certain historical specificity. It has arisen in the context of modern, industrial, mass society, and it is expressly designed for use by that society, employing, as it does, the characteristic productive forces of that society, viz., mass technologies, in order to deliver art to enormous consuming populations.

Mass art, unlike popular art *simpliciter*, is not the sort of art that might be found in any society. It is the art of mass, industrial society, and is designed for the purposes of such societies. Undoubtedly, though mass art is an historically specific category, one cannot date its advent with great precision. Mass society itself begins to emerge gradually with the evolution of capitalism, urbanization, and industrialization, and mass art develops in tandem, making an early appearance with such inaugural mass information technologies as the printing press, which itself made possible the popularization of nascent mass art genres such as the novel. As industrialization and the information technologies that are part and parcel of it expanded, photography, motion pictures, radio, telecommunications, and now computerization have been added to the printing press so that technologically produced and disseminated art has progressively become the mark of an epoch beginning at least since the late nineteenth century and continuing with exponentially rising intensity into the twenty-first century.

Mass art, in short, is designed for mass consumption. It is designed to be consumed by large numbers of people. This is because mass art makes possible the simultaneous consumption of the same artwork by audiences often divided by great distances. Vaudeville was a popular art, but it was not a mass art for the obvious reason that, on the vaudeville circuit, a W. C. Fields could only address one audience of a limited size in one theater at a time. However, when he translated his routines for the cinema, he could "play" on both sides of the tracks in Peoria, London, and even Philadelphia at the same time. As this example indicates, in refusing to label this phenomenon popular art, I do not deny that there is frequently an historical connection between popular art, broadly so-called, and mass art. Quite often, mass art evolves out of already existing popular art. Ballads, first disseminated through live performances and preserved in memory, in turn, give way to ballad sheets and sheet music, and, ultimately, evolve into records. Carnival freak shows perhaps develop into horror movies, while nineteenth-century stage melodramas provide a repertory of stories and techniques to be mined by early films, just as storytelling, stylized joking, and badinage, and finally stand-up comedy remain the provenance of much late-night television, not to mention sitcoms.

But of course, not all traditional forms of popular entertainment, broadly construed, have been transformed into mass art forms. Cock-fighting, for example, has not found its way into mass art. And mass art has developed certain forms that evince no debt to traditional popular arts. For instance, music video owes its heritage to pre-existing mass art forms such as film. In short, though all mass art may belong to the broader, ahistorical class of popular art, not all popular art is mass art.

Ex hypothesi, what marks off mass art from the broader class of ahistorical popular art is, as the label "mass art" signals, that it is produced and disseminated by means of mass industrial technologies, technologies capable of delivering multiple instances or tokens of mass artworks to widely disparate reception points. Like the mass manufacture of automobiles, mass art is a form of mass production and distribution, designed to deliver a mutiplicity of artworks to frequently geographically remote, mass consuming audiences.[4] Mass art is the art of mass society, predicated on addressing mass audiences by means of the opportunities afforded by mass technologies.

Mass art is produced and delivered by mass media. These media are called *mass* because they make the product available to relatively large audiences simultaneously. It is important to stress that these media are called *mass* because they make their products technologically available to large audiences, even if they do not actually command large audiences. Television, that is, was a mass medium in this sense before large numbers of people possessed television sets.[5] The products of mass art are, in principle, produced for a plurality of recipients, and mass technology contributes to the realization of this aim by, as John B. Thompson puts it, extending "the availability of symbolic forms in space and time."[6]

However, though production and delivery by mass media technologies represents a necessary condition of mass art, it is not sufficient to identify a candidate as a mass artwork, since avant-garde artworks can also be produced and delivered by mass technologies. Robert Ashley uses the same, broadly speaking, sound-recording technologies as do The Rolling Stones and Madonna, while filmmakers like Michael Snow and Jean Luc Godard deploy the same cinematic apparatus that David O. Selznick and Victor Fleming did in their production of *Gone With The Wind*. Yet clearly, avant-garde artworks, when produced by means of mass media, are not mass artworks proper, for they are not designed for consumption by mass audiences. Quite frequently, they are expressly designed to confound mass audiences – to outrage bourgeois sensibility – and even when they are not directly intended to do this, they invariably do so nevertheless, since it is a necessary condition of being avant-garde that the works in question subvert or, at least, go beyond conventional expectations.

Avant-garde artworks are not designed to be immediately accessible to mass audiences. They are meant to challenge or to transgress the common understandings and expectations that the mass consuming audience has with regard to the relevant artforms. This is not to say that an avant-garde work cannot be a best seller: Salman Rushdie's *The Satanic Verses* was. However, the explanation in this case has more to do with the fact that people in places like Iowa defiantly refused to allow an Iranian dictator to tell them what they might read, and less to do with their appreciation of Rushdie's disjunctive narrative strategies.

Indeed, I conjecture that Rushdie's book, though widely purchased, was not widely read. For in order to be read with understanding and appreciation, *The Satanic Verses* requires a background of literary history, of literary theory, and of the related discourse of the divided subject that is not at the fingertips of most of the Anglophone reading public.

The Bridges of Madison County (to stay in Iowa) is a mass artwork, but *The Satanic Verses* is not. What is the difference? The former is designed to be accessible to the mass reading public and the latter is not. All things being equal, any literate consumer should be able to understand *The Bridges of Madison County* without any specialized background, save the ability to read and a rudimentary mastery of the practice of fiction. *The Satanic Verses*, on the other hand, requires a special background in order to be understood, though, of course, that background can be acquired autodidactically.

Avant-garde artworks can be produced and delivered by mass technologies, but they are not mass artworks. For though produced and delivered by mass technologies, such avant-garde artworks are not structured for ready assimilation and reception by mass audiences. Indeed, they are designed to thwart ready assimilation. In the most benign cases, avant-garde artworks are intended to stretch common sensibilities, while in the more standard case, they are designed to confound them for the sake of disrupting what are perceived to be aesthetic and/or moral laxities.

Indeed, throughout the epoch of mass art, it has been the defenders of the avant-garde aesthetic (e.g., Collingwood, Adorno, and Greenberg)[7] who have been the harshest critics of mass art. For them, the avant-garde has been both the historical and the conceptual antithesis of mass art. Inasmuch as the avant-garde is the antithesis of mass art, it provides, in an Hegelian fashion, insight into the "thesis" – mass art – from which it draws its program and its purpose. Avant-garde art is designed to be difficult, to be intellectually, aesthetically, and often morally challenging, to be inaccessible to those without certain backgrounds of knowledge and acquired sensibilities. Mass art, in contrast, is designed to be easy, to be readily accessible to the largest number of people possible, with minimum effort.

Avant-garde art is esoteric; mass art is exoteric. Mass art is meant to command a mass audience. Thus, it is designed to be user friendly. Ideally, it is structured in such a way that large numbers of people will be able to understand and to appreciate it virtually effortlessly. It is made in order to capture and to hold the attention of large audiences, while avant-garde art is made to be effortful and to rebuff easy assimilation by large audiences.

Insofar as mass art is meant to capture large markets, it gravitates toward the choice of devices that will make it readily accessible to mass, untutored audiences. Comic books, commercial movies, and television, for example, narrate by means of pictures. And pictures are symbols whose referents are recognized, all things being equal, immediately and automatically by viewers simply by looking. Pictorial recognition, that is, is acquired in tandem with object recognition in such a way that one is able to recognize a picture of something, say of an apple, where one is already able to recognize perceptually, "in nature," the kind of thing – such as apples – that the picture depicts. Children, for example, often learn what things are like from pictures, before they actually see them.[8] Picture recognition requires no appreciable training. Thus, mass artforms that rely on pictures as basic constituents will be accessible in a fundamental way to virtually unlimited audiences. Indeed, it is this feature of movies – of motion *pictures* – that primarily contributed to the international popularity of silent films, which became a global artform just because they could be understood by almost everyone across national, class, religious, and educational backgrounds.

The search for what is massively accessible even tends to influence the choice of content in mass entertainments. Action/adventure scenarios are so serviceable for the purposes of mass art because physical competition between the starkly defined forces of good and evil is easier for almost anyone to track than are complex psychological dramas, which may require background cultural information that the common viewer is apt to lack. That is, it is easier for the randomly selected plain viewer to understand *Mortal Combat* than *Blow Up*.

It is the point or function of mass art to address mass audiences. This may be driven by the profit motive in capitalist states or by ideological purposes in totalitarian countries. And this, in turn, dictates certain desiderata concerning the internal structures of mass artworks, viz., that mass artworks will gravitate toward structures, like pictorial representation, that will be accessible virtually on contact, without specialized background training or effort by vast numbers of people. Mass artworks tend toward a certain kind of homogeneity exactly because they aim at engaging what is common among huge populations of consumers.

Frequently, it is this tendency toward homogenization that critics – generally avant-garde critics – single out for loathing when it comes to discussions of mass art. However, the search for common denominators in mass art, at the levels of both style and content, is not a flaw, but rather a design consideration given the function of mass art. For it is the point of mass art to engage mass audiences, and that mandates an inclination toward structures that will be readily accessible virtually on contact and with little effort on the part of audiences with widely differing backgrounds.

Gathering together and amplifying some of these observations, we may attempt to define the mass artwork by means of the following formula:

> x is a mass artwork if and only if 1) x is a multiple instance or type artwork 2) produced and distributed by a mass technology, 3) which artwork is intentionally designed to gravitate in its structural choices (e.g., its narrative forms, symbolism, intended affect, and even its content) toward those choices that promise accessibility with minimum effort, virtually on first contact, for the largest number of relatively untutored audiences.

I have arrived at the first condition by stipulating that my domain of concern is mass *art*, not mass culture, which would represent a broader category. That is, my concern is with those items of mass culture that are more narrowly identifiable as art – such as dramas, stories, and songs rather than news programs, cooking shows, or sporting events. Since mass artworks are not avant-garde, there should be little problem classifying items in terms of whether or not they fall into already entrenched artforms – such as drama or song – or in terms of whether they discharge classically recognized artistic purposes like representation or expression. That mass artworks are what are called multiple or type arts is a feature of the works that, if not already obvious, will be explicated in the next section of this essay.[9]

The second condition – that mass artworks are produced and distributed by mass technologies – should also be fairly obvious. Mass art emerges historically; it has not always been with us. It arrives on the scene only when technologies capable of mass production and delivery do. Thus, mass art is not popular art *simpliciter*. It requires a mass production and distribution technology where such a technology is defined as one that is capable of delivering multiple (or at least two) tokens of a mass artwork type to more than one reception point simultaneously. Walter Benjamin spoke of mass art in terms of mass reproducibility.[10] This does a nice job for things like certain photographs, but it does not capture the possibility of simultaneous broadcasts. Rather, it is more fruitful to think of mass artworks as ones that can be delivered to multiple reception sites simultaneously.

The notion of a discrete reception site here is a bit tricky. It cannot be specified in terms of measurable distances between reception sites. An average-sized household with two television sets has at least two discrete reception sites, whereas Mount Rushmore defines one reception site, though it can be viewed by many people from many different standpoints, which encompass an area greater than that of the average household. What counts as a discrete reception site depends upon what is the normatively correct focus of audience attention within a given practice. Mount Rushmore has a single, spatially continuous reception point covering an indeterminately large expanse, whereas two television sets are, in standard conditions, two reception sites.[11]

Each theater stage has a discrete reception site, though, unlike in the case of television, in theater it is impossible to deliver the same token performance of a play to two different reception sites simultaneously, whereas this capability is a *sine qua non* of a mass technology art like television.

However, though the production and distribution of the relevant artworks by mass industrial technologies is an essential feature of mass artworks, it is not sufficient to identify a candidate as a mass artwork, since, as we have seen, it appears counterintuitive to count avant-garde artworks, like films by Stan Brakhage, as mass artworks. Such artworks may be produced and delivered through the agency of a mass medium, but they cannot be reasonably expected to enlist mass untutored audiences. They are not readily accessible cognitively and emotively to plain viewers. That is why Brakhage introduces his films with lectures: he is trying to educate his audiences in the way in which to view his films. Mass artworks proper are ones whose design choices are made with an eye to guaranteeing their accessibility to viewers who, with no specialized background, can understand and appreciate them virtually on contact, while expending little effort.[12]

Rock music, for example, in addition to its harmonic simplicity, employs a readily detectable backbeat that helps organize the rest of the sound. This beat is a pronounced or foregrounded frame of reference whose repetitiveness grants easy entry into the rhythmic structure that converges on it. As the old Beatles song "Rock and Roll Music" has it: "It's got a back beat, you can't lose it." Most people can pick it up quickly and move to it, at least in terms of toe and finger tapping, and rhythmic nodding. It is this internal structural feature, among others, that makes rock music accessible globally.

One might think that insofar as most rock is song-in-a-natural-language, it would not travel well. However, sociologists have discovered that listeners do not primarily attend to the lyrics in rock, but rather to the broad emotive contour of a piece.[13] Thus, students in Moscow can savor the same tones of euphoria or defiance that their opposite numbers in Liverpool do.

Insofar as my definition of mass art emphasizes its search for structures that can command mass audiences, the formula suggests a rich empirical research program for studying mass art, viz., that, with mass artworks, an always useful question to ask concerns what it is about the relevant works that enables them to command the attention of large audiences. That the cutting rates in MTV videos average 19.94 shots per minute[14] helps explain why music videos rivet viewers to the screen, since such a pattern provides little opportunity for attention to flag. Indeed, given the way our perceptual system operates, i.e., given the involuntary tendency of our attention to reawaken (for sound adaptive reasons) upon the onset of new stimuli, MTV might be said to be exploiting our hard wiring in such a way that most viewers find themselves irresistibly drawn to its imagery.[15]

II. The ontology of mass art

Having defined the nature of the mass artwork, I would now like to turn to the question of its ontological status – to the question of the way in which the mass artwork exists. The strategy that I will adopt is first to attempt to characterize the ontological status of motion pictures in order to go on to see whether that characterization can be generalized, with appropriate adjustments, to other mass art forms such as photography, sound recording, broadcast radio, and telecommunications.

A useful way to get at the ontology of film is to focus on the difference between theatrical performances and film performances.[16] Say that there is a performance of *The Master Builder* tonight at eight o'clock at the local repertory theater, and a performance of *Waterworld* at the same time in the neighborhood cinema. One might go to either. In both cases, we are likely to be seated in an auditorium, and each performance might begin as a curtain rises. But despite these surface similarities, there are ontologically profound differences between the two performances.

Undoubtedly, this assertion will seem odd to some philosophers. For if one distinguishes between two kinds of arts – those that are singular and those that are multiple – then film performances and theater performances appear to be ontologically on a par; both the theater performance and the film performance will count as tokens of a type. In each case, the performance is a token of an art type – *The Master Builder*, on the one hand, and *Waterworld*, on the other – in the sense that any token of the type in question may undergo destruction – say, by fire – while the type continues to exist.[17]

Clearly, the type/token distinction, though helpful in locating the ontological distinction between certain paintings and sculptures, on the one hand, and things like plays, films, novels, and symphonies, on the other, is not fine-grained enough to distinguish between film performances and theater performances. In order to get at this distinction, it is instructive to consider the different routes by which we get from a play-type to a dramatic performance token, on the one hand, versus the route from a film-type to a performance (i.e., a showing) of a film.

To get from a film-type to a token performance, we require a *template*; to get from a play-type to a token performance, we require an interpretation. Moreover, the different routes from type to token performance in theater, versus from film-type to film performance, explains why we regard theatrical performances as artworks in their own right, while, at the same time, we do not regard film performances (i.e., film showings) as artworks.

The film performance is generated from a template – standardly a film print, but it might also be a videotape, a laser disk, or a computer program coded in a physical medium. Such templates are themselves tokens; each one of them can be destroyed and each one of them can be assigned a spatial location, though the film-type – *Waterworld* – cannot. Nor is the negative of the work the film-type. It is one token among others. The original negative of Murnau's *Nosferatu* was destroyed as a result of a court order, but the film still exists.

Each film showing is a token of the film-type; each token showing gives us access to the film-type. But in order to present a token performance of a film, we require a template – a film print or a video cassette or a laser disk – which is itself a token of the film-type. The token film performance is generated from the template mechanically (or electronically), in accordance with routine technical procedures. Thus, the token film performance – the film showing – is not an artistic performance and does not warrant aesthetic appreciation.

Of course, one may complain if the film is shown out of focus, or if it burns up in the projector, but these complaints are not aesthetic. They are complaints about the mechanical expertise of the projectionist. The expertise of the projectionist, undoubtedly, is a precondition for access to the artwork qua film-type. But it is not an object of *aesthetic* commendation.

The account is very different when it comes to plays. The difference, in part, is a function of the fact that plays may be considered as literary works, or as performance works. When a play, like *Strange Interlude*, is considered as a literary work, then my copy of *Strange Interlude* is a token of the art-type *Strange Interlude* in the same way that my copy of *The Warden* is a token of Trollope's novel. But when regarded from the perspective of theatrical performance, a token of *Strange Interlude* is a particular performance which occurs at a specifiable time and place.

Whereas a film performance is generated from a template, and not an interpretation, a theatrical performance of *Strange Interlude* is generated by an interpretation and not a template. When used in the context of performance, the play-type *Strange Interlude* by Eugene O'Neill functions as a recipe which is to be filled in by other artists – by directors, actors, set designers, and the like. O'Neill composed the play – which is a type – but the play must be brought to life by an interpretation, or a conjunction of interpretations (by directors, actors, etc.), and, furthermore, this interpretation governs the performance tokens of the play as it is offered to the public from night to night.

Moreover, this interpretation is a type; the same interpretation of a play can be revived after a substantial temporal hiatus and can be tokened in different theaters with numerically different but qualitatively identical sets. So, the performance token of a play-type is generated through an interpretation, which is itself a type. Consequently, theatrical interpretations are types within a type.[18] We get from a play-type to a performance through an interpretation which is a type. This contrasts with the route from a film-type to a token film showing, which is mediated through a template that is itself a token.

Earlier I noted that a film performance – that is to say a film showing at your local theater – is not itself an artwork, while matters stand differently with theater. Theatrical performances are artworks in their own right. It takes artistry and imagination to embody an interpretation, whereas film performances require nothing more than technical competence. In theater as we know it, the play, the interpretation, and the performance are each candidates for aesthetic appreciation.

In the best case, the play, its interpretation, and its performance are integrated, though we recognize that these are discriminable layers of artistry, even if one person writes the play, directs it, and acts in it as well. For there are many cases where a bad play finds a commendable interpretation, embodied in superb performances, while, at other times, a good play is poorly interpreted but performed well, and so on. That we make these distinctions so easily indicates that there are different ontological strata of artistry when it comes to the stage, strata of artistry that we do not obtain in film in the same way. For if with theater the play-type is a recipe that directors and other artists interpret, yielding different, though related, artworks, with film the recipe (e.g., the shooting script) and the artistic interpretations of the director, actors, etc., are nondetachable constituents of the same artwork. We do not evaluate shooting scripts independently of the film production, and we do not evaluate film showings *aesthetically* at all.

It is fairly standard to regard works of film art as types. But if the preceding comparison with theater is persuasive, then we can characterize films in a more fine-grained way, viz.: a film is a type whose token performances are generated by templates that are themselves tokens. Our next question is whether this pattern of analysis can be generalized to other forms of mass art, including photography, radio, telecommunication, music recordings, and best-selling pulp fiction.

Best-selling pulp fiction, like literature in general, is a type-art. My copy of *The Gift* is a token of Danielle Steele's novel in the same way that my copy of *The Magic Mountain* is a token of Thomas Mann's novel. In either case, the destruction of my copies would not standardly occasion the destruction of Steele's or Mann's novel. Indeed, every graphic token of Steele's novel might be burnt up and yet the novel might continue to exist if, à la *Fahrenheit 451*, one person remembered the text. Of course, it strains English usage to call these tokens of *The Gift* performances; so, it is perhaps better to speak of token instances, or of token reception-instances, rather than of token performances, as we expand our characterization of the pattern of analysis that we have already developed with respect of film to other mass art forms. Moreover, as in the case of film, we have access to works of pulp literature through token reception instances that are themselves generated from templates, including hard-type and programs and, perhaps at the limit, memory traces.

Turning from pulp fiction to photography, the first thing to be noted is that it may not be the case that photography is uniformly a multiple art form from an ontological point of view. For there may be, due to their method of production, photographic artworks that are one of a kind, such as daguerreo-types.[19] Such photographs have an ontological status that is characteristic of the status of paintings.

Like the *Mona Lisa*, if a daguerreotype by Nièpce is destroyed, we have lost the daguerreotype, even if photographic reproductions of it remain, in the same way that if the *Mona Lisa* in the Louvre were shredded, we would lose da Vinci's masterpiece, despite the continued existence of all those museum postcards. With such single instance photographs, the so-called reproductions thereof are not tokens of the work in question, but documentations of it. Thus, I do not wish to call single-instance photographs mass art proper for the same reason that the *Mona Lisa* is not an example of mass art, despite the fact that it has been endlessly documented photographically in art history texts and travel books.

On the other hand, in addition to single-instance photographs, there are many photographs that fall squarely into the category of mass art. Predictably enough, given the photographic basis of film, the pattern developed to analyze cinema suits such photographs quite nicely. For token reception instances of such photographs are generated from templates, like negatives, which are themselves tokens, and the works in question continue to exist even if the negatives and most of the other tokens of the relevant photograph are lost or destroyed.

Considering radio and television, the first point to make is that in a great many cases, programs in these media are recorded on such things as audio magnetic tape, kinescopes, videotapes, or digital programs for subsequent broadcasting. This practice became fairly standard in radio by the late 1940s. And in cases like this, the pattern of analysis matches the one introduced for film, since the token instances of tape serve as the requisite templates that make token reception instances possible. But what of one-time broadcasts that are not taped or artistically modified (by things like mixing) at the message source?

Clearly, one-time broadcasts in radio and television should count as exam-ples of mass art, since they can simultaneously afford a multiplicity of token reception instances of the same work – a song or a drama – in reception sites that are geographically remote from each other. But what is the template in these cases? My suggestion is that the template is the transmission signal or the message signal that has been derived from the message source by coding and modulating devices for the purpose of transmission, and which is received by demodulation and decoding devices such as household radios and televisions. Each token reception instance is derived from the template by a mechanical/electrical (as opposed to an artistic) process. Just as projecting a film is neither artistic nor interpretive, neither is turning on or tuning a radio or a television. The token reception instances of the programs in question are physical processes. The broadcast signal is a physical structure and certain token reception instances of these programs can be destroyed, by jamming, for example, while the radio mass artwork and the television mass artwork continue to exist. Of course, where the program signal derives from a magnetic template, we find a relay of templates, including the transmission signal, as well as a tape, mediating the mass art type and its token reception instances.[20]

Where the one-time broadcast involves a script, in the case of a drama, or a score, in the case of music, we have no problem thinking that we are dealing with a type that, in principle, can be tokened more than once. However, a problem may appear to arise when one thinks of broadcasts that involve improvisation (and no taping or mixing), since one may worry that in such cases we will be unable to specify the type of which the reception instances are tokens. Here I think that our anxieties rest on the intuition that improvisations are one-of-a-kind events.

I believe that there are two ways to handle this problem. The first is to concede that improvisations are singular artworks and to argue that, as in the case of single instance photographs, reception instances of improvisations are documentations rather than tokens of the works in question. However, the second solution to this problem, and the one I prefer, is to deny that improvisations are, in principle, single instance artworks. For improvisations can be memorized and played again by the original artists or by someone else; they can be notated, as they are in the classical tradition, and played again; and in the age of mass art they can be taped and/or memorized by listeners who, in turn, can notate them and/or reproduce them. An improvisation continues to exist as long as token performances of it can be executed. A painting ceases to exist when the "original" is destroyed; but in this sense, there are not, strictly speaking, originals in the case of improvised musical or dramatic productions. It is conceptually possible to replicate an improvisation, but it is not possible to replicate paintings under the standard concept of a painting.

Improvisations are not, in principle, singular artworks. Thus, the pattern developed to characterize film artworks can be applied to broadcast improvisations. That is, we see and/or hear token reception instances of the improvisation type through the mediation of a token transmission signal template.

The story to be told about popular sound recordings resembles the account of typical broadcasting, for the straightforward reason that most typical broadcasting of popular music already involves sound recording. In sound recording, a microphone transforms aural vibrations into electrical pulses, which are amplified and conveyed to a recording head, which is an electromagnet that produces patterns on the coating of the recording tape. This process, in turn, is reversed in playback when the magnetic patterns are converted back into vibrations, amplified by some type of loudspeaker or headphone. Once again, the musical work, which is a type, generates a token reception instance in my living room, via a token template, which in this case is a magnetic pattern or a relay token thereof.

However, as with some of the media we have already examined, with sound recording we may wish to distinguish between two kinds of cases: pieces created in the studio by mixing, dubbing, etc., which we might regard as constructed, mass art types, and pieces of music that are virtually unvarnished documentations of independently existing musical performances.[21] Though the former probably have the best claim conceptually, and I suspect statistically, to be considered mass music proper, the latter have played an undeniable role historically in the evolution of mass culture, even if the future seems to belong to studio-constructed mass music.[22]

Provisionally, then, the pattern of analysis developed to isolate the ontological status of film appears to work across the board for mass artworks in general. Mass artworks are multiple instance or type artworks. Specifically, they are types whose token reception instances are generated by templates, or by relays of templates, that are themselves tokens. This serves to distinguish the works in question from singular artworks, on the one hand, and from type artworks whose tokens are generated by interpretations. Of course, this does not separate the works in question from certain nonartworks, such as television news programs, that are also produced and delivered by the relevant mass technologies. Television news programs and situation comedies share the same mode of existence, inasmuch as they are the same kind of types. Where they differ is in their claims to art status.

III. Objection #1: All art is multiple

In my attempt to isolate the ontological status of mass artworks I have, in part, relied upon a distinction between singular and multiple arts. However, this distinction has been challenged by Gregory Currie in his exciting and important monograph *An Ontology of Art*.[23] There Currie advances the Instance Multiplicity Hypothesis, according to which all art is multiple.[24] There are no singular arts on Currie's view, our intuitions about paradigmatic cases of fine art, such as painting and sculpture, notwithstanding. Thus, to the extent that my theory of the ontology of mass art depends on a distinction between singular arts and multiple arts, it appears to rely upon a distinction where there is none.

Currie introduces his defense of the Instance Multiplicity Hypothesis by claiming that there is a presumption in favor of any ontological theory of art that offers a unified perspective of the field – that says either that all art is singular or that all art is multiple. Moreover, it is fairly obvious that it cannot be the case that every art is singular. Consider literature. So, the hypothesis that all the arts are multiple has a better chance of providing a unified theory of the field. In other words, Currie thinks that there is a presumption in favor of the view that artworks are multiple across the board. Thus, if there are no considerations that threaten to defeat it, the Instance Multiplicity Hypothesis is the ontological theory that we should endorse.

Currie argues that it is logically possible to produce molecule for molecule versions of any work of fine art. Imagine a super-Xerox machine that can replicate any painting, sculpture, and so on. Since the replica is identical, molecule for molecule, to the original, it has the same perceptible structure as the original. And since the replica is counterfactually dependent on the original in the sense that every feature in the replica is causally dependent on a corresponding feature in the original, then the presence of features in the replica are explained by the same historical, contextual, and intentional factors that explain the presence of those features in the original. Thus, these super-Xeroxes deliver the same aesthetic stimulation as the original and grant access to the historical significance of the original. Therefore, they are perfectly satisfactory targets for artistic (i.e., aesthetic plus historical) attention – from the viewpoint of appreciation. That is, they are on a par with originals. Indeed, Currie writes as though all fine art is, via his super-Xerox machine, mass art (at least in principle). His argumentative strategy, in effect, is to challenge opponents to find something wrong with his conjecture.

Most of Currie's energy is spent showing what is misguided about possible objections to his theory. However, I think that there are some pretty decisive considerations that he never addresses and that indicate that the Instance Multiplicity Hypothesis does not offer a general theory for all the arts. For example, Currie never thinks about site-specific works of art – that is, sculptures and architectural artworks that take their character from the environment in which they are constructed and which are altered over time by the conditions of the surrounding environments in ways that are intended to constitute part of what viewers are to take as their object of appreciation. That is, works of sculpture and architecture interact with the specific sites upon which or in which they are constructed, and that interactive process can itself be intended to be part of what is significant about the piece.

Robert Smithson's *Spiral Jetty* was constructed on a site notable for its unique possession of a certain strain of algae that afforded the reddish hue that he was after, and the shape of the jetty was a response to the formation of the surrounding site. Moreover, part of what was to be appreciated in the work was the differing appearances of the jetty as the water levels altered. Similarly, Walter De Maria's *Lightning Field* was situated as it was because of the high intensity of electrical activity in the environment and because of the way in which the surrounding mountains framed that activity. And, of course, part of the piece involved the way in which the piece engaged recurrent lightning storms.[25]

These pieces are representative of an important genre in contemporary art, sometimes called "earthworks." Their relevance to the discussion of singular versus multiple arts is, of course, that the very vicissitudes these works undergo as they interact with their environments are part of what these artworks are about. These works are involved with processes, not merely with products. It is hard to imagine that, in the known physical universe, one could replicate the exact processes undergone by the original site-specific works by means of Currie's super-Xerox machine. Let us grant that Currie's super-Xeroxing machine can replicate a site-specific structure and its surrounding environment at time T1. Yet, it is unimaginable that physically all the events that the original undergoes from time T2 through Tn will occur in the putative replica. But if the future histories of the supposed replica do not experience the same events as the original, then the artworks are not identical. It is highly unlikely, given the structure of the physical universe, that Currie's super-Xeroxes of site-specific works will standardly weather in exactly the same way that the originals do. But since the weathering process can be an element of artistic attention in site-specific works, site-specific works are singular artworks, works that are not, in principle, multipliable in the known physical universe. For in the known physical universe, the probability that the original site-specific work and all the super-Xeroxes thereof might undergo the same physical transformations is wildly freakish.

Nor can these considerations be turned aside on the grounds that the works cited are of contestable artistic status. The same case can be made on the basis of acknowledged architectural masterpieces such as Frank Lloyd Wright's Taliesin and Fallingwater. Furthermore, site specificity is arguably a central feature of Greek temple architecture.[26] At one point, Currie briefly considers architecture, and surmises that the surrounding environment is irrelevant to the identity of the work – perhaps because he realizes that if his super-Xeroxes must replicate entire, indeterminately bounded environments and their vicissitudes, they will seem immensely implausible, even in principle. But he is just wrong if he thinks that a unique environment and its vicissitudes cannot be part of a site-specific work. And that error spells the defeat of the Instance Multiplicity Hypothesis, for the reasons I have already rehearsed.

Currie says that there is a presumption in favor of a unified theory of the ontology of art and that the view that all art is multiple is the most credible unified theory. I see no reason to believe that there is such a presumption and, in any case, if the facts are otherwise, all claims about such a presumption must be retired. Furthermore, I think that the fact of site-specific artworks of the sort to which I have alluded shows the so-called presumption to be extravagant. There are at least these singular artworks, and that is enough to sustain the distinction between singular and multiple arts that I have invoked in developing my theory of the ontology of mass art. Even if super-Xeroxing were possible, there would still be a contrast class of singular artworks. Not all art is, in principle, super-Xeroxable. There is still a distinction with a difference worth marking here. Moreover, even if it were the case that all art is multiple in the way that Currie speculates, my theory of the ontology of mass art would still be informative, since I draw a contrast between multiple art whose token instances are generated by interpretations and mass art whose tokens are necessarily generated by templates that are themselves tokens, and/or relays of tokens.

IV. Objection #2: Mass art is irrelevant

An objection to my initial claim in this essay that mass art is a worthy topic for aesthetic investigation might be that mass art is already obsolete. On this objection, the subject does not possess the urgency with which I invest it, since it will turn out to be a mere blip on the historical screen. Mass art is on the way out. The evolutionary trajectory of communication technology is away from mass art and toward customized art. The consumer of art in the future will not be part of a mass audience. Consumers in the near future will be empowered by new information technologies such that they will be able to personalize their artistic menus, often interactively. Indeed, perhaps we will all become artists in the coming cyber-utopia.

It may be further argued that mass art, as I conceive of it, will be but a brief faltering moment preceding the glorious emergence of highly individualized, technological art consumption (and production). To a limited extent, the pros pects for customized art are already evident in the existence of cable and satellite channels for specialized viewers, who may select among cartoon channels, science fiction channels, comedy channels, history channels, and so on. But this is only a hint of what is to come. Alleged synergies between telephonic, computer, satellite, and video technologies promise an era of personalized art consumption which will create a demand for the production of technological artworks that are of an incredibly diverse variety. When the mass audience disappears, that is, mass art will disappear with it. And that eventuality is just around the corner.

In my opinion, such prophecies are excessively premature. The kind of "customization" that we have before us in the form of comedy channels, cartoon channels, children's channels, and the like[27] are not evidence of the passing of mass art, since the choices these channels afford are merely between types or genres of mass art. The structures of the programs on the comedy channel and the science fiction channel are not really different in kind, because they are all mass artworks designed to be available to the common untutored viewer for fast pick-up with minimum effort. The programs in question could just as easily appear on networks that are not dedicated to single genre programming. They are gathered together on a single channel, but a single channel that is still devoted to being accessible to large, heterogeneous audiences. Structurally, the programs on such channels are still examples of mass art. The parallel editing on *Babylon 5* and *Amazing Stories* is the same as that employed in *Bewitched*, *The Dick Van Dyke Show*, and *The Jeffersons*.

Nor am I convinced that mass art is about to disappear with the advent of technologies that might have the potential to afford a more diversified fare. There are several reasons for this. First, the economies of scale that are available in technological media incline the communication industries toward the production of "mass-produced, common-denominator, mass-audience media."[28] These industries are not likely to divest themselves readily of the advantages of these economies of scale and of the profits they deliver. Of course, these interests control not only their own mass art productions, but also the relevant mass media technologies of dissemination and distribution. And we can be assured that they will not kill the goose that lays the golden eggs.

Furthermore, audiences will not change just because technological means alter. A taste for easily accessible art will not evaporate, nor will the pleasure to be had in sharing artworks with large numbers of our fellow citizens disappear. That is, the sociability that mass art affords in several ways – as a common source of discussion and criticism, and as a reservoir of common cultural symbols – supplies a powerful motivation for the persistence of mass art. And, in addition, it is far from clear that vast majorities crave the vaunted capacities for interactivity and selectivity that are putatively in the offing.[29] Thus, there are economic and psychological counterpressures that militate against the emergence of the personalized communications-utopias heralded by pundits of the information revolution. Mass art is here to stay for the foreseeable future. And, therefore, it is incumbent upon philosophers of art to begin to take account of it theoretically.

Notes

1   Patrick Maynard, "Photo-Opportunity: Photography as Technology," *Canadian Review of American Studies* 22 (1991): 505–6.

2   I prefer the term "mass art" to "entertainment," since the phenomena that I am discussing in this paper are obviously descended from acknowledged artforms and genres, such as the drama, the novel, and oil painting. The term "entertainment," to date, is far looser than the term "art." Furthermore, by stipulating that my concern is with mass art, I am excluding from my inquiry mass media genres, like television news and sporting events, that are not descended from the arts.

3   For more elaborate defenses of the definition of mass art propounded in this section see: Noël Carroll, "The Nature of Mass Art" and "Mass Art, High Art and the Avant-Garde: A Response to David Novitz," in *1992: Philosophic Exchange* (Brockport, New York: Center for Philosophic Exchange, State University of New York, College at Brockport, 1993).

4   Interestingly, radio, as conceived by Marconi, was from a single broadcasting point to a single reception point. The notion of multiple reception points was pioneered by DeForest. I owe this point to Patrick Maynard.

5 Similarly, a country and western recording counts as a mass artwork, even if few people listen to it.

6 John B. Thompson, *Ideology and Modern Culture: Critical Social Theory in the Era of Mass Communication* (Stanford University Press, 1990), p. 221.

7 See Noël Carroll, "Philosophical Resistance to Mass Art," in Gerhard Hoffman and Alfred Hornung (eds.), *Affirmation and Negation in Contemporary American Culture* (Heidelberg: Unversitätsverlag C. Winter, 1994), pp. 297–312.

8 In a private communication, Patrick Maynard has referred to this as "reciprocal" transfer.

9 Tangentially, I might mention that not all mass media technologies have spawned mass art forms. The telephone, as such, does not seem to have given birth to a mass art form of its own, though it has functioned as an element in artworks and as a delivery system for some mass artworks.

10 Walter Benjamin, "The Work of Art in the Age of Mechanical Reproduction," in *Illuminations*, ed. Hannah Arendt (New York: Schocken Books, 1969), pp. 217–253.

11 The caveat – "in standard conditions" – is meant to exclude cases such as those where different television monitors convey parts of a single image after the fashion of a mosaic (as in some of the work of Nam June Paik).

12 Although in this essay I only discuss mass art, popular art, and avant-garde art, it is not my contention that these are the only relevant forms of art. There is also folk art, middle-brow art, and the forms of traditional art that existed before the advent of modern mass art (such as the paintings of daVinci). For further discussion of these other forms of art and their relation to mass art, see Noël Carroll, "Nature of Mass Art"; Noël Carroll, "Mass Art, High Art and the Avant-garde"; and Noël Carroll, *A Philosophy of Mass Art* (Oxford: Oxford University Press, 1998).

13 Roger Jon Desmond, "Adolescents and Music Lyrics: Implications of a Cognitive Perspective," *Communications Quarterly* 35 (1987): 278; Simon Frith, *Music For Pleasure* (New York: Routledge, 1988), p. 154; and Quentin Schultze et al., *Dancing in the Dark: Youth, Popular Culture and the Electronic Media* (Grand Rapids, Michigan: William B. Eerdmans, 1991), pp. 160–163.

14 Donald L. Fry and Virginia H. Fry, "Some Structural Characteristics of Music Television Video," a paper presented at the meetings of the Speech Communication Association in Chicago in November of 1984 and cited in *Dancing in the Dark*, p. 206.

15 Perhaps what is called channel surfing is a related phenomenon. As our attention sags, we try (often subconsciously) to reactivate it by changing the channel, thereby introducing a burst of new stimulation. What we do to ourselves by way of channel surfing is roughly what MTV editing does for us automatically and at a much faster pace.

16 This account of the ontology of film builds on earlier attempts of mine, including: "Towards an Ontology of the Moving Image," in Cynthia A. Freeland and Thomas E. Wartenberg (eds.), *Philosophy and Film* (New York: Routledge, 1995); and "Defining the Moving Image" in my *Theorizing the Moving Image* (New York: Cambridge University Press, 1996).

17 The application of the type/token distinction to art derives from Richard Wollheim in his book *Art and Its Objects* (Cambridge: Cambridge University Press, 1980), especially sections 35–8.

18   See R. A. Sharpe, "Type, Token, Interpretation, Performance," in *Mind* 88 (1979): 437–40.

19   Patrick Maynard has pointed out to me that some modern photography printers count individual daguerreotype prints as one of a kind.

20   One complication should be mentioned here. Suppose a television program is being shot before a live audience. In such cases, we might want to talk about two artworks. There is the work of theater, which is performed in front of the specific studio audience, and there is something else. In one case, where what is broadcast is being edited and structured (e.g., in terms of close-ups, long-shots, etc.), there is another artwork, which is a mass artwork, one that differs in important respects from what the studio audience sees. And in another case, where there may be no additional structuration (a prospect some might deny is a live one), the something else is a documentation of the theatrical artwork, something on a par with a museum postcard of the *Mona Lisa*. Similar distinctions can be drawn with respect to live radio broadcasts which will comprise a live performance artwork for the immediate studio audience, and either a straight documentation of it (if there are such things) or, more standardly, a mass artwork which has been modulated, mixed and enhanced electronically for the radio audience.

21   Many might wish to deny the possibility of what I call unvarnished recordings and, therefore, regard all musical sound recording in terms of the category of constructed, mass art types. For an extended, though controversial, discussion of the ontological significance of sound recording for rock music, see Theodore Gracyk, *Rhythm and Noise: The Aesthetics of Rock Music* (Durham, NC: Duke University Press, 1996).

22   It perhaps pays to remark here that rock music played by garage bands, bar bands, and the like is not mass art proper by my construal. It may count as popular art, but it is not mass art because it is not, in the basic case, delivered to multiple reception sites simultaneously.

23   Gregory Currie, *An Ontology of Art* (New York: St Martin's Press, 1989).

24   See ch. 4 of *An Ontology of Art*.

25   Descriptions and photographs of the pieces by Smithson and De Maria can be found in John Beardsley, *Earthworks and Beyond: Contemporary Art in the Landscape* (New York: Abbeville Press Publishers, 1989).

26   See, for example, Vincent Scully's *The Earth, The Temple and The Gods: Greek Sacred Architecture* (New York: Frederick A. Praeger, 1969).

27   There is even a game-show channel, though, of course, it is not a purveyor of mass art in my sense, since game shows are not art.

28   See W. Russell Neuman, *The Future of the Mass Audience* (Cambridge: Cambridge University Press, 1991), p. 13.

29   Similarly, there is no reason to predict that just because the technology is there that people will exploit it so as to become so many da Vincis, creating unheralded art at their computer work stations ferverishly. Whatever psychological and social forces disincline people to experiment artistically on their own now will not disappear merely because of the advent of a new technology.

2

Modernity and the Plasticity of Perception

In "Seeing and Showing," Arthur Danto energetically and eruditely challenges a certain view of the plasticity of human vision, namely, that human vision changes over history and that artistic representation plays a significant role in effecting such transformations. Sentiments like these can be heard frequently in certain precincts of the humanities today, notably, in departments of art history and film. Danto, however, is preoccupied with the version of the view that he finds in the writings of the late Marx Wartofsky. Against what he takes Wartofsky to be saying, Danto argues, marshalling cross-cultural evidence, that perception is cognitively impenetrable and that, as such, it does not have a history, let alone one shaped by art history.

The level of perception that concerns Danto is the ability to recognize what naturalistic pictures are pictures of. For instance, normal viewers of widely varying cultural backgrounds are able to recognize human faces in pictures of human faces on the silver screen. *Ex hypothesi*, no amount of cultural conditioning will succeed in making normal viewers worldwide literally see such faces as cross-sections of centipedes. The way the world looks – in terms of the nonconceptual content of perception – to normally sighted humans is a function of our biological hard-wiring, and, to the extent that pictorial systems activate those hard-wired perceptual capabilities, humans from one cultural background are able to recognize what pictures from alternative cultural styles are pictures of. Thus, Danto points out that the Chinese were able to recognize, without specialized training, what pictures in the Western style of perspective represented.

"Modernity and the Plasticity of Perception," *Journal of Aesthetics and Art Criticism* 59(1) (2001): 11–17.

For Danto, then, there is some substratum of perception that is universal, or nearly universal, and, therefore, rooted in human nature, biologically speaking. The capacity to recognize certain kinds of pictures is a consequence of this. These pictures do not transform human perception – in the sense of rewiring our biological endowments – but rather merely activate the perceptual capacities we already possess. The human perceptual apparatus – at the level of seeing how things look and recognizing them on that basis – does not change, and, therefore, art does not change vision, at least in the sense of restructuring the human capacity for recognizing things perceptually on the basis of how they appear fundamentally to all human viewers.

Xanthippe would look to me (had I a time machine) pretty much the way she looked to Socrates, and no pictures of Xanthippe would fundamentally restructure the hardware that either Socrates or I would employ when recognizing Xanthippe. The difference in conceptual backgrounds and artistic enculturation between Socrates and me would make no difference in our literal, basic perceptions of Xanthippe.

Danto thinks that this line of argument refutes Wartofsky's claim that art transforms human perception. But it is not clear to me, despite Wartofsky's dramatic way of putting things, that Wartofsky's thesis is as strong as the one that Danto sets out to rebut. For in his essay "Art History and Perception," what Wartofsky seems to be talking about is learning from pictures, and that possibility hardly seems controversial.[1]

If I understand Wartofsky correctly, the transformation of perception that he has in mind is the sort of thing that happens when after attending to paintings by Cézanne and remarking upon the busyness of the contours around his objects, I come to notice in everyday life that the longer I look at the edges of things, the more they appear to vacillate. That is, I can learn about features of how the world looks that I heretofore neglected, and this can change me indelibly. Perhaps I will never see fruit in exactly the same way after studying certain still lifes by Cézanne. Perhaps this will even modify my own neuroperceptual system in some very subtle way. Perhaps whole subcultures could be taught to notice what Cézanne noticed. But, in any event, if the idea that art transforms perception amounts to no more than that we can learn about the way the world looks – and notice visible features of it that we had previously ignored – from pictures, then the claim seems scarcely exceptionable.

Indeed, the changes in perception that Wartofsky champions may even presuppose the kinds of perceptual regularities that Danto defends, since in order to learn the lesson of Cézanne's contours, we must first recognize, at the level of perception that concerns Danto, that the relevant patches of color represent objects, say fruit. Thus, there is a way in which Wartofsky's position about how art transforms perception and Danto's views can, with little or no strain, be reconciled consistently.[2]

Nevertheless, although Wartofsky may not be quite the target that Danto is looking for, the transformation of perception thesis does seem to have found favor among a significant number of art historians and film historians, especially among those who wish to mark off modernity as a distinctive historical epoch. These writers have claimed that modernity is characterized by, among other things, a new kind of perception. Thus, it would appear that the issues Danto raises are quite timely, even if Wartofsky himself did not commit the error Danto attributes to him.

A touchstone for the aforesaid approach to modernity is Walter Benjamin's classic essay, "The Work of Art in the Age of Mechanical Reproduction." There Benjamin claims:

> During long periods of history, the mode of human sense perception changes with humanity's entire mode of existence. The manner in which human sense perception is organized, the medium in which it is accomplished, is determined not only by nature but by historical circumstances as well. The fifth century, with its great shifts of population, saw the birth of the late Roman art industry and the Vienna Genesis, and there developed not only an art different from that of antiquity but also a new type of perception. The scholars of the Viennese school, Riegl and Wickhoff, who resisted the weight of the classical tradition under which these classical forms had been buried, were the first to draw conclusions from them concerning the organization of perception at the time. However far-reaching their insight, these scholars limited themselves to showing the significant formal hallmark which characterized perception in late Roman times. They did not attempt – and perhaps, saw no way – to show the social transformations expressed by these changes in perception. The conditions for an analogous insight are more favorable in the present. And if changes in the medium of contemporary perception can be comprehended as decay of the aura, it is possible to show its social causes.[3]

For Benjamin, "the aura" is a response-dependent property of objects that enjoins us to experience them "at a distance" – not a literal distance, but what some might call "aesthetic distance."[4] Modernity, however, it is alleged, leads to a decay of this kind of distance, presenting us with objects and situations in a way that abets "the urge to get hold of objects at very close range."[5] Photographs and cinematic close-ups both reflect this putative urge and encourage it. For example, from the close shots of small gestures in the movies, we are said to become sensitized to the psychopathology of everyday life, or, as Benjamin puts it, "film has brought about a similar [similar to Freud's] deepening of apperception."[6]

But the urge for closeness is not the only dimension along which perception has changed for Benjamin. In a fairly illustrative summary of recent interpretations of Benjamin's viewpoint, Jonathan Crary says that in Benjamin's writings,

> We encounter an ambulatory observer shaped by a convergence of new urban spaces, technologies, and new economic and symbolic functions of images and products – forms of artificial lighting, new use of mirrors, glass and steel architecture, railroads, museums, gardens, photography, fashion, crowds. Perception for Benjamin was acutely temporal and kinetic; he makes clear how modernity subverts even the possibility of a contemplative beholder [the kind of beholder who correlates with the aura]. There is never a pure access to a single object; vision is always multiple, adjacent to and overlapping with other objects, desires and vectors.[7]

Modernity, in other words, brings forth a new kind of perceiver, one of whose major modes is exemplified by the Baudelairean *flâneur* who is, according to Crary, "a mobile consumer of a ceaseless succession of illusory commodity-like images."[8] Wandering through the rapidly expanding cities of late-nineteenth- and twentieth-century modernity, these ambulatory observers are constantly shifting their attention from one thing to another – from one event, scene, sensation, spectacle, or product to the next.

Such observers may have thought that this way of strolling around and looking around was natural, but it was, according to modernity theorists, a new form of attention, one that was complicit with the cultural logic of capitalism, whose vested interests keep folks always on the lookout for new things to acquire.[9] Moreover, for some film historians, motion pictures, with their shifting points of view (film editing), both reflect this mobile, attention-switching mode of perception and also acclimate and perhaps even condition the modern city dweller to its hastening rhythms.[10]

There can be little doubt that, at least most of the time, authors like Crary believe that the modernity thesis contradicts "a persistent, and most often unexamined, Kantian prejudice that perceptual and cognitive capacities are ahistorical; that is, they are unchanging and permanent, and most significantly independent of an external social/technological milieu that is in constant flux."[11] But it is exactly the claim that some perceptual capacities are ahistorical that Danto examines and defends. Who has the better of it – Danto or the modernity theorists?

The modernity thesis claims that perception changes. But what does this mean? The most straightforward reading is that the *faculty of perception* changes. After all, the claim that people's *perceptions*, rather than their faculty of perception, change with modern life is not a very interesting claim. People's perceptions are changing all of the time. Of course, people's perceptions change with modern life; there are lots of new things to see. However, since proponents of the modernity thesis frame their conjecture linguistically in terms of "perception," rather than in terms of "perceptions," it seems reasonable to surmise that they intend to be speaking about some deep structural change in the faculty of perception across a significant human population.

That the faculty of perception across a significant human population might change is scientific possibility, given the theory of evolution. The processes of mutation and natural selection could bring about such a transformation. And perhaps with immense sophistication, genetic engineering might someday also be able to bring about a change like this self-consciously. So the claim that the faculty of perception might change is not inadmissible.

However, the modernity thesis is more specific. It claims that the faculty of perception did change some time around the late nineteenth century and early twentieth century. But if that happened, since we do not yet possess the requisite super-science of genetic engineering, it would have had to result from the normal processes of natural selection. And that takes a great deal of time – far more time than the amount lived through by the two or three generations that witnessed the transition to modernity. So on evolutionary grounds, we have substantial grounds, in principle, to be suspicious of the modernity thesis.[12]

But the modernity thesis is not just advanced as marking a transition that is possible in principle. Proponents are explicit about some of the precise changes in the faculty of perception that they believe occurred. These primarily have to do with attention. The modern city is bustling with things to see in every direction. There are things you want to see – like shop windows and billboards – and things you have to see – oncoming, high-speed traffic – everywhere. The modern city dweller has to be able to shift her or his attention rapidly. This mode of attention allegedly contrasts with what went before, when, for example, attention was directed to contemplating the aura. Moreover, this change in the faculty of perception/attention occurred as a result of the situation of modernity, not as a result of the process of natural selection.

This is a very tangled hypothesis, and it calls for some unraveling. Let us grant, for the purposes of argument, that city dwellers shift attention more frequently than do people down on the farm. Does this amount to a change in the faculty of perception? I cannot see that it does. The human perceptual apparatus, at the level of anatomical and physiological structure, is constantly in motion, constantly scanning the environment. This adaptive feature is longstanding; it served our prehistoric forebears advantageously, keeping them on the alert for predators and prey – for danger and for opportunities of all sorts, including not only food and shelter, but also companionship. The human eye rarely fixates; saccadic eye movement is the norm. We did not suddenly become attention-switching *flâneurs* in the late nineteenth century; we have been natural-born *flâneurs* since way back when.

Perhaps the modern city gave us more to scan; perhaps it accelerated our innate rhythms of scansion in some systematic way, though it is hard to imagine how anyone could know this. But if the modernity thesis is simply that the conditions of the modern city prompt us to shift our attention more often than less stimulating environments, that hardly constitutes a change in the deep structure of the faculty of perception. The faculty of perception was already calibrated for rapid attention shifting. *Even if* the modern city elicits more attention shifting than previous environments, it did not invent the capacity, but only engaged the faculty of perception further in a long-familiar activity.[13]

But what of the contrast that friends of the modernity thesis draw between modern vision and the supposedly antecedent form of contemplative perception associated with "the aura" (which sort of perception Benjamin says is decaying in the contemporary period)? I think that that contrast is a confused, and, for that reason, false one. If what has been already said is true, then the natural inclination of perception has always been to rove, not to contemplate. There is no discontinuity in the faculty of perception between what preceded modernity and what came after.

Moreover, what is called perception of the aura does not characterize ordinary, everyday perception in the time preceding its alleged demise. It is what some call aesthetic perception, distanced perception, the practice of looking at artworks and sacerdotal images. Juxtaposing how people are said to attend to those things, perhaps as a result of acculturation, with how they attend to city traffic is a false comparison. The fact that there is a difference between how people perceptually negotiate ordinary city life and how they "distance" themselves in the presence of certain kinds of images, like artworks, does not mark a historical rupture in the faculty of perception, but different enduring ways of using the perceptual faculty: one, the line of least resistance, that involves roving attention, and another, generally cultivated through socialization, involving fixated, contemplative attention, usually of certain kinds of objects, such as artworks, relics, and other foci of veneration.

Furthermore, the possibility of the kind of fixated, distanced, contemplative attention that we often train ourselves to direct to artworks, relics, and, sometimes, even to everyday objects did not disappear with the onset of modernity. People still frequently suppress their natural proclivities to let their attention roam and instead fixate, contemplate, or aesthetically distance themselves in art galleries, museums, theaters, on nature walks, in churches, and the like. The two ways of perceiving coexist today, as I suspect they always have. Modernity did not retire contemplative gazing.

Benjamin says that in contrast to pre-modern distancing, in modernity there is a craving to see things close up. Cinema satisfies this craving and even tutors perception by teaching us through cinematic object lessons (close-shots) about the significance of small gestures. Certainly no one knows the extent to which cinema influenced viewer sensitivity to small gestures. To do that, one would need to know about pre-cinema sensitivities amongst the relevant cultural groups. And how would one discover that?

Nevertheless, it is plausible to claim that cinema drew the attention of some people to the significance of gestures and that this had some transfer value in everyday life. In my own experience, I can even cite some examples of this. But the question before us is whether this constitutes a change in the faculty of perception.

In order to answer this question, I think we need to stipulate a broad, provisional distinction between seeing and noticing. "Seeing," in this context, refers to what the faculty of visual perception does automatically; "noticing" refers to the way in which we can organize what we see, often as the result of learning. "Noticing," for my purposes, is a matter of focusing on details of what we see, of finding certain objects or structures salient. Given the distinction between seeing and noticing, I think that the most charitable interpretation we can give of Benjamin's hypothesis is that cinema (TV and photography) afforded and continues to afford the possibility for some to learn to notice certain features of the world which, though previously seen, went unheeded.

Whereas I *see* what the experienced tracker sees, she or he *notices* the telltale signs that an animal has been this way. In the best of cases, I can learn to do this as well. It does not require a change in my faculty of perception, however. It involves learning a certain way of organizing what I literally see. Likewise, this seems the most that a friend of the modernity thesis can derive from considering cinematic close-ups of small gestures. The case is parallel to that of our earlier discussion of Cézanne. One can learn to see features of the world hithertofore unremarked by looking at artworks, including films, but that does not constitute a change in the faculty of perception.

The distinction between seeing and noticing may also be useful for blocking another way of attempting to bolster the claim that modernity changed perception. Surely, it might be said, modernity ushers in a host of new concepts, for example, that of the neurotic. And with the advent of new concepts – and the abandonment of old concepts – moderns see what their forebears did not. However, what the relevant concepts do is to enable us to organize our visual field, to highlight phenomenologically elements of what we would literally see sans the pertinent concept in bold relief, so to speak. Looking under the guidance of the kinds of concepts we are talking about, in other words, falls primarily into the category of what I am calling "noticing." To employ an ultimately unsatisfactory metaphor, a change in concepts of the relevant sort is a change in software, not hardware.

The modernity thesis appears to claim that there was a change in the faculty of perception as the nineteenth century became the twentieth century. We have explored several reasons for rejecting strong readings of this hypothesis. But the modernity thesis also claims certain relations between the arts, notably, cinema and photography, and this alleged change in perception. So in what remains, let me comment on the second part of this thesis.[14]

The cinema, to take Benjamin's leading example, is somehow bound up with the change of perception that heralds modernity. This is obviously true, but uninteresting; undeniably cinema arose during the period identified as modernity and reflects modernity by being an example of it. But there are further, more ambitious claims lurking in this neighborhood: that, at the level of perceptual change, cinema reflects modernity and/or that it is somehow an agency of modernity.

Of course, cinema reflects modernity in some sense. But does it reflect it in any systematic way that is relevant to the hypothesis about changes in perception? If there had been a change in perception (which I deny) and if cinema reflected it, there seem to me to be two ways of understanding what such reflection would amount to: either cinema was somehow a causal consequence of the alleged change in perception or analogies can be drawn between cinema and the putatively new forms of vision.

The idea that changes in perception due to some new form of vision spawned by modern urban living provides a causal condition for the dissemination of cinema seems unlikely, since rural populations, including rural populations in lands remote from Western industrialization, such as the Indian countryside, easily assimilated cinematic representation without the preparation of living amidst the visual frenzy of the modern city.

Nonetheless, does not cinema reflect modern vision insofar as analogies can be found between perceptual features of modern life and cinema – for example, between an alleged increase in shifting attention in daily life and film editing, on the one hand, and the barrage of stimuli in urban centers and the sensational content of films, on the other hand? Yet analogies like these are not very compelling, especially since they are too easy to come by.

If one is selective enough and imaginative enough, one can probably find analogies between cinema and ancient Egyptian life, particularly if the terms of the analogy are broad enough. But, even if it makes sense to try to compare them, is the tempo of modern life really reflected by film editing (all film editing?) in any way that is revelatory? Phenomenologically, film editing from the early twentieth century never seems as harried as Times Square on a busy day. Nor does it appear actually informative to subsume the magical transformations so popular in early films under the same category of sensation that is employed to characterize the experience of the modern city.[15]

Lastly, it is claimed that cinema contributes to modernity, again at the level of changing perception fundamentally. If we put to one side the possibility that we might be able to learn to notice different features of the world from viewing art or film, the basic question boils down to whether any form of visual representation can change the faculty of perception. My own disposition is to argue that the pictorial arts have developed in ways that already suit our nearly unchanging or only glacially mutating perceptual capacities, instead of the causal influence running in the opposite direction.

But perhaps these are matters better left to experimental investigation rather than to armchair speculation. For we can, once we have segregated the relevant variables precisely, test to see whether the perceptual faculties of children differ systematically before and after exposure to cinema. If changes are in evidence, then that might at least show that the kind of transformation of perception advertised by the modernity thesis is empirically plausible. But, given the repeated failed attempts to corroborate scientifically the claim that exposure to television shrinks attention spans, one should reserve the right to remain skeptical about the prospects for comparable hypotheses concerning the influence of cinema, or of any other art form, on our faculties of visual perception/attention.

Undoubtedly, some readers will complain that I interpret the modernity thesis in too strong a manner. They will allege that it claims something less than an assertion that the faculty of perception changes literally under the influence of the arts. But if this is so, why do art historians and film historians, as well as others in the humanities, feel so compelled to speak as though perception were utterly plastic? What is really at stake in the use of such extravagant language? But that, of course, is a topic for some other symposium.

Notes

1   Marx W. Wartofsky, "Art History and Perception," in John Fisher (ed.), *Perceiving Artworks* (Temple University Press, 1980).
2   Wartofsky does briefly allude to the theory/observation debate in the philosophy of science, suggesting that pictures supply something like the framework for vision that theories are said to provide for scientific observations. However, his comments are too fleeting to warrant sustained criticism. Were this position developed more fully, it might certainly call for the type of criticisms Danto raises. Jerry Fodor, for example, raises objections parallel to Danto's against the thesis of the theory-ladenness of observation in the philosophy of science. See Wartofsky, "Art History and Perception," p. 24; and Jerry Fodor, "Observation Reconsidered," *Philosophy of Science* 51 (1984); Jerry Fodor, "A Reply to Churchland's 'Perceptual Plasticity and Theoretical Neutrality,'" *Philosophy of Science* 55 (1988).
3   Walter Benjamin, "The Work of Art in the Age of Mechanical Reproduction," *Illuminations*, trans. Harry Zohn (New York: Schocken Books, 1969), p. 69.
4   One thing that makes it very difficult to evaluate claims about changes in perception in modernity is that commentators do not always seem to agree about the nature of those changes. Indeed, at times they seem to have diametrically opposed phenomena in mind. For example, the influential theorist Wolfgang Schivelbusch claims that modernity as a result of the experience of nineteenth-century train riding gave rise to a panoramic form of perception. But such a form of perception would be distanced. Therefore, Schivelbusch's hypothesis seems incompatible with Benjamin's claims about the deterioration of the aura. Who is right? Don't we need to settle this question or to discount both Benjamin and Schivelbush's conjectures in order to address concretely the issue of whether perception changed? Mustn't we know what we are looking for? Unfortunately, some commentators appear to accept both Benjamin's and Schivelbush's claims without realizing the tension between them. This makes arguing about the change of perception thesis pretty slippery. See Wolfgang Schivelbusch, *The Railway Journey* (University of California Press, 1986).

5   Benjamin, "The Work of Art in the Age of Mechanical Reproduction," p. 223.
6   Ibid., p. 235.
7   Jonathan Crary, *Techniques of the Observer: On Vision and Modernity in the Nineteenth Century* (MIT Press, 1992), p. 20.
8   Ibid., p. 21.
9   Jonathan Crary, "Dr Mabuse and Mr Edison," in Russell Ferguson (ed.), *Art and Film since 1945: Hall of Mirrors* (Los Angeles: Museum of Contemporary Art, 1996), p. 265.
10 Sometimes commentators ground claims about the mobility of modern perception on both Schivelbusch's speculations about panoramic vision and Benjamin's discussion of the *flâneur* without realizing that Benjamin's claims about the deterioration of aura do not fit nicely with Schivelbusch's panoramas.

It should also be noted that, though often unacknowledged, there seems to be an implicit disagreement among commentators about the exact role that cinema plays in the production of a new form of vision. Some seem to think that cinema helps acclimate viewers to the brave new visual world of modernity, some claim that it abets the culture of visual sensation by supplying even greater shocks to the visual system than does city life, and some claim that cinema helps stabilize or fix perception in a world of flux. These alternatives do not all seem compatible. Which one should we focus on when evaluating the modernity hypothesis?

11 Crary, "Dr Mabuse and Mr Edison," p. 262. Crary also says of Benjamin, "This organization of experience for him [Benjamin] was above all the obliteration of a Kantian model of apperception and its replacement by the perceptual fragment or ruin" (ibid., p. 272).

The caveat – "at least most of the time" – is included above to acknowledge that once in a while in the midst of articles about changing vision, Crary inexplicably will say things such as "vision may not have changed in the nineteenth century" ("Dr Mabuse and Mr Edison," p. 268). I do not know what to do about these incongruities in Crary's writing, except to say that, "most of the time," it seems to me that he embraces the transformation of vision hypothesis. It should be said, in addition, that it is often difficult to interpret what Crary is claiming, since he often appears to slide illicitly from speaking about what people thought about perception at a certain time to how people actually perceived at that time. This can lead to egregious confusion, since historically dated theories about perception very often fail to track the phenomena accurately.

12 For further argumentation, from an evolutionary point of view, against the notion that media change perception, see Noël Carroll, *A Philosophy of Mass Art* (Oxford: Clarendon Press, 1998), ch. 2.

13 I say "even if" because it is not obvious to me that when walking down a city street I scan the scene more often than did my prehistoric ancestors warily crossing some savanna, fearful of potential dangers from every direction.

Also, it is interesting to note that many contemporary city dwellers do not scan their environment but keep their gaze glued to the pavement so as to avoid the attention of street crazies. Needless to say, this perceptual practice, provoked by conditions in contemporary cities, does not amount to a change in the faculty of perception. But is the learned custom of browsing the displays in sidewalk shop windows different in principle?

14 Of course, I agree that cinema changed perception in the trivial sense of giving us a new kind of thing to see, namely, film. And, of course, film changes film perception. But this is not the claim that I will be examining in what follows. What we want to ask after is whether film either reflects or causes changes in the way we see the real world, not the film world.

15 For a trenchant, detailed discussion of the modernity hypothesis with respect to early cinema, see David Bordwell, *On the History of Film Style* (Cambridge, MA: Harvard University Press, 1998), pp. 141–6.

3

The Ties that Bind

Characters, the Emotions, and Popular Fictions

The issues

From Plato to Collingwood, philosophers have regarded the arousal of emotions as the characteristic calling card of the popular arts. Though far from pleased by this aspect of popular fictions – for Plato, the tragedies of his own day – he nevertheless was convinced that this was the inevitable destiny of any art that aspired to popularity, since the general populace, he believed, lives by its guts rather than by its mind. Consequently, Plato reasoned, anyone who wished to curry favor with the common run of the citizenry would have to appeal – Plato would say *pander* – to their emotions instead of to their brains.

Whether or not one shares Plato's low estimates of the emotions and those who allegedly live by them, one can agree that addressing the emotions is a central feature of what are called the popular arts, and perhaps even concur that these arts are popular in large measure because they engage the emotions, especially the garden-variety emotions, as effectively as they do.[1] This is particularly obvious with popular fictions – whether literary or visual; whether novels, short stories, plays, films, comic books, or graphic novels; whether a song or an entire musical; or whether still photos, sculptural ensembles, radio broadcasts, or TV shows. Popular fictions command our attention by provoking emotional responses which, in turn, keep us riveted to them as they unfold.

"On the Ties that Bind: Characters, the Emotions, and Popular Fictions," in William Irwin and Jorge Gracia (eds.), *Philosophy and the Interpretation of Popular Culture* (Lanham, MD: Rowman & Littlefield, 2007), pp. 89–116.

The emotions, to an arresting degree, are the ties that bind us to popular fictions. This chapter is about the affective address of popular fiction.[2]

Needless to say, Plato not only noticed that arousing the emotions was a primary strategy for absorbing audiences in popular fictions; he also realized that an indispensable means for doing so – for holding onto audiences affectively – was via their relationships to fictional characters. And though this is clearly not the only mechanism by which popular fictions enlist audiences in their agenda, I have to agree with Plato that it is, indisputably, a major channel for securing our attention emotively. Thus, for the remainder of this chapter, I will follow Plato in attempting to limn the ways in which popular fictions engage their audiences emotionally by exploring the various kinds of affective relationships popular fictioneers propose between viewers, readers, and listeners, on the one hand, and the fictional characters whose adventures preoccupy us, on the other hand.

In short, this chapter is an examination of the emotive address of popular narration in terms of the way in which that process is implemented through our relation to fictional characters. Of course, it goes virtually without saying that there is no *one* relation here, but many.[3] How many exactly? I must confess that I do not know. Thus, this chapter is only a preliminary sketch, offering several crude distinctions that will undoubtedly benefit from future refinement. My only justification for presenting such an unfinished project at this time is that one has to start somewhere.

In order to begin this exploration of the affective bonds between characters and popular audiences, I will start with the most ancient and maybe still the most popular proposal about the nature of this relationship – namely, that it is a matter of identification. I will critically review both simple and sophisticated versions of the notion of identification, not merely for the sake of dismissing this idea, but, more importantly, in order to reveal how much more diverse and complicated our relationships with fictional characters really are than is suggested by the identification model.

Next, I will examine and reject the recently fashionable concept of simulation as a comprehensive account of our relation to fictional characters. I will argue that we rarely, if ever, resort to simulation in trying to understand the emotions of fictional characters or to explain and/or to predict their behavior.[4]

Like the idea of identification, that of simulation promotes the notion that sharing the selfsame or congruent emotive states with fictional characters is key to our affective bond with at least the protagonists in popular narratives. However, I will maintain that a much more comprehensive model of our emotional stance to characters is captured by concepts such as care, concern, and sympathy – pro-attitudes that we have *for* others rather than emotional states we share *with* them. That is, whereas we feel sympathy for the immiserated family, that is not an emotion they bear toward themselves, and it therefore is not an emotion that we *could* share with them. Thus, if you pace the identification and simulation approaches, it would appear that the most frequently recurring relationships between ourselves and fictional protagonists are not ones in which we reproduce the same emotional states but ones in which we, the audience, mobilize an affective stance toward the relevant characters that is different from the one, if any, that they are undergoing. Or, so I shall argue.

Before concluding, however, I will also consider one sort of audience-character interaction where it does seem that we should concede that there is an undeniable degree of shared affect. This is the case where the audience automatically mimics the facial and/or postural expressions of the characters in order to ascertain approximately what they are feeling. These may be called *mirror reflexes*. These reactions play a significant role in popular audiovisual fictions. Moreover, understanding the way in which these processes operate may also suggest the grain of truth that makes notions like identification and simulation seductive.

Identification

Perhaps the earliest theory of our emotional bond with fictional characters was proposed by Plato in his *Republic*. There he hypothesized that audiences take on board the emotions – notably pity and fear – of the characters they encounter in tragedies. Plato did not think this politically advisable, since guardians who pitied either themselves or the enemy, or who feared for their own death, would scarcely make ideal warriors. Although most have parted company with Plato's worries about the civic danger of taking on these emotions, the idea that such a transfer of emotional states occurs upon exposure to fictional characters remains an article of faith among ordinary audience members and professional critics alike. Both groups speak freely of *identifying* with characters, by which they most often appear to mean that they suffer the selfsame emotional states – the same joys and fears – that possess the relevant fictional personae.

Furthermore, on this view, it may be suggested that a large part of the attraction of fiction is that it affords us the opportunity to experience vicariously the emotional states of the characters in question – most notably the protagonists. This is what accounts putatively for our interest in such fictions. When this possibility is not available – when we are said to be unable to identify with the characters – that then is often given as a reason why the fiction has failed to grip us. How often has one heard the refrain "I could not identify with so-and-so (usually the hero or heroine)" offered as a reason for why some or another popular fiction failed?

The notion of identification is so commonplace that one readily forgets that it is a highly theoretical hypothesis with a long philosophical lineage. It is a piece of theory that has seeped into ordinary language where it evades close scrutiny. However, the idea, at least in its most blatant form, has little to recommend it. If identification were the characteristic mode of our emotional involvement with characters, we would expect audiences to be in the same emotional states as the characters to whom they are exposed. But more often than not, this is not the case.

A young couple in a TV drama blissfully walks down the garden path holding hands, while, unbeknownst to them, they are being stalked by a serial killer. Seeing this, we are consumed by fear for them, although from their point of view, things could not be better. Such scenes recur with numbing frequency in suspense fictions. The emotional frisson they engender cannot be explained in terms of identification, since the audience is in a radically different mental state than the protagonists. Likewise, when a Harold Lloyd type is embarrassed, we are apt to be comically amused, but he is disconsolate. And when Oedipus is wracked with guilt, we do not share his remorse but feel pity for him. Whereas the theory of identification predicts shared emotional states between characters and spectators, quite often – perhaps most often – our emotions go in different, and sometimes even opposite, directions.

Moreover, this is not only true with regard to protagonists. When the villain is frustrated ("foiled again!"), we are likely to feel joy, while, as he is gloating about his imminent triumph, our ire mounts. Whereas the notion of emotive identification would appear to presuppose symmetry between the emotional states of characters and audiences – why else would it be called "identification" – in a vast number of cases, the pertinent relationships are asymmetrical. So, at the very least, identification cannot provide us with a general account of our emotional relationship to characters.

Of course, one response to this observation might be that it is not our emotions that are the substance of identification here; rather, we are identifying with the character. But if we were identifying with the character – one of the aforesaid young lovers – and contemplating the situation as he or she understands it, then we would not be feeling consternation. We should be feeling bliss. But that is not the case. So there does not seem to be any theoretical gain in saying that it is the character with whom we identify – at least not if it is our intention to explain our emotional engagement in terms of identification.

Perhaps it will be granted that identification is not a comprehensive account of our emotional bonding with characters. There are all those cases of divergent reactions of the sort to which I've already alluded. Instead, it might be claimed that identification merely accounts for a great many instances of the emotional connection between characters and audiences. For example, when the protagonist is angry with his nemesis, so are we; when the heroine is disgusted by the monster, we are too. There are a great many cases like these. Are they not cases of identification?

Even if some may be, many clearly are not. I may be angry with the villain for the same reasons that the hero is. This no more implies that I identify with the hero than my dislike of a certain political candidate implies that I identify with everyone else in my party who shares this dislike with me. For we have all arrived at this appraisal through our own route. I have not become possessed by the feelings of some or another member of my political persuasion.[5] It is my own emotive appraisal. For a mental state to count as a case of emotive identification, we should not only share emotive states, but I should be in an emotive state like yours *because* you are in that state. It is in this respect that identification appears to be something akin to emotional contagion. But I may be angry with the villain because he acts wrongfully and be repulsed by the monster because it is disgusting, and *not* because the hero is angry or the heroine is disgusted. Sharing similar emotional states will not count as identification unless the state is not only similar but is a causal consequence of the character being in that state. And in an immense number of cases of converging emotional states, audiences are in the emotional states they are in because they appraise the fictional situations in the same way the characters do, and not because characters, in like states, have infected the audiences with their passions. To suppose the latter in most instances is to add an unnecessary bit of theoretical baggage, since the impurity of the monster and the evil of the antagonist respectively is enough to motivate the horror of the audience, on the one hand, and their anger, on the other.[6]

Another sort of evidence that might be mistakenly adduced on behalf of identification would be to note that quite often the emotional states of the audience appear to converge qualitatively with those of the relevant fictional characters. The characters suffer, and our hearts go out to them; we feel compassion. Our emotional states seem coordinated or synchronized with those of their fictional objects. This obviously happens. But, at the same time, it is not proof of emotional identification, since our emotional states, though compatible and even consilient, are not identical. Compassion is something that we feel toward the fictional characters, not something that they feel toward themselves. Indeed, with regard to your average popular melodrama, the emotive difference is even more pronounced, since we usually feel both pity *and* admiration for the victims of adversity, like Stella Dallas, whereas they evince neither of these emotions toward themselves. Indeed, would we so admire Stella Dallas for being self-sacrificing if she admired herself for being so?

This last example, moreover, illustrates the way in which the notion of identification frequently obscures the complexity of our emotional relations to fictional characters. Suppose we are confronted with a character plagued by the loss of a loved one; the character feels grief. The object of the character's emotional state is her loved one. We, in turn, are moved by the character's plight; let us say we feel sorrow. But our sorrow is not the same as the character's grief, since our sorrow has a different object. The object of our sorrow is the grief-stricken character; that the character is in anguish is part of the reason we feel sorrow for him. We are not grieving at our loss of a loved one but are saddened that the character's loss pains him. We are not in the same emotional state, since the object of our emotional state is different and more encompassing than the object of the character's emotional state; the object of the character's emotional state is only the loved one, whereas the object of our state is someone who has lost a loved one.[7] Inasmuch as it is generally the case (1) that the object of the audience's emotional state includes the character *and* the object of his state and (2) that the object of the audience's state is not reducible to the object of the character's emotional state, the claim that the audience's emotional state is identical to that of the character will be typically suspect. Talk of identification merely tends to flatten out our understanding of the emotional relationships of audiences to fictional characters rather than to acknowledge their complexity.

Of course, it is not only the case that the constituency of the objects of the audience's emotions differ significantly from those of fictional characters. It is also the case that there is an ontological difference here. Presumably, in the world of the fiction, the characters' emotions are grounded in their beliefs, whereas, given our metaphysical location, our emotional responses arise from simply entertaining or imagining certain thoughts about that world.[8] Furthermore, this probably contributes to yet another palpable difference between the emotional states of audiences and those of characters – namely, that the former are generally presumed to be felt less intensely, all things being equal, than the latter.[9] And, of course, another salient difference in this ontological neighborhood is that the emotions of fictional characters are still connected to the agent's action-behavior system, while the audience's emotions are disengaged, undoubtedly because of the way in which they have been decoupled from certain beliefs about the existence and urgency of the situations the fiction has invited us to imagine. All these differences should underscore that the relationship betwixt the emotional state of fictional characters and those of their audiences can rarely, if ever, be that of identity, thereby suggesting that the notion of identification is moot.[10]

But it may be argued that the idea of identification that I am criticizing is too simplistic. Identification, it might be said, is not something that happens to me as a result of what the character feels. It is something that, in part, I bring about. The fiction invites me to imagine that I am the character in certain circumstances and then to further imagine aspectually what I would feel so situated.[11] For example, I imagine I am the child of a farmer who has been bushwhacked, and then I imagine the desire for revenge that would overtake me, including the passion of hatred with which I would regard my father's murderers.

However, I distrust this more sophisticated version of identification on several counts. First, it is overly elaborate. What motivates postulating our imagining that we are the character? If our own sense of justice has been violated by the murder of the farmer, then that will account for our indignation toward his killers and our desire for their punishment. That is, we can find an explanation sufficient to our emotional reaction without adding identification – including aspectual identification – to the story. So why do so? It offends the principle of explanatory parsimony.

Second, I wonder whether it is even plausible to suggest that the fiction invites us to imagine being the character. How is it marked? For certainly it should be marked, since no one wishes to claim that we imagine being all the characters. How could we? When would we have the time? That is, there is the question – especially with respect to films, TV dramas, and plays – of how we would find the opportunity to indulge in these imaginings while still keeping up with the story as the production evolves rapidly in real time.

But maybe an even deeper problem with this version of identification is that it courts paradox. For if I really did imagine that I was the aggrieved child in search of revenge, shouldn't I resent the fact that the fictional character is beating me to the punch? Or, to see how extensive this problem is, suppose that I am imagining that I am the central character and that I am in love? Shouldn't I be jealous of that guy on the screen who is courting my baby? Or imagine that the character with whom I am identifying is bidding for a job. Wouldn't I resent the competition and find his hopefulness offensive? But none of these paradoxes arises. Why not? Presumably because I am not imagining that I am the character and/or that I have taken on his emotions, motives, and desires – not even aspectually.[12]

The emotional states of the audience may be coordinated with those of the characters in various ways. They may share the same emotive valence. For example, when the character is miserable and the audience feels pity, both are in dysphoric emotional states. These states converge vectorially – they both belong on the negative, distressful, or painful side of the scale of the emotions. Likewise, when the character is joyous and we are happy for her, our emotions converge vectorially on the euphoric side of the scale.[13] But though our emotions are similar in their valence, they are not identical. Thus, the fact that our emotions are often coordinated does not in any way support the notion of identification, unless that means nothing more than a somewhat similar feeling. But why invoke the notion of *identity* to describe that?

Simulation

We appear to be emotionally tied to popular fictions predominantly through our relations with certain characters, particularly those called protagonists. But what is the nature of that relationship – at least in the largest number of cases? We have just argued that the concept of identification does not seem to do it justice. Perhaps it is what is nowadays called "simulation."[14]

Simulation is a concept from the philosophy of mind that has recently been imported into aesthetics. In the philosophy of mind, the idea is that we understand and explain others, ascertain what they are feeling, identify their intentions and motivations, and predict their behavior by simulating them. That is, we input their beliefs and desires into our own off-line cognitive-conative system. Since, ex hypothesi, our cognitive-conative architecture is the same as theirs, if we run their belief-desire program on ourselves – their software on our hardware – then we should be able to derive a reasonable fix on that which people just like us (folk psychologically speaking) are likely to think, feel, plan, want, and so forth. That is, we put them into our shoes – or, equally metaphorically, we put their beliefs and desires into the black box that outputs our emotions, decisions, and behaviors – in order to project what they are likely to feel, think, or do.[15] This, moreover, is done on the presupposition that with respect to processing beliefs and desires into emotions and deliberations, we are structurally the same.

This theory – called simulation theory – is counterposed to another view in the philosophy of mind of the way in which we go about understanding others – which alternative view is called the theory theory, that is, the *theory* that we understand what others are about by applying something like a scientific *theory* to their behavior. Simulation is thought to have several advantages over the theory theory when it comes to reading the minds of others, because, on the one hand, the theoretical framework ostensibly presupposed by the theory theory would be monumentally complex – too complex, indeed, to postulate with great confidence – and, on the other hand, even if there were such a theory, it would take an immense amount of time to deploy in real time to particular cases, whereas we frequently size up people's emotional states and intentions in the blink of an eye.

But what does all this have to do with aesthetics – specifically with the question of our emotional relationship to the protagonists in popular fictions? Putatively, our relationship with fictional characters is generally like the relationships we have with other people in the world outside of fiction. The fiction invites us to understand them, to apprehend what they are feeling and intending, to speculate about what they will do next, and so forth, just as we must mind read our conspecifics in everyday life. In order to do so – in order to follow the fiction (the unfolding of the intentions and feelings of fictional characters) – we simulate them, or at least the leading ones, notably the protagonists. We input their beliefs and desires into our cognitive-conative architecture and discover what they are thinking and feeling by coming to think and feel broadly similar things, as our own system runs through its paces on their steam. Consequently, on this view, we are engaged emotively with the fiction by being immersed in a virtually continuous process of replicating the emotions and desires of (especially) the protagonists.

Unlike the proponent of identification, the simulation theorist does not claim that the emotions allegedly reproduced in us are identical, either thoroughly or aspectually, with those attributed to the protagonist. At best, they are only approximately similar. However, this still leaves the simulation theorist open to one objection that was leveled at the friends of identification – namely, the charge that simulation theory can be nothing near to a comprehensive theory of our emotional relationship to fictional characters because of the staggeringly vast number of cases where the emotions of the audience are different from and even opposed to those suffered by the fictional characters. When the protagonist rushes home joyously to tell her spouse that she's been promoted at the same time that we know she will find her family massacred, our despondent emotive state is nothing at all like hers. Moreover, if we were simulating her psychology, we would not be following the story appropriately. Furthermore, since similar asymmetries are so often the rule in popular fictions, simulation cannot be anything like a comprehensive account of our emotive engagement with characters.

Of course, sometimes the emotions of the audience and the characters do converge. Perhaps simulation explains those cases. However, this seems unlikely. Fictions, especially audiovisual ones, proceed at a pace that would seem to be uncongenial for simulation. Supposedly one advantage of simulation theory over the theory theory is that it is more suited temporally to sussing out the emotive states of conspecifics. But be that as it may, simulation takes time too, and one wonders whether one typically has sufficient breathing space to simulate in reaction to a spritely edited audiovisual array.[16]

Yet even deeper than the question of how simulation can occur in these cases is whether or how often it does occur. Simulation theory in the philosophy of mind is advanced as a view of how we go about determining what our conspecifics are feeling and thinking – a way of understanding and predicting their not transparently fathomable behavior. But popular fictions are not like everyday life. They are designed to be understood; indeed, they are designed to be understood quickly and clearly by untutored audiences.[17]

Moreover, that aspiration extends to the way in which the fictional characters are constructed. Perhaps in our ordinary experience our conspecifics strike us as opaque in a way that calls for simulation. I would not say this never happens, though I am not convinced that it is happening all the time. Nevertheless, I will argue that the kinds of situations that call for simulation occur rarely with respect to fictional characters, especially those who inhabit popular fictions, because those characters are expressly contrived in such a way that they wear their feelings and their thoughts on their sleeves. Thus, there is little or no need to hypothesize the operation of simulation in response to popular fiction, since we usually know exactly what the fictional characters are feeling and thinking faster than it would take to simulate these fictional beings.

This is most evident with respect to literary fictions. Most popular fictions employ the device of free, indirect discourse, which means that the author can narrate what the character is thinking and feeling from both the outside and the inside. We have his or her context described for us, often in emotionally suggestive terms; her physical state is delineated; and then we are also made privy to her thoughts. In such situations, there is no call for simulation. We are just told what the character is feeling and thinking. Perhaps some readers use the text as a script for attempting to raise similar emotions in themselves. I don't, but I wouldn't claim that others are like me in this respect. Nevertheless, it should be clear that there is no pressure to mobilize simulation theory in cases like this to explain how we come to understand the feelings and thoughts of the protagonists. We are told them outright.

Of course, this feature of literary fictions is not as common in audiovisual fictions. We do not as frequently enter the mind of the protagonist in films and TV dramas. But it is true that quite often they do tell us how they are feeling and what they are thinking, frequently by way of dialogue with interlocutors. And even in those cases where the characters do not explicitly articulate their states of mind, I would still contend that the characters in those fictions manifest their feelings and thoughts so openly that simulation is effectively beside the point.

How is this possible? Perhaps one way to get at this is to ask whether, with respect to everyday experience, simulation and the theory theory exhaust our ways of gaining access to the feelings and thoughts of others. Arguably, they do not. Often – indeed, probably most often – we impute thoughts and feelings to others on the basis of schemas, scripts, prototypes, contextual cues, and heuristics, rather than on the basis of a theory, which stratagems, in turn, enable us to infer the inner states of others.

Confronted with a coworker who has just been fired or a friend who has lost a loved one, we infer, all things being equal, that they are down. If their shoulders are slouched and their eyelids heavy, we recognize these as signs of distress. We have no need to perform a simulation, because, through experience, we have amassed a repertoire of schemas, heuristics, and contextual and recognitional cues to alert us to the inner states of conspecifics.[18]

When we hear that a relative has secured a long-sought-after job, all things being equal, we suppose that the relative is happy, and we rejoice for her. There is no need for simulation. We have access to a body of prototypes regarding emotional responses in certain contexts, as well as recognitional cues, such as facial expressions and postures, that enable us to assess the emotional states of others. These are not theories, and they are not applied by subsuming particular situations under nomological generalizations, as the theory theory might have it, but they are prototypes – schemas, heuristics, and recognitional cues – employed by *analogy*. Such is a reasonably reliable means for tracking the emotional states and thoughts of conspecifics, and I am confident that we depend on it in everyday life far more than we do on simulation. For, quite frequently, simulation would just be too time consuming.

Moreover, this has important ramifications for popular fictions. Inasmuch as popular fictions are designed to maximize accessibility, they gravitate naturally toward the use of the schemas, heuristics, and contextual and/or recognitional cues that abound in the cultures of their target audiences. Indeed, it is part of the art of designing a character for the purposes of popular fiction that one be able to streamline the details of the character's persona so that it calls forth the schemas, heuristics, and cues that fit it almost automatically.

In the situation comedy *Sex and the City*, the character of Samantha snugly fits the schema of the carnal woman – the sensual woman who loves sex (e.g., the Wife of Bath). When her eyes open wide as a handsome swain glides by, we do not need to simulate Samantha in order to determine her internal state. We can infer it based on our prototype for Samantha and the recognitional cues she supplies. Moreover, with respect to this particular TV series, our surmise will almost always be confirmed when Samantha slyly, albeit redundantly,[19] confides her desires to her friends, Carrie, Miranda, and Charlotte. Nor does this seem to me to be a peculiar example of the way in which the characters in popular fictions function.

But if this is a fair observation, then there appears to be little urge to hypothesize the operation of simulation in response to the characters in popular fiction. The problem that simulation is supposed to solve with respect to understanding the feelings and thoughts of others in everyday life does not generally arise with regard to popular fictions because popular fictions intensively exploit the schemas, heuristics, and contextual and recognitional cues that constitute our prototypes for discerning the inner lives of others.

Popular fictioneers build characters, economically sculpting their features, precisely to trigger quickly and effortlessly the mobilization of those prototypes by audiences. Thus, the need to postulate the operation of simulation as the means by which we apprehend the emotions and thoughts of the characters in popular fictions is largely otiose. But if we are not simulating the emotions of said characters, then it is not the case that we are emotionally bound to them by a continuous process of sharing congruent feelings.

Sympathy[20]

We are emotionally tied to popular fictions generally due to our relationship with characters, especially the protagonists. Neither the notion of identification nor that of simulation appears to explain the usual structure of this relationship satisfactorily. Whether or not identification or simulation ever occurs, they occur far more rarely than is often supposed, and therefore neither can afford a relatively comprehensive account of the emotive address of popular fiction. One thing that both identification and simulation have in common is that they postulate more-than-less closely shared emotional states between audiences and fictional characters. Moreover, it is the unlikelihood that such states are the norm that calls into question the adequacy of these accounts respectively. So maybe the way to go is to look for an emotional bond where the audience's emotional state is categorically different from those of the fictional characters.

One obvious candidate is sympathy. Sympathy is not an emotional state that persons bear toward themselves. It is, by definition, directed at others. For our purposes, we will construe sympathy roughly as nonfleeting care and concern, or, more broadly, as a nonpassing pro-attitude, toward another person (or a fictional character). Sympathy is a supportive response. Sympathy, conceived as an emotion, involves visceral feelings of distress when the interests of the objects of our pro-attitude are endangered, and feelings of elation, closure, or satisfaction when their welfare is achieved. The emotion in question has as a component the enduring desire for the well-being of its object – a desire that things will work out well for her. In order to be the object of this pro-attitude, the person in question must be thought to be worthy of our benevolence as a result of our interests, projects, values, loyalties, allegiances, or moral commitments. When X is appraised to be worthy of our nonpassing desire that things work out well for her, and this is linked to positive feeling tones when gratified and negative ones when frustrated, then we are in the emotional state that I am calling sympathy. If *sympathy* strikes you as having connotations of being too saccharin, you are welcome to refer to this emotive state merely as a pro-attitude.

The suggestion that sympathy plays a role in our emotional involvement with characters is surely unobjectionable. However, I am claiming more for it than that. I want to argue that it, along with antipathy (about which I will have little to say in this chapter), constitutes the major emotive cement between audiences and popular fictions. This, of course, requires me to say why I believe that sympathy holds this place of privilege and also how it is able to do so.

Obviously, in the course of a popular fiction, one undergoes many emotional states. One is angry for a while, then sad, then happy, then gripped by suspense, and then happy again. Sometimes sympathy for the protagonist is so strong that you can feel it. At other times, it appears to take the backseat for an interlude of comic amusement. Why select out sympathy as the most crucial lever for moving the audience's emotions with regard to popular fictions?

The first reason might be called its breadth. Sympathy for the protagonist is the most pervasive emotion from beginning to end of a popular fiction. As soon as sympathy is secured, unless it is later intentionally neutralized by the creator of the fiction, it stays on the alert, tracking the protagonist's fortunes, registering distress as her fortunes waver and pleasure as they rise. Sympathy, once enlisted, is constantly on call throughout the fiction. Generally, no other emotive stance – save antipathy for the antagonist – is as long lasting. The indignation we feel toward the surly guard who cuffs the hero comes and goes, but our sympathy for the protagonist endures. It provides the emotive optic through which we survey the narrative from one end to the other. Each event in the story is weighed in light of our sympathy for the protagonist; of every event, it is pertinent to ask whether it advances or deters her fortunes, even if the answer in some cases is neither.

The protagonists in popular fictions have goals and interests that are hard to miss. The narrative trajectory usually involves the accomplishment of those goals and the satisfaction of those interests in the face of various obstacles. We follow this quest from the perspective of sympathy, cheering the protagonists on as they advance and feeling consternation as they falter. Of course, sometimes our sympathy for the characters puts us out of sync with them – when we believe a character is falling for the wrong guy, for example. But still we track the unfolding narrative from a sympathetic viewpoint, one that disposes us to care about her best interests rather than her subjective assessment of them.

Sympathy is the most persistent emotional bond that we have with respect to the fictional protagonist; in this sense, it generally has more breadth than other emotions elicited by popular fictions. Furthermore, sympathy also has what might be called depth. It is our sympathy toward the protagonist that shapes our overall reception of the fiction. When we are angered by the way in which the heroine is mistreated, that anger itself is subsidiary to the sympathy we bear toward her. It underlies and reinforces our anger. It is our sympathy for the character that disposes us to regard her as inside our network of concern and, therefore, to assess an injustice done to her as something perpetrated against one of "our own." The negative emotions we muster in response to the protagonist's setbacks are a function of our sympathy for her. Sympathy is the foundation here. That is why we say it has depth.

Two reasons, then, suggest that sympathy is the major emotional bond between audiences and leading fictional characters, namely that sympathy appears to have greater breadth and depth than any other emotion we undergo while consuming a popular narrative. The obvious exception here may be the antipathy, distaste, and hatred that we often bear toward the antagonists in popular fictions. However, since this antipathy is generally the reverse side of – and indeed a function of – the sympathy we bear toward their rival protagonists, this case seems less of a counterexample to our conjecture than a corollary.

Admittedly, sometimes the influence goes in the opposite direction; there are cases – involving the enemy-of-my-enemy-is-my-friend syndrome – where sympathy may be a function of antipathy. Yet, in the main, in popular fictions, I would guess as a matter of empirical speculation that antipathy is usually an offshoot of sympathy. Nevertheless, in any event, the two are always connected so as to permit us to adjust our hypothesis and to propose that sympathy-cum-antipathy is the fundamental axis of the emotional address of popular fiction. Moreover, since it is neither the case that protagonists sympathize with themselves nor that antagonists hate themselves, pace both the notions of identification and simulation, our major emotional bond with popular fictions is, on this account, not a matter of our sharing the same or closely similar emotions with fictional characters.

If sympathy – or, more cumbersomely, sympathy-cum-antipathy – is the crux of our relationship to characters in popular fictions, there remains the question of how it is mobilized. In everyday life, we extend our sympathies to those with whom we share interests or projects or loyalties, or those who exemplify values of which we approve, or those who fall under the protection of certain moral principles. Of course, most of the interests, projects, and loyalties that we base many of our quotidian sympathies upon are highly specific to us. Needless to say, the creator of popular fictions cannot hope to activate the individualized interests of every member of the audience on behalf of her protagonists. Consequently, she must aim at engaging the audience at a fairly generic level of interests, projects, and loyalties. She must try to find some common ground amongst the diverse audience membership which will encourage us to find the protagonists to be worthy of our goodwill.

This is a design problem for the popular fictioneer; he must find some way to elicit from a variegated audience the converging desire that the protagonists do well – that is, our conviction that it would be good for them to do well, or that they deserve to do well. Moreover, as an empirical generalization, I hypothesize that the most common solution to this problem is to create protagonists who command the audience's moral endorsement. That is, morality provides the popular fictioneer with an interest, or project, or loyalty upon which target audiences from the same cultural background are likely to converge, at least broadly speaking.[21] Thus, by presenting protagonists who are morally appealing, the creator of popular fictions secures the criterial wherewithal to garner the sympathy that is required for her intended audiences to be emotionally absorbed by the story. That is, said protagonists meet the criterion of being deserving of our benevolence because they are morally deserving. It is no accident that the protagonists in popular fictions are good guys. Good guys are precisely what are likely to engender a pro-attitude from heterogeneous audiences of otherwise varied and often conflicting interests and loyalties. Morality, of the fairly generic sort found in popular fictions, is something that people from different backgrounds are apt to agree upon, at least roughly. Few, for instance, would disagree that Maximus was wronged when his family was slaughtered in *Gladiator*.

Characters in popular fictions are presented as morally right. This is obviously so in the greatest number of cases. But even so-called antiheros usually oppose some form of conventional/corrupt moral order in the name of some deeper sense of justice. Hard-boiled detectives always discover that society is even more rotten than they are. Alienated gunslingers protect the little folk against greedy cattle barons and bullying railroad magnates. Disaffected teenagers really care about problems that adult society culpably neglects or misunderstands. And so on. No matter how antisocial the protagonist appears at first glance, he or she is quickly seen to be prosocial at heart. Moreover, this is how it should be if sympathy is to take hold across a diverse audience whose likeliest point of convergence is apt to be morality very broadly construed.

By "broadly construed," I do not simply mean that the audience shares some rough and ready principles, but also a sense of what counts as virtuous. Protagonists enlist our moral approval, and thence our sympathy, because they are portrayed as persons of a variety of virtues, including a sense of fairness, justice, respect for others, loyalty, honor, honesty, and dignity; respect for the family; and concern for the weak, the lame, the halt, the elderly, and children, as well as less morally charged and more pagan virtues such as strength, cunning, and wit. These virtues, in turn, engender in audiences the palpable desire that the protagonists do well and that their rivals do badly.

Often in popular fictions, it is not the case that the protagonists are what we would call morally upright, and yet they still win our sympathy. Consider, for example, caper films. However, when one examines the structure of these exercises, one notices that the fictional universe has been constructed in such a way that the characters we might normally upbraid as criminals are presented in such a way that they are the most virtuous characters in evidence.[22] The forces of everyday society are either kept offscreen so that their countervailing claims never impinge on our sympathies, or they are shown to be venal and/or culpably stupid.[23]

In short, mobilizing sympathy for the protagonists – and the corresponding ill will toward the antagonists – in popular fictions generally relies on establishing that the protagonists are representatives of a value – generally a moral value – widely shared among the mass audience for popular fictions. This approval, then, is what grounds the audience's sympathy for the protagonist, which sympathy, in turn, binds the audience emotionally to the fiction. For example, it is undoubtedly the shared conviction in the moral rightness of the survival of humanity that makes science-fiction films – like *Independence Day* and *Jurassic Park* – such international blockbusters, since a pro-attitude toward humanity's continued existence is at least one thing upon which most members of the worldwide audience can agree. Perhaps this is the reason that science fiction (and, for related reasons, fantasy) can lay claim to being among the presiding popular genres of globalization.

Mirror reflexes

Thus far, I have been stressing that the most important affective bonds between popular audiences and their fictions involve us in marshaling emotional responses to characters, which emotional states are categorically quite different from the states undergone by the relevant fictional beings. And though I think that this hypothesis is generally accurate when it comes to describing the *emotional* relationships between audiences and characters, it is not a complete account of our *affective* engagement with popular fictions, especially audiovisual ones. For there is a stratum of affective communion that involves charged visceral feelings, which, though not exactly full-fledged emotions, nevertheless resonate congruently in the breasts of audience members and protagonists alike. What I have in mind may be called mirror reflexes.

Occasionally, when speaking to another person, we suddenly realize that we have adopted her facial expressions. She is frowning; we start to frown. Or she is smiling, and we find ourselves smiling. The same is true of gestures and postures. We watch the outfielder reach for a fly ball, and the muscles in our arm tug slightly in that direction. If our informant bends to us, we bend toward him. And so on. We have an involuntary tendency to mirror automatically the behavior, especially the expressive behavior, of our conspecifics.[24]

Putatively, we do this in order to gain some sense of what they are feeling. By configuring our own facial expression after the fashion of our interlocutor's – smiling, for example, when she is smiling – we gain an inkling of her inner state. The feedback from the disposition of our facial muscles buzzes our autonomic system in a way that is presumably isomorphic to what is going on in her system, if she is not dissembling. This does not give us full access to her emotional state, but it provides an important clue, since it yields something like a facsimile of the bodily feeling component of her overall state. Similarly, gestures and postures are often mimicked – though usually only in a highly truncated manner – in order to gather information about what is percolating inside our conspecifics. Moreover, this mimicry is predominantly automatic, not intentional. It is, in all probability, part of our biological endowment.

Children on their caregiver's knee evince mirror reflexes in abundance.[25] Clearly this behavior is a boon in learning the emotional repertoire – and much else – of one's culture, for it enables the child to discern the situations the caregiver associates with feelings of distress or elation. Among adults, mirror reflexes are also highly adaptive, since they facilitate social coordination.[26] Albeit subliminally, one can gauge – at least very broadly – the temperament of a room or the disposition of one's spouse by using your body as a detector of the kind of internal sensations that are apt to be associated with the manifest expressions of others.[27] The human capacity for mirror reflexes is, in all likelihood, an asset from the perspective of natural selection, since they are a means for both gaining information about conspecifics and for synchronizing our moods in joint ventures, from face-to-face conversations to cheerleading.

Aestheticians have been aware of the phenomenon of mirror reflexes at least since the work of Theodor Lipps.[28] And Sergei Eisenstein attempted to exploit Lipps's insights explicitly in his theory of filmmaking.[29] Though neither he nor Lipps used the terminology of mirror reflexes, Eisenstein included close-ups of stereotypical facial expressions and of body parts, such as clenched fists, in his films, in the hope of inspiring the sort of mimicry in audiences that would prepare them viscerally for the kinds of emotional states that he wished to arouse in them.[30] Less theoretically inclined filmmakers also discovered the importance of such affective modeling intuitively, and it has been a staple of popular cinema since the twenties. This is a legacy, further-more, that movies have bequeathed to TV. Undoubtedly, a significant amount of the affect stirred up by audiovisual entertainments is connected to the way in which they educe muscular mimicry in their audiences.

Watching a videotape of *Riverdance*, the audience taps its feet, accessing a simulacrum of the spirited pulse of the dancers. As Bruno in Hitchcock's *Strangers on a Train* reaches for the lighter he has dropped into the sewer, our arm muscles flex, within the abbreviated ambit of our theater seat, in a man-ner like his in order to help us feel his intention with our body. And even before we see the monster onscreen, the screaming visage of the victim, etched in horror, prompts us to tense our face analogously in a way that sends a signal through our muscles that things are about to get unpleasant.[31] The activity onscreen primes mimicry of a limited and circumscribed variety which may deliver information about the internal states of characters which we sample in terms of similar sensations in ourselves. Though not full-scale emotions – but only feelings sans objects – these sensations may be neverthe-less a serviceable source of the affective grip that such spectacles have on us in at least two ways.

First, they contribute to keeping the excitement level in our body elevated, thereby realizing one of the promises of popular audiovisual fictions. And second, they may make available information that we can integrate into our more encompassing emotional responses to the characters. The bodily feeling of distress the protagonist feels that is imprinted on his twisted features is relayed into us by our selective imitation of his expression so that we can use the dysphoric taste of that sensation as a recognitional cue for the kind of emotion he is undergoing and as an indicator of the kind of vectorially con-vergent emotion that is appropriate on his behalf – as, for example, sorrow would be apt if he is feeling some sort of pain. That is, mirror reflexes may function as subroutines in the formation of our emotional responses to fic-tional characters, not only alerting us to the general valence – whether posi-tive or negative – of their mental state but also calibrating the kind of passion we need to send back their way.

Mirror reflexes are not examples of emotional identification, since they do not involve the replication of complete emotional states but only feelings, which need not be the same feeling states but only similar ones. They are not simulations of emotions either, since they do not involve beliefs and desires, and they do not appear to require going off-line, if I understand that metaphor correctly. On the other hand, they are important elements in the affective address of audiovisual popular fictions like movies and TV. They can make our bodies vibrate with feeling in the presence of certain characters, and, even more importantly, they can facilitate our recognition of character emotion and modulate our own emotional response to it. In this regard, it would appear that audiovisual popular fictions have resources for exciting the affective reactions of audiences that popular literary fictions lack.

Summary

In this chapter, I have attempted to explore the affective address of popular fictions by focusing on the way they structure the audience's relationships to characters. I began by exploring two models for characterizing this subject – identification and simulation.[32] These approaches have in common the hunch that the nature of the audience's relationships to fictional characters, especially protagonists, involves sharing the selfsame or nearly the same emotions that the characters suffer. I have argued that this seems to be rarely if ever the case. Alternatively, I maintain that a better view of our emotional response to the characters in popular fictions is that it generally comprises a pro-attitude; it is a matter of care, concern, or sympathy – an emotional state that we have for and not with the characters in question. However, even if this is the dominant form of our emotional relation with characters, it is not the only affective relationship that is important in our commerce with popular fictions, especially audiovisual ones. There are also mirror reflexes. These responses engender in us something like an echo of the *feelings* that fictional characters are represented as undergoing by virtue of their expressive behavior. No account of our affective bond to such fictions would be complete without acknowledging these responses. Moreover, it is probably mirror reflexes that give rise to the claim that audiences emotionally identify with characters, whereas it might be more accurate to say that said reflexes enable us to sample something like the bodily feelings of fictional personae on our way to responding emotionally to them.

Notes

1 See Noël Carroll, *A Philosophy of Mass Art* (Oxford: Oxford University Press, 1998).
2 It is important to note that I use the concept of affect to include not only emotions but also moods, phobias, and reflex responses such as the startle response and what, in this essay, are later called mirror reflexes. For me, the notion of the emotions, properly so called, refers narrowly to mental states that take objects and that have

at least an appraisal component as well as a feeling component. Other affective states may differ from emotions in the sense that they lack objects and/or cognitive appraisals. In this essay, mirror reflexes are singled out as an important type of affect found in audiovisual popular fictions which are different from emotions. Though not discussed in this essay, startle reflexes are also a significant form of affect available to audiovisual popular fictions which are not emotions. Startle responses, however, are not discussed herein, since they need not involve the audience's connection to fictional characters, whereas mirror reflexes do.

3   Though in a recent article, Amy Coplan does not list me as a pluralist in this regard, I have always been so. See, for example, my "Film, Emotion, and Genre," in Carl Plantinga and Greg M. Smith (eds.), *Passionate Views: Film, Cognition, and Emotion* (Baltimore, MD: Johns Hopkins University Press, 1999), 21–47. See also Amy Coplan, "Empathic Engagement with Narrative Fictions," *Journal of Aesthetics and Art Criticism*, 52 (2004): 141–52.

4   I stress that my concern here is with the extent to which audiences deploy simulation in response to the characters in popular narrative fictions. I am neutral about the degree to which simulation is employed in everyday life and even somewhat agnostic about whether it is employed at all (though, on most days, I lean in the direction that it is, at least to some degree). In any event, I leave the latter two issues to philosophers of mind to adjudicate.

5   And, in any event, wouldn't there be too many other people for me to identify with – many of whom I have no knowledge?

6   This argument from explanatory parsimony has often been overlooked by my critics. Amy Coplan, for example, invites us to imagine a case where we witness a student being humiliated by a professor and then "share" the student's anger at the professor. I agree that mutual anger at the professor is readily conceivable in such a situation. But I do not see why we need to postulate an intervening stage in which I share the student's humiliation (though I concede we may feel pain or distress on his behalf). Why doesn't the professor's boorishness and insensitivity suffice to explain our anger? What – once our reaction to that is taken into account – remains to be elucidated?

Consider, for example, the construction of the entrance scene of the monster in a horror film. Here are two possible ways of doing it. First, the monster, oozing with slime, rises from his hoary gravesite and stalks toward the camera. No other character sees him. Yet we are horrified by its appearance. Alternatively, a gravedigger sees the monster, and this is interpolated into the scene by means of several point-of-view shots. Again, we are horrified. *But,* why suppose in the second case that our horror has been channeled, so to speak, through the gravedigger? That is, why imagine that we have identified with the gravedigger and, in consequence, have "caught" his horror?

For there is no need to suppose that our horrified response to the first scene is any different than to the second scene. But if we can explain our emotional responses to the first scene in terms of the way in which it has criterially prefocused our attention and kick-started our own emotional processing (sans any link to some human character in the fiction), then why must we add an identificatory epicycle to explain the way in which we arrive at the same emotional state in the second instance? See Amy Coplan, "Empathetic Engagement with Narrative Fictions."

7 That is, the object of the audience's emotional state is typically the character's situation, which includes the object of his emotion. Standardly, the object of the audience's emotional state is not simply identical to the object of the character's state.

8 That is, a fiction mandates that we suppose or imagine its propositional content, not that we believe it.

9 Discussing empathy apart from the case of fiction, Edith Stein remarks on these phenomenological differences, "The subject of the empathized experience, however, is not the subject empathizing, but another.... [W]hile I am living in the other's joy, I do not feel primordial joy. It does not issue from my 'I.' Neither does it have the character of once having lived like remembered joy." See Edith Stein, *On the Problem of Empathy* (Washington, DC: ICS Publishers, 1989), 11–12.

10 Though I am very dubious about the idea that identification ever occurs, I am not claiming that I know that it does not. Rather, I am arguing that it is not a particularly comprehensive model of our emotional interaction with narrative fictions, a claim that most friends of identification have advanced. Since my argument concerns the generality of the notion of identification, it is not to the point to respond to my objections, as some have, by observing that I have not shown that it is self-contradictory to assert that spectators might identify with characters or that identification is in any other way, in principle, precluded. That may be so; however, that is not incompatible with my central allegation which is that we have little to gain by adverting to identification to account for our emotional responses to fictional characters in the largest number of cases.

Philosophical debates often follow a predictable trajectory. One side begins with a bold claim – like: everything is really mind. After a series of objections, the position gets refined drastically down to "it has not been shown that it is logically impossible that everything is mind" or "it has not been shown that there is not some evidence of the existence of mind."

At one time, it was believed that identification was the whole story or, at least, a major part of it, with respect to our emotional responses to narrative fictions. Perhaps for some, this conviction is still firm. It is this view that I am denying. Whether identification might be logically possible in some circumstances or whether it actually obtains on rare occasions is not an option that I claim to have foreclosed categorically. What I have argued is that identification, as it is usually understood, is extremely unlikely.

11 This approach is defended by Berys Gaut in his interesting article, "Identification and Emotion in Narrative Film," in Plantinga and Smith (eds.), *Passionate Views: Film, Cognition, and Emotion*, 200–216. For criticism of this view, see Noël Carroll, "Sympathy for the Devil," in Richard Greene and Peter Vernezze (eds.), *The Sopranos and Philosophy* (Chicago: Open Court, 2004), 121–36.

12 Amy Coplan appears to think that identification, which she calls "empathy," in cases like these involves suffering the self-same emotion type while, at the same time, differentiating oneself from the character. This is certainly logically possible. However, it would be a rather ad hoc solution to the paradox I've imagined, since it is more economical to suppose that the problem does not arise to begin with because we are not identifying with the character than it is to posit that we are identifying with the character while simultaneously we are also *differentiating*

ourselves from the character. Unless something motivates postulating identification in the first place, there is no reason to conjecture differentiation in the second place. But as I have argued earlier, identification is not a wheel we need to add to this mechanism, since the operation of our own emotive apparatus – with no assistance from character contagion – can explain our feelings toward the protagonists.

13 Similarly, it should be noted that not only do our emotional states vis-à-vis characters vary systematically in terms of convergence. There are also systematic relationships in the way they diverge. For example, when the villain is frustrated, the audience is apt to feel joy, whereas when he is happy, we are likely to feel anger – as when he strokes the fair heroine's cheek with his clammy fingers. That is, sometimes when certain characters are in euphoric states, our emotions diverge vectorially toward an opposing dysphoric state, and vice versa.

14 The locus classicus of the application of simulation theory to fiction is Gregory Currie's "The Moral Psychology of Fiction," *Australasian Journal of Philosophy*, 73 (1995): 250–59. This article is criticized in Carroll, *Philosophy of Mass Art*, 342–56.

15 Though the proponents of simulation seem to think that insulating our target's beliefs and desires from our own is not a problem, I suspect that when we put others in our shoes (or, ourselves in their shoes), it is probably very unlikely that we can prevent seepage from our own character, beliefs, desires, and so forth from contaminating the outcome. Thus, the *similarity* that is supposed to obtain between our emotional responses and our targets may be exceedingly rough.

16 Though he does not discuss the case of popular fictions, Jose Luis Bermudez points out that there may be real-time problems with respect to simulation theory. See José Luis Bermudez, "The Domain of Folk Psychology," in Anthony O'Hear (ed.), *Minds and Persons* (Cambridge: Cambridge University Press, 2001).

17 Indeed, such accessibility is arguably a necessary condition for mass art. See my *Philosophy of Mass Art*.

18 Likewise, we generally rely on heuristics rather than simulations or theories when we design our behavioral responses to conspecifics. As Bermudez points out, if we are engaged in iterated negotiations with others, we typically adopt a tit-for-tat heuristic, sans simulation.

19 Redundancy is a feature of all effective communication, but it is especially crucial in mass fictions where a premium is necessarily placed upon accessibility.

20 Though I do not agree with his conclusions, especially regarding empathy, this section has been influenced by Stephen Darwall's thinking about sympathy and caring. See Stephen Darwall, "Empathy, Sympathy, and Care," *Philosophical Studies* 89 (1998): 261–82.

21 The importance of morality for engendering audience allegiance to fictional characters is defended in my "Toward a Theory of Film Suspense," in *Theorizing the Moving Image* (Cambridge: Cambridge University Press, 1996); and "The Paradox of Suspense" in *Beyond Aesthetics* (Cambridge: Cambridge University Press, 2000).

22 Since, for example, the recent remake of *Ocean's Eleven*.

23 Sometimes the moral standing of the protagonists relies on his being lesser than the evils that surround him. See my "Sympathy for the Devil," which attempts to explicate our sympathy for Tony as grounded in our apprehension of him as the least vicious of the prominent denizens in the fictional world of *The Sopranos*.

24 Elaine Hatfield, John T. Cacioppo, and Richard L. Rapson, *Emotional Contagion* (Cambridge: Cambridge University Press, 1994), especially ch. 2.

25 This begins quite early on. Twelve-to-twenty-one-day-old infants show evidence of mimicry. See A. N. Meltzoff and A. K. Moore, "Imitation of Facial and Manual Gestures by Human Neonates," *Science* 198 (1977): 75–78.

26 See Hatfield, Cacioppo, and Rapson, *Emotional Contagion*.

27 Of course, if through mimicry we detect that our spouse is "hot under the collar," that need not suck us into a comparable emotional state of anger. Instead, we may use that affective information to be wary – to be on guard lest we trigger the wrath of our antecedently upset mate.

28 Theodor Lipps, "Empathy and Aesthetic Pleasure," in Karl Aschenbrenner and Arnold Isenberg (eds.), *Aesthetic Theories: Studies in the Philosophy of Art* (Englewood Cliffs, NJ: Prentice Hall, 1965), 403–14.

29 David Bordwell, *The Cinema of Eisenstein* (Cambridge, MA: Harvard University Press, 1993), 116.

30 Though it is probably by osmosis that most filmmakers pick up on the efficacy of mirror reflexes for modulating audiences affectively, Eisenstein's writings have figured in film pedagogy in many countries and possibly may have alerted at least some fledgling filmmakers to the existence of this resource.

31 Since the appearance of the monster onscreen should, all things being equal, be sufficient to raise horror in audiences, a question may arise about why affective cues like the reaction of the character to the monster is included at all. One reason is that it is an added, although redundant, means of clarifying exactly how the spectator should take what is happening in the film. Redundancy, of course, is an indispensable in popular entertainments, given their commitment to utter accessibility. And perhaps there is also another consideration. Like laughter and crying, screaming itself tends to be infectious. Thus, the way to set the viewers off on a screaming jag is to start it up from inside the film. As football games have cheerleaders, horror films have scream leaders – characters, like the one played by Faye Wray in *King Kong*, whose job it is to get the audience worked up. In such cases, the filmmakers hope that abundant screaming echoing throughout the theater will convince the viewers that the movie is scary enough to recommend to their friends.

32 When this chapter was originally presented as a talk at the State University of New York at Buffalo, members of the audience asked me why I did not discuss empathy. The reason is that I have found this notion to be exceedingly ambiguous and ultimately too confusing. It means many different things to different theorists. Some of these views I find unobjectionable. In other cases, the notion of empathy is pretty close to what I call identification in this essay. I have not addressed the identification view of empathy at length in the text, since I feel what I have said about identification does not need to be repeated.

In his *The Nature of Sympathy* (London: Routledge and Kegan Paul, 1954), Max Scheler thinks of empathy as a sort of pathological identification, as occurs in schizophrenia. Since this does not seem to be a conception of empathy that most aestheticians have in mind when they invoke the concept, I do not think that I need to address it here.

On the other hand, in a less idiosyncratic vein, by *empathy*, some simply have in mind that I understand another's point of view. But since I may understand the plight of another – may comprehend where she's "coming from" – without feeling precisely what she feels, I have no qualms about this variant of *empathy*. I can *hear* you, without feeling your pain.

To "empathize" with someone else often means to acknowledge that her feelings are warranted. Insofar as this does not require exactly parallel emotions, I have no problems with this construal either.

Empathy may refer to *sensing* the emotions of others. But I can sense that my chairman is dispirited without being unhappy myself. My own emotional state may be contrary to his. Sensing that he is down may make my day. So this notion of empathy is acceptable in principle from my viewpoint. Even if, instead, my response is complementary to my chairman's mental state – that is, for example, sensing his dolors induces a feeling of troubled concern for him in me – this does not involve identification, since our emotions, though suited to each other, are not the same.

Indeed, if empathy only involves broadly congruent – that is, vectorially converging – emotive states, I am happy to agree that it occurs quite often in response to narrative fictions. I only draw the line when theorists use the label *empathy* to mark what I have challenged under the rubric of identification. I concede that this is how many, though far from all, use the term *empathy*. Of them, I ask that they consider my objections to identification.

Amy Coplan contends that my acceptance of empathy as involving nothing more than broadly congruent emotional states between fictional characters and audiences belies my confusion of empathy with sympathy. Empathy, she contends, involves sharing the same emotions but not necessarily in a way that elicits care for the other. But, she points out, in one of my examples of vectorially convergent empathy – where the character feels sorrow and I feel pity – my state does involve concern for the character, and, therefore, is a state of sympathy. Nevertheless, I would respond that it is not the case that empathy in my sense always collapses into sympathy, even if it does in the preceding example.

Given the difference in the information available to us, a fictional character may feel fear due to his superior knowledge, whereas the audience feels, at most, disquiet or unease: let us imagine that he is an experienced tracker, savvy in the signs of the jungle, whereas we, unlike him, do not know exactly what and how dangerous that which is headed toward us really is. This would be an example of the broadly congruent sense of empathy that would not be reducible to a case of sympathy. I think that cases like this obtain in narrative fictions, so the distinction between empathy and sympathy that Coplan respects can be made out on my view, though I agree that empathy of this sort is often mixed with sympathy. On the other hand, even Coplan would have to acknowledge that empathy and sympathy – in either her sense or mine – often overlap and are continuous.

Amy Coplan's carefully argued article against my position only reached my desk as I was struggling to meet the deadline for this article. Thus I have not had the opportunity to give it the close attention it merits. However, it is my general impression that she takes empathy to be what I treat as identification and that she fails to grapple with my argument from explanatory parsimony, which is one of my leading objections to the identification hypothesis.

Of course, Amy Coplan is not the only philosopher to equate empathy with identification. I suspect this also occurs in Douglas Chismar, "Empathy and Sympathy: The Important Difference," *Journal of Value Enquiry* 22 (1988): 257–66.

For a discussion of empathy in relation to film, see Carl Plantinga, "The Scene of Empathy and the Human Face," in Plantinga and Smith (eds.), *Passionate Views*, 238–55.

4

Character, Social Information, and the Challenge of Psychology

I. Introduction

One common, recurring view of the function and value of fictional characters is that they afford readers, viewers, and/or listeners social information – information about various kinds of people and how they behave. By engaging with such characters, it is thought, we improve our skills in predicting and explaining how actual people – people outside of fictions – will act.[1]

Presumably, a flesh-and-blood agent has a network of traits, which we call her *character*. This network is what gives rise to her behavior. It is in virtue of this network of traits that we predict and explain her actions. Likewise, fictional characters can be seen as composed of a package of integrated traits which we are mandated to imagine by their authors. For this reason, it is possible for certain fictional characters to model the kinds of characters observed in actual persons. In the process of focusing upon such characters in our commerce with fiction, we expand upon our skill in discerning various, diverse kinds of characters as they can be observed in living-and-breathing people, as well as our ability to understand what makes them "tick" and our capacity to predict their behavior.

Our interest in character is undoubtedly one of the major attractions of fiction. We devour fiction because we take pleasure in learning about others – in their intentions, desires, beliefs, emotions and the ways in which these

"Character, Social Information, and the Challenge of Psychology," in Garry Hagberg (ed.), *Fictional Characters, Real Characters: The Search for Ethical Content in Literature* (Oxford: Oxford University Press, forthcoming)

apparently shape what they do. Since we are intensely social animals – animals that depend on living in society and that are, consequently, highly dependent upon having and exhibiting social *savoir faire* – it is adaptive that we take such pleasure in the lives, including the inner lives, of others. Nature, in other words, has equipped us with an incentive to search for the kind of social information we need in order to thrive by disposing us to desire and enjoy its acquisition.

The institution of fiction, then, is founded upon this innate curiosity that we have about our conspecifics. It presents us with fictional characters about whom we are as inquisitive as we are with regard to our neighbors. Fiction provides us with the opportunity to practice and enhance our capacities for gathering social information, for gaining insight and understanding into the various configurations of character, and for developing our skills in inferring their intentions, desires, beliefs, and emotions and for predicting how these will combine and issue in behavior. In this way, literary, motion picture, and theatrical narratives, while, at the same time they are immensely pleasing, also function to educate us socially. Indeed, it is possible to comprehend them as on a continuum with the little boy's GI Joes and his sister's Barbies, fictional characters in their own right that exercise social skills through imaginative play.

This in brief outline is one view of the function and value of fictional characters. On it, the aptitudes and insights that we acquire from scrutinizing fictional characters can be transferred to everyday life and our intercourse with others. When we explore fictional characters, we exercise social talents that have carry-over value to actual encounters and we may even learn of new social worlds that "have such people in it." But this view rests on the presumption that in the world outside of fiction humans have the kinds of character-structures that the authors of fiction invest in their creations.

However, recent experimental work in social psychology has begun to question whether folks really have the sorts of consistent characters that what can be called the common view attributes alike both to flesh-and-blood people and the inhabitants of fictions.[2] Instead, it is argued that situation is far more important than what we think of as character in the determination of action, including moral action. What is the upshot of "situationalism" for the common view of the transfer value of engaging with fictional characters? Does it show that it rests on a mistake and maybe even that the conception of fictional characters is nothing more than a disreputable fragment of an obsolete folk psychology?

In this essay, I would like to argue for *one* way of defending a modified version of the common view that we derive social information from fictional characters. I emphasize that my ambition here is only to advance *one* defense in this piece. I believe there are other defenses to be pursued in future papers. Here, I intend to do no more than to initiate a counterattack to situationalist skepticism about the notion that fictional characters afford social information with carry-over value to the world outside of fiction.

I will begin by reviewing the common view through the thoughts of one of its founders, Aristotle. Then I will rehearse the challenge that situationalism presents to the common view in greater depth than bruited so far. Once we grasp what situationalism involves, we will be in a better position to see how certain of the functions of fictional characters in the service of social information which is claimed for them by the common view need not be threatened by situationalism. To this end, I will attempt to illustrate the function that I have in mind by taking a close look at its operation in the fictional narrative *The Big Country* – a 1957 novel by Donald Hamilton which was made into a motion picture in 1958 by William Wyler.

II. Aristotle, poetry, and character

In his *Poetics*, Aristotle argues that

> the poet's function is to describe, not the thing that happened, but the kind of thing that might happen, i.e. what is possible as being probable or necessary. The distinction between historian and poet is not in the one writing prose and the other writing verse – you might put the work of Herodotus into verse and it would still be a species of history; it consists really in this, that the one describes the thing that has been, and the other a kind of thing that might be. Hence poetry is more philosophic and of graver import than history, since its statements are of the nature of universals, whereas those of history are singulars. By a universal statement I mean one as to what such or such *a kind of man* will probably or necessarily say or do.[3]

Here, we see that Aristotle maintains that poetry – which, for our purposes, we may construe as fiction – trades in generalizations. These generalizations are about what certain kinds of men "will probably or necessarily say or do." That is, poetry tells us what certain kinds of people – people with this or that character-structure – are likely to say (to decide) and to do in certain situations.[4] Poetry, for example, shows us how someone like Creon will behave when his proclamations are disobeyed.

What poetry says about the characters with such characters – as, for example, Creon's inflexibility – is putatively of universal significance. So what we are shown about characters with such characters applies not only to the denizens of tragedy, but to those living beings with characters like Creon's whom we meet on a daily basis in the course of everyday life.

Aristotle thinks that the primary pleasure that we derive from poetry is the pleasure of learning. The learning dispensed by tragedy comes by way of imitation – the imitation of actions as those actions flow from the agents with certain discernible and recurring patterns of intentions. Aristotle maintains that the plot is the primary element of tragedy, since he associates plot with the main action of the narrative. But what we learn about that action is not simply *that* it happened but *how* it was determined by the character – the network of traits – of the major character (for example, Oedipus) in the tragedy.

Tragedy, on Aristotle's view, teaches us certain scenarios – certain regularities or tendencies in the course of human affairs – that are apt to occur when people with this or that set of dispositions or character traits are placed in various situations. In these cases, the constitution of their character will explain the ensuing pathway of events, which in tragedy usually trends badly. But since these tendencies are universal, given the character-structures that are in place in the pertinent situations, they will be operative not only inside the theater, but outside as well. Thus, by limning the characters of dramatic characters, poets illuminate the springs of action of certain of our actual conspecifics, delineating their characters by means of fictional models – a process otherwise known as *mimesis*.

In Aristotle, we see a clear affirmation of the common view. By contemplating what the dramatist has a certain kind of person do or say in a certain situation, we comprehend various regularities of human life as those are determined by agents with certain character-structures. These regularities pertain not only to human events as represented in fictions, but to social interactions outside the amphitheater. Scrutinizing fictional characters is not only entertaining; it is good for us. We learn from it lessons that apply to life – lessons about general patterns of the way in which people of a certain type (people with this or that kind of character) will or will be likely to react when various situations arise. And this social information is advantageous when it comes to predicting, explaining, and understanding their behavior.

III. Social psychological skepticism about character

What I have called the common view, as articulated by Aristotle, assumes that there is such a thing as character – that people have relatively stable networks of traits or characteristics which enable us to predict, explain, and/or understand their actions. Mary is a cheapskate so we predict that she won't order wine with her complimentary airline meal, because she would have to pay for it. On the other hand, if the wine were free, we would anticipate her asking for it, and even requesting more than one glass. When it is brought to our attention that Mary recycles her Christmas gifts, we explain this to ourselves by saying "Well, of course, she's a cheapskate." Her character is such – call it penurious or stingy – that there is no expense that Mary will not attempt to avoid. On the common view, fictional characters, such as Moliere's miser or Dickens's Scrooge, model an array of character types in ways that abet our prediction and explanation of their flesh-and-blood counterparts. But, this presupposes fictional characters have such counterparts. That is, it assumes that the folks we encounter at work and play have fixed characters in the preceding sense. And this is precisely what many social psychologists are calling into question.

In an impressive number of experiments, social psychologists have shown that in the relevant cases, people's behavior is not best explained by what we might suppose is their character, but by situational factors.[5] One of these experiments involves seminarians from Princeton Theological Seminary and it goes something like this.[6]

After reading a passage recounting the parable of the Good Samaritan, they were instructed to go across campus to deliver a short, extemporaneous lecture on the subject. Some were told they had barely enough time to reach the lecture hall; others that they had ample time. Furthermore, on the way to the lecture hall, the psychologists planted a stooge, feigning need of assistance. It turned out that the seminarians who were in a hurry were far less likely to behave like Good Samaritans than the ones who were not in a rush.

Let us suppose that seminarians are the kind of people who are characteristically predisposed toward helping behaviors, perhaps especially after reading and thinking about the parable of the Good Samaritan. On this basis, we would predict that they would be likely to stop, given the relatively stable network of trait that makes for a seminarian, particularly one who is thinking about the Good Samaritan story. Yet, the important explanatory variable in this experiment was the amount of time the seminarians had to reach the lecture hall. A situational factor, call it the *hurry*-factor, rather than their alleged character-structures, explained how they acted.

Similarly, in another experiment, researchers observed that people who had just found a dime in the coin return slot of a telephone booth (which dime had been placed there by the experimental team) were twenty-two times more likely to help a woman whose papers were scattered on the ground than those who were not so "lucky." That is, helping behavior of the sort that we might typically presume issues from the deep springs of character may sometimes really depend on something as apparently inconsequential as whether or not one has found ten cents.[7] In other experiments, situational features, such as the level of exacerbated ambient noise, like the sound of a lawnmower, appears to influence at rates that are not random the subjects's inclination to help an injured man who has dropped some books; at normal noise levels, people proffer aid at a rate five times greater than those who are bombarded by louder noise levels.

Situational features that we are apt to think are irrelevant to the explanation of our behavior, when investigated statistically, seem to tell a different tale. Subjects tend to think that the number of people witnessing an event that calls for a response has no influence on their behavior, but that's not what the numbers say. Furthermore, some of the pertinent experiments have darker portents than the ones alluded to so far.

One experiment in 1976 had to be terminated almost as soon as it began because the volunteers who were role-playing prison guards started to abuse the subjects who were role-playing their prisoners. That is, the situation rather than their putative everyday character determined their behavior. Likewise, during the infamous Milgram experiments, in which college students were instructed to administer electric shocks to other subjects continued to raise the voltage even though the people they were supposedly electrocuting (of course, they were really actors) screamed for them to stop.

In these last two experiments, in other words, subjects behaved in what we might describe as a sadistic manner at variance with what we would presume about their behavior in everyday life. In everyday life, we would not attribute a sadistic character to them. Rather, they behaved sadistically because of the structure of the situations in which they found themselves.

The theme that unifies the various experiments that I have rather hastily put before you is the following hypothesis: situational factors, including ones that might seem irrelevant to the subject and even sometimes rather inconsequential, seem to have far more determinative influence on what people do than their alleged characters. Indeed, the behavior that we would predict in a number of these cases on the basis of postulating stable character-structures in the subject population surprisingly fails to occur.

From data like this, the situationalist might mount the following argument:[8]

1. If behavior is typically the outcome of relatively stable character formations, then systematic observation will disclose pervasive behavioral consistency.
2. Systematic observation does not disclose pervasive behavioral consistency. (Recall the seminarians, the victims of ambient noise, those who "found" a dime, those in smaller crowds rather than larger crowds, and so on).
3. Therefore, behavior is not typically the outcome of relatively stable character formations.

Furthermore, since the common view presupposes that behavior is typically the outcome relatively stable character formations, the preceding conclusion calls into question the common view. That is,

4. If the common view is correct, then behavior is typically the outcome of stable character formations.
5. Therefore, the common view is not correct.

That is, the common view reassures us that the character modeling we encounter in fictions reveals something about the characters of living and breathing agents such that we can use what the models "tell" us in order to predict, explain, and understand behavior. But since real-life character formations do not typically possess this predictive and/or explanatory power, neither will their fictional models. Although we think we are deriving social information by contemplating fictional characters, we are not really doing so. Perhaps if Lex Luthor found a dime in a telephone booth instead of Superman, he wouldn't have become bent on world domination.

IV. A defense of a modified version of the common view

Skepticism about something like the common view has been abroad at least since L. C. Knight poked fun at the impossibility of answering the question of the number of children had by Lady Macbeth. Literary critics have protested loudly and repeatedly that literary characters are not like real people. Obviously the common view could not be accurate for all literary fictional characters, since many fictional characters behave as they do in order to satisfy the exigencies of the plots that they inhabit.

Consider the way in which the worm turns in the penultimate scene of many comedies. Throughout, he has been portrayed as a meek and mild weakling. But when the bully makes off with his beloved, he somehow suddenly musters the courage and *the strength* to rescue the object of his affections. This hardly seems accurate modeling of the character-type *homo nerd*. Rather, the comic plot needs this incongruous turn of events. Moreover, a case can be made that this is not rare – fictional characters are very often artfully designed to serve structural purposes.

Examples like this call into question whether fictional characters are reliably like actual people. However, the skepticism about character that derives from recent experimental psychology makes a different point: namely that actual people don't have character-structures of the sort that folk psychology frequently attributes to them. To put the point playfully, as Yogi Bera might: it is not merely that fictional characters are not like real people; real people aren't that way either.

That is, the common view is dubious because it relies upon the controversial notion that real people have character-structures that are determinative of their behaviors, whereas faith in power of these putative character-structures is now open to serious scientific question. In short, you can't provide an accurate model of what doesn't exist. So, fictional characters cannot be providing readers, viewers, and listeners with viable social information.

The common view, as I have articulated it, holds that fictional characters provide us with social information that we can apply to the world *because* fictional characters possess character-structures like those of actual people. That is, fictional characters "work" the way real people "work" – or, at least, the way that real people with supposedly, highly integrated and pronounced character-structures "work." So we can apply what we learn contemplating from the one, to the other.

Although they are connected, we can divide the common view into at least two parts: the epistemic part and the transfer part. The epistemic part claims that literary characters accurately model the character-types of at least certain actual kinds of people. The transfer part says that the social information garnered from contemplating fictional characters can be transferred to our ongoing social lives. The common view holds that transfer is feasible because of the epistemic accuracy of at least some fictional characters. But what if we decouple the two parts of the common view and modify it so that this new version of the common view merely claims that the social information conveyed by fictional characters can be transferred to our negotiation of life with our conspecifics?

Notice that the social psychological findings that we have been reviewing so far raise problems, if they do, for the epistemic component of the common view – namely, the claim that fictional characters accurately model the determinative character-structures of actual people. This claim becomes rather shaky, if, as some of the social psychologists allege, real people do not really have the kind of determinative character-structures that folk psychology (and much fiction) seems to presuppose. For the purposes of this article (and only this article), let the skeptics have this much. It still does not entirely vanquish the common view, or at least a modification of the common view, if it can be shown that, despite its epistemic limitations, the new common view can still maintain that fictional characters convey social information that has carry-over application to everyday living.

How is that possible? The strongest form of skepticism that can be made-out on the basis of the social psychological experimentation is that character, of an allegedly fixed nature, is not as determinative in explaining and predicting behavior as are various situational factors. So, modeling such character-structures, as some claim fictional characters do, does not give us a leg up on explaining and predicting the actions of our conspecifics. That is, it does not give us useful social information. We may think that we are getting reliable social information from contemplation of fictional characters. But we are deceiving ourselves.

However, the denial of the acquisition of useful social information here is too quick. Undoubtedly, honing insight into explaining and predicting the behavior of others counts as useful social information. But it is not the only sort of useful social information. It is what we might broadly call factual social information. Factual information, in this sense, tells us how the world is. But there is also useful social information that is normative.

By "useful social information," here, I mean social information that is applicable in orienting ourselves to social life. Being able to predict and explain how others are likely to behave is eminently useful in this respect. However, so is knowing how people are *supposed* to behave where the people in question include not only others, but ourselves. So even if fictional characters do not enable us, for the reasons canvassed above, to explain how actual people act, they may still provide us with useful social information about what to expect – for example, morally – from their behavior.

That is, even if fictional characters do not supply us with predictive models with respect to actual persons, they may nevertheless afford social information that we may use to *evaluate* people's behaviors – again, both the actions of others as well as our own. Thus, even if it turns out that the direction of fit between fictional characters and the world is never such that fictional characters correspond to the way the world is, that leaves open the possibility that fictional characters indicate the way in which the world should be, from the social point of view.

This is a very abstract conclusion and, admittedly, it has been reached in a rather armchair fashion by means of an exercise of logic. But the conclusion is really very commonsensical and readily confirmed empirically. Fictional characters frequently indicate to us how people should be (and shouldn't be). Whether they sometimes inform us about how people are, one can nevertheless affirm that they often provide models (exemplars) of the way in which people, in a given culture, should carry themselves and behave.

This is certainly a major, indisputable function of the founding epics, and the heroes therein, of cultures and civilizations virtually everywhere. In these cases, it seems undeniable that fictional characters supply readers, listeners, and/or viewers with useful social information. They provide role models for various social roles – from warriors, like Ulysses, to their spouses, like Penelope. In this, they enact norms which we may use to evaluate the behavior of real people in terms of whether they live up to those norms or fail.

Cultures, of course, have as one of their most abiding interests the reproduction of the ethos that makes them the cultures they are. That ethos includes a network of values, beliefs, roles, norms, obligations and so forth. Individuals need to be recruited into this cultural system as informed participants in their social environment. They need to learn how people like them should act. Cultures supply their citizens with multiple, redundant channels for acquiring this information. But among these channels of information, one of the most privileged vehicles involves the characters in the narratives the culture tells itself.

Characters – such as those found in the great myths and later in the fictions (and especially the popular fictions) of secular culture – are a crucial, recurring mechanism for imparting social information about the way in which members of that culture, given their role or station in it, should comport themselves. In this fashion, fictional characters function to provide norms for evaluating ourselves and others.

In a great many fictions, the ensemble of traits that comprise the characters (particularly the central characters) involve a cluster of virtues and/or vices that the characters exemplify to varying degrees. In a staggering number of cases, characters embody the virtues and vices that are at the core of the ethos of the culture of the author who has created them. Readers, listeners, and viewers absorb the virtues and vices of the culture from their exemplification in concrete characters more easily than they assimilate such social information from abstract rules which, in any event, need to be given particularized applications in order to be operationalized. In this regard, fictional characters may satisfy our craving for social information even when they fail to give us accurate models of how people do in fact act. Moreover, this is to be expected, since there would be no need to explicitly articulate norms, if people always acted in accordance with them, so to speak, naturally.

Of course, not all fictional characters have this function, nor is it my intention to suggest that they do. But, by the same token, a substantial number of them, perhaps even the majority, do serve this purpose, perhaps among others. Nor is it only the case that this is true of popular fiction (although it is especially true there). For we find normative modeling in ambitious fiction as well, such as Mann's *Magic Mountain*. Nor, it pays to remember, is this normative modeling only positive. It may be negative, as is the case of Pyotor in Dostoyevsky's *Demons*.

A broad re-construal of the common view is that fictional characters afford us useful social information that we can apply to our actual environment. This would appear to be a highly defensible position, at least for a great many fictions. But, if this is acceptable, then a remnant of the common view can be recuperated even in the face of the most radical skeptical extrapolation of the findings of social psychologists regarding the determinative significance of character for explaining and predicting action. This may not be the most robust response to skeptics about the common view, nor does it reinstate Aristotle. Consider it instead as an opening move in a larger campaign.

In order to clarify the function of fictional characters that I have introduced here and to demonstrate its relevance to the way in which fictional characters afford social information, I will illustrate my points by looking at how character functions in *The Big Country*. This will not only enable me to amplify the argument so far, but will also allow me to demonstrate an important narrative structure for the articulation of the virtues and vices of a given culture – a structure that I call *the wheel of virtue*.[9]

V. *The Big Country*

The Big Country is the title of a novel by Donald Hamilton that was subsequently made into a motion picture by William Wyler.[10] It is a popular fiction, an example of the genre of the western. I have chosen to discuss it in this context for several reasons. The western genre itself, at least up until the revisionism of the late sixties, functioned as something like an American myth, projecting character-types that embodied contemporary norms of character.[11] In *The Big Country*, we are offered an exploration of the concept of manliness, albeit of a very period specific sort, that projects models of what counts as real manliness and what doesn't. Presumably the positive image of manliness, manifested in the fictional character of Jim McKay, is not only presented as something to be admired and emulated, but also as a model against which to assess actual men in terms of whether or not they possess the ensemble of virtues that make for a truly manly character.

The title of both the film and the novel is *The Big Country*. The location in question is Texas and constant reference is made to its immense scale, often with a not so subtle hint of pride when observed by Texans. In the film, the enormity of the landscape is a conspicuously recurring visual theme as people, places, and events are repeatedly framed in awesome long shots in which said people, places, and events are dwarfed by the vast expanse that surrounds them. I suspect that no other western movie has made so much the sheer size of the landscape. In this regard, the visual design of the film, though rarely acknowledged, is brilliant in its thoughtful, consistent use of space, especially empty space.

Landscape, of course, is often emblematic of the identity of a nation, as the forest is of Germany. The landscape in the *The Big Country* is as American as all outdoors: it is a wilderness, one whose manifest destiny is to be settled and civilized, a fact acknowledged by characters in the fiction. The vast empty spaces invite the idea of a future in which they will eventually be filled. The question of the fiction poses is: what kind of men (and, to a lesser extent, women) should populate it? As the painter Thomas Cole commented upon the significance of representations of impressive American landscapes: "the mind's eye may see far into futurity. Where the wolf roams, the plough shall glisten; on the grey crag shall rise a temple and a tower – mighty deeds shall be done in the now pathless wilderness; and people yet unborn shall sanctify the soil."[12]

If, as Cole suggests, an empty landscape encourages thoughts about the people who should occupy it, *The Big Country*, in effect, explores the issue in terms of the options involving the kinds of people who deserve to inherit this empty earth, this big country, which subject, when broached in the nineteen fifties, becomes a question of how we, now born, should be.[13] Specifically, it is the question of what kind of man should inhabit this land – what kind of man should the American man be.

The *man* recommended to us in this fiction is Jim McKay.[14] He is a retired sea captain of means. He heads to Texas to marry Patricia Terrill, the daughter of Major Henry Terrill, the owner of a sprawling ranch called Ladder. Almost immediately after he arrives in town and meets his betrothed, questions about his manhood arise.

As they drive to Ladder, McKay and Pat are accosted by the Hannassey gang, led by Buck, the son of the patriarch of the family, Rufus. The Hannasseys have a longstanding feud with the Terrills, and Buck and his boys take pleasure in humiliating the son-in-law-to-be of Henry Terrill. They lasso him, drag him around, and shoot at this bowler hat. As Buck leaves, he comments that McKay "ain't much of a man."

Interestingly, just before the harassment begins, Pat reaches for her Winchester, but McKay takes it from her, not believing that the Hannassys's drunken pranks warrant lethal retaliation. This signals to the audience that McKay is a man who will avoid unnecessary violence and, even then when called for, he will only employ it proportionately. He is not only a man from the East, but a man from the future. However, his refusal to agitate for blood revenge rather than being respected for its moderation and judiciousness raises the suspicion that he is a coward.

McKay's father, it turns out, was an avid duelist. In fact, he died in a duel. But McKay has no truck with ostentatious honor codes. He cares little for what others think of him, but only what he thinks of himself. He disdains what he regards as petty challenges to his manhood. He eschews the weight of appearances as interpreted by others, and steers by what he believes is his real inner nature.

His rival, Steve Leech, the foreman of Ladder and an admirer of Pat, tries to trick McKay into riding a nasty, unbroken horse, named Old Thunder, who throws off everyone who mounts him. McKay realizes a scheme that is afoot, and declines to fall for it, which leads to some sneering remarks from Leech, intended to further impugn McKay's manhood.

Shortly afterwards, McKay attempts to stop the Major from raiding the Hannessey's compound in retaliation for Buck's earlier effrontery. McKay doesn't think that the dust-up is worth a full-scale counter-attack. But his forbearance – his unwillingness to take the hazing as all that serious – makes him suspect, rather than earning him respect for having the nerve to argue with the Major.

While the Hannassey compound is being pillaged, back at Ladder, McKay secretly mounts Old Thunder. After being thrown again and again, he finally tames the horse, but he has the stable hand who witnesses this promise not to tell anyone what he has done. Again, the point is made that McKay doesn't care what others think of him, but only what he thinks of himself.

After the passage of some time, McKay decides to see some of this big country on his own. With a compass and a map, he sets off, instructing the stable hand to inform Pat and the Major that he will be back in a few days but that they should not worry. In fact, he navigates his way to a ranch called the Big Muddy, which is owned by Julie Maragon. This is a spread which both the Terrills and the Hannasseys covet intensely as a source of water. McKay buys the ranch from Julie, a friend of Pat's and a schoolteacher, as a wedding present for his future wife.

While he is away, the Terrills decide that he is lost and frantically send out search parties to find him. Finally, he, in a manner of speaking, finds one such search party, led by his rival Leech. Leech accuses him of being lost, an accusation McKay firmly denies. When they return to Ladder, Leech repeats the charge that McKay was lost. This time, when McKay claims to have known his location every step of the way, Leech calls him a liar, taunting McKay with the intention of provoking a fight. Predictably, McKay declines.

Pat turns from him in shame and later accuses McKay of humiliating her. "Don't you care about what people think?" she says. "No, I'm not responsible for what people think. Only for what I am," he replies. Then he decides to find lodging in town so they can both cool off a bit. But before leaving Ladder, he goes to Leech's bunk and, after securing Leech's agreement that their fight will remain their secret, they battle the night away to a draw. When it is all over, McKay asks Leech what has been proven; Leech admits "nothing." McKay, in other words, isn't afraid to fight Leech whose equal in fisticuffs he shows himself to be. He just refuses to do so because that's what people think he should do. As they say, he's his own man, a man utterly independent of the opinions of others.

The feud between the Terrills and the Hannaseys heats up. Thinking that Julie Maragon still owns the Big Muddy, the Hannasseys kidnap her, ostensibly to force her to sell her ranch, but really to coax Major Terrill into attacking the Hannassey compound again, where an ambush awaits. The Major takes the bait. Meanwhile, McKay, whom we suspect has fallen for Julie, also rides off to the rescue, thinking that he can retrieve her on his own, thereby averting a bloodbath. However, in order to do so, he must fight an old fashioned duel with single-shot pistols with Buck, the very iconography of the ritual again raising the question of what is a man or, maybe, who is a gentleman. Buck reveals himself to be a coward in the face of McKay's steely resolve and, when Buck attempts to shoot an unarmed McKay, Buck's father Rufus kills his son.

By this time, Major Terrill's men have entered Blanco Canyon, and have fallen into the Hannassey ambush. McKay convinces Rufus Hannassey that the feud is really just between him and Henry Terrill and that there is no reason that so many other people should be sacrificed to the pride of these two old men. Rufus challenges the Major to a duel with Winchesters, the two old men kill each other and peace comes to the land, but not before McKay and Leech exchange glances, recalling to mind the end of their earlier stand-off, which, the viewer remembers, proved nothing. Macho displays of violence in the name of honor, never do, the film implies which is, of course, McKay's credo.

McKay has a very fixed character. Again and again, he shows two recurring traits. He will not do something just because that is what others expect, especially where this involves proving that he is courageous. What "people" think of as honor, he appears to regard as showing off. He is autonomous, true only to himself and his own convictions.[15] Second, and related to this, his relation to violence is measured. He is averse to the violent exhibition of his prowess, though he is a formidable person, and he consistently attempts to limit or tone down the level of force in proportion to what the situation calls for. In these respects, he stands in contrast to the other leading male characters in the fiction.

Perhaps, he is most starkly different from Buck who is a braggart and a bully, but who consistently shows himself to be a coward when the chips are down. Buck is an alpha-male wannabe. He swaggers, boasts, and threatens, but cringes under pressure. The difference is also underscored visually; Buck is slovenly, whereas Mckay seems to always have his tie on. Whereas a manly man like McKay, is confident, Buck is falsely confident.[16]

Major Henry Terrill, like McKay, looks like a gentleman. His clothes, like his house, are fine. He is well-spoken; his rhetoric is high-toned and seems principled, but as McKay reveals, the Major is a hypocrite, employing lofty language to mask his selfish interests. Publicly, the Major talks the talk, and impresses others. But for all his grand words, he is also a bully, scaring the women and children of the Hannassey compound by raiding it when the cowboys are away. The Major may convince others of his probity. Yet that perhaps only underlines the theme of the untrustworthiness of public opinion.

Steve Leech and Rufus Hannassey prove themselves to be better men than Buck and the Major. Leech indicates this by developing a grudging appreciation for McKay and by objecting to some of the Major's more questionable actions. But Leech is still a prisoner of the cowboy code of honor according which one must prove oneself to others by responding forcefully to every challenge with one's guns or one's fists. Rufus also reveals a deeper sense of justice than does the Major, but he is still not the mature man that McKay is. Even though he recognizes that he has deceived himself about his true motives with respect to Terrill, he is still not man enough to let go of his hatred and forge a peaceful *modus vivendi* with his neighbor.

McKay's character is articulated in two ways. First, he behaves in accordance with a consistent pattern of action. He does not give in to the demands of others that he prove himself, usually in terms of violence; and, though not afraid to employ force, he does so only when *he* feels it is necessary and then only to the degree he believes the situation calls forth. However, it is not only through his own actions that McKay's character is clarified. His character is also cast in bold relief by means of comparisons with the other leading male characters. For example, McKay's commitment to the principle of proportionate violence is made salient in contrast to the Major's tendency towards inordinate displays of force, as when he retaliates to Buck's harassment of McKay with a full-scale attack on the Hannassey compound.

This second strategy for highlighting the exemplary character of a figure like McKay is what I call the wheel of virtue. This structure is quite common in narrative fiction, popular and otherwise. When we approach a narrative fiction, we rarely encounter a random collection of personalities. Instead, the cast of characters generally exhibits notably strong, highly structured, systematically varied and subtly polarized relations of comparison and contrast to each other. Characters like McKay and Buck are opposites, setting off each other's qualities in process of reciprocal reflection. Likewise, other features of McKay are underscored by contrasting him to Major Terrill who, although superficially resembling McKay vis à vis civility, is really a brutal self-serving demagogue. In other words, he is what McKay is not, since McKay is a self-effacing, peaceful man, genuinely concerned about others.

The wheel of virtue involves arraying characters in a comparative/constrastive structure that calls to mind a color wheel. However, what are displayed are not colors, but virtues (and vices).

Moreover, virtue wheels need not be merely a way of tabulating the differences between the various characters. Virtue wheels can be arranged in such a way that they have the potential to direct our evaluation of the characters who are being held up for comparison.

In Dickens's *Great Expectations*, for example, we encounter a virtue wheel with respect to parenting. There is Pip's sister, her husband Joe Gagery, Miss Havisham, and Abel Magwitch. Reflecting on this array, it is hard to resist the conclusion that Joe Gagery is the only figure under consideration who exemplifies the virtues of a good parent. In contrast to Miss Havisham and Magwitch, Joe's commitment to his charge is one of selfless love, whereas the other two are using the relevant children to subserve their own psychic needs. Pip's sister is also out of the question, since she regards Pip as a bothersome chore. The way this particular wheel of virtue is articulated makes unavoidable the conclusion that Joe is the representative of a good parental character.

Clearly, *The Big Country* employs the very common structure of the wheel of virtue in a way comparable to Dickens's deployment of the structure in *Great Expectations*. That is, it is not only used to take note of various modes of manliness, but it is designed so that one of the spokes in the wheel stands out as the qualitatively best one. The other ways of being a man in *The Big Country* pale in comparison to McKay's mode for being in the world. In this respect, McKay's character functions as an exemplar of what, in the culture of nineteen-fifties America, a manly man should be: autonomous, independently minded, cool-headed, inwardly self-confident, and peace-loving, unless provoked (usually in the defense of others).

It seems highly unlikely that Mckay's character was intended simply to reflect the prevailing character of American men in the nineteen fifties. For patently even in those days there were more Buck Hannasseys, Henry Terrills, and Steve Leeches than there were Jim McKays. Indeed, something like this conclusion is even suggested by the relevant wheel of virtue. McKay functions as the norm against which we are encouraged to assess the rest. If McKay modeled men as they were, there would be no *raison d'être* for the wheel of virtue in the first place.

By means of the structure of the wheel of virtue, *The Big Country* is able to convey important social information to viewers and readers. This social information is not about how men at the time of the production of the fiction were, but how they are supposed to be. *The Big Country* doesn't report on character, it recommends a certain aspirational character-structure, perhaps especially to its male viewers.[17] It is the character of the manly man as embodied by Jim McKay, a character who exemplifies a norm of manliness to be achieved, rather than an imitation of the character of the males as they are. Indeed, with respect to the way existing males are, Jim Mckay represents something like an evaluative norm for assessing their behavior.

VI. Summary

One of our interests in character is connected to our appetite to acquire social information that is transferrable from fiction to everyday life. On one view, this is possible because fictions model the kind of character-structures that determine the behavior of comparable living-and-breathing people. Contemplating fictional characters affords us the opportunity to practice explaining and predicting the behavior of various character types as well as offering us clues about what makes them tick. This is a very common view. Perhaps something like the germ of it can be found in Aristotle's *Poetics*.

However, this view looks like it may run afoul of the situationalist approach to social psychology which argues that situational factors are more determinative of behavior than the allegedly fixed characters of folk psychology. Thus, fictional characters cannot be modeling the determinative characters of our conspecifics, because there are not the relevant sorts of determinative characters out there in the world to be modeled.

As an initial response to this worry, I point out that not all social information is connected to the explanation and prediction of behavior. Much social information is normative. It is about how people should comport themselves. The common view that fictional characters may supply us with social information that can be transferred to everyday affairs can be defended then against even the most radical extrapolations from situationalism by pointing to the undeniable fact that in a great many cases, fictional characters provide readers, viewers, and listeners with the means for evaluating their neighbors. This is an unexceptionable function of fictional characters in every culture, even if it is not the function of every fictional character. In the pertinent cases, fictional characters afford the sort of normative social information that is indispensable for orienting oneself to one's social environment. And by supplying readers, listeners, and viewers with this kind of information, cultures are able to reproduce themselves.[18]

My major example of this function of fictional characters was that of Jim McKay in *The Big Country*. He models a kind of character prized in the nineteen fifties – a man of quiet strength who knows his own mind and stays true to himself as opposed to the opinions of others. It is against this model that readers and viewers are encouraged to assess the behavior of, for example, loudmouths and bullies. Moreover, like many narratives *The Big Country* makes its advocacy of McKay's version of the manly character manifest by means of the structure of the wheel of virtue where in contrast to the other ways of being a man, as represented by other characters, McKay's is advanced as the best.

Notes

1   The view that our insatiable appetite for social information is a leading reason for our interest in literary characters is a major theme of Blakey Vermeule's interesting book *Why Do We Care about Literary Characters?* (Baltimore, MD: Johns Hopkins University Press, 2010).

2   The tension between the common view and the emerging situationalist persuasion in social psychology was first brought to my attention by Jacob Berger in an unpublished seminar paper for a class in the Philosophy of Art at the Graduate Center of CUNY in 2008. Skepticism about fictional character is also discussed in Gregory Currie, *Narratives and Narrators: A Philosophy of Stories* (Oxford: Oxford University Press, 2010), pp. 199–218.

3   Aristotle, *Poetics*, in *The Complete Works of Aristotle*, vol. 2, ed. Jonathan Barnes (Princeton, NJ: Princeton University Press, 1984), pp. 2322–3 (emphasis added).

4   In Aristotle's claim that the poet knows what such and such a man will probably say, I find it hard not to hear an echo of Ion's suggestion, regarding the craft of poetry, that the rhapsode "will know what it's fitting for a man or a woman to say – or for a slave or a freeman or a follower or a leader." Aristotle, it seems to me, is returning to this attempt to define the craft of poetry which, of course, Socrates rejects. But Aristotle, it appears, wants to work it out with greater precision in order to advance his counterattack on Plato's dismissal of poetry. Among other things, Aristotle maintains the poet knows something, something close to philosophy, namely, recurring tendencies in the trajectories of human action. For Ion's attempt to define the poetic craft, see Plato, *Ion*, in *Two Comic Dialogues*, trans. Paul Woodruff (Indianapolis, IN: Hackett, 1983), p. 32.

5   See Maria W. Merritt, John M. Doris, and Gilbert Harman, "Character," in *The Moral Psychology Handbook*, ed. John M. Doris and the Moral Psychology Research Group (Oxford: Oxford University Press, 2010), pp. 355–401.

6   John M. Darley and C. Daniel Batson, "From Jerusalem to Jericho: A Study of Situational and Dispositional Variables in Helping Behavior," *Journal of Personality and Social Psychology*, vol. 27(1) (1973), pp. 100–108.

7 Information about the experiments referenced in this section can be found in Merritt, Doris, and Harman's "Character."

8 The first part of this argument is derived from Merritt, Doris, and Harman, "Character."

9 This structure is discussed at length in Noël Carroll, "The Wheel of Virtue," in my *Art in Three Dimensions* (Oxford: Oxford University Press, 2010), pp. 201–234.

10 Donald Hamilton, *The Big Country* (New York: Dell, 1957).

11 I should also mention that I have chosen a fiction that is over fifty years old in order to illustrate my points because I think it is easier for us to note what is culturally distinctive about such phenomena at a temporal remove.

12 Thomas Cole as quoted by Yuriko Saito in her *Everyday Aesthetics* (Oxford: Oxford University Press, 2007), p. 74. For further comment on the national significance of landscape, see also pp. 246–249.

13 Perhaps needless to say, there is only one mention of Native Americans in the film and no mention of African-Americans (although there is a paternalistic or condescending view of Mexican Americans as comically well-intentioned). This fiction is, as might be expected, about the ideal character of a manly White man. My purpose in this paper is not to politically endorse this prejudice, but only to demonstrate that it is the primary function of the fiction to broadcast social information about how to inhabit this role and to analyze how this is done.

14 I will recap the plot of the motion picture since it is probably better known and more accessible (the book is out of print).

15 Perhaps here it pays to mention that Jim McKay is played by Gregory Peck, a star often associated with roles like this one. McKay is very reminiscent of Peck's version of Atticus Finch in *To Kill a Mockingbird* – only sexier and a little less avuncular.

16 The notion of the *manly man* derives from Harvey C. Mansfield, *Manliness* (New Haven, CT: Yale University Press, 2006).

17 There is also an abbreviated wheel of virtue that pertains to women in *The Big Country*. This involves the explicit contrast between Pat Terrill and Julie Maragon. Pat is concerned with what people will think; Julie thinks that a woman should believe in her man. Rather than judging McKay as others may superficially do, being in love for Julie means trying to understand the situation from your mate's perspective. Whether either or neither of these positions is defensible is not my point here. I only mention it in order to reinforce the point that *The Big Country* employs the wheel of virtue structure in order to equip audiences with social information relevant to evaluating the comportment of their friends, neighbors and fellow citizens.

18 Needless to say, this is not the only source of this information. But it is a very effective one, given how very vivid narratives are.

Section II

The Philosophy of Motion Pictures

5

Movies, the Moral Emotions, and Sympathy

I. Introduction

Movies are a mass art form. By "movies" here I am, of course, referring to mainstream, motion-picture, narrative fictions, whether seen on the silver screen or TV (where many TV programs are themselves movies, in my sense of the term). *Movies*, in the way that I am using it, are intended to command large audiences. Typically nowadays they are made in order to make substantial profits and, in order to do so, they need to be capable of engaging the multitudes.[1] Movies succeed, when they do succeed, in large measure, by addressing the emotions of spectators. The emotions are able to perform this function so well, because the emotions, or, at least, the emotions usually stirred up by the movies, are broadly convergent across vast populations, populations, indeed, that generally enjoy being thrust into the relevant emotional states, so long as they do not have to pay the price that those states standardly exact (as sadness, for example, correlates with personal loss). That is one of the reasons that viewers flock to the movies. The emotions not only contribute to the intelligibility of motion-picture narratives, but they do so in a way that promotes pleasure.[2]

In this essay I will argue that the moral emotions are one of the important, if not the most important, levers available to moviemakers for recruiting the mass audiences that movies are designed to enlist. I will outline how the moral emotions underpin our reactions to the persons, actions, events, and scenes that movies depict and then conclude with a discussion of the way in which sympathy (and antipathy), as motivated by moral concerns, support

"Movies, the Moral Emotions, and Sympathy," *Midwest Studies in Philosophy* 34(1) (2010): 1–19.

our other emotional responses to the movies, including our moral-emotional responses. However, before examining the operation of the moral emotions in the movies, something needs to be said about the broader relationship of the emotions in general to the movies.

II. Emotions and movies

Possibly since Homer sang of the wrath of Achilles, but, at least from Plato's *Republic* onwards, the arts have been associated the emotions in the West, not to mention *rasa* theory in the East. The relation between the movies and the emotions is especially pronounced; many of the leading movie genres take their very names from the emotions they are designed to arouse – horror, suspense, mystery, thrillers, and tear-jerkers. Others, like comedy and drama, though not wearing their relation to the emotions upon their sleeves, are clearly linked to the emotions – to comic amusement, on the one hand, and to pity, anger, joy, sadness, and so forth, on the other.

People often go to the movies to have their emotions aroused – to have a good cry or a good scare. Although such experiences may be unwelcome in life outside the movies, they are coveted when they come cost-free – where, for example, our fear is not tied to real danger. Movies afford an intense, visceral experience, an invigorating emotional bath, if you will, one for which customers are willing to pay good money. Thus, it should come as no surprise that profit-seeking moviemakers should be disposed to rely so heavily upon arousing emotions as a basic strategy.

Moreover, inasmuch as the emotions are part of our biological equipment, most of us share if not certain basic emotions, then, at least, certain emotional domains – certain concerns, such as those involving harm, to which different cultures craft sometimes diverging but also often converging paradigmatic emotional-response patterns. Because some emotions are arguably nearly universal, while many others are recognizably connected to recurring human interests, the emotions are an ideal medium for those, such as moviemakers, who aspire to conquer a mass market. Movies exploit the potential of the emotions to be positively exciting for most people worldwide. That is why movies made in southern California are sought after by kids growing up in Lebanon. That is why a film like *Avatar* can clear over a billion dollars early on in its initial global run, stimulating, as it does, across continents the emotions of moral indignation, awe, fear, loathing, admiration, joy, as well as feelings that have no precise names in our vocabulary.

Although the movies may be said to be made for the emotions, the emotions, as is obvious, were not made for the movies. Our emotions are biological adaptations shaped by natural selection in order to protect and advance vital human interests. Fear, for example, alerts the organism to danger and prepares it to freeze, flee, or fight. Anger signals that a wrong has been done to me or mine and readies us for retaliation. Disgust focuses upon pollution and initiates bodily responses like gagging, choking, and vomiting where the impurity at issue is a foodstuff or a stench. Bonding emotions of all sorts – like patriotism – are the foundation of communal activity and the achievement of group ends and purposes. The emotions enable us to negotiate the world – in many cases, almost automatically.

That is, in contrast to slow cognitive processes like deliberation, the emotions rapidly size up situations in terms of our abiding interests and generally prime some or another behavioral response to our plight and/or our prospects. Deliberation is methodical and, well, deliberative; emotional appraisal is fast. And a speedy decision was often just what the moment called for in our ancestral environments, where a sudden motivating apprehension of fear at the possible presence of a predator was a better policy than sitting down and reasoning one's way through the evidence. Back then, it was better to be safe than sorry. Often, it still is.

The emotions are appraisals of our interests that give rise to bodily reactions – some physiological, some phenomenological – which, in turn, generally lead to an action tendency of some sort, as when angered we are prompted to "get even." These appraisals can be very fast; they may even bypass processing in the frontal cortex of the brain and stimulate our behavioral response systems directly. Moreover, with respect to the speed at which the emotions deliver their appraisals, the emotions and the movies are well suited to each other, since the pace of the action in the movies is very fast, often faster than in life outside the movies. At present, many movies are cut a rate of three shots a minute. In order to follow all this flurry of activity, a rapid-response, tracking system like the emotions would have to be in place. And, of course, it is and it is no accident that moviemakers have taken advantage of it.

Another feature of the emotions that has been a boon to fictioneers in general and to moviemakers in particular is that the emotions can be ignited by imaginings. That is, emotions do not require our belief in the existence of the objects, persons, and events that elicit them. We may send a shudder of anxiety down our own spine by imagining that we are in the process of cutting off our index finger with a meat cleaver, even while we are aware that the event in question is not happening.

Undoubtedly, the human capacity to be moved emotionally by contrary-to-fact, imagined situations was adaptive, since it enabled our forebears to be apprehensive about places and things not immediately present to them. Tribal elders, for example, could instill fear in the hearts of children by telling them stories about how they would be devoured by crocodiles if they wandered too close to the riverbank, thereby increasing the likelihood that the kids in question would mature and reproduce.

Although the emotions did not evolve in order to make movies possible, the fact that the emotions can be engendered by imaginings is a prerequisite for movies becoming a mass art. For had it not been the case that with respect to our cognitive architecture that fictions could provoke emotional responses, then the movies would lack the affective calling card that gathers vast audiences before them. The movies in this regard exploit mental powers that developed to deal with something else, just as the movies take advantage of the speed of emotional processing that evolved to scope out situations where time was of the essence rather than to keep up with fast-moving stories.

Even if the benefits to moviemakers of engaging the emotions are obvious, the way in which moviemakers succeed in achieving this may be theoretically less apparent. But here it pays to remind ourselves that the emotions are primarily appraisal mechanisms. They evaluate persons and objects, actions and events, with respect to vital human interests.

Jealousy, for example, alerts one sibling to another sibling's perceived encroachment upon his/her parents's affection and, therefore, concern. That is, jealousy, in such cases, detects challenges to the conditions of one's well-being and triggers alarm when they are threatened. Disgust zeroes in on impurity, fear on perceived danger or harm, and so on.

In the latter cases, the emotions in question evaluate the circumstances in terms of protecting, first and foremost, our physical integrity. But the emotions may also function to advance our sense of social standing, as contempt does by assessing others as inferior to ourselves.

Yet note: if the emotions involve appraisal, there must be some standard or criterion, however implicit, against which the particular objects of our emotional states are being assayed. Anger, for example, is the appraisal of an event as a wrong done to me or mine: you willfully step on my foot; I assess that to be a wrong, thereby setting off a train of physical events and sensations and, most likely, a desire for retribution.

These appraisals can originate near the site of perception without any further need for computation: the self-regarding preacher spills water on himself and we laugh; our perceptual pattern-detectors recognize that an expected pattern has been broken. Nevertheless, on other, probably less frequent occasions, our emotional appraisals emerge only after extended cognitive processing and rumination – as when we finally put together all those subtle signs of favoritism that the boss has been bestowing upon our office rival.

However, whether specific emotive reactions arise with perception or result from cognitive processing downstream, these episodes are appraisals relative to certain criteria, as, for instance, perceived danger is a criterion for fear – i.e., the emotive appraisal of a situation as dangerous.

In the ordinary course of events, when an emotion engulfs us, it focuses our attention on those features of the situation that are pertinent to the human interests or themes it is the function of the relevant emotion to advance or protect, while, at the same time, filtering out aspects of the situation that are not germane to the presiding emotional theme. We focus on the car speeding toward us – assessing its dangerousness – while not registering the numbers on its license plate.

The emotions are selectively attentive in terms of the interests they govern. In the first instance, the emotions batten upon prominent elements of the situation that threaten our interests or that afford opportunities to advance them. But then feedback, reinforced at the hormonal level to this initial assessment of the situation leads us to scan the scene further, selecting out more features of the situation that are pertinent to the dominant emotional concern. For example: that the driver in the aforesaid automobile is aiming it at us – that he intends to kill us.

When in the grip of an emotion, the state selectively organizes or gestalts the situation under the aegis of its central theme or concern. It structures attention selectively in light of criteria, namely, the criteria appropriate to the abiding interest it is the function of the emotion to protect or advance. In the preceding car scenario, fear gestalts the scene in terms of perceived harm. Perceived harm is the criterion of relevance for the emotive appraisal that we call fear.

Turning from the ordinary course of events and back to the movies, we can immediately note one striking difference between them. In life, our emotions do most of the work of organizing the events that come our way. We size-up the situation, picking out and appraising, albeit under the guidance of the emotion, what is relevant for our attention. What is relevant, of course, is what falls under the criterion or the criteria of the presiding emotional state. In this respect, we may say that our emotive appraisal is criterially focused.

However, when it comes to the movies (as well as the other arts), we notice that a great deal of the selection that it is up to the emotions to secure in life has already been done by the moviemakers. Whereas in most instances in life the emotions have to start the process of gestalting the stimulus from scratch, with movies a great deal of that work has already been done for us by the moviemaker who has designed the fictional situation in such a way that its criterially pertinent variables stand out saliently in ways that make our emotive appraisal of it in the manner the moviemaker intends virtually unavoidable. If in everyday life our emotions criterially focus events for us, movie events have been, to an appreciable extent, criterially *prefocused* for us.

For example, were we to film the car sequence imagined above, we would economically select just those details needed to mobilize and exacerbate the fear appraisal – perhaps we would include a shot of the car headed toward us and then maybe a close-up of the malevolent driver staring us down. We wouldn't include a shot of the license plate or of the back seat of the car. The sequence would be selectively prefocused criterially – in this case by means of editing – in terms of features appropriate to inspiring fear – the appraisal of the event as dangerous then leading to a gut reaction.

Movies have a panoply of means for engendering emotions in audiences. Undoubtedly the most obvious structure for eliciting spectator emotion is the narrative. Clearly, the narrative structure is an instrument for making certain events and the various components of those events salient. Comedies, for example, will often favor incongruous trains of events – the heretofore physically inept hero suddenly and unexpectedly rises to the challenge of saving his beloved and vanquishes his imposing adversaries (think Buster Keaton here) – where perceived incongruities are criterial for comic amusement.[3]

Dialogue and voice-over commentary can also call attention to the emotively relevant features of the fictional events before us; fictional characters, including fictional narrators, can bring our attention to those elements in a scene that we are mandated to focus upon, as do the off-screen voices in *The Magnificent Ambersons* which voices shape our assessment of young George's behavior.

Although the use of narrative and dialogue as a means of criterially prefocusing the audience's emotive appraisal is shared by movies with theater and, indeed, with many other art forms (including narrative painting, opera, song, and so forth), there are also certain devices available to function in this way that are more historically characteristic of the movies (including video and TV) than they are of the other arts. One thing that I have in mind in this respect is variable framing – the alteration of what is made visually salient to the viewer by scaling (making the object of attention larger in the visual field), indexing (by pointing the camera toward the object) and by bracketing (placing the object within a frame that excludes that which is irrelevant). These processes of variable framing can be implemented by editing, camera movement, or by the deployment of lenses of varying focal lengths. Variable framing insures that viewers will be looking where the moviemaker intends them to be looking precisely when the moviemaker wants them to be looking there.

If the moviemaker wishes to stimulate pity in the audience, she may show us a close-up of a character, previously established by the narrative to be praiseworthy, as that character's face writhes in agony in response to a flogging administered by a merciless prison guard. However, emotion may not only be elicited by moving the camera in. Expanding the field of vision may also be effective in engendering suspense as when the moviemaker cuts from the close-up of the heroine bobbing above and below the water line in a fast-moving stream to a broader shot of the ominously cascading waterfall toward which the erstwhile heroine seems inevitably headed.

The variable framing selectively picks out or criterially prefocuses the elements of the sequence that are pertinent to the affect the moviemaker wants to prompt, and with those appropriately valenced or charged items dominating our attention, we are, all things being equal, smoothly led to make the apposite, viscerally inflected appraisals – such as pity on the one hand, or suspense on the other. Call the audience's share here *emotive uptake* where emotive uptake is the aim of the creator's activity of *criterially prefocusing* certain features of the movie world.

Of course, there are other devices available to moviemakers for the purpose of criterial prefocusing. Sound, both noise and music, digetic and nondigetic, can be deployed in the service of criterial prefocusing. Loud, off-screen sounds may alert us to oncoming menace – as, for example, when we hear trees snapping and something very large approaching the altar where Ann Darrow is bound in the original version of *King Kong*. Likewise, non-digetic music may underscore (literally) the emotive significance of an event as when a march cadence annotates the gathering of the forces of the right-eous in a Western.

Perhaps needless to say, variable framing does not even exhaust the visual means available to moviemakers for the purpose of criterial prefocusing. Other devices include lighting, masks (like irises), and racking focus, all of which enable the moviemaker to control what the spectator sees – what she focuses upon. For example, in order to provoke fear, the moviemaker may first show us the protagonist standing against a background in soft focus; suddenly a blur appears; then the moviemaker reverses the field of focus and the blur metamorphoses into that incarnation of evil, Michael Myers. By racking focus in this way, the moviemaker criterially prefocuses the protagonists's circumstances in light of imminent danger, thereby setting up for emotive uptake in viewers in terms of the emotional appraisal that we call fear.

Emotional appraisal, of course, can occur before we have a fully determinate conception of the nature of the particular object of our attention. For instance, fear may begin to take hold before we recognize that the blur in the previous example is none other than the death-dealing Michael Myers. That it is large, advancing, and obscure may be enough to set off an alarm of apprehension. For obvious reasons of security, the emotions are typically hair-triggered, often discharging before we have fully cognized the object in question and relying instead upon very basic processes for recognizing patterns and deviations therefrom.

In summary, the emotions – the glue that keeps the movie audience in their seats – depends heavily on what we called criterial prefocusing; criterial pre-focusing is what predisposes us to the varieties of emotional arousals that ideally the moviemaker intends to elicit. Such emotional arousal may also be called emotive uptake. As we shall see in the next section, the elicitation of the moral emotions by the movies is, as might be expected, simply a special case of provoking emotional arousal in response to movies. It involves criterially prefocusing scenes and sequences so as to facilitate emotive uptake. The way in which the elicitation of the moral emotions differs from the elicitation of the nonmoral emotions is primarily a matter of that which is criterially prefocused in the moral cases versus what is critierially prefocused in the other cases.

III. The moral emotions and the audience's response to movie characters, actions, events, and scenes

The moral emotions are a subcategory of the emotions in general. As we have seen, the emotions in general are normative inasmuch as they are appraisals. The moral emotions emerge naturally from the nonmoral emotions, since they are evaluative, albeit evaluative in a very special manner – specifically, the moral emotions are emotions that respond to actions and events that conform or that fail to conform to moral standards.[4] The moral emotions enlist, so to say, the non-moral emotions for moral purposes.

Anger, for example, has an evaluative dimension – it is an emotional response mobilized by the perception of a wrong done to me or mine. Moral anger or moral indignation specifies the relevant sort of wrong in terms of things like injustice. Moral fear responds to harm where the harm in question is an evil, perhaps a great evil, such as genocide. Moral contempt is contempt, but contempt which assesses others to be *morally* inferior, while moral disgust targets *moral* pollution – that is, impurity with a moral dimension, like gang rape. The examples so far involve negative moral emotions. But there are positive moral emotions as well. Admiration is an emotional response to excellence in persons; moral admiration appraises the moral excellence of persons. It is a form of moral judgment.

It should not be surprising that the emotions are connected to moral judgment, since, as we have seen, the emotions are naturally selected adaptations for making assessments rapidly. The emotions are a form of value judgment. Hence, since moral judgments are evaluative, albeit ethically, it is most likely that they will possess some relations to the emotions in general. Indeed, many moral judgments are rooted in moral-emotional responses.

We are constantly making moral judgments in the course of everyday life. We are always judging the character and the actions of the people who surround us. Most of these judgments are borne in emotion, as when we angrily disapprove, if only to ourselves or to our confidants, of the permissive parent who allows her noisy children to run up and down the aisle of a crowded airplane.

The idea that moral judgments are rooted in the emotions may appear to fly in the face of common pictures of moral judgment. Usually, we (especially philosophers) tend to think of moral judgments as being issued after a chain of reasoning. However, although this may happen sometimes, there is evidence that a great many moral judgments are based on gut reactions. Recent research by social psychologists, such as John Haidt, indicates that moral judgments are generally fast, automatic, intuitive appraisals;[5] in short, they are emotions.

For example, when subjects are asked to morally evaluate a situation involving a brother and sister who agree to try incest, but in secret, only once, and employing several methods of birth control, subjects assess the behavior of these siblings as morally wrong, despite the fact that the case has been set-up in such a way as to undermine certain standard objections to incest, including that it will set a bad example, that it will spiral into an addiction, and that it will lead to physically compromised offspring. Nevertheless, even though their objections do not hold up, most subjects will not budge from their initial negative appraisals. Those appraisals, thus, are probably not based on reasons; instead they are most likely based on emotional responses. This hypothesis, moreover, is supported by the fact that when pressed to support these moral assessments, subjects give as reasons issues that have already been precluded by the story, such as the threat of birth defects.[6]

On the account emerging from contemporary moral psychologists, upon recognizing certain patterns, the stimuli, such as the suggestion of incest, are processed rapidly, triggering, almost immediately, feelings of approval or disapproval. Reasoning, if it comes into the emotion process at all comes into play after the initial intuitive appraisal takes hold, monitoring our gut reactions, sometimes modifying them, and often, if asked, confabulating after-the-fact rationalizations to back up our emotional responses. The moral intuitions here are cognitive, at least in the sense that they depend on pattern recognition, but they need not be front-loaded by reasoning. Indeed, some moral psychologists claim they never are. I am not convinced that they are right in this matter, although the evidence suggests that many more instances of moral judgment fit the intuitive model than fit the rationalistic one.

As previously mentioned, we undergo these flashes of moral intuitions almost incessantly. If you doubt it, observe yourself observing other drivers on a busy highway. Moreover, this sort of relentless activation of our moral emotions is possibly even more saturated in response to the movies, if only because movies are more condensed – in a mere two hours or so, there are so many more occasions to approve or disapprove of the characters – of their traits and their actions – than most comparable two-hour stretches outside the cinema. Furthermore, the rights and wrongs that exercise our moral emotions in the course of an ordinary day are typically not as salient as those we find in the movies, since in the majority of cases in daily life, those rights and wrongs have not been framed deliberately for our scrutiny.

Like the emotions in general, the moral emotions serve the purposes of the movies expeditiously. Not only are they a source of pleasure – we enjoy approving and disapproving of the action of others, especially when their actions do not impinge directly on us and our interests – but the moral emotions also orient the spectator to the narrative by parsing the dramatic conflict, most often in terms of good versus evil, and they do this rapidly, allowing the movie to hurtle forward at the characteristically accelerated pace of cinema, thereby enabling us to track the characters and the action in a constant rhythm of approval and disapproval.

Needless to say, the movies, by definition, are products designed to attract mass audiences. And they are capable of acquitting this function in large measure because the moral emotions they activate fall into nearly universal domains of concern or, at least, can be recognized as belonging to domains of concern acknowledged cross-culturally.[7] Thus, Hollywood movies can inspire the moral emotions of viewers not only of subcultures state-side, but in South America, while the Hong Kong and Bollywood cinemas also move transnationally. *Animé* is popular in Madison, Wisconsin as well as Tokyo to an appreciable extent because the moral emotions in which it trades cross borders as well as continents.

One of these domains of concern might be called, following the current literature, welfare. It concerns harm. Characters who inflict harm – particularly in terms of pain, and especially, where the victims are the young, the old, the disabled or the otherwise defenseless – provoke fast, intuitive, other-condemning, emotive appraisals, such as anger, indignation, loathing, and contempt.[8] The film – or rather the films – *Funny Games* are predicated upon raising our moral ire again and again at the unmotivated wanton terror that the intruders inflict upon the altogether innocent family and its neighbors.[9]

Moreover, the audience is not only encouraged to appraise the agents of harm with various grades of opprobrium. The victims also typically claim a degree of compassion from us. The event is not only an occasion for the condemnation of others, but for compassion for the harmed. Thus, at the same time that the Cossacks on the Odessa Steps in Sergei Eisenstein's *Battleship Potemkin* provoke moral indignation, moral compassion is also engendered for those who are ruthlessly destroyed. They include two minors, one an infant, a group of elders, two mothers, and then an older woman whose face is slashed by a cavalryman's saber. In this film, as in others, including his *Alexander Nevsky*, Eisenstein is exploiting a widely distributed, ethical proclivity to cultivate moral allegiance with – or attraction toward – the prototypically weakest members of society, while, at the same time, eliciting compassion for "the people" (the citizens of Odessa) by representing them synecdochically in terms of these innocent victims.

In westerns, the peaceable sheep-herders are savaged by the brutish gunfighters who have been hired by the tyrannical cattle ranchers to drive the shepherds from their pastures. As the newcomers are beaten by the bullies, the harms inflicted upon them raise our righteous rage while simultaneously eliciting pangs of distress for the goodly folk.

Horror movies also revolve around the theme of harm. The aliens from outer space invade our planet with the intention of making it their own and enslaving us. Our moral loathing mounts as the moviemakers highlight the pain and suffering, physical and often psychological, undergone by the hapless humans whose only crime is that they inhabit the real estate that the Martians covet. As one of these slimy, autocratic monsters rises up behind and then prepares to strike at some harmless earthling (frequently a woman), our feelings of suspense are freighted with the moral concern that a wrong is about to transpire, virtually inexorably. And as the beast snaps it prey between its mandibles, a lump of moral sorrow weighs upon our hearts.

Westerns and horror movies are only two genres that specialize in endangering and restoring the welfare of characters. So many other genres foreground harm as their abiding moral theme, including war movies, crime films, ninja sagas, spectacles (ancient, medieval, and modern), psycho-stalker flicks, social protest movies, and so forth. In short, an impressive proportion of movie genres focus on harms, notably harms directed at the undeserving. And where the moviemakers criterially prefocus the harm wreaked upon the undeserving, there is predictably a response involving moral animus and even moral hatred that reaches across the mass audiences that the moviemakers seek to engage so eagerly.

Our concern for the welfare of certain characters not only animates our negative intuitive appraisals of circumstances and characters that mete out harms to the innocent. Our concern for the welfare of various characters also makes us sensitive to acts of aid, succor, benevolence, generosity, and helpfulness on the part of certain characters on behalf of other characters. Such gestures are apt to elicit felt, intuitive appraisals in terms of moral admiration of varying magnitudes. This is key to the emotional address of many melodramas (a.k.a. tear-jerkers). Such movies introduce us to characters who go out of their way to do good for (and to alleviate the misfortune of) others (e.g., *Blindside*).

In one particular variation of the melodrama, a relative, say a mother, as in the case of *Stella Dallas*, sacrifices her own desires to benefit her kin, for example her daughter. We, in turn, cry for joy – our tears are shed in part out of pity for the loss the self-sacrificing mother suffers, but we also, at the same moment, feel positively and admiringly toward her – morally uplifted by the criterially prefocused spectacle of her selflessness in a way that makes us proud to be, in a manner of speaking, in her corner. Thus, even melodramas quite frequently ride on engaging our moral sentiments. And we don't even need to speak of religious films here.

Movies trade in moral emotions connected with concerns about human welfare because that is a domain of ethical concern that is global. Along with a concern for the welfare of certain characters, audiences also share a sense of justice – the desire that fairness should prevail, that rights be upheld, that exploitation be eschewed and that individuals be respected. This concern with justice, of course, is very often linked to the concern for the welfare of various characters, since a very obvious way of perpetrating injustice is to harm people who have done no wrong. When characters who are portrayed as praiseworthy or, at least, blameless, are physically abused, exploited, tortured, or humiliated, a righteous anger is raised in the collective gorge of the audience and a passion for just retribution keeps viewers in their seats for the duration of the film, until the last of the marauding bandits have been vanquished by the villagers and the Magnificent Seven (or their Samurai brethren). The moral redress of injustice is the moral motor that drives the plot and our interest in it with respect to countless action films and thrillers, not to mention motion pictures of serious social criticism.

The themes of justice and injustice – of revenge, retribution, and restoration – are staples of the movies because these moral emotions and the criteria that govern them are so widely shared by masses of people that they are ideally something that large numbers of viewers are willing to flock to see for the purpose of having said moral emotions excited. So often the movies are denounced as being immoral – often in terms of their sexual content. Yet I would speculate that if one could count up the number of times that the movies incite acceptable moral emotions versus the instances of dubious titillation, the former would way outweigh the latter.

Such movies, needless to say, not only traffic in moral revulsion toward those who revel in injustice, but also in moral admiration toward those, like Atticus Finch, who work tirelessly for the sake of justice. Think of the scene at the end of the trial in *To Kill a Mockingbird* when Scout is told to stand up because her Daddy is passing by. The climactic thrill that the audience experiences at that moment is grounded in the moral awe we are encouraged to feel in response to the courage that Lawyer Finch has displayed for the sake of justice, and, perhaps again, we also feel a bit of pride on our part for being on his side.

Of course, this concern with justice need not be as epic as the examples cited so far. The injustices can be interpersonal as when the executive treats the elevator operator played by Shirley Maclain in *The Apartment* as merely a means or when the disabled woman is humiliated in *In the Company of Men*. Indignation at the prospect of violations of the audience's conception of justice is a fine emotive fixative to keep masses of viewers who share the same conception collectively tied to the screen.

A third domain of moral concern that appears nearly universal is what has been called "the ethics of community."[10] This category involves rules pertaining to issues of social relationships, including both relations between individuals and between the individual and the group or groups to which he or she belongs. The moral rules relevant to the ethics of community apply to family relations, social rank, obligations to one's institutional affiliations, including the state, and to the apportionment of communal resources.[11] Violation of these rules tends to elicit moral anger, indignation, and contempt. Although the particular rules associated with the ethics of community show variation from culture and subculture to culture and subculture, the possession of rules in this category occurs everywhere.

Cultures globally establish to whom and to what their inhabitants owe deference, respect, fealty, loyalty, and patriotism. When those norms are violated, bitterness and rancor ensue, often mobilizing a retaliatory response toward the offender. Obedience with regard to these rules, especially conformity of an especially supererogatory degree, in contrast, provoke palpitations of admiration, joy, perhaps pride, and even awe.

For example, families can be found everywhere. Cultures generally have norms of rank, respect, and obligations of mutual aid between family members. When those rules are flouted – as when sons disrespect fathers – observers become disturbed, angered, often contemptuous, and even morally disgusted. When we witness special, mindful attention given by a character to a family relation, our response is a warm feeling of approval or admiration and, in pronounced cases, something like elevation.

Given the pervasiveness of the ethics of community, it should be no surprise that the movies deploy it in their endeavor to assemble mass audiences. In some cases, the ethics of community of diverse audiences may converge; but even where the codes of different audiences vary, most viewers will be able to access something of the feeling for what is at stake on an analogy with the rules of family ties with which they are familiar.

For these reasons, probably most audiences will be enraged and saddened by the way in which Sarah Jane, the mixed-race daughter who is trying to pass as white, rejects her black mother, Annie Johnson, in *Imitation of Life*. Likewise, when the grown children of Barkley and Lucy allow their elderly parents to be parted, most likely forever, at the end of *Make Way for Tomorrow*, one feels not only dispirited but disgusted by the lack of gratitude involved. Of course, we may not only be ethically moved when children betray parents; disapproval can flow in the other direction as well. For instance, in *Parenthood*, when the overzealous Nathan Huffner starts grooming his preschooler daughter for the Ivy League at the expense of childhood fun, it is hard not to be morally aggravated by him.

Needless to say, family life is not the only area presided over by the ethics of community. One's relations to one's nation or one's people also fall into this category. Thus, patriotic pride and joy are frequent positive emotional reactions that moviemakers attempt to curry, particularly during times of wars that a nation supports, as was the case with Hollywood movies during the World War II. Think of films such as *A Guy Named Joe* or *Thirty Seconds over Tokyo*. Indeed, patriotic films of that war can still stir up pride in the hearts of American audiences as witnessed by *Saving Private Ryan*.

Moreover, disloyalty can engender surges of hatred in viewers as does the behavior of the scientist in Howard Hawks's *The Thing* who appears to favor the giant carrot from outer space over the human race. Similarly, those who take more than their fair share, like the pigs in the cartoon version of *Animal Farm*, or who pretend to social status they don't deserve, like Ziggy, in the TV series *The Wire*, are very likely to earn the visceral contempt of the audience. The criterially prefocused exploitation of factory workers, as in *Strike* and *Metropolis*, can also be a cause for moral indignation in virtue of counting as a violation of the ethics of community, although it may, at the same time, also be compounded by constituting a harm to others, namely the workers, as well as a violation of their rights.

Another domain of moral concern ripe for articulation by moviemakers is that of purity, and, especially, violations thereof. Of course, the primary emotional response to impurity is disgust. And genres, such as the horror movie, take the elicitation of disgust to be their brief. As the moldering mummy with missing facial parts reaches out to touch the bare shoulder of the heroine, we instinctively recoil; as the zombie, dripping with blood and putrefaction, takes a bite out of the aging preacher, we gag.

Originally disgust is an emotion that has been adapted to guard the intimate borders of the human body – mouths, nasal passages, genitals, and so forth. Thus, foodstuffs (notably spoiled ones), stenches, sexual acts, and practices are apt targets of disgust. Milk that has soured makes us retch; certain odors, like vomit, make our stomachs churn, while the contemplation of certain sexual acts may make us involuntarily exclaim "ugh."

These reactions are deployed first and foremost in our own case: we choke when we swallow the fetid milk. But the response can also be launched when we observe others, for example, being tricked into eating something impure. Indeed, it is this capacity for disgust to be engendered by the actions of third parties which enables moviemakers – including the masters of horror – to activate it so easily by means of their imagery.

Undoubtedly, what I've said so far will strike you as unexceptionable. However, on second thought, you may ask yourself, "Why is he talking about disgust in the context of moral concern?" For, disgust, as we have been using that term, is primarily a response to physical stimuli, not moral stimuli. So, what does disgust have to do with ethics; is it even a moral emotion?

As noted, disgust originates as a device to defend the body against the ingestion of noxious substances such as decaying food. However, the presence of sexual practices on the list of disgust elicitors indicates that disgust can be triggered by things other than inedibles. Things involving bodily fluids, such as blood, mucus, semen, and so forth are also disgusting as are, by extension, a great many slimy things. Thus, practices involving the exchange of bodily fluids can be disgusting metonymically, so to speak. Furthermore, disgust can be associated with things, such as tabooed foods, that have no natural propensity to make us gag. And what is true of foods can be extended to activities of all sorts, thereby dragooning disgust in the service of morality, reinforcing other cultural dictates, as exemplified by the practices of the Hindu caste system.

That is, disgust can be extended as a response to practices and behaviors other than those involving a bodily focus; it can be expanded as a reaction to violations of moral norms where it can serve to guard the boundaries of other moral domains. Hence, we may say of someone who breaks some moral rule – such as the prohibitions against lying or adultery – that her behavior is disgusting.[12]

The extension of disgust into the moral realm is an especially useful form of moral rhetoric in the hands of moviemakers. In D. W. Griffith's *Birth of a Nation*, the African American legislature is depicted as disgusting as a means of highlighting Griffith's belief that their very presence in the assembly is a moral wrong. The questionable cleanliness of these delegates, their vulgar way of eating, and their general obliviousness to social decorum are meant to signal their moral turpitude by way of attempting to elicit from the audience a visceral reaction of repugnance. In the western, *The Big Country*, the utter moral unscrupulousness of the uncouth younger Hannassey is underscored by representing him as saliently unwashed, focusing the moral disgust with which we are intended to regard him by means of his physically disgusting appearance. Likewise, when monsters and psychopaths tear their victims apart, the criterially prefocused gore they incur is disgusting in a way that reinforces our convictions about the evil of their actions.

In these instances, disgust is being employed to amplify a moral judgment rather like the way in which Dorian Gray's portrait is intended to. But there is also something that we may think of as moral disgust. This disgust pertains first and foremost to immoral behaviors that we already regard as disgusting – ones often connected to the body, such as the forced fellatio and rape scenes in *The Girl with the Dragon Tattoo*. However, we are also prone to describe and experience excessively evil actions or persons as disgusting, like Gordon Gekko in Oliver Stone's *Wall Street*.

Undoubtedly, it may seem strange that something like disgust that originated as a response to physical impurities can be extrapolated to the moral realm. Perhaps one reason for the transportation into the ethical domain is that many cultures think of the spirit as being in an initial pure state that can be polluted by moral infractions, like sin. The body is a temple containing the soul, which can be breached and infected as some nasty liquid can turn one's stomach. Just as disgust staves off physical impurity, it also does double duty fending off spiritual impurity. Moviemakers, as a result, can mobilize moral disgust against screen characters, like the Nazi commandant in *Schindler's List*, whose sadism audiences find repugnant. Moreover, if excessive evil, suitably foregrounded and criterially prefocused, can elicit moral disgust, an excess of goodness or moral goodness can elicit awe, an emotion many moviemakers strive to evoke in motion pictures involving Jesus Christ.

IV. Sympathy/antipathy, morality, and the movies

As we have seen, most of our emotional responses to movies are focused upon characters and their circumstances. Many of those reactions, in turn, are moral emotions. We are riled by the injustices suffered by protagonists and innocent bystanders, angered by children who fail to pay proper deference to their parents, while feeling a sort of moral satisfaction and even admiration towards characters who protect the weak and worthy, and we experience a sense of elevation or joy when justice is restored. In order for these emotions to take hold, however, we need to have an antecedent, positive, affective investment in some characters, their situations, and their prospects, while, at the same time, bearing a negative attitude toward an opposing set of characters, their situations, and their prospects. Call the former group of characters the protagonists, and the latter group the antagonists. My hypothesis is that to a large extent what bonds us to the protagonists affectively is sympathy which emotional attachment is secured primarily by moral considerations and that, contrariwise, what engenders antipathy toward the villains is their discernible moral failings.

That is, in order to be angered by threats to the protagonists, we need to be on their side. We need to be in sympathy with their agenda. In order to curry that sympathy, moviemakers chiefly depend upon addressing our moral sentiments of approval. To take pleasure in the defeat of those who would harm the protagonists, we must typically regard them in a negative light. And moviemakers typically engineer that attitude by portraying the antagonists as immoral if not downright evil, as Billy Wilder portrays the ruthless newspaper man, played by Kirk Douglas, in *Ace in the Hole* who not only arranges to have the rescue of the Indian curio dealer blocked, but who also, while doing so, seduces the man's wife.

Sympathy and antipathy – conceived of as underlying pro and con attitudes – govern the activation of our moral emotions toward said characters in specific scenes and situations as the movie unfolds. Moreover, these overarching attitudes toward the various characters are secured by criterially prefocusing their virtues and their vices.

In order to see how this works, let's start with sympathy. Roughly, sympathy is a non-passing attitude of care or concern – a pro-attitude – toward another person or group (fictional or nonfictional, including anthropomorphized beings of every stripe). Sympathy, construed as an occurrent emotion, is a supportive reaction. It supplies a supportive impulse of benevolence toward its object (although this impulse is often not acted upon in everyday life, insofar as it frequently conflicts with our interests). Sympathy, *qua* occurrent emotion, involves visceral feelings of distress when the interests of the objects of our overarching pro-attitudes are compromised or imperiled; and feelings of elation or satisfaction when their well-being is advanced or achieved. Sympathetic emotional responses appraise circumstances positively when things go nicely for the objects of our concern, but assess situations negatively when the projects of the objects of our concern are frustrated or aborted. Moreover, these evaluations are connected to some degree of euphoria, on the one hand, and dysphoria, on the other hand.

We are saddened when the ancient Hebrews are enslaved by Pharaoh, but gladdened by their escape across the Red Sea. Because of our sympathetic or pro-attitude toward the oppressed Hebrews, we feel moral indignation when the Egyptian lash bloodies the backs of the apparently blameless workers; and when Pharaoh's chariots sink beneath the waves, we experience a species of joy that might be called moral elevation or moral triumph.

A practical question for moviemakers and a theoretical question for philosophers of the motion picture is: how is that sympathetic or pro-attitude typically put in place? Sympathy, as noted, involves a benevolent disposition toward the object of our attitude. In order to warrant that benevolence, the person or persons in question must be thought to be worthy of our pro-attitude in virtue of our interests, projects, values, loyalties, commitments, and allegiances. Consequently, the question for moviemakers and philosophers alike is: what needs to be foregrounded or criterially prefocused so that the massive audiences moviemakers seek after will find the pertinent characters deserving of our good will on their behalf?

Just because moviemakers are aiming for mass audiences, the answer to this question is not obvious. For mass audiences are comprised of people with different and sometimes even conflicting interests, projects, values, loyalties, commitments, and allegiances. This is the case not only when the desired audience spans cultures, countries, and continents, but even within single countries and cultures. After all, the makers of *Spider Man* want liberals and conservatives to get behind the eponymous web-slinger.

As an empirical conjecture, I hypothesize that the most commonly recurring solution to this design problem – by a long shot – is for moviemakers to create protagonists (and the other characters meant to warrant our concern) in such a way that the audience will recognize them to be, broadly speaking, morally good.

That is, morality, especially of a widely shared and often nearly universal variety, provides the moviemaker with the touchstone she needs to assure the convergence in sentiment on behalf of the protagonists from peoples of the same and different cultures. The moviemaker needs to find something upon which disparate audiences agree, despite their otherwise diverging interests. And, as one may observe through the examination of countless movies, that something is generally a shared moral sense.

The protagonists uphold justice, do not harm unavoidably, show respect and friendliness toward one and all. They are pro-family, courteous, and mostly pro-social (deep down this is even true of apparent anti-heroes and rebels without causes). These characters are honest and they stand by their promises to good people. Indeed, they are themselves good people. This forges alliances between heterogeneous audiences on their behalf for the duration of the motion picture which sympathy underlies the moral elation we feel in response to their victories and the moral indignation we experience at their defeats.

By designing protagonists who are morally appealing, the moviemaker purchases the criterial wherewithal necessary to elicit the pro-attitudes required to underwrite the audiences's moral responses to the story, thereby sustaining the audience's absorption in the movie. By being morally upstanding, the relevant characters satisfy the conditions for being worthy of our benevolent wishes because they are morally deserving in ways that can be recognized by mass audiences with otherwise highly diversified interests. These characters exhibit virtue and the audience rewards virtue with sympathetic concern. Morality, understood very generously, is a project that audiences with otherwise widely variegated commitments can share.

Protagonists are usually good guys, since good guys are precisely what are likely to command pro-attitudes from mass and massively mixed audiences. These characters are attractive because they are morally attractive or appealing. Their virtue wins the audience's allegiance. We side with Dorothy rather than the Wicked Witch, because Dorothy is a good person, kind to those less fortunate than herself, whereas the Wicked Witch terrorizes the weak. Even the superficially alienated antiheroes of the movies in the end turn out to win our admiration because they do the right things, as Rick does at the end of *Casablanca*.

An underlying pro-attitude toward the protagonists is central to the emotions, including the moral emotions, which we muster for these characters throughout the motion picture. Of course, over the duration of a given movie, we may undergo a gamut of different emotional reactions to these characters including moral indignation at the way they are treated, on the one hand, and moral satisfaction or elevation at the success of their just causes. But it is the sympathy that we feel with these characters that generally plays the major structuring role vis à vis whatever accompanying feelings may emerge, including our affective moral reactions. We are proud of the hero's victory over evil and morally angered by the way the villains mistreat him because his well-being is an object of our concern. Moreover, that sympathy on his behalf has been instilled in us by representing him as deserving in virtue of his goodness.

Of course, sympathy is not the only factor that structures our emotional responses to movies. Another, related factor is antipathy. Most movies confront the protagonists and the other goodly folk with some adversaries, a.k.a. the bad guys. We are not only invited to embrace the righteous as fellow members of a generic "Us"; their opposing number constitutes a "Them" toward whom the audience is prompted to react with ill will. Furthermore, if the pro-attitude engendered in viewers towards the "Us" is encouraged by criterially prefocusing their moral worthiness, the antipathy channeled toward the "Them" is generally sustained by representing them as morally defective. Where the protagonist is nice to nice people – showing good manners and respect to everyone regardless of rank – the villain is rude to anyone weaker or socially inferior to him and often much worse than merely disrespectful. The antagonists pillage, cheat, lie, kill, and so on.

The hero picks up the lollipop the child has dropped; the villain is more likely to throw it further afield, if not eat it himself. Because the negative moral attitude that we bear toward the antagonists, we greet his successes in battle with moral outrage and his defeats with a feeling of appropriateness – a sensation of moral closure. When the Nazi leadership is burned to the ground at the end of Quentin Tarantino's *Inglourious Basterds*, the heart quickens with a joyousness rooted in conviction that Hitler and his accomplices have been dealt their just moral desserts.

Sympathy, motivated by morality, inclines us to assimilate the protagonists as belonging to Us. But this bond is usually further deepened by ranging one or more enemies against Us where these enemies are typically recognizable because they have been fashioned as morally bad people. That is, most movies involve instilling two kinds of attitudes in audiences: a pro-attitude to the protagonists and their associates, and a con-attitude toward the antagonists and their allies; and these attitudes, in turn, provide the basis for our emotional responses to these characters, including our affective moral appraisals of them. The spectators feel allied to the protagonist and opposed to the antagonist. Indeed, the antagonist engenders anger, hatred, and even disgust in us where these antipathetic emotional reactions are most often moral in nature.

Whereas sympathy in the ordinary run of events tends to be something that we extend, all things being equal, by default to most of the people we encounter, in movies sympathy must be induced. In movies (and other popular fictions) this is usually accomplished by making the pertinent characters morally attractive. The viewer's affiliation with these characters is further reinforced by setting an array of nemeses against them whom we find repelling, generally due to their criterially prefocused moral failings, which can range from petty vices to pronounced viciousness.

In most cases, I hypothesize that it is the sympathy with which we regard the protagonists that is the leading source of our emotional responses to the characters. However, sometimes antipathy toward the villains is enough to win some characters sympathy on the rebound, in a manner of speaking. That is, the moviemaker may exploit the "enemy-of-my-enemy-is-my-friend" phenomenon as when the dastardly space invaders, wielding their deadly Z-rays, evaporate thousands of law abiding earthlings without a blink of their eyes (usually more than two). Our hatred for these merciless marauders from galaxies far, far away is enough to enlist our sympathies for our fellow earth folk which, in turn, sparks the moral indignation that we feel in response to the abuses to which they are subjected.

Inciting our moral emotions is key to the success of most movies. The possibility of inspiring those emotions in the viewer depends upon nurturing attitudes of sympathy and antipathy toward the various characters in the movie. Yet, securing those attitudes is typically accomplished by criterially prefocusing certain characters as virtuous and others as morally blemished, if not vicious.

V. Concluding remarks

We began by pointing out that the movies seek mass markets. This makes the arousal of emotion especially attractive to moviemakers for a number of reasons. Many emotions (and especially the ones in which the movies typically traffic) are widely shared, due to their biological origin, and can thus provide the terms of engagement with which to address potentially immense audiences. By exciting the emotions, moviemakers thereby render their stories accessible to the many.

Moreover, those audiences possess an interest in having these emotions aroused inasmuch as emotional arousal can itself be pleasing, especially if it does not endanger any of one's interests. Hence, moviemakers are naturally drawn to inciting the emotions of viewers, not only as a means for making their stories intelligible for the masses, but also as a means of doing so in a way that has the added benefit of affording pleasure.

Even if this observation is almost a platitude, perhaps the extent to which moviemakers seek to elicit moral emotions is less obvious. Consequently, I tried to show how many of the standard emotional themes of the movies invoke widespread, nearly universal (albeit often overlapping) domains of moral concern, such as welfare, justice, communal order, and impurity.

Emotional responses, including moral ones, towards characters and their situations generally require overarching pro and/or con attitudes toward the relevant fictional beings. I call these attitudes sympathy and antipathy respectively. Interestingly, as induced by movies, these attitudes appear to be founded primarily upon moral themes. In movies, we are usually mandated to sympathize with the virtuous, the characters we love to love, and to disdain the vicious, the characters we love to hate.

Although frequently rebuked as the acme of moral decadence, the movies are moral through and through. This is especially evident when one considers the ways in which the movies engage the affective responses of their audiences. For those affective reactions quite often take the form of moral-emotional responses which, in turn, are undergirded by pro and con attitudes that themselves depend upon moral factors. Therefore, despite the recurring jeremiads of pundits, the movies and morals belong together. Indeed, it is hard to imagine how movies could have ever taken hold without the support of the moral sentiments.

Notes

1   The qualification is meant to allow for movies made by communist states and other organizations that are not made for profit but are aimed nevertheless at mass audiences.

2   Emotions in daily life solve the frame problem; they organize the buzzing confusion in terms of our interests. Similarly, by engaging our moral emotions, moviemakers

enable us to organize the incoming stimulus coherently, very often, as we shall see, by stoking our sense of good and evil.

3 See Noël Carroll, "Two Comic Plots," in my *Art in Three Dimensions* (Oxford: Oxford University Press, 2010).

4 Jesse Prinz, *The Emotional Construction of Morals* (Oxford: Oxford University Press, 2007), p. 118.

5 John Haidt, "The Emotional Dog and its Rational Tail: A Social Intuitionist Approach to Moral Judgment," *Psychological Review* 108 (2001), pp. 814–34.

6 Ibid.

7 See John Haidt and C. Joseph, "Intuitive Ethics: How Innately Prepared Intuitions Generate Culturally Variable Virtues," *Daedalus* 133 (2004), pp. 55–66. See also P. Rozin, L. Lowery, S. Imada, and J. Haidt, "The CAD Hypothesis," *Journal of Personality and Social Psychology* 76 (1999), pp. 574–86. Throughout this section I rely heavily upon the notion of globally recurring domains of moral concerns, like the ones discussed in the previous articles, because I am trying to explain the *mass* reach of the movies and these domains cross cultures. Further evidence that emotions are to a certain extent nearly universal is suggested that infants apparently possess proto-moral predispositions. See Paul Bloom, "The Moral Life of Babies," *New York Times Magazine* (May 9, 2010), pp. 44–9, 56, 62, 63, 65. See also Paul Bloom, *How Pleasure Works* (New York: W. W. Norton, 2010).

8 Other-regarding, moral emotions are, I predict, more common in response to movies, since spectators are generally in the position of witnesses, though there are exceptions, as when the spectator is nudged towards evaluating his or her own responses. Certain popular films, such as Alfred Hitchcock's *Strangers on a Train* and *Rear Window* have been said to have the effect of making the viewer feel guilty in recognition of his implicit endorsement of the moral infractions of certain characters – such as L.B. Jeffries' voyeurism in *Rear Window*.

9 Perhaps this film at a second remove is also designed to elicit self-regarding moral emotions; maybe we are supposed to condemn ourselves as paying customers to enactments of sadism of the sort that *Funny Games* exemplifies.

10 R. A. Shweder, N. C. Much, M. Mahapatra, and L. Park, "The 'Big Three' of Morality," in P. Rozin and A. Brandt (eds.), *Morality and Mental Health* (New York: Routledge, 1997); P. Rozin, L. Lowery, J. Haidt, and S. Imada, "The CAD Hypothesis," *Journal of Personality and Social Psychology* 76(4) (1999), pp. 574–596.

11 Jesse Prinz, *The Emotional Construction of Morals*, 72.

12 In earlier writing, I attempted to restrict disgust exclusively to the physical realm, but I now agree that it may extend to the moral realm as well.

6

The Problem with Movie Stars

Introduction

In *The World Viewed*, Stanley Cavell offers the brilliant critical observation that "In *Ride the High Country*, the pathos of the aging cowboys (Randolph Scott and Joel McCrea) depends upon their being enacted by aging men whom we can remember as young cowboys."[1] For Cavell, the earlier roles of stars can affect our reception of their subsequent characterizations. Humphrey Bogart's portrayals of protagonists with checkered histories, in movies like *Casablanca*, succeed so well, in part, because we recall, as Cavell puts it, his outlaw past[2] – that is, the series of films, such as *Angels with Dirty Faces*, where Bogart played heavies on the wrong side of right.

The phenomenon to which Cavell adverts is hard to gainsay. Once established, most movie stars, save perhaps chameleons like Daniel Day-Lewis, come to us with an established persona, rooted in their previous films, and that persona can have expressive ramifications which we often use to fill in our sense of the character before us in the present instance. This is quite obvious with respect to parodies, such as *The Freshman* and *Analyze That* in which Marlon Brando's and Robert DeNiro's comic portrayals of gangsters play off their earlier dramatic portrayals of mafia chieftains. But serious films also exploit the penumbra of film history that follows the movie star onscreen.

A very clear cut example of this is Billy Wilder's *Sunset Boulevard*. Especially for its first audiences, the fading silent-movie queen Norma Desmond had all

"The Problem with Movie Stars," in Scott Walden (ed.), *Photography and Philosophy* (Malden, MA: Wiley-Blackwell, 2008), pp. 248–64.

the more resonance for being enacted by Gloria Swanson, whom many of the initial viewers of the film recognized as a genuine silent movie star whose career was in eclipse. Likewise, when her butler Max asserts that he, along with D. W. Griffith and Cecil B. DeMille, were once the leading film directors in Hollywood, the line is particularly moving because it is spoken by Erich von Stroheim, who, as well as being a well-known actor, had indeed been a silent film director of the highest stature. And for the viewer who might have forgotten these well-known facts of movie fandom, the creators of *Sunset Boulevard* include some footage of *Queen Kelly*, a film directed by Stroheim and starring Swanson.

Though *Sunset Boulevard* is quite overt in this matter, references to star personae, though in a subtler register, are quite pervasive. When a casting director ponders whether the audience will accept a certain actor in a certain role, she is thinking about whether, given the persona that the actor has forged thus far over his or her career, it enriches or, at least, meshes with a viable interpretation of the character at hand.[3]

Although I am reasonably sure that Basil Rathbone was pleasant enough with his friends and family, at a certain point in his career it would have been hard to imagine him portraying an affable, ordinary traffic policeman. Of course, he could have been cast as an extraordinary policeman whose self-confidence bordered on arrogance. But an ordinary, nice guy – never! And even if he could have, in some sense, pulled it off, the producers would have vetoed the suggestion. Glen Ford would be a better bet, they'd say.

Indeed, movies are often written with specific stars in mind. Sofia Coppola's *Lost in Translation* was said to have been conceived from the start with Bill Murray in the leading role. Here the author herself was using Murray's star persona to flesh out the character in the expectation that viewers would continue to do the same.

Movie stars have personae that accumulate associations as their careers progress and it is part of the art of the producer, writers, the casting director and so forth to match up current projects with suitable, ongoing, star personae. They do this because they know that viewers will use that information to round out their comprehension of and, in consequence, their affective response to the characters.

That we react to certain characters as we do is often abetted by employing actors whose careers are freighted with certain publicly available associations. We usually begin by presuming that a character played by Gregory Peck is a decent guy because he appeared in so many films where he earnestly struggled to do the right thing. We presume that Clark Gable will stand up for his rights and for the rights of others because his screen persona is that of a stand-up kinda fellow. He is brash and aggressive, never passive. Confronted, he barks rather than whispers. He could never have been cast as Ashley in *Gone with the Wind*.

Responses of this sort are not flights of fan fantasy. They are premeditated effects; the film has been designed to elicit them through the way in which the relevant movie stars have been chosen for their roles.

Perhaps, all this sounds very obvious and unexceptionable. Reacting to movie stars in this way is a pattern of spectatorship that most of us pick up almost by osmosis, as we are inducted into the practice of movie-going. However, acknowledging the existence of this channel of communication between the screen and the auditorium can very quickly head us toward paradox.

Why?

Most popular, commercial movies – that is, the kind of movies in which movie stars star – are fictional. Furthermore, many of our responses to fictions, including fictional films, depend upon restricting our attention to the story world of the movie and to what it presupposes. It is fictional in the film that the hero is dangling over a precipice and it is presupposed in the fiction that, were he to fall, he would be crushed to death against the ground below. That is what we need to be thinking about at this moment in the movie, if we are to feel suspense.[4] We should keep our minds focused upon what is contained within the bounds of the fiction operator – that is, on what fills in the blank in the formula: "It is true in the fiction that ——." For, if we help ourselves to certain information that does not belong under the scope of the fiction operator, suspense will not obtain.

Which information? For example, film-viewing commonplaces such as that the hero always escapes from tight predicaments like the one just mentioned. If we dwelt upon our knowledge of that bit of motion-picture lore, we would have not have call to fret about the plight of the hero. If we brought to mind what we know of how such popular movies are constructed, in other words, most of the curiosity required to sustain our interest in such films would evaporate.[5]

In order to be effectively drawn into the question of whether the boy will get the girl, we need to relegate to the back burner of our consciousness our "real-world" knowledge that this is almost always how it goes when the top-billed star and starlet are thrown together. Yes, they bicker, but the veteran film viewer *knows* this is but a prelude to a kiss. And yet, we do not let that knowledge push its way to the forefront of our mind, since, were it to take over, it would be difficult to remain inquisitive about the outcome of this prospective courtship.

As we imaginatively entertain a fiction like this one, we need to bracket our quite considerable command of the ways in which the plots in popular movie genres generally unfold. That is, in order for many movie plots to work their emotional magic upon us, we need to put our fund of movie lore on hold. We must discount our grasp of the principles that govern popular-movie, plot construction when it comes to entertaining the probabilities of what is likely to transpire or not in the fictional world; since that involves knowledge that is outside the legitimate scope of the fiction operator.

But isn't it precisely that sort of movie lore that we are mobilizing when we use a star's persona to fill-out the character he or she is playing? Thus, it appears that successful movie going both requires access to extra-fictional or external movie lore, while also demanding that we bracket such lore from our imaginative engagement with films. A contradiction seems in the offing.[6] The purpose of this article is to avert it.

The problem

Although the recommendation – that successful engagement with a fiction requires us to focus imaginatively upon what falls inside the fiction operator – is, broadly speaking, correct, it is very important not to misinterpret this maxim. For, in order to understand any fiction, we must generally access information that is unstated and/or not shown in the work. We need not only to attend to what is explicitly given in the fiction, but also to what is presupposed by it. That is, we will have to fill-out the description or the picture of the fictional environment with which the creator presents us; and to do this, we must go beyond the explicit boundaries of the fiction operator, strictly construed, albeit in a principled way.

But how will we know how to fill-in what is presupposed by the fiction in a principled way? To a great extent, we achieve this by using our beliefs about the actual world to help us along. When in the course of a movie about World War II, a British soldier fights alongside of an American soldier and against a German one, it does not have to be explained to the typical American viewer that the "Tommies" were our allies; that is knowledge from the "real world" that the intended viewer uses to fill-in or make sense of the fiction. Likewise, when we are shown that the fiction is set in the Forbidden City in Beijing, the average, prepared audience-member does not have to be told that the Emperor is Chinese, since that is a belief about the actual history of the world that the viewer almost naturally brings to bear on the fiction on the screen.

In short, imaginative narratives make reference to the world outside the fiction in multiple ways and, in order to follow such fictions, cinematic and otherwise, audiences must employ and, indeed, they are expected to resort to many of their standing beliefs, convictions, (and emotions) regarding the extra-fictional or "real world" in order to flesh out what is presupposed by the fiction. Moreover, this involves not only historical and geographical facts, but also biological and social ones – such as, *ceteris paribus*, persons drained of blood die, and mothers are likely to attempt to protect their offspring.

These suppositions, of course, can be over-ridden by the presiding rules of a genre or explicitly by the specific way in which the narrative at hand evolves. For example, persons drained of blood may return as the Undead in vampire films. Nevertheless, to a perhaps surprising extent, following a fiction involves using what we believe about the actual world and how it works in order to fill-in and make sense of what is onscreen. Thus, what might be called the *realistic heuristic* is often our default assumption when processing a cinematic fiction.[7]

Generally, we respond emotionally to the situations in cinematic fictions and anticipate their likely outcomes in accordance with the realistic heuristic.[8] We are not meant to calibrate our reactions to what transpires in the fiction in the expectation that it will abide by the rules that govern the plot construction of popular fictions. If we know that the boy will get the girl, or vice versa, or that good always wills out, where's the *frisson* in that? So, we go with the realistic heuristic and the kind of probabilities it makes available.

We do not key our emotional responses to the conventional plot trajectories and their subtending probabilities which we know rule Hollywood-type plot construction, since they have little to do with our beliefs about what is probable in the actual world as it thrives outside our cineplexes. That is, we do not typically deploy the movie-going lore pertinent to the plot construction of popular entertainments, unless we are watching a film about Hollywood plot construction (for example, *Boy Meets Girl*).

Standardly, the beliefs about how the fictional world works, up on which our cognitive and emotional responses to the movie depend, rely upon the realistic heuristic and not on film lore about plot construction. Although film lore about plot construction reflects how movies go, it does not reflect what we know of the way of the actual "non-cinematic" world. For, what we believe is probable of a movie *qua* movie is radically different from what we believe to be probable *in* a movie conceived of as a creditable fictional world.

But do the prescriptions of the realistic heuristic also preclude our using what we know of the past careers of movie stars in order to augment our affective response to the character before us on screen? When we recall John Wayne with a twinge of wistful recognition as a truly beautiful young cowboy while watching the (intentionally exaggeratedly) dilapidated and besotted version of him in *True Grit*, are we in violation of the realistic heuristic?

At first blush, it may appear that we are. For, supposing that the realistic heuristic discounts the transmigration of souls as an explanation, how would we account for any relation of continuance between the Ringo Kid, for example, and Rooster Cogburn? Nor is reincarnation a presupposition of the western genre, as it is of the mummy genre. So, isn't our melancholy in this case as ill-advised here as would be our invocation of the inevitable happy ending with respect to any number of suspense sequences? In both cases, we are going outside of the fiction and our realistic default assumptions about how the fictional world works and is intelligible. In both cases, we are using what we know about movies in order to engender our reaction to the movie before us.

Film, photography, and allusion

And yet, once again, it pays to re-emphasize that we do allow that fictions can make reference to the world outside the fiction.[9] A fiction can make reference to air travel and invite us – even bid us – to use what we know about air travel in order to fillout the story. *United 93* does not explain to us what those metal carts that the stewardesses push are; it presumes that we know what they are and that we use that information to explain to ourselves why they are available for smashing in the door of the cockpit.

But the creators of fictions may not only refer to the actual world with *literal* intent – with the intention that we apply literally what we believe of the real world to the circumstances of the fiction. The creators of a fiction may also refer to things outside the fiction with what might be called *figurational* intent – that is, with the intention that we apply figuratively what we associate to the stretch of reality referred to by fiction to elements within the fiction, or even to the totality of the ongoing fiction as a whole.

A fiction, including a pictorial one, for example, may refer to Christ in order to encourage audiences to apprehend a certain character within the fiction in terms of attributes that they associate with Jesus, as is the case of the character played by Ian Hunter in Frank Borzage's *Strange Cargo*. Here the allusion to Christ is a way of underscoring the redemptive aura of the character. The use of figuration in this way does not violate the realistic heuristic, since it does not involve claims about what is literally true in the fictional world nor how it operates.

As I understand *Strange Cargo*, it is only committed to the view that the character is Christ-like, not that he is necessarily Christ; just as the monster in *Bride of Frankenstein* is pictorially associated with the crucified Jesus when the villagers chain him to a pole. The monster is not literally identified with Jesus here, though the allusion serves to analogize his situation to that of Christ's as the victim of an unruly and unjustified mob.[10] And, as this case should make abundantly evident, one can allude for purposes of figurative comparison in a fiction to things outside the fictional world with no impropriety – not logical, conceptual, ontological, nor even aesthetic.

Moreover, a fiction may also allude to a fictional character. During the movie *In Her Shoes*, the character Rose twice runs the dogs she has been hired to exercise up the steps of the Philadelphia Art Museum. In doing this, the film alludes to the fictional character of Rocky Balboa from the movie *Rocky*. Via this allusion, we are encouraged to regard Rose's new life – previously she had been an uptight, corporate lawyer – as some sort of personal triumph for her, as a similar run up that staircase had been for Rocky.

In a written fiction, an author may allude to a movie character, saying, for example, that so-and-so's muscles rippled like Maciste's. There is no reason to think that comparable allusions cannot be achieved pictorially as well, as the case of the allusion to Rocky during *In Her Shoes* indicates. Indeed, in both written and pictorial fictions, one can even allude to movie stars; the character played by Raymond Massey in the movie version of *Arsenic and Old Lace*, for example, is explicitly compared to Boris Karloff.

But what has this to do with our problem with movie stars? Namely: that in the cases before us, the images of the pertinent movie stars, among other functions, allude to the actors in question. That is, it is my contention that when we encounter established movie stars on screen, it is sometimes the case that we may experience them – and may be encouraged to experience them – in a two-fold manner. On the one hand, they portray the character in the fiction before us; on the other hand, in certain cases, their image may also serve as an *allusion* to the screen persona they have cultivated over the course of their career. This, moreover, probably has to do with the photographic basis of the traditional fictional film which itself can be two-fold in a parallel manner.

The traditional, photographically based image of a person in a fiction film both represents a character (as Cesar Romero *nominally portrays* Cortez in *Captain from Castile)*, while it also refers to *(physically portrays)* its actual model (in this case, Cesar Romero).[11] The same shot of Cesar Romero can appear in the fictional motion picture *Captain from Castile* where, first and foremost, it represents or nominally portrays Cortez; or it can appear in a documentary on the TV program *Biography* where it refers to Cesar Romero (playing Cortez). Every image, populated with particularized people, in a traditional, photographically constructed fiction-film has at least this potential for doubleness.[12] In this respect, such images have built into them the possibility of referring (by way of physical portrayal) to the actual models of the characters that they nominally portray within the fiction.

Furthermore, as we shall attempt to demonstrate in the next section, it is possible to mobilize physical portrayal and nominal portrayal in the self-same shot or sequence of shots in a given film. Consequently, due to the possibility of simultaneously enlisting physical and nominal portrayal at once, it is conceivable that when movie stars nominally portray one character on screen, they may also, by way of the photographic physical portrayal of themselves, be referring, or, more precisely, *alluding* to their screen persona in a way that beckons us to bring to bear associations we have regarding their earlier roles upon the character currently on screen before us.

Were we to recruit what we know about the construction of popular plots – for example, that the hero always escapes in thrillers – we would not be able emotively to process the majority of fictional movies in the way they are designed to be assimilated. This is because they are designed to be imaginatively engaged in accordance with the realistic heuristic and the aforesaid strategies of plot construction are usually so improbable that they are scarcely realistic. In most cases, the mandated emotive uptake of a fiction requires the realistic heuristic, or the realistic heuristic modified by the relevant genre pre-suppositions, or something quite like them. If we track the story in terms of the principles of popular plot construction, as a script doctor might, there would not be any affective friction in the fiction.

Although most of us know the likely plot trajectories that shape popular films from Hollywood through Hong Kong and on to Bollywood, we do not take those structures to be part and parcel of the ontological laws that govern the pertinent fictional worlds. The relevant laws for following what goes on in most movies approximate what we would surmise deploying the realistic heuristic. Were we to allow knowledge of movie-going lore about plot development to figure in our calculations of whether the heroine can save the infant from the mounting, enveloping flames, we would be treating the pertinent, popular plot-construction strategies as though they were literally principles that govern the fictional world (as opposed to principles that govern the fabrication of the fictional world in our real-world movie studios). However, those plot stratagems are outside the fictional world of the motion picture; they are not literally part of the fictional environment.

Contrariwise, allusions are not presented as literally elements of the fictional environment, nor do they intersect literally with the causal laws that we presuppose to be operative in the fictional world. Allusions are figurative asides. They are not of a piece with the literal content of the fictional world, but are of the nature of meta-comments about the literal content of the fictional world. Their relation to the fictional world is tropological not ontological.

If we were to adopt plot-construction strategies – such as: the boy always wins the girl – for following the evolution of the fiction, we would be treating those strategies as functioning causal patterns operating within the ontology of the fictional world. However, they actually belong to our world where the producer, often for financial purposes, demands a happy ending from his writers and director. Thus we should not think of them as material to the sequence of events as they emerge within the fiction.

Furthermore, neither are these strategies of plot construction to be understood figuratively. They are not, for example, usually allusions intimated by the discourse that conveys the fiction; since, although a fiction might allude to the "happy ending" motif, as Bertolt Brecht does at the end of *The Three Penny Opera*, we typically have no reason to believe that most fictions that exploit such plot constructions are alluding to the popular narrative conventions that determine them. Thus, movie-going lore about the conventional trajectories of popular fictions is generally out of bounds when it comes to our imaginative engagement with movies.

Knowledge of these tendencies is precluded by the realistic heuristic from our cognitive processing of how the fictional world of the movie literally works (unless the fiction itself is about how popular-movie-makers construct popular-movie plots). Moreover, except where marked appropriately, movies that employ these conventional structures are not to be taken to be referring to them figuratively. So, we may not access these plot schemas on the grounds that the movie is alluding to them. On the other hand, it may be the case that we can entertain the movie lore we know about star personae, since the image of the stars on the screen may be functioning as a trope.

Allusions do not refer directly to states of affairs or causal chains within the fictional world. They are *figural*. So just as the metaphorical dissolves in Eisenstein's *Strike* do not propose that the spy has literally turned into a monkey in the fictional world, when a movie image (containing a character played by Joel McCrea) alludes to Joel McCrea and his star persona, the image does not imply that Joel McCrea or any of his previous characters are inhabitants of the fictional world of *Ride the High Country*.

The movie lore that we are not mandated to access concerns the artistic strategies for construing the laws of probability that govern the story world from inside the scope of the fiction operator. However, that principle is not violated when we explore the figurative allusions available in the cinematic array.

So far, then, we have found a reason why certain prohibitions concerning our access to movie-going lore may not bar our remembrance of the star's persona when configuring our emotional response to the character that he or she is portraying on screen. The reason is that the photographically based image of the star is alluding to the star's persona as that has evolved over his or her past roles and, moreover, this kind of figuration is perfectly compatible with a literal approach to what is true in the fiction. The star persona is part of the connotative dimension of the movie, as literary scholars use that phrase, rather than being part of the denotative dimension. This is surely a conceivable solution to the problem of movie stars. But how plausible is it to suppose that sometimes movies are really alluding in this way to star personae?

The movie star as allusion

Whereas our knowledge of movie lore can be applied to the fictional world when it is alluded to figuratively, as may be the case with star personae, knowledge of movie lore about popular plot conventions should not be enlisted literally in our processing of the fictional world. Perhaps this distinction gives us a way to explain why filling out the characters by reference to star personae is acceptable, while filling out the laws that govern happenings in said fictional worlds with reference to our knowledge of popular plot conventions, like the happy-ending motif, are not appropriate. But why think that star personae are actually used in this way? Why think film makers are alluding to star personae? What is the evidence?

We began with Stanley Cavell's inspiring analysis of the casting of *Ride the High Country*. One might balk at it on the grounds that the film does not explicitly invite us to recall the earlier careers of Scott and McCrea. Why suppose that it is a *donnée* of movie-going that viewers should use established star personae to illuminate the characters before them on screen? Perhaps Cavell was simply allowing his mind to wander.

But one reason in favor of supposing that there is this donnée in operation is that there are some movies that explicitly invite us to access star personae. An incontestable example is Don Siegel's *The Shootist,* which starred John Wayne. This film opens in a way that almost seems to be informed by Cavell's interpretation of *Ride the High Country.*

The film concerns the last days of a gunman or shootist, named John Bernard Books (a character loosely based on John Wesley Hardin). John Bernard Books is played by John Wayne. The film opens with a montage of what is putatively John Bernard Books's earlier days. The viewer, however, recognizes that this montage is composed of shots from some of John Wayne's 68 other westerns, including cuts from *The Big Trail* and *Rio Bravo.* In short, we are overtly invited, indeed nudged, to formulate our emotive response to John Bernard Books by recalling central moments in the evolution of John Wayne's star persona – we are almost instructed outright to attribute to Books associations we have formed over the years and over many films toward John Wayne, the actor portraying Books. For, in *The Shootist,* the earlier moments in the development of Wayne's star persona are recalled before our very eyes.

Nor can there be any doubt that this was intended. According to William Self, one of the producers of the film, George C. Scott was, at one point, being contemplated for the role of John Bernard Books. However, that idea was dropped immediately when it was learned that John Wayne wanted to play the part. For, in Self's own words, it was anticipated that Wayne would bring an *iconic* dimension to the portrayal – where by "iconic," Self appears to have in mind something like what I mean when I speak of a movie star's allusion to his or her star persona.[13]

Moreover, the producers of *The Shootist* intended the opening montage to set the tone of the film; as asserted by the film's screenwriter, Miles Hood Swarthout, the creators of the movie wanted viewers to fill-in Books's back-story[14] by alluding to Wayne's long tenure as an actor in Westerns, thereby suggesting not only something of Books's courageousness, but also something of his righteousness and adherence to a cowboy code of honor.

At the time of the release of the film, this opening montage was sometimes compared to François Truffaut's use in *Love on the Run* of footage of Jean-Pierre Léaud from earlier films in Truffaut's Antoine Doinel cycle – such as *Bed & Board* and *The 400 Blows.* However, Siegal's use of the Wayne footage is very different from Truffaut's use of the Léaud footage. For, Truffaut's footage is essentially a matter of flashbacks to earlier events (culled from earlier films in the same cycle) in the life of Antoine Doinel who happens to be played throughout this series of films by Léaud. There is no allusion to Léaud's star persona. On the other hand, John Bernard Books's celluloid biography is assembled from strips of film representing utterly disjoint fictional worlds. What they have in common is that all these different fictional characters were played by John Wayne and that all these films contributed to his established star persona as a western icon. For this reason, they function not only as ostensible flashbacks to Books's past, but also as allusions to Wayne's star persona.

Moreover, Wayne's is not the only star persona dragooned by *The Shootist*. In the final gun battle, Books is ranged against, among others, characters played by Hugh O'Brien and Richard Boone, stars of the TV series *Wyatt Earp* and *Have Gun Will Travel*, respectively. Since these actors never lost a fight in the programs that made them stars, we can use their star persona to surmise that they are very formidable opponents.[15] So even if one were skeptical about whether or not star personae are functioning allusively in a film like *Ride the High Country*, the possibility of this sort of figurative reference is virtually indisputable in the case of *The Shootist*, both in terms of its salient – shall we say "impossible to miss" – expressive orchestration of what is on screen and also on the basis of the subsequent documentary testimony of the creators of the film.

Likewise, in Ida Lupino's *The Bigamist*, there is also an important allusion to a star persona. The bigamist in the film, who is played by Edmond O'Brien, remarks that the social worker, who is investigating him, looks just like Edmond Gwenn. Of course, the social worker *is* being portrayed by the actor Edmond Gwenn. The point of this allusion is to insinuate that the social worker is benevolent, since Gwenn, recently the lead in *Miracle on 34th Street* (in which he played Santa Claus), possessed a star persona that radiated avuncularity. That this association is not a wayward or idiosyncratic one on our part, moreover, is made abundantly clear in the film when, on a guided bus tour of Hollywood, the bigamist is shown what we are told by the tour guide is the home of Edmond Gwenn who, in turn, is explicitly cited for his role in *Miracle on 34th Street* (a film, by the way, that the bigamist announces he enjoyed completely). In short, there can be no doubt that Lupino intends to be alluding to Gwenn's star persona in this film, most probably in order to incite our associations with him as a generous and caring figure – someone who, in other words, can be trusted.

In *The Shootist* and *The Bigamist*, there can be little doubt that the allusion to the star personae of the actors playing the pertinent characters is apposite, since the allusions are so out in the open, in a manner of speaking. Cases like this show that allusion to star personae is both an existing and a viable expressive device. But it would also appear that allusions need not be always as explicitly pronounced as they are in these cases.

In *Indiana Jones and the Last Crusade*, we are introduced to Indiana Jones's father, a scholar like his son, but decidedly more professorial, older, stuffier, and far less adventurous. Nevertheless, we readily accept that he charms the beautiful Dr Elsa Schneider almost as effectively as does his son.

But why do we feel so persuaded by this possibility? Probably because Indiana Jones's father is played by Sean Connery, a star with a persona linked associatively – since his days as James Bond – with being an irresistible seducer. Moreover, there can be little doubt that the producers of *Indiana Jones and the Last Crusade* considered the casting of their film with respect to the iconic status of its players no less than did the producers of *The Shootist*. They intend us to use the allusion to Sean Connery's star persona in order to influence our conception of the character of Prof. Henry Jones Sr., just as the creators of *The Shootist* deployed John Wayne's star persona in order to build up John Bernard Books's character.

In part because there is what might be called the practice of allusive casting, viewers test what they know of the star personae of actors they recognize in order to see whether it sheds light associatively on the characters in question. This, of course, does not always succeed, since sometimes actors choose to perform against the grain of their star persona, as Gregory Peck did when he played Dr Mengele in *The Boys from Brazil*. But where there are salient parallels between the character and the star persona, we regard that as a signal of an intended reference and allow the star persona to enrich our sense of the character.[16]

For, in the context where the practice of allusive casting is well entrenched, and widely acknowledged – and where so much money hangs on getting the casting just right – a reasonable default assumption is that the intersection of the character with the star persona of the actor is not accidental, but rather is intentional. That is, within the context of Hollywood-type casting, a coherent mesh between a character and a star persona supplies us with the grounds for presuming that we are in the presence of an allusion whose full significance it is up to us to explore as we might explore a metaphor.

Undoubtedly, some are likely to dismiss the sort of associations evoked in viewers by star personae as wildly subjective. Of course, many viewers may have very personal associations with their favorite stars. Who cares if Cate Blanchett reminds you of your cousin? Nevertheless, there is also generally an intersubjective core of converging response regarding a great many star personae. Consider this thought experiment. You can cast any star, living or dead, as Mother Teresa. Would you cast Bette Davis or Pamela Anderson in the role? Would Greer Garson be a better choice? Which one would you choose? Now ask the person sitting next to you who of the three actresses she would choose? Isn't she likely to agree with you? Try it.

As indicated earlier, I think that the practice of allusion to the star personae of featured movie actors took root so spontaneously in traditional, photographically based motion pictures because of the possibility of that kind of film to produce images that could be taken equally as two different species of representations – as physical portrayals of their models and as nominal portrayals of fictional characters. The images in movies whose provenance is photography are, thus, potentially double-barreled. In many cases, this possibility lies dormant. But where the narrative context of a fiction triggers recognition in the character of aspects of the star persona of the actor, we permit ourselves to exploit further the star persona to enlarge our conception of the character expressively.

Perhaps some evidence for this hypothesis is that we seem far less prone to rely upon star personae when it comes to live theater than when viewing films. Orson Welles' star persona weighs heavily on his Falstaff in *Chimes at Midnight*. To our minds, this Falstaff is like Orson Welles, or, at least, like his star persona, in a way that illuminates this version of the character of Falstaff for us. But it is hard to think of theater actors whose history of roles infects their current performances so insidiously. Maybe the reason for this contrast is that theatrical representation does not possess the kind of representational doubleness that we have attributed to photographically executed films.

Whereas the film image physically portrays the actor himself on film while nominally portraying the fictional character, there is only one level of representation on the theater stage. The theater actor only nominally portrays the fictional character. Save some Brechtian prompted experiments, the actor in theater does not standardly represent himself. He or she *is* himself and not a physical portrayal thereof. Typically, allusion to one's star persona does not seem to occur in theater, because theatrical representation does not possess the kind of doubleness of representation that we claim occurs in photographically engineered motion pictures.

One objection to this attempt to solve the problem with movie stars in terms of allusion might be that, if we are to suppose that there is an allusion to John Wayne's screen persona in a film like *The Shootist*, then we must take that allusion to be continuous throughout the film. That is, whenever John Wayne is on the screen, we must assume that the film is alluding to his star persona. But this is suspect, because, it may be argued, allusions are local not global.[17]

When Lloyd Bentsen told Dan Quayle that he was no Jack Kennedy, that allusion was a one-off remark. Yet if *The Shootist* is alluding to John Wayne's star persona, it would appear to do so whenever Wayne is on camera.

However, this objection rides on a faulty premise. There is no reason to deny that allusions are continuous in the relevant sense. *Ulysses* by James Joyce is said to allude to the Catholic Mass. Allusions to the Catholic Mass are distributed progressively throughout the text from one end to the other. The allusion is not local but global. And if you reject this example, remember that the whole of Joyce's *Ulysses* involves a continuous network of allusions to Homer's *Odyssey*.

Similarly, in the indeterminately large number of fictions that allude to Christ by way of Christ-like figures, the characters are often Christ-like through and through and not just here and there. And, in a less exalted vein, the episode of *South Park* that eviscerates the 2004 presidential election in the United States, the allusion to the Bush/Kerry debacle, re-configured as a contest between a giant douche-bag and a turd-sandwich, is continuous throughout.

Summary

Many movie stars have what we have called star personae, clusters of associations that they have accumulated over their careers in virtue of the roles (and the kind of roles) they have played. Viewers often use these star personae to fill-out their understanding of and response to the characters the actors are playing in movies that represent utterly distinct fictional worlds – as the fictional world of *Rio Bravo* is distinct from that of *The Shootist*. Furthermore, it seems that viewers are intended to do this by the established practices of casting.

And yet this raises a problem. In a great many cases, it seems as though viewers should put their knowledge of movie lore on hold, if they wish to enjoy a film in the way it is designed to be enjoyed. Forget that you know that in a Hollywood film the hero never dies in a car crash in the middle of the film. Dwelling on that piece of movie wisdom will stifle suspense.

But why is it appropriate to put our knowledge of star personae to work when watching a movie, but not our knowledge of how popular plots go 99.9% of the time? Why is access to one kind of movie lore legitimate and the access to the other kind not?

In this essay, I have tried to resolve this apparent problem with movie stars by arguing that the invocation of star personae is a matter of figuration. Films allude to star personae; the history of the star's previous roles and the characters he played are not presented as literally connected to the character. Moreover, the possibility of alluding to the star persona appears to grow out of the capacity of the photographically based motion-picture to physically portray the movie star who is nominally portraying a character in the fiction.

Notes

1 Stanley Cavell, *The World Viewed: Reflections on the Ontology of Film* (New York: Viking Press, 1971), p. 75.
2 Ibid., p. 71.

3   This is true not only of stars, of course, but of stock players in minor roles, like Donald Meek (whose name says it all).

4   For an account of suspense, see Noël Carroll, "Film, Genre, and Emotion," in Noël Carroll and Jinhee Choi (eds.) *Philosophy of Film and Motion Pictures* (Oxford: Blackwell, 2006).

5   On the role of curiosity in sustaining audience interest in popular entertainments, see my "Narrative Closure," *Philosophical Studies* 35 (2007), 1–15.

6   This problem is broached by Jonathan M. Weinberg and Aaron Meskin in their "Imagine That!" in Matthew Kieran (ed.), *Contemporary Debates in Aesthetics and the Philosophy of Art* (Oxford: Blackwell, 2006), p. 230.

7   I think that this idea originally stems from David Lewis, "Truth in Fiction," in *Philosophical Papers*, vol. 1 (Oxford: Oxford University Press, 1983), pp. 261–281.

8   This requires some qualification. Though we may start by assuming the realistic heuristic, it may have to be waived or, at least, modified, under certain conditions. In some instances, the genre in question mandates that the realistic heuristic be retired with respect to certain situations. For example, in a science-fiction adventure, such as an episode of *StarTrek*, space ships may travel through black holes, though we know that, in reality, an attempt to do so would be short-lived. Call this a genre dispensation. Similarly, in other cases, in order to render a fiction coherent, we may have to repeal the realistic heuristic in favor of entertaining the divergent beliefs of the culture that originally produced the fiction. So, although we may not believe that ghosts are possible, we may suppose they are in order to feel our way into Hamlet's plight.

9   On allusion, see Stephanie Ross, "Art and Allusion," *Journal of Aesthetics and Art Criticism* 40 (1981): 59–70; William Irwin, "What is an Allusion?" *Journal of Aesthetics and Art Criticism* 59 (2001): 287–297; and William Irwin, "The Aesthetics of Allusioin," *Journal of Value Inquiry* 36 (2002): 521–32.

10 This sort of visual allusion is well precedented in painting, as when David figures the assassinated Marat as a savior by arranging his limbs after the manner of those typical of the expiring Christ.

11 On the distinction between physical portrayal and nominal portrayal, see Noël Carroll, "Concerning Uniqueness Claims for Photographic and Cinematographic Representation," in *Theorizing the Moving Image* (Cambridge: Cambridge University Press, 1996), pp. 45–48. See also Monroe Beardsley, *Aesthetics* (New York: Harcourt, Brace and World, 1958), especially ch. 6, sec. 16. See also Göran Hermeren, *Representation and Meaning* (Lund: Scandinavian University Books, 1969), especially ch. 2.

12 The qualification "at least," above, signals our acknowledgment that a cinematic image might also *depict* a class or collection of objects. On depiction, see my "Concerning Uniqueness Claims." In virtue of depiction, the said image have the potential not only for doubleness, but for *tripleness*.

13 Information about *The Shootist* in this essay derives from the short "The Shootist Legend Lives On," on the 2001 DVD of *The Shootist*, which is distributed by the Paramount Widescreen DVD Collection.

14 Ibid.

15 Maybe there is even another layer of allusion here. Since Boone and O'Brien were essentially TV cowboy stars and Wayne was a movie cowboy star, perhaps it is being insinuated that Wayne belongs to a better class of gunfighter.

16 Salient parallels here would seem to be a reasonable clue since we presume, quite rationally, that the filmmakers know whom they have cast.

17 Michael Leddy, "The Limits of Allusion," *British Journal of Aesthetics* 32 (1992): 111–14. This article is discussed critically by William Irwin in his "What is an Allusion?"

7

Cinematic Narrative

If by *narrative* we mean the mere recounting or representation of any event and/or state of affairs through some interval of time, then the overwhelming numbers of motion picture shots, save for freeze frames, are narratives, albeit in many, many cases, minimal ones. However, in most usage, the concept of narrative is reserved for representations of states of affairs and events of a greater degree of complexity and structure.

Prototypically, most narratives involve at least two, but generally more, events and/or states of affairs which are related or arranged temporally and causally (where the causation in question may include mental states such as desires, intentions, and motives). "Charlemagne was crowned Holy Roman Emperor in 800 and, in 1945, Japan surrendered unconditionally to the Allies" is not a narrative in the aforementioned sense, although "After being tested in New Mexico, atomic bombs were dropped on Hiroshima and Nagasaki" is, since it comprises three events of which the first temporally preceded and was causally related to the other two. Most motion pictures – including most fictions, nonfictions, and even some abstractions – are narrative in the sense that they involve a number of events and states of affairs standing in temporal and causal relations to each other (Carroll 2001, 2007b).

Narratives may be very broadly sorted into two major categories: *episodic narratives* and *unified narratives*. Episodic narratives are composed of a string of smaller narratives or episodes, frequently connected by the recurring presence of a central character, but without strong causal linkage between one story and

"Narrative Closure," in Paisley Livingston and Carl Plantinga (eds.), *The Routledge Companion to Philosophy and Film* (London: Routledge, 2009), pp. 207–16.

the next. In the ancient world, epic poems recalling the adventures of Hercules would be an example of this. Likewise, the *Odyssey* is another example of the episodic narrative. It is made up of individual stories of the wanderings of Ulysses, but one of his adventures – say his encounter with the Cyclops – does not figure causally in bringing about his encounter with Circe, or the Sirens, or Scylla and Charybdis. The movie serial *Rocketman* and the television series *Superman* are also episodic narratives, as are most sit-coms. So are soap-operas, however, instead of rotating around one or a few central figures, their casts usually involve a larger revolving gallery of recurring characters.

A unified narrative, as Aristotle put it, has a *beginning*, a *middle*, and an *end* (Aristotle 1996). Although undoubtedly this sounds spectacularly uninformative – can't anything that is extended through space and/or time be subdivided in this way? – these terms should not be understood in their bland, ordinary sense. Rather they are technical terms. By "the end," Aristotle means an event which secures the feeling of closure in an audience – the almost palpable sensation that the story has finished-up at exactly the right spot. Nothing that needed to be told has been left untold, nor has the story gone on superfluously. At most we learn that the prince and the princess lived happily ever after, but we are not informed of their subsequent adventures. That would be the stuff of other, further stories.

The *beginning*, in turn, is just what the audience needs to know in order to start to follow the story. We are introduced to a locale, and a set of characters. We learn of their desires, aspirations, relations, struggles, and so forth. Perhaps we learn about certain conflicts between them, as when we witness the enmity between Achilles and Agamemnon at the opening of Wolfgang Petersen's *Troy*. The beginning typically supplies us with the background that we need to understand in order to track with understanding that which happens next.

Often the narrative of a motion picture begins with an establishing shot that depicts a state of affairs and tells us where and when the story will unfold. Then we meet a number of characters. Some change intrudes which calls for action, or reaction. Helen absconds with Paris to Troy. This complication generates a response – alliances are forged between various Greek forces in preparation for war. And with this complication, we enter the middle of the narrative which concludes or ends when the problem that ensues or the questions (Who will win? Who will die?) that are provoked by the complications – in this case the Trojan War – are resolved.

A narrative of this sort is unified in as much as each part leads smoothly to the next. Given the situation and the people who inhabit it, the kind of change or complication that is introduced causes certain problems to be raised or questions to be asked; then these queries will gradually be further complicated and eventually answered by the action of the characters, and, precisely when all the presiding questions are settled, the story proper ends (though there may also be a brief coda). Such a narrative is unified insofar as it appears rhetorically to be held together tightly by the logic of questions and answers.

Of course, often in Hollywood movies, there is more than one story – there is frequently a problem to be solved (in *Casino Royale*, James Bond has to entrap the international arms-merchant/gambler), while there is also a romantic subplot about whether 007 and his beautiful co-spy will become a couple (Bordwell et al. 1985). Nevertheless, these two stories usually get intertwined so that the romance often results in or contributes to the solution of the problem. Indeed, as many as 60 percent of classical Hollywood films have been said to exhibit this structure (Bordwell et al. 1985).

Aristotle's theory of the unified narrative has influenced the way in which screenwriters construct narratives. Syd Field (1994) wrote an influential guide to popular screenwriting in which he divided screenplays into three parts or *acts*: a beginning (often the first 25 percent of the motion picture), a confrontation (frequently, 50 percent of the movie), and a resolution (25 percent or whatever is left over after the first two acts) with turning points inbetween. Paul Joseph Gulino (2004) thinks that the popularity of Field's book was a major influence on the notion of the Hollywood film possessing a "three-*act* structure," although the Danish director Urban Gad recommended that filmmakers construct their works in acts as early as in 1912 (Bordwell 2008).

Others have refined the three-part structure, not in a way that refutes Aristotle, but which instead limns with greater clarity the grounds for the interlocking coherence in the kind of story that Aristotle had in mind. For example, Kristin Thompson (1999) sees four acts where Field says there are three. Hers include: the set-up, the complication, development, and climax; whereas, David Bordwell (1985) describes the classical Hollywood plot as a six-part structure: introduction of setting and characters, explanation of state of affairs, complicating action, ensuing events, outcome, and ending. But despite the varying numbers, it seems fair to suggest that all these authors belong to the school of Aristotle; they do not contradict his *Poetics* as much as they make more explicit the interconnected elements that render such stories so unified.

Motion pictures articulated in the Aristotelian tradition not only are structurally unified; they *feel* unified or of a piece. That is, as mentioned earlier, when "The End" flashes onscreen or, as is becoming more routine nowadays, when the end-credits start crawling up from the bottom edge of the image, the audience has a strong sense of finality and completeness. Unlike the episodic narrative, which, in principle, seems like it could keep going on and on, the unified narrative appears as though it has to end just where it does, rather like the sonnet that feels as though it concludes on exactly the right word, or the song that closes on just the correct note. Whereas the episodic narrative gives the appearance of an assortment of adventures, of which some might be subtracted with no irreparable loss to the feel of the saga, the unified narrative leaves us with the impression of one, indissolubly integrated whole from which nothing can be left out, save at the cost of a tangible experience of perturbation. That is, once again, this sort of narrative engenders a powerful feeling of closure, the sense that every salient element that has been set in motion in the story has been, as they say, wrapped up.

This is not to say that closure is altogether an alien factor in episodic narratives. Within episodes in an episodic narrative, closure may obtain. In each episode of the television series, *Have Gun Will Travel*, for instance, Paladin's assignment for the week was successfully discharged. Of course, in some episodic narratives, like motion picture serials of the sort referred to as cliff-hangers, the closure of one adventure might be deferred to the beginning of the next install-ment in order to ensure that the audience returns in the subsequent week in order to discover the way in which the heroine escaped her fate worse than death. But, at the same time, very complicated episodic narratives with large storylines, like soap operas, over time become too intricate to wrap up. If they go off the air, they may have no other option, but to leave viewers hanging, as the TV series *The Sopranos* did with stylish *élan* at the conclusion of its final season.

In one way or another, closure plays a role in our experience of the vast number of the motion picture narratives that we encounter, including episodic and unified narratives. As we shall see, closure is not a universal feature of narrative motion pictures and moviemakers may have important reasons to foreswear closure. Yet, it is reasonable to say that most motion picture narra-tives aspire to instill closure in spectators.

As already indicated, we signal our feelings of closure by saying of a movie that "it appears to wrap things up" or "it seems like it tied up all the loose ends." But can we be less metaphorical than this? Can we account for the nar-rative structures in the movie that account for these impressions?

In this regard, one important suggestion comes from David Hume's essay "Of Tragedy" (1998). Hume writes:

> Had you any intention to move a person extremely by the narration of any event, the best method of increasing its effect would be artfully to delay inform-ing him of it, and first excite his curiosity and impatience before you let him into the secret. (Hume 1998)

That is, Hume recommends that the way in which a narrative can take hold of an audience's attention is to engender their curiosity about what happens next. He calls that which they want to know "a secret." Similarly, in his discus-sion of what he labels "the hermeneutic code," Roland Barthes dubs it "an enigma" (Barthes 1974: 18–20). For our purposes, we may adopt less inflated terminology and simply say that what Hume has in mind is that a story sus-tains our attention, often irresistibly, by presenting us with *questions* that we want answered – questions that the narrative implicitly promises to answer and which we expect will be answered. Hume, of course, was offering advice to playwrights; but it has been accepted even more eagerly by screenwriters.

What does this have to do with bringing about the impression of closure? Closure will obtain when all of the saliently posed questions that the narrative has served up are answered. For instance, recall this archetypal plot: boy meets girl and they are attracted to each other; enter some oily Lothario bent on seducing the girl – will the boy be able to unmask his rival and regain the girl's affections? This is what the audience wants to know. And, finally, the boy gets the girl. The End. Closure.

The movie does not go on to tell us that the couple then bought car insurance, because that was not part of the story. That is, whether or not the couple bought an insurance policy is not a question about which the movie has encouraged us to be curious. Were this episode to be added to the movie, the feeling of closure would be diluted; the movie would not strike us has having ended at the right spot. It would have gone on beyond the point where closure would obtain.

On the other hand, if after establishing the existence of a happy family, their beloved infant is abducted, the audience will want to learn whether the child will be rescued. The complications that unfold contribute to sustaining or answering this question. The movie, then, is over when that question is answered one way or another. Suppose, as is usually the case, we learn that the infant has been saved. The impression of closure will correspond with that revelation. In ordinary suspense movies, we will feel frustration rather than closure, if that answer is not forthcoming. And if the movie goes on to show us the child getting a flu shot, that will feel like a narrative, non sequitur, since whether or not the baby needed a flu shot is not part of the story – not one of the forcefully advanced questions that have come to preoccupy our attention as spectators. That is, were the scene with the flu shot added, rather than wrapping things up, a *loose end* would be added.

It is to be hoped that this discussion of closure in the unified narrative suggests that a major source of the sense of the completeness and coherence evident in this species of narrative – to which, arguably, most motion pictures belong – is what we can call *erotetic*. "Erotetic logic" is the logic of questions and answers. By extension, there is also erotetic narration. This is narration that proceeds by generating questions that the narration then goes on to answer. Closure obtains when all of the pronounced questions the movie has elected to put emphatically before us have been answered. This hypothesis can be confirmed by turning off the projector as the last reel of the movie is about to wind onto the screen. Irritated, the audience will jump up and demand to know, for instance, whether the baby was rescued. They want their closure.

Erotetic narration not only imbues a motion picture with an aura of completeness and completion. The evolving network of questions and answers also holds the story together – renders it coherent – throughout the unified narrative. That is, scenes and sequences are connected to other scenes and sequences by a skein of questions and answers.

The motion picture standardly begins by answering the kind of questions we automatically ask whenever we are introduced to a novel situation. We want implicitly to know: where the action is set and when; who are these people; what do they want and why are they acting like this. The opening of the typical motion picture will answer these basic questions at least to the extent that we have enough information to understand the further questions that the subsequent changes in the initial states of affairs and their accompanying complications elicit.

Some scenes and sequences simply raise questions to be answered down the line by other scenes and sequences. In early American cinema, two-shot films, involving stories of kidnappings, began with an opening shot in which a child was kidnapped, thereby raising the question of whether he or she could be recovered; and then the second shot delivered the answer, as the child was rescued from the clutches of some stereotypically swarthy Eastern or Southern European immigrant.

In other, more complex motion pictures, scenes and sequences may function in order to prolong, as Hume advised, the delivery of the answers to our questions. This may be the result of a subsequent scene only partially answering an ongoing question. For example, once we learn the child has been kidnapped, part of what we are apt to want to know, if we haven't witnessed the abduction, is "by whom?" This may be partially answered by learning that the kidnapper is a woman with a limp, but exactly which woman with a limp remains a live question.

Likewise, a later scene may sustain an earlier question by keeping our questions aloft. For instance, the escaped convict eludes apprehension in one scene, thereby iterating the question of whether he will be caught in the next scene or a subsequent one. Or, the fearless vampire killers close in on Dracula's lair, but he transforms himself into bat and flies away, leaving us wondering if they will be able to stake him another day.

Sometimes when scenes answer one of our questions, they will replace one question with another. When King Kong is subdued on Skull Island, the inquiring minds in the audience want to know what Carl Denham intends to do with him. And, of course, new characters, forces, and situations can be established at any point in the diegesis, bringing in their two new questions to be answered as they interact with what has already been given about the storyworld up to that point.

Scenes and sequences in erotetic narratives function to raise and/or answer questions, to answer questions partially, to cause questions to be iterated, and to answer some questions in a way that opens onto others. Because scenes and sequences are bound together by this network of questions and answers, unified narratives give the appearance of coherence – everything seems to belong or to fit, specifically to fit into the network of questions and answers.

The questions and answers that hold together the typical motion picture narrative come in hierarchically differentiated orders of magnitude. For convenience sake, we can make the following rough distinctions. First, there are *presiding macro-questions*. These include the question that dominates the motion picture globally from one end to the other. Will the boy be able to get the girl? Can Goldfinger have his way with Fort Knox? Will the village survive in *Seven Samurai*?

Of course, a film may have more than one presiding macro-question. Buster Keaton's *The General* has several, including: Will Johnny be able to enlist in the Southern army? Will Johnny be able to recover his locomotive, *The General*? Will he be able to rescue his love, Annabelle Lee? Will he be able to alert the Confederates of the encroaching Union attack in time? These are the interlocking, indeed, in this case, piggy-backed, macro-questions that keep us riveted to the story in the expectation that they will be answered. When they are answered, *The General* is effectively finished. We do not ask what Johnny will do after the Civil War, because that is not one of the presiding macro-questions that we have been invited to entertain. When all of the presiding macro-questions in a unified movie narrative are answered, closure is usually secured and we feel that Keaton's movie has been completed and is complete (Carroll 2007a).

However, motion pictures are not merely unified by overarching or presiding macro-questions. There are also more localized questions that call forth or propone answers of a more limited scope. In *The General*, in one scene, the Union hijackers pile debris on the rail tracks in other to derail Johnny who is in hot pursuit. These activities raise the question of whether or not Johnny will be derailed in a subsequent scene or sequence. And, of course, subsequent scenes or sequences answer such questions. Johnny doesn't get derailed.

We may call these local erotetic networks *micro-questions* and *micro-answers*. They generally provide the glue that holds the trail of scenes and sequences together on a local basis, while, at the same time, also not letting go of our attention. Moreover, these micro-questions and answers are typically hierarchically subordinated to the presiding macro-questions that animate the narrative. For example, the question/answer network involving Johnny's possible derailment in *The General* provides information in the direction of answering the presiding macro-questions of whether he will save his engine, his love, the Confederacy, and, ultimately, whether he will win his uniform and enlist.

Finally, it should be added that there are erotetic structures that are neither presiding macro-questions/answer networks nor micro ones. These are question/answer complexes that span large parts of a motion picture, but not the entirety of the work. For example, the question of what is going to happen to Marion in Alfred Hitchcock's *Psycho* dominates the opening of the film, but is resolved once Norman Bates kills her. The macro-questions about her fate organizes a large part of the film, but not the whole of it, since once she is eviscerated in the shower sequence, questions about Marion's future are replaced by questions about whether her murder and her murderer will be discovered. Since the question about Marion is sustained over many micro-questions/answers – like: will the suspicious-looking cop further investigate her? – it is a macro-structure, but since it is not sustained across the entire film, it is not a *presiding* macro-structure. It does not provoke closure. Answering presiding macro-questions is what educes closure.

Although I have spoken of the narrative organization of motion pictures in terms of its erotetic, rhetorical address, narrative exposition is also impor-tantly concerned with the temporal order of the depicted events. Events in films occur before, after, and simultaneously with respect to each other. Nor need the procession of events in a film be that of a progressive linear move-ment. There can be flashbacks and flashforwards.

It is a fact about narration that the time of the telling or recounting of the tale (sometimes called *the discourse*, or in a related vein, *syuzhet)* need not follow the order of events as they occurred in the tale (sometimes called *the story* or *fabula*) (Chatman 1978; Bordwell 2008). This is as true of movies as it is of other kinds of narratives. Although the story is told in a progressive fashion, moving forward in unbroken real time from the opening credits to the end credits, the events that comprise the tale in the storyworld need not be projected consecutively in our world, the world of the audience-outside-of-the-fiction. *Mildred Pierce* begins in the present of the storyworld with a man being shot and then moves backwards in the time of the fiction – that is, flashes back – in order to answer the questions of who shot the man and why.

Likewise, *Easy Rider* flashes forward to an image of a burning motorcycle in order to prompt the question of who is going to die. Or, if there is a flash forward to a shot of Petulia throwing something through a shop window, it primes us to ask "why?" That is, even though the temporal order of the nar-ration is a level of plot structure that is distinguishable from its erotetic organ-ization, it is not altogether unrelated, since typically the manipulation of time by the discourse of the narration will be in the service of supplying the kinds of questions and answers that contribute to narrative closure.

Similarly, breaks out of the forward flow of the narrative and into the tem-porally suspended fantasies of characters – as in *Billy Liar, Lord Jim*, and *The Pawnbroker* – also serve to answer narrative questions, often concerning the desires of the characters and thusly they can serve the designs of narrative closure by disclosing the deepest wishes of these protagonists in a way that bids us to wonder whether they will be realized or not.

If so far I may have inadvertently suggested that all motion pictures that depict a series of events in time involve closure, then I have misled you, and not only because some motion pictures that strive for closure botch the job. For there are also things like home movies that show the major events in the life of a family – birthdays, vacations, weddings, etc. – in the temporal order in which they occurred. Yet, these, and comparably arranged, chronologically ordered event-series, are best thought of as not yet fully prototypical narratives, properly so-called, but only as chronicles, and, for that reason, they are bereft of closure (Carroll 2001). And, in addition, even some full-fledged narratives, like the individual installments of cliff-hangers, such as *The Perils of Pauline*, avoid closure at the end of each episode in order to drum up future business.

Moreover, there are also unified narratives that eschew closure at the level of the depiction of the events and actions of the storyworld in order to achieve unity at a higher level or plane of organization or signification. For example, at the end of his masterpiece *Rashomon*, Akira Kurosawa refrains from announcing, from an omniscient viewpoint, what really happened when the bandit, the husband, and the wife met in the forest. Our questions about what actually went down in the storyworld go unanswered, but in a way that prompts us to ask about Kursosawa's artistic motivation or intention in withholding this information from us.

That is, the transparently purposive avoidance of closure at the level of the action of the story disposes us to attempt to interpret the significance of this decision on Kurosawa's part. It encourages what we might name "interpretive ascent." What is Kurosawa trying to communicate by this obvious subversion of the erotetic model? And once having ascended to that level of interpretation, thoughtful viewers regularly grasped that the point or theme of *Rashomon* is to suggest a form of epistemological perspectivism.

Likewise in *L'Avventura*, Michelangelo Antonioni seems simply to drop the question of why the character played by Lea Massari has disappeared in order to tantalize the viewer into inferring an other-than-narrative significance to the story – such as the insinuation of the existential meaninglessness of contemporary life, an acknowledgment, that is, of the possibility that life does not come – as unified movies do – with answers clearly stamped upon the face of it.

There are, of course, other objectives that may lead motion picture makers to forgo closure at the level of the story. It may be done to enhance the expressive unity of a film. That we never learn whether Irena in *The Curse of the Cat People* is a ghost or a psychological projection contributes to the eerie, ambiguous, uncanny feeling the film emits. Furthermore, realistic films, like *Amacord*, often loosen the erotetic grip of the narrative structure in order to appear more "lifelike" – to contrive a rhythm more akin to the everyday flow of often directionless events as opposed the propulsive forward pace of erotetic narration.

Moreover, reflexive films, such as *Last Year at Marienbad*, pose questions they refuse to answer in order to induce the viewer to reflect apperceptively upon the way in which this strategy discloses the degree to which we normally expect answers to the questions that narratives stimulate in us. Ordinarily those questions are tacit, despite the fact that they structure the way in which we follow movies with understanding. Modernist exercises like *Last Year at Marienbad*, in contrast, bring this tacit process of question-formation to the surface, where the ambitious viewer may use it to flash a searchlight upon her own default, motion-picture processing dispositions and procedures.

Thus, not all motion picture makers intend closure nor do they employ erotetic narration to its fullest, natural advantage. Nevertheless a great many do – indeed, most do, including documentaries and narrative television. This, furthermore, is a major factor contributing to the surpassing clarity that most motion pictures possess, especially in contrast to our far more desultory and diffuse mundane lives. In this way, erotetic narration and the closure it brings to the unified narrative is a crucial element in accounting for the power of movies. As neurobiologists have begun to prove, the brain has a preference for clarity. So in this regard, the kind of narratives that are most common across motion pictures are just the sort of brain food we crave.

Moreover, even motion pictures that defer the full effect of erotetic narration by forfeiting closure, nevertheless also frequently exploit it indirectly, since averting closure, where that evasion appears intentional, may inspire the viewer to ask "why?" And this may lead to an enhanced appreciation of the motion picture in terms of, among other things, its expressive and/or aesthetic qualities and/or its thematic significance.

Although not all narratives are motion pictures and not all motion pictures are narrative, narration and the motion picture have come together so often that theirs would appear to be at least a common law marriage, and, therefore, no philosophy of the motion pictures can be truly complete without a consideration of cinematic narrative and its most habitual, recurring structures, such as erotetic narration and closure.

References

Aristotle (1996) *Poetics*, trans. M. Heath. London and New York: Penguin Books.

Barthes, R. (1974) *S/Z*, trans. R. Howard. New York: Hill and Wang.

Bordwell, D. (2008) "Three Dimensions of Narrative Film," in *Poetics of Cinema*. London: Routledge.

Carroll, N. (2001) "The Narrative Connection," in *Beyond Aesthetics*. Cambridge and New York: Cambridge University Press.

Carroll, N. (2007a) *Comedy Incarnate: Buster Keaton, Physical Humor and Bodily Coping*. Oxford: Blackwell.

Carroll, N. (2007b) "Narrative Closure." *Philosophical Studies* 135 (August): 1–15.

Chatman, S. (1978) *Story and Discourse: Narrative Structure in Fiction and Film*. Ithaca, NY: Cornell University Press.

Field, S. (1994) *Screenplay: The Foundations of Screenwriting*. New York: Dell.

Gulino, P. J. (2004) *Screenwriting: The Sequence Approach*. New York and London: Continuum.

Hume, D. (1998) "Of Tragedy," in *David Hume: Selected Essays*. Oxford: Oxford University Press.

Thompson, K. (1999) *Storytelling in the New Hollywood: Understanding Classical Narrative Technique*. Cambridge, MA: Harvard University Press.

Further Reading

Bordwell, D. (1985) *Narration in the Fiction Film*. Madison: University of Wisconsin Press.

Bordwell, D. (2006) *The Way Hollywood Tells It: Story and Style in Modern Movies*. Berkeley: University of California Press.

Bordwell, D., Staiger, J., and Thompson, K. (1985) *The Classical Hollywood Cinema: Film Style and Mode of Production to 1960*. New York: Columbia University Press.

Carroll, N. (1996) "Toward a Theory of Film Suspense," in *Theorizing the Moving Image*. Cambridge and New York: Cambridge University Press.

Carroll, N. (2008) *The Philosophy of Motion Pictures*. Oxford: Blackwell.

Livingston, P. (2001) "Narrative," in B. Gaut and D. Lopes (eds.), *The Routledge Companion to Aesthetics*. London and New York: Routledge.

Thompson, K. (2003) *Storytelling in Film and Television*. Cambridge, MA: Harvard University Press.

8

Cinematic Narration

Most of the motion pictures we encounter – whether nonfiction or fiction – are narrative in nature. Motion pictures, of course, are not the only medium in which narrative figures prominently. Nevertheless, narrative motion pictures are so pervasive that a discussion of cinematic narration is an unavoidable topic for the philosophy of the moving image.

Because it seems reasonable to presuppose that narration implies a narrator (Chatman 1990), a question naturally arises about the nature of that narrator. Who or what is the cinematic narrator? The answer might appear to you to require little thought. The narrator is just the motion picture maker or makers responsible for the work at hand. If we are talking about a nonfiction film, like *The Fog of War*, then Errol Morris is the narrator. If we are speaking of a fiction film, such as *No Country for Old Men*, then the narrators are the Coen brothers. However, even if the answer seems fairly straightforward when it comes to cases of nonfiction, many philosophers suspect that works of fiction are more complicated. In order to see why, it is useful first to take a brief detour into literary theory.

With respect to the study of literary fictions, distinctions are often made between the actual author, the implied author, and the narrator. The actual author is the real person who wrote the text and is presumably collecting royalties for it. The implied author is the author as he/she manifests himself/herself in the text. The implied author may in fact share all the actual author's beliefs, desires, attitudes, allegiances, and so forth, but, equally, may not. The

"Narration," in Paisley Livingston and Carl Plantinga (eds.), *The Routledge Companion to Philosophy and Film* (London: Routledge, 2009), pp. 196–206.

actual author – a romantic at heart – may don the persona or mask of a cynic for the purpose of telling the tale in a certain way. The implied author is the agent who is responsible for the way the fiction is written – its tone, structures, ellipses, emphases, etc. *qua* fiction.

Yet in addition to the actual and implied authors of a literary text, there may also be so-called narrators. These are fictional creatures. They are part of the fictional world as it is presented by the text. Indeed, they are the fictional presenters of the text. Often these presenters appear as characters in the story, as in the case of Henry James's *What Maisie Knew*. Watson is the explicit narrator with regard to the adventures of Sherlock Holmes. He, as a character, is overtly introduced in the fiction as its narrator; he inhabits the fictional world of the story that he is presenting to us.

But in addition to overt or explicit narrators, like Watson, it is also argued that there may be implicit fictional narrators. For example, in Ring Lardner's classic short story "The Haircut," there is an explicit narrator, the barber, but it is not he, with his blinkered understanding of the situation, who lets us know that Jim Kendall was actually murdered. Yet, it is reasonable to suppose that we have been told that this is true in the fictional world of the short story. But, if narration requires a narrator, who told us this was so? An implicit, fictional narrator.

Why must we believe that there are such implicit fictional narrators? The argument goes like this: A fiction is something that we are mandated to imagine. We are mandated to imagine the events in the fiction as true – as obtaining in the world of the fiction. Where an explicit fictional narrator is telling the tale, we typically imagine what he or she reports as true in the world of the narrative (unless we have some reason to suspect the explicit narrator is unreliable or limited in one way or another). However, where there is no explicit narrator in evidence, it is argued that we still have reason to suspect there is an implicit one nearby – that is, a narrative agency that asserts or reports what is true from inside the world of the story.

Why? First, recall that it is being presupposed that there is no narration without a narrator. But when it comes to fiction, it is alleged that the narrator cannot be the actual author or the implied author. The actual author cannot report things as true in the story world; what the actual author does is establish that it is *fictional* that thus and such (rather than asserting that or reporting what is true that thus and such). Margaret Mitchell made it *fictional that* Scarlett O'Hara lived at Tara; Mitchell did not perform the illocutionary act of asserting "Scarlett O'Hara lived at Tara." Had Mitchell done that, she would have uttered a falsehood.

The same problem besets the implied author, since the implied author is responsible for *Gone with the Wind qua* fiction. Both the actual author and the implied author stand, so to speak, on the wrong side of the fiction operator (the "it is fictional that ..." operator) with respect to making assertions or reports about what is the case in the fictional world. Implied authors can make assertions about what is fictional, but not about what is true in the narrative.

Yet it is a true, narrative assertion in the fiction that Scarlett O'Hara lived at Tara. Who made this narrative assertion along with all the others we imagine to be true in the fictional world of *Gone with the Wind*? If there is no explicit narrator in view, we are urged to postulate an implicit fictional narrator, a narrational agency who (unlike the actual author) believes Scarlett O'Hara, Rhett Butler, Ashley Wilkes, and the rest exist and who reports their trials and tribulations to us as facts which we then go on to imagine. Moreover, the implicit fictional narrator is, like explicit fictional narrators, a denizen of the fiction – a fictional character – even if he or she is unacknowledged by the other fictional inhabitants of his or her world.

The question for the philosophy of the moving image is which of these literary distinctions carry over to motion pictures and to what extent (i.e., if there are implicit fictional narrators, for example, how frequently do they occur: always, sometimes, or never?). Obviously motion pictures have actual authors – as Zhang Yimou is the actual author of *Ju Dou* – whose manifestation is implied in the film whether sincerely or not. Motion pictures may also have explicit narrators – like Lester Burnham in *American Beauty* – who are characters in the story – or explicit narrators in the form of voiceover commentators, as in the case of *The Magnificent Ambersons*. But do motion picture fictions have implicit fictional narrators and, if so, how extensive is the phenomenon?

There may be some reasons to deny the postulation of implicit, fictional narrators across the board. Putatively, we are forced to posit the aforesaid narrator universally or ubiquitously because narration presupposes a narrator. But perhaps the possibility that the actual author is the narrator has been dismissed too quickly. Why suppose that there must be an act of asserting or reporting inside the fictional operator in order for such and such to be true in the fiction?

Rather, what makes something true in the fiction is that the actual author has mandated that we imagine (i.e., entertain as unasserted) certain propositional contents – for example: it is true in the fiction *Psycho* that Norman Bates is psychotic just in case Alfred Hitchcock and his team of fictioneers have mandated that we imagine the propositional content "that Norman Bates is psychotic." In other words, there is no apparent pressure to presume that there are acts of assertion going on within the fiction. That appears to require of the viewer one thought too many or, at least, one thought that is not necessary.

Defenders of the implicit narrator hypothesis argue that it is natural to imagine that there is a continuous activity of reporting going on as a novel unfolds (Wilson 2007). But claims of naturalness are not likely to carry the day here. Not only do I not find myself entertaining the report model, I see no necessity in doing so. When I watch a play, it would seem strained to think that I am watching a report, so why think that I am reading one upon encountering, for instance, a dialogue novel in the fashion of Ivy Compton-Burnett?

That is, the report model hardly fits every case of narration. It does not fit what Plato called *mimesis* in Books 2 and 3 of the *Republic*. Hence, claims on behalf of the report model will have to be made on a case by case basis, not summarily. And to the extent that the report model does not obtain comprehensively, there is no reason for the blanket postulation of implicit fictional narrators, since their postulation would appear to rest upon the report model. Yet, since the report model occurs at best occasionally, so will the need for introducing implicit fictional narrators.

Friends of the report model may find it natural because they endorse the notion that fictions are props in games of make-believe and that the consumption of a fiction involves the reader in making-believe that he or she is reading a report. But again, although some readers may behave this way, it is idiosyncratic enough that asserting that it is natural is immensely controversial. For, how many of us are aware of playing this game? So the defender of implicit fictional narrators may be involved in attributing to audiences two more thoughts than are needed – the idea that there is a report before us and the idea that we are making-believe that we are reading one.

Another reason to be suspicious about the postulation of ubiquitous, implicit, fictional narrators is that they often lead to self-contradiction. For example, readers often learn how things turn out in a story where, at the same time, it is given that no one in the fiction ever learnt what happened (Currie 1996). But, if there is a implicit narrator who dwells in the fictional world, then there is someone or some agency in the fiction who knows what went down and who is reporting it to us. So, in cases like this, we are driven to the unhappy conclusion that no one in the fiction ever learnt the outcome of the story and yet someone from the fiction is telling us the outcome. Of course, the way to avoid this logical contretemps is simply to abstain from postulating the existence of the implicit fictional narrator in the first instance.

Thus far the arguments against the ubiquity of implicit fictional narrators have applied alike to both literary and cinematic examples. But, it might be alleged that there is something about motion pictures that especially warrants hypothesizing them and which so far our objections have left untouched. Specifically, some may contend that it has to do with the way in which we interact with the visuals in a motion picture.

On their account, when we see a house onscreen, it is natural for us to suppose that "I imagine seeing a house" (or, that "I am seeing the house imaginarily"). So when presented with an establishing shot of the little house on the prairie, I imagine seeing the little house on the prairie. But for some philosophers, this raises the question of who in the fictional world is responsible for showing us the house; they maintain that reason demands an answer to this question (Levinson 1996).

Ostensibly the actual filmmakers cannot be showing us the house, since the house is fictional and they are merely showing us an actual house that is being used to represent the fictional house. So, it is argued, we must postulate some fictional presenter at work here. It is this implicit fictional presenter who makes it possible for us to perceive imaginarily the sights and sounds of the fictional world, something the actual filmmaker cannot do, since he/she only has entrée to the actual world.

Nevertheless, insofar as this argument rests upon the notion of seeing imaginarily, it falters. For, the notion of seeing imaginarily does not seem very compelling. Watching a gun battle in the 2007 version of *3:10 to Yuma*, I find myself curiously unscathed, nor do I imagine myself ducking bullets. Yet if I were imagining that I was seeing a gun fight close up, wouldn't I have to imagine that my life was endangered? Can I be imagining that I'm seeing a gun battle from a vantage point inside the line of fire and not imagine bullets bursting midair around me? And if I were imagining that, would I continue eating my popcorn so nonchalantly? However, I do eat my popcorn nonchalantly because I don't imagine myself amidst a blizzard of flying steel and if I don't imagine that I am amidst the fire fight, how can I plausibly imagine that I am seeing it?

Similarly, many camera positions are such that were I to imagine myself to be an eye-witness inside the fictional world, I would also have to imagine myself in some very unlikely places. In *Casino Royale*, a building in Venice sinks into the lagoon. Do I imagine myself submerged? Do I imagine myself wet, when I am dry? Of course, I don't imagine these things. But how then can it be the case that I am imagining that I am having a close encounter of the third kind within the world of the fiction?

And what do I imagine seeing when there is an onscreen dissolve or a wipe? That the world is dematerializing or erasing itself in my presence? Cuts are also a problem. One moment we are shown Paris and the next moment Moscow is before us. If we imagine seeing these two sights in rapid succession, then wouldn't the question of how I moved across Europe so quickly arise? Yet it doesn't, nor do I feel any pressure to imagine how I pulled off this miracle – just because I wasn't seeing imaginarily in the first place.

In other words, if I were seeing imaginarily, I would have to perform a wealth of unlikely supplemental imaginings in order to account for how I came to be able to perform my primary feats of imaginary seeing (Currie 1996). But I do not appear to perform the requisite, supplemental imaginings. So the notion of imagining-seeing appears dubious. Instead of seeing imaginarily, it seems that a more plausible account of my relation to the visual array is that I *literally* see representations of actors on screen which I use to imagine the fiction. In other words, we may jettison talk of seeing imaginarily. And, if the hypothesis of imagining-seeing is supposed to support the hypothesis of the implicit fictional narrator/presenter, then the two ideas fall together.

Another problem, apart from that of improbable supplemental imagining, is that the hypothesis of the fictional presenters who guide our imagining-seeing is that it can lead to self-contradiction. For example, in the TV series

Six Feet Under, the character Nathan Fisher buries his wife in the desert; in the fiction, it is given that no one sees this. Yet, if there is an implicit, fictional narrator/presenter, who enables us to see the burial imaginarily, then someone has witnessed the event. But this yields the contradiction that it both is the case that, in the fiction, no one witnessed the burial and that someone witnessed the burial. In order to avoid this problem, the obvious solution is to eschew the notion of an implicit fictional narrator/presenter (Currie 1996).

However, not only does the implicit fictional narrator/presenter lead to untoward consequences, but the reasoning in its behalf appears ill-motivated. Supposedly we are in need of these fictional intermediaries because actual and implied authors lack the right metaphysical relationship to the world of the fiction. They cannot provide us with the proper metaphysical access to the fictional world because they live on the wrong side of the fiction operator. But if the contents of the fictional world are inaccessible directly to actual authors, implied authors, and their audiences, why would the same problem apply to the alleged fictional presenters as well as to the named fictional characters in the motion picture? If there is any problem with making contact with the fictional world from outside the fiction operator, that problem, *ex hypothsi*, would persist with respect to making contact with an implicit fiction narrator/presenter (Kania 2005).

That is, if we need a fictional intermediary to secure access to whatever is fictional, and the implicit narrator/presenter is fictional, then in order to make contact with the first implicit fictional narrator/presenter, we will need to postulate a second, fictional narrator/presenter, and then, for the same reason, a third, and so on *ad infinitum*. The thinking behind the idea of such a narrator threatens to drag us in to an endless regress such that we could never secure access to the fictional world. But we do have access to fictional worlds. Thus, so much the worse for the implicit, fictional narrator/presenter (Carroll 2006)

One way to mute some of the objections to the notion of the implicit, fictional narrator/presenter is to think of this narrative agency as a documentary motion picture (Wilson 2006). Instead of imagining that we are seeing the world of the fiction under the guidance of an implicit narrator who beckons us to look here and then there, we are to imagine that we are viewing a documentary film produced in the world of the fiction. Just as we are supposed to imagine reading the novel *A Tale of Two Cities* as a report from inside the fiction, when we watch the movie adaptation of the novel, we are to imagine that we seeing a nonfiction film about happenings that occurred during the French Revolution.

This will dodge many of the previous objections involving supplemental imaginings, for if what we imagine seeing is a movie then we don't have to explain to ourselves why we weren't wounded during the gunfight, or dampened during *Casino Royale*, nor do we have to imagine a story about how we manage to get across Europe in less than a second nor need we be perplexed about what we are to imagine seeing when confronted with visual effects like dissolves and wipes. We can account for all this and more on the supposition that it is a movie, albeit a nonfiction movie, that we imagine we are seeing.

Although the documentary version of the report model succeeds quite well with some of the problems of supplemental imagining, it has a number of liabilities. First, it seems plausible that many viewers encounter motion picture fictions before they are exposed to nonfictions. This may be true of children and people in remote areas. These viewers may not yet have the concept of nonfiction film or any idea of how such films are made. Thus, they would not be capable of imagining that they are seeing a nonfiction documentary. But they show no confusion over how they are to process the motion pictures in question.

Furthermore, there is the problem of historical films, like *Quo Vadis?*, *Attila the Hun*, *Hannibal*, or *Gladiator*. Are we to imagine seeing a documentary centuries before moving picture cameras were invented? And, in addition, the documentary hypothesis does not dispel the problem of motion picture events that we are to imagine were witnessed by no one. Surely we are mandated to imagine at the end of *Greed* that there are no onlookers when Marcus and McTeague die in the desert. But this is incompatible with the documentary hypothesis which would place a camera crew within spitting distance of the doomed men. Moreover, the documentary hypothesis not only incurs a logical problem here; it would force most viewers to raise ethical questions about the morality of the film, given the callousness of the supposed documentary filmmakers who idly stand by as these two men perish.

One way to blunt these objections is to claim that we imagine that these documentaries are not human artifacts. They are naturally occurring objects – specifically they are naturally iconic representations or images, perhaps like mirrors (like the ones owned by wicked witches) (Wilson 2006). If we imagine that something of this sort is what transmits the images that we imagine seeing, then the problem of motion picture representations of witness-less events disappears, since these natural icons are not humans. Nor are movies whose events antedate the invention of cinema troublesome, so long as we presuppose that these natural iconic representations have been around since the dawn of time.

One might respond to the idea of natural iconic representations by objecting that imagining that we are encountering such entities has implications as unlikely as many of the implications involved in imagining we are confronting things like gun fights face-to-face. How do these naturally occurring iconic representations work? Exactly what are we supposed to imagine – simply that there are such things? But is that any less outlandish – or, at least, any less "magical" – than imagining that somehow, on a single cut, we are able to move across Europe faster than the speed of light? If the consequences of face-to-face, imaginary seeing strains the bounds of sense, how much better off are we with these allegedly natural, iconic representations?

Moreover, if these naturally occurring iconic representations are supposed to answer the question of who is narrating, then doesn't this process have to be an agent of some sort, like a human or, at least, an anthropomorphic person? But haven't natural iconic representations been introduced precisely to avert the problems that arise when we imagine we are dealing with the work of a human documentarian?

Of course, it might be stipulated that the natural iconic representations constitute some sort of image maker, but if that image maker is a person, then we are back to the problem of reports of putatively witness-less events. So, there appears to be a dilemma in the offing here: either the natural iconic representation is not an agent of some sort (violating the demand that narratives have narrators) or the natural iconic representation is an image-maker (returning us to the problem of witness-less events) (Carroll 2006).

One way of attempting to repel this kind of criticism is to maintain that when we are mandated to imagine thus-and-so regarding the world of the fiction, we are not thereby mandated to imagine everything about how thus-and-so came to be, although we will suppose that it came about somehow. *The Son of Kong* features a scion to the one-of-a-kind King; we suppose the son to be legitimate and imagine he inhabits Skull Island, but we need not imagine how he got there with no Queen Kong in evidence.

Fictions leave much concerning that which we are mandated to imagine indeterminate and unexplained, but we are not, it may be argued by the defenders of the implicit fictional narrators/presenters and/or natural iconic representations, mandated to fill in the gaps. Thus, we are not mandated to imagine how natural iconic representations work nor whether they are agents. Nor are we prescribed to imagine everything such posits entail. We just imagine that, howsoever these things operate, they are producing the images of goings-on in the fictional world.

Indeed, in the old *Flash Gordon* serials, there was a viewing device that enabled one to see anywhere in the galaxy with no recording devices in evidence. Ours was not to reason why or how. We were simply to imagine that there were such machines in Flash's universe.

Thus, we may think likewise of the alleged naturally occurring iconic representations. The implicit, fictional presenter/narrating agency has access to or is identical with an equally unexplained and narratively underdeveloped mechanism which allows us to see imaginarily the pictures it produces, although we know not – and cannot even imagine – how. Just as you can imagine that you are in bed with your favorite celebrity – without imagining how you got there – so we may imagine seeing all sorts of images without imagining how we gained access to them. If such images appear to provoke certain anomalies – such as recordings of putatively unrecorded events – we need not imagine how the events were recorded in such a way that evades this apparent contradiction. We merely imagine that the images are somehow available, *sans* absurdity, for us to imagine seeing.

However, this suggestion will not do, for it is not true that when processing a fiction that we are not mandated to imagine a great deal of what is presupposed or implied by what is given in the world of the motion picture. When assimilating a fiction, we constantly need to fill in many of the details that the creator of the story has left out, including things entailed by the narrative, although not stated outright or shown in it. For example, we are mandated to imagine that Philip Marlowe has a heart and that if he is shot in it, he will die.

This supplemental imagining is governed by a default assumption – unless otherwise instructed by the fiction, assume that the world of the fiction is like our world and imagine accordingly. Since this is a default assumption, it may be overridden. Some genres, for example, presuppose things, at variance with the way of actual world – for example, that mummies can be brought back to life. And stories from other cultures and times may come with presuppositions at odds with the way in which we believe the world works and, in order to process these fictions, we will need to adjust our imaginings to alien views. However, our default response to a fiction is to fill it in in terms of our beliefs about how the world is. This is called the realistic heuristic. Moreover, this heuristic raises problems for the attempt to save the hypothesis of the implicit fictional presenter/narrator by means of the bold assertion that we are not mandated to worry in our imaginings whether natural iconic representations provoke contradictions.

For, insofar as there is a realistic heuristic, it is wrong to contend that we are not mandated to imagine altogether that which has not been said or shown in the fiction. We are mandated to imagine that Philip Marlowe has a heart, that a bullet can stop it, and that, because of this, Marlowe will tread cautiously when a firearm is pointed his way. Similarly, when we deploy the realistic heuristic to the fiction of naturally occurring iconic representations, then, if there are salient implications such a device would have in the world as we know it, then we are entitled to imagine they prevail in the fictional world, *unless it is stipulated otherwise.*

The realistic heuristic can be overridden. If we are told that Philip Marlowe is invulnerable, then we will suspend the realistic heuristic and we will not be nonplussed when he survives repeated blastings. Likewise, we do not wonder about the how the viewing device works in the *Flash Gordon* serials, because we have been told that it works and not to worry our heads about it. But notice that in these cases, the realistic heuristic can be retired because the fiction has explicitly told us to do so. Flash Gordon's all-seeing television has been introduced into the story straightforwardly and we have been overtly reassured that it works in the Flash Gordon universe. But the same is not true of the implicit fictional narrator/presenter or of naturally occurring iconic representation. Therefore, if these postulations fall afoul of the realistic heuristic with respect to the supplemental imaginings they enjoin, then the disturbance they represent for our imaginings is genuine (Gaut 2004).

In fact, by definition, no fiction tells us that it possesses an implicit, fictional narrator/presenter or an implicit, naturally occurring image-maker. So, on the one hand, we have no reason to postulate the existence of one on the grounds of the default assumption of the realistic heuristic. On the other hand, if we are told that there are such things by some theorist, then, since within the fiction the realistic heuristic has not been suspended, we can, again by dint of the realistic heuristic, wonder whether it is logically intelligible. If these theoretical postulations presuppose or entail any absurdity – such as an event given as unrecorded which has been recorded – the contradiction cannot be evaded by appealing to the idea that we need not imagine that which the recommended postulation entails *because*, without a stipulation to do otherwise, we are to imagine that the kinds of logical, physical, and psychological implications that obtain in the actual world obtain in the world of the fiction. And, of course, if these postulations are *implicit*, then it has not been stipulated that we should think otherwise.

Another consideration against the notion of the naturally iconic image-maker is that it seems far too complex a posit to attribute to any viewers, save those steeped in analytic metaphysics. As we have seen, the notion of naturally occurring image-making emerges from an intense dialectic and is designed to deflect certain counter-examples and conundrums that beset the notion of ubiquitous, implicit, fictional narrators/presenters. Such a mechanism is extremely unlikely to occur to most viewers. It is not apt to be part of their imaginative processing of fictional motion pictures, since they lack the concept.

And yet most do assimilate such movies successfully. Thus, they must be doing it without the benefit of the various metaphysical hypotheses presented so far in the debate (Carroll 2006). Perhaps if normal viewers can do without such things, motion picture philosophers can do so as well.

Still another problem with the naturally iconic image-maker as a solution to the perplexities raised by the implicit narrator/presenter is that even if we could imagine some natural process that might give rise to individual motion picture images, what conceivable natural process could edit them into a coherent story. The natural iconic image-maker does not merely present single images; those images get organized into narratives. However, there is no Flash Gordon, Dale Arden, or Dr Zharkoff directing the image-maker where to look and in what order. Even if naturally occurring iconic images were conceivable without too much effort, can entire naturally produced motion picture narratives be imagined as readily?

The friends of ubiquitous, implicit narrators/presenters with respect to fictional movies maintain as their starting point that if we get visual information about the fictional world from the movie, rationality compels us to ask how we get it (Levinson 1996). The implicit fictional narrator is their answer. But why do we stop there in our quest to learn about the provenance of this information?

Obviously, postulating the agency of an implicit narrator may lead us to ask what appear to be silly and irrelevant questions – such as, how does the implicit fictional narrator know that *x* when it is given by said narrator himself that no one within the boundaries of the fiction knows that *x*. For the sake of forestalling such questions, the defenders of the implicit narrators declare that our questioning about the way in which we learn about the fictional world should stop as soon as we surmise that the fictional narrator has informed us that *x*.

Yet isn't stopping just here arbitrary? Why has reason suddenly become so easy going? If we really felt driven to learn how we get the relevant information, won't we want an account of how the implicit narrator gathered it, especially where it conflicts with the assumption of the realistic heuristic?

But perhaps if we all agree that the pursuit of such questions is silly, then the best way to stop these questions before they start is by refraining from postulating the existence of an implicit, fictional narrator/presenter, since once we get rid of him, these absurdities will disappear.

References

Carroll, Noël, "Film Narrative/Narration: Introduction," in Noël Carroll and Jinhee Choi (eds.), *Philosophy of Film and Motion Pictures* (Oxford: Blackwell, 2006).

Chatman, Seymour, *Coming to Terms* (Ithaca, NY: Cornell University Press, 1990).

Currie, Gregory, *Image and Mind* (Cambridge: Cambridge University Press, 1995).

Gaut, Berys, "The Philosophy of the Movies: Cinematic Narration," in Peter Kivy (ed.), *The Blackwell Guide to Aesthetics* (Oxford: Blackwell, 2004).

Kania, Andrew, "Against the Ubiquity of Fictional Narrators," *Journal of Aesthetics and Art Criticism* 63(1) (2005): 47–54.

Levinson, Jerrold, "Film Music and Narrative Agency," in David Bordwell and Noël Carroll (eds.), *Post-Theory* (Madison: University of Wisconsin Press, 1996).

Wilson, George, *Le Grand Imagier* Steps Out: On the Primitive Basis of Film Narration," in Noël Carroll and Jinhee Choi (eds.), *The Philosophy of Film and Motion Picture* (Oxford: Blackwell, 2006).

Wilson, George, "Elusive Narrators in Fiction and Film," *Philosophical Studies* 135(1) (2007): 73–88.

Further Reading

Alward, Peter, "Leave Me Out of It: *De Re*, But Not *De Se*, Imaginative Engagement with Fiction," *Journal of Aesthetics and Art Criticism* 64(4) (2006): 451–60.

Bordwell, David, *Narration and the Fiction Film* (Madison: University of Wisconsin Press, 1985).

Walton, Kendall, *Mimesis as Make-Believe* (Cambridge, MA: Harvard University Press, 1990).

Wilson, George, *Narration in Light* (Baltimore, MD: Johns Hopkins University Press, 1986).

Wilson, George, "Narrative," in Jerrold Levinson (ed.), *The Oxford Handbook of Aesthetics* (Oxford: Oxford University Press, 2003).

Wilson, George, "Transparency and Twist in Narrative Fiction Film," *Journal of Aesthetics and Art Criticism* 64(1) (2006): 81–96.

9

Psychoanalysis and the Horror Film

Because I have expressed reservations about the application of psychoanalysis to film studies in general and to the horror film in particular, I have been invited to contribute a comment to this volume on the relevance of psycho-analysis to the horror film. The editor's intention to include dissenting voices in this anthology is as laudable as it is generous and frankly unexpected. But I don't know for whom this opportunity is scarier: me or the psychoanalysts. For I must enter the lair of the Other, while they must suffer the presence of a wolf in philosopher's clothing. I guess it all depends on who you think the monster really is.

Is psychoanalysis relevant to the analysis of the horror film?[1] I think that the simple answer to this question is "Of course." It is certainly relevant, even apposite, to the analysis of many horror films, because many horror films presuppose, implicitly or explicitly, psychoanalytic concepts and imagery. *Forbidden Planet* (1956), for example, is frankly Freudian. Its monster is called the Id, a phenomenon explained in explicitly psychoanalytic terms within the world of the fiction. Anyone interpreting *Forbidden Planet* is thereby licensed to explicate the film psychoanalytically for the same reason that an exegete of Eisenstein's *The General Line* (1929) would be correct in adverting to Marxist ideology. In both cases, the hermeneutical warrant is historicist. If interpreta-tion is, at least in part, the retrieval of a film's intended meaning and an explanation of its design, then, where a filmmaker intends psychoanalytic significance, it is incumbent on the interpreter to attempt to unravel it.

"Psychoanalysis and the Horror Film," in Steven Jay Schneider (ed.), *Horror film and Psychoanalysis: Freud's Worst Nightmare* (Cambridge: Cambridge University Press, 2004), pp. 257–70.

Minerva's Night Out: Philosophy, Pop Culture, and Moving Pictures, First Edition. Noël Carroll.
© 2013 Blackwell Publishing Ltd. Published 2013 by Blackwell Publishing Ltd.

This does not mean that one must interview the filmmaker to establish that she intended her work to carry psychoanalytically inflected significance. The best evidence for such a message is the film itself. One can infer a psychoanalytic intention on the basis of the film, just as an interpreter of Thomas Mann's *Doctor Faustus* might appeal to Nietzsche's philosophy to explicate some of the more obscure aspects of the text. For some authors, like Norman Mailer, psychoanalytic concepts so infuse their writing that, were they to deny it, we would suspect irony, if not downright lying.

Similarly, an example is the horror filmmaker and author Clive Barker. His writing and imagery show familiarity with psychoanalysis at every turn. He wears it on his sleeve, so to speak, which is where Dante shows his Thomism and Brecht his Marxism. Using these frameworks interpretively, including psychoanalysis, with respect to the relevant texts need not involve going outside of the text, as they used to say, but is grounded by attention to the text.

So far my examples have been of filmmakers and authors who are rather self-consciously psychoanalytic. However, psychoanalytic interpretation may also be plausibly warranted with regard to less self-conscious filmmakers and authors. For in addition to being a medical practice, psychoanalysis has also become a common idiom of thought throughout Western culture; its concepts, scenarios, and metaphors have seeped into everyday language. Just as ordinary speakers may employ psychoanalytic frameworks without being aware of doing so, so may artists.

Psychoanalysis, understood as a cultural myth, like Christianity, pervades the thinking of literate Westerners (and many non-literate ones as well); we can overhear it in elevator conversations between people who can neither spell "psychoanalysis" nor differentiate it from any other form of psychology. Likewise, we can see its concepts, scenarios, and imagery in the work of filmmakers and authors with no express commitment to psychoanalysis.

In a Christian culture like ours, we can attribute Christ-imagery to a film – e.g., call a character a "Christ-figure" – even where that might not be the description the filmmakers would have offered. We can do this because we presume it is likely that the filmmaker arrived at this pattern because he is steeped in a culture where Christ-imagery is pervasive. Thus, we infer that the filmmaker tacitly or un-self-consciously intends his character to have a Christ-like effect, though this is not how he might put it. Likewise, psychoanalytic imagery and concepts are so culturally widespread that we may infer psychoanalytic significance to films that are not fully self-conscious about its presence.

One last analogy: The idiom of Social Darwinism has suffused our culture since the late nineteenth century. People who may never have heard of Darwin mouth its platitudes. Thus, it makes sense to interpret a film like *King Kong* (1933) – which drips with pop-Darwinian imagery – in terms of evolutionary metaphors, despite the fact that the filmmakers, in all likelihood, would not have described them as such. Nevertheless, they did access from the ambient cultural atmosphere readily available material vibrating with Social Darwinian resonances, and they did intend it to move audiences who were prepared culturally to respond to it in certain predictable ways. And this is what licenses bringing to bear the framework of Social Darwinian concepts, scenarios, and imagery in an explication of *King Kong*.

Similarly, it is reasonable to hypothesize that, given the pervasive psychoanalytic coloration of our culture, often filmmakers and filmgoers share enough tacit, albeit generally vague and fragmented, knowledge of psychoanalytic concepts, scenarios, and imagery and, consequently, that they can be said to be trading in psychoanalytic meanings, even if that is not how they would put the matter. Hence, for the purpose of explaining the design and the uptake of such films, exegetes may resort to explicit psychoanalytic terminology, and this can be unexceptionable, even on historicist grounds. For example, calling Luke's relation to Darth Vader "Oedipal" should raise no hermeneutical eyebrows.

This defense of the relevance of psychoanalysis to the horror film, however, does not entail that psychoanalysis is relevant to the interpretation of *all* horror films. For, pervasive though psychoanalytic thought may be, it is not the case that in every horror film one will find evidence of psychoanalytic concepts, scenarios, and/or imagery. And where there is no evidence of the pertinent authorial intentions, either explicit or tacit, psychoanalytic interpretations cannot be warranted on historicist grounds.

Moreover, this sort of defense also places limitations on the specificity of the psychoanalytic framework one may mobilize with respect to a given horror film. As indicated, many of the psychoanalytic ideas available to filmmakers and their audiences are extremely general, rather vague, and even inchoate. These the interpreter must approach gingerly. In such cases, one's deployment of psychoanalytic concepts should be correspondingly general. For on historicist grounds, it will not do to apply a piece of recondite Lacanian conceptual machinery to a film whose only psychoanalytic commitment is something like the nostrum that sexual repression is unhealthy.

For example, a Lacanian analysis of the original *Cat People* (1942) could not be motivated on historicist grounds, though a specific psychoanalytic interpretation could be defended on the grounds of the film itself and the popularity of certain watered-down psychoanalytic ideas in the culture from which it emerged.[2]

This is not to say, I hasten to add, that there could not be a Lacanian horror film worthy of a Lacanian interpretation. But that would depend on whether Lacanian concepts, scenarios, and imagery were sufficiently evident in the film such that it is plausible to hypothesize that the filmmaker intended them as such. Moreover, I have no doubt that we will be seeing many Lacanian horror films soon as more and more filmmakers and filmviewers are trained in university programs with film analysis classes where Lacanese is the vernacular.

The conclusion that psychoanalysis is relevant to the analysis of *some* horror films seems unavoidable, if only on historicist grounds. Lest my use of the qualifier "some" sound too grudging, let me explicitly state that I think that probably *many* horror films warrant psychoanalytic interpretations for the reasons I've given, just as many Italian Renaissance paintings warrant the use of interpretive frameworks informed by Catholic theology. The interpreter need not embrace these interpretive frameworks because they are true or because she believes them to be true, but only because psychoanalysis and Catholicism are sources of concepts, scenarios, and imagery that so suffuse their respective cultures that they can be postulated as influencing artists, audiences, and their mutually adaptive responses.

But just as not every Italian Renaissance painting mandates an interpretation informed by Catholicism, not every horror film warrants a psychoanalytic interpretation. Many space invasion films, like *Independence Day* (1996) – which agitate literally for the survival of the species – may be more fruitfully examined from a Darwinian perspective than from a psychoanalytic one (not because Darwinism is true and psychoanalysis is not, but because Darwinian concepts, narratives, and imagery also suffuse the culture *and* are more evident in *Independence Day* than psychoanalytic ones).[3]

This hermeneutical defense of the relevance of psychoanalysis to horror films grants the psychoanalytic critic a field of study. Indeed, I suspect that many psychoanalytic interpretations of horror films, though undertaken by exegetes convinced of the truth of psychoanalysis, could, without much strain, be recuperated instructively as the observations of participant-observers in a culture suffused with psychoanalytic thinking. However, I also suspect that many psychoanalytic critics are likely to spurn this concession, because, though I agree that *many* horror films deserve a psychoanalytic interpretation (at least in part), they believe that *all* horror films should be interpreted psychoanalytically.

One reason why many psychoanalytic critics are apt to reject what I've called the hermeneutical defense of their practice is that they believe that psychoanalysis is true, whereas the preceding hermeneutical defense does not require that psychoanalysis be any less wacky than scientology to be apposite in a given case. That is, the preceding hermeneutical defense only asks that psychoanalysis be culturally pervasive. Moreover, it is because the psychoanalytic critic believes that psychoanalysis is a comprehensive theory that she believes its laws apply to everything in its putative domain; whereas, according to the preceding hermeneutical defense, the warrant for psychoanalytic interpretations only extends as far as the historically concrete distribution of psychoanalytic ideas across filmmakers, films, and their intended audiences. That is why, under its aegis, one would look to scientology to initiate an interpretation of *Battlefield Earth* (2000) and not to psychoanalysis.

Insofar as psychoanalytic critics defend their practice with regard to the horror film on the grounds of the truth of psychoanalysis as a general theory of human nature, the debate is clearly too gigantic to be engaged here. There are too many different brands of psychoanalysis and too many different claims to be adjudicated *ad seriatim*. So, for the sake of argument, let us suppose that there is some truth to psychoanalysis. Is this enough to warrant a psychoanalytic approach to all horror films?

If we assume that whatever is true about psychoanalysis is universally true – in the sense that it applies to every aspect of human behavior – then we might suppose that psychoanalysis will always have something to say about every horror film, inasmuch as every horror film is a specimen of human behavior. However, I predict that this assumption will be too heady for even most, if not all, of the friends of psychoanalysis. Some human phenomena are not on the psychoanalytic radar screen. Surely, Freud thought this. Consequently, the case for explicating all horror films psychoanalytically will depend on showing that there is something in the very nature of the horror film that is peculiarly suited for psychoanalysis. That is, the psychoanalyst needs to establish that there is something in the essence of horror – something without which a film would not be a horror film – that is only explicable or that is best explained psychoanalytically.

This defense of the psychoanalytic interpretation of horror would not be based on interpretive protocols, like historicism. Rather, it would be a theoretical defense. It relies on identifying a comprehensive feature of all horror films, which feature, in turn, is theorized most compellingly by psychoanalysis.

In the past, I've denied that psychoanalysis has succeeded in adducing such a feature. For example, one of the most persuasive attempts to advance such a generalization can be derived from Ernest Jones's *On the Nightmare* (1971). Jones argues that the horrific creatures of folklore are symbolic expressions of repressed wishes. This hypothesis, if convincing, would do a nice job of explaining the ambivalent reaction of horror fiction audiences – their tendency to be both attracted and repelled by horror films. The attraction comes from the fact that a wish is being manifested and thereby gratified, while the repulsion springs from the fact that it is a *prohibited* wish, a wish that occasions psychic punishment. So, for Jones, a vampire figure expresses the desire of the living for the return of a deceased loved one for the purpose of sexual congress, a wish that then elicits disgust from our psychic censor.

However, though this repressed-wish hypothesis promises certain explanatory advantages, it does require that we be able to locate in every horror film a symbolic expression of a repressed wish. And this, I have argued, cannot be done. Many horror films do not contain enough of the relevant kinds of details to motivate the postulation of any latent content, such as a repressed wish. A radioactively enlarged anything, tramping about the countryside killing everything, suffices to make a horror film, but neither the language or the imagery of the film has to suggest any repressed psychosexual portent, let alone a wish. The monster need only be abnormally large and lethal to be horrific; it may not be connected to anything psychically deeper than that. Therefore, the hypothesis that all horror shares the feature of expressing a repressed wish, insofar as it is insufficiently comprehensive, cannot support the conviction that all horror films are to be psychoanalyzed.

That is, horrific creatures can be manufactured formulaically through various strategies, including combinatory ones (for example, put an insect's head on a dog's body). With a specific film or text, this anomaly need not be associated with anything further to be horrifying. Hence, the horrific beings who serve to identify instances of the horror genre can be contrived disconnected from any wishes, repressed or otherwise. And yet the films in which they figure will still count as horror films – indeed, horror films immune from psychoanalysis – for anyone not in the thrall of Jones's theory.

Of course, this argument, if it is convincing, only shows that the universal applicability of psychoanalysis to the horror film cannot be derived from Jones's initially seductive proposal that all horror traffics in the fulfillment of repressed wishes. Yet might there be other psychoanalytic hypotheses that will succeed where the one derived from Jones failed?

Recently, such a proposal has been offered by Steven Jay Schneider. Schneider returns to Freud's 1919 essay "The 'Uncanny'" for inspiration. Schneider points out that in Freud's characterization of the uncanny, which he finds useful for modeling horror, Freud indicates that not only repressed wishes, but also surmounted beliefs, can function to trigger the sense of uncanniness (2000: 172). These surmounted beliefs include things like infantile beliefs in the omnipotence of the will and the belief that the dead can return to life. By portraying possessed children with telekinetic powers or revenants from the crypt, horror films reconfirm such surmounted beliefs, thereby presumably affording pleasure. Moreover, Schneider goes on to develop an interesting typology of horrific creatures in terms of the surmounted beliefs they reconfirm (2000: 183).

Schneider's conception of horror in terms of repressed wishes *and* surmounted beliefs is certainly more comprehensive than the account derived from Jones. However, it is plagued by a serious incongruity. If horror is a function of the reconfirmation of surmounted beliefs, then how can it be possible for people who have not surmounted the beliefs in question to be susceptible to horror fictions? A leading example of surmounted belief for Schneider is that the dead can return to life. This archaic belief underwrites all sorts of horrific beings, from zombies and vampires to ghosts and haunted houses. But, of course, many horror viewers believe that the dead can return to life.[4] They believe in channeling, and séances, not to mention ghosts, haunted houses, and zombies, and some perhaps even believe in vampires. Because these folks have never abandoned (or surmounted) these beliefs, then they should not be horrified by horror movies. But this prediction seems improbable.[5]

Under this category of horrific beings, Schneider includes "embodied souls," of which the demonically possessed are the prime example. Should we then suppose that a screening of *The Exorcist* (1973) in the church basement to an audience of Catholics who believe in possession will evoke no tremor of horror? Not very likely.

Another important family of reconfirmations of surmounted belief for Schneider comprises figures that embody the omnipotence of thought. But again there are horror fans who believe in the omnipotence of thought; for example, there are people who believe in voodoo. When such a person reads a horror novel, like Hugh Cave's *The Evil Returns*, in which the nefarious borcor Margal controls minds from afar, how will Schneider explain the horror they feel, or the horror felt by reverential Fundamentalists who read Christian horror novels like *The Mark*? Surmounted belief just does not seem to be the elusive secret of horror that Schneider takes it to be.[6]

Nor does it appear to be the case that horror films that fail to be explained in terms of surmounted belief will nevertheless be explicable in terms of repressed wishes. To see this, we need only combine the counterexamples we used to challenge Jones and Schneider. Imagine a horror film, watched by believers in ghosts, about a spirit of whom not enough is said, shown, or implied to allow us to infer anything about its latent import. Nor is enough psychosexual detail indicated about the humans it besets to enable one to isolate a network of psychic associations. In such a case, the generalization that all horror films involve either the expression of repressed wishes or surmounted beliefs would seem to be falsified.

There does not appear to be a general feature, or disjunctive set of features, shared by all horror films such that they are always best explained by psychoanalysis. Needless to say, I've only canvassed two proposals about what that general feature might be – Jones's and Schneider's. But because these are among the strongest contenders, noting their limitations should indicate that the burden of proof here rests with the psychoanalysts. It is up to them to produce the relevant sort of general feature before they lay claim to being the privileged interpreters of all horror films.

Of course, that psychoanalysis might not be applicable to all horror films does not entail that it cannot clarify some. Psychoanalysis is a vast and complex body of ideas, including not only meta-psychological theories but also observations of hithertofore scarcely noticed patterns of human behavior. Some of these ideas, if they are well founded and if they track the phenomena on the screen, may illuminate otherwise perplexing aspects of particular horror films.

Consider, for example, James Whale's *Bride of Frankenstein* (1935), the sequel to *Frankenstein* (1931). On the eve of Henry Frankenstein's (Colin Clive) marriage, the wizened Dr Septimus Pretorius approaches him in the hope of enlisting the younger scientist to experiment once again in the creation of life. Ernest Thesiger plays Pretorius in a style that we have since come to call camp. He tries to charm, cajole, and tempt Henry, though Henry resists, having had an unhappy experience with reanimation in the previous film. Pretorius flirtatiously importunes, promising knowledge and grandeur; Henry fidgets, nervously and darkly. If you turn off the soundtrack it is easy to imagine that we are witnesses to an attempt at homosexual seduction. But, of course, the object of the seduction is not directly sexual, but rather involves the prospect of two men creating life together.

Another notable feature of Pretorius's mien is his sneering attitude toward Henry's wife-to-be, Elizabeth (Valerie Hobson), and the upcoming nuptials. Indeed, Pretorius behaves almost as though he is jealous of Elizabeth, as if she were a rival. In any case, there is an undeniable sexual undercurrent here.

Part of what film interpretation is about concerns making sense of characters, explaining why they are as they are, notably where there is something mysterious and opaque in their behavior. With respect to *Bride of Frankenstein*, one question that arises about Pretorius is why he is so venomous about Henry's prospective mate and their marriage. Of course, part of the reason for Pretorius's opposition is that it may deter Henry's participation in the experiment. But Pretorius's dripping sarcasm is so marked and excessive that it suggests that something deeper is at stake. What could it be?

Here psychoanalysis may suggest an answer. In *Symbolic Wounds*, Bruno Bettelheim cites evidence for the existence of what might be called womb envy, a recurring male desire to possess the reproductive power of women. This longing, Bettelheim maintains, is re-enacted in the symbolism of many puberty rituals. Supposing the behavioral pattern to be well founded, the interpreter of *Bride of Frankenstein* might conjecture that Pretorius's animus is energized by the desire to realize this male "birth" fantasy. He wants to bring forth life, but with a man as his partner rather than a woman. The notion of subtracting the woman from the conventional birth equation is perhaps accentuated by the pointedly fey mannerisms that Thesiger brings to his role.

But, in any event, the logic of the admittedly weird plot of *Bride of Frankenstein* and Pretorius's pronounced aversion to marriage can be rendered intelligible interpretively by speculating that the film is underwritten by a male, in this instance possibly homosexual, desire to appropriate the female powers of reproduction. Indeed, this might even be an example of the kind of surmounted belief that Schneider emphasizes.

This use of a psychoanalytic concept to clarify an opaque pattern in a horror film would not be defended on the grounds of historicism. It is unlikely that the creators or the intended audience of *Bride of Frankenstein* had the concept of birth envy in their conscious cognitive stock. Nor is the preceding interpretation grounded in the supposition that all horror fictions can be interpreted psychoanalytically. Rather, this interpretation is motivated by the need to explain certain specific incongruities in the film. That those incongruities can be made intelligible by reference to a recurring behavioral pattern that has been recognized by psychoanalysis counts in its favor.

It need not be the case that the creators of *Bride of Frankenstein* be aware of the pattern as discovered by Bettelheim. They may be enacting it through the partnership of Pretorius and Frankenstein without realizing that that relationship struck them as comprehensible, intelligible, and fitting because it adhered to an unacknowledged psychic scenario. They had access to it, albeit unconsciously, because, *ex hypothesi*, it rehearses a naturally recurring form of envy. Here interpretation retrieves their unconscious intentions.

So if a psychoanalytic interpretation rests on empirically well-founded observations and theories of human behavior, if it accords with the details of the film, if it does not ignore or contradict countervailing evidence, and if it explains the incongruities of the film better than or equally well as competing interpretations, it will be well warranted. That may sound like a lot of "ifs," but it is by no means obvious that these conditions cannot be met in a particular case. Moreover, these conditions are pretty much default conditions that we expect to be met by any interpretation of fictional representations of fictional affairs. So if the preceding psychoanalytic interpretation of *Bride of Frankenstein* meets these conditions, all things being equal, it should be acceptable.

Thus far, we have found two ways in which psychoanalysis is relevant to the analysis of horror films: where it is motivated by historical or contextual considerations, and where it otherwise meets our general interpretive protocols. My own suspicion – and it is only a hunch – is that where most psychoanalytic interpretations of horror films succeed, it is on historicist grounds, but that may only reflect my skepticism about how many well-founded, uniquely psychoanalytic observations there are to be had about recurring patterns of human behavior. But since I concede that there may be some, then it follows that there may be some well-warranted interpretations of horror films that rest on them. This has to be the case, because in general, we allow as a default presupposition, that interpreters, including ordinary viewers, may legitimately make reference to well-founded, general patterns of human behavior when attempting to make sense of fictional representations of human action, including horror films.[7]

Before concluding, it may be useful to offer some brief remarks about two tendencies in psychoanalytic film criticism that have not yet been mentioned. We might call these illustrative criticism and demonstrative criticism. By illustrative criticism, I mean the use of fictional examples to serve as illustrations of psychoanalytic concepts. Perhaps Freud's use of Sophocles' play to explicate the "Oedipal complex" is an example of this. A more recent example, and one closer to the topic of this article, is Slavoj Žižek's employment of Robert Heinlein's novel *The Unpleasant Profession of Jonathan Hoag* to exemplify the notion of the Lacanian Real.

After quoting a passage from the novel, Žižek writes: "What is this 'grey and formless mist' if not the Lacanian Real – the pulsing of the pre-symbolic substance in all its abhorrent vitality? But what is crucial for us here is the form, or more precisely the place, in which the Real interferes; it irrupts on the very boundary separating the 'outside' from the 'inside', materialized in this case by the car window" (1999: 18–19). Heinlein's imagery here is used to indicate something about the Lacanian Real, its liminality.

Žižek's purpose does not seem to be to explain Heinlein's text, but to give his audience a concrete handle on a difficult piece of Lacanian terminology. In this, Žižek strives to make the text fit the concept, rather than to find a concept that models the text. Given Žižek's aims, this is not an error – but, let me suggest, neither is it textual criticism. It has the wrong direction of fit: the concepts in question need not illuminate the text; the text is supposed to illuminate the concept. Likewise Freud's use of Sophocles' play tells us little about the specific text of *Oedipus Rex*. Would we even say, on the basis of the play, that Oedipus had the famous complex that bears his name, since he did not know that Laius was his father and Jocasta his mother?

The use of films to illustrate psychoanalytic concepts can be found frequently in books devoted to introducing readers to poststructuralist ideas. That this practice can have heuristic value should not be denied. Just as the preacher may use some current event to elucidate a theological doctrine, so a film instructor may turn a film or a part of a film into a parable about some psychoanalytic concept. But insofar as parables take the phenomenon at hand out of context and shape them for their own heuristic purposes, we do not count them as analytic, because the direction of fit between the concept and the phenomenon runs in the wrong direction.

Applying these observations about illustrative criticism to the question of the relation of psychoanalysis to the horror film, we can say that where the psychoanalytic criticism in question is essentially illustrative in nature, it is, strictly speaking, irrelevant to the analysis of the horror film. For in most cases, the illustrative criticism at issue will not be about the horror film; it will be about psychoanalytic concepts. That is, it will have the wrong object of inquiry. On the other hand, where examples of illustrative criticism do tell us something about how a specific horror film or subgenre works, that will be due to the fact that, in addition to pursuing illustrative purposes, they also abide by the protocols of interpretation discussed above. But the bottom line is that illustrative criticism need not abide by those protocols and, therefore, criticism that is as such merely illustrative of psychoanalytic concepts guarantees little insight into the horror film.

One last species of psychoanalytic criticism that deserves mention is what I call demonstrative. Demonstrative criticism in general is criticism aimed at getting people to notice features of artworks, including films. The demonstrative critic may achieve her aim by pointing to an artwork – getting us to feel the tension in the painting by pointing to one part of it and then to another so that the imbalance between two figures jumps out at us. Or the demonstrative critic may redescribe the work, perhaps using metaphors, analogies, and comparisons to other artworks and the like to bring certain qualities of the work to our notice. A dance critic, for example, may call a movement "silky" to draw our attention to important features of the choreography, such as its smoothness, seamless transitions, and lightness.

Psychoanalytic concepts can also be used in this way. Steven Schneider (1999: 72) calls attention to the repetition in the shower sequence in *Psycho* (1960) by reminding readers of what Freud said about repetition. Rhetorically, this gets one to see and to appreciate an important structural feature of the scene. And I suspect that many film instructors use psychoanalytic concepts as a way to begin to encourage students to notice cinematic articulations that would most likely go unheeded. In this way, as an instrument of demonstrative criticism, psychoanalysis may be a very serviceable medium for film pedagogy.

Demonstrative criticism is a very important, though frequently overlooked, form of criticism. One is truly fortunate when one has a good demonstrative critic as a guide. However, the aim of demonstrative criticism is not analysis or interpretation. It employs redescription, metaphors, analogies, comparisons with other works, allusions, and so forth to get us to notice what we might otherwise overlook. Its aim is pragmatic, not analytic. It succeeds if it enables audiences to grasp features of works that might ordinarily be neglected. To that end, the demonstrative critic can employ almost whatever it takes to get the job done, including exaggeration. The output of demonstrative criticism is not ultimately a meaning or an interpretation, but an experience – the viewers' coming to take note of the pertinent features of the work.

And for that to occur, a false theory may be serviceable. For example, though arguably flawed, Freud's work alerts us to many important joke structures. That is one reason that I frequently teach it. It directs my students' attention to what they ought to be thinking about, even if I believe they should not be thinking about it Freud's way. Sometimes a weak theory can provide useful demonstrative criticism.

But, then, even if the psychoanalysis of horror films can function heuristically as salutary demonstrative criticism, that does not entail that it is directly relevant to the *analysis* of the horror film. Getting people to see what needs to be analyzed and analyzing it need not converge. And, for that reason, I would caution the friends of psychoanalysis against counting the pedagogical advantages psychoanalysis may afford them as evidence of its relevance to the analysis of the horror film. For in many cases, their successes may be better described as a function of their excellence as demonstrative critics.

I began with the question of the relevance of psychoanalysis to the analysis of the horror film. I have argued that one cannot presuppose that psychoanalysis has any proprietary authority when it comes to analyzing horror. Though many practitioners more or less presume that psychoanalysis is relevant to the analysis of all horror films, I think this presumption is mistaken. I have also denied that certain psychoanalytic practices with respect to the ostensible criticism of the horror film – notably illustrative criticism and demonstrative criticism – need to be regarded as contributions to the analysis of the horror film.

But these negative conclusions do not foreclose the possibility of the relevance of psychoanalysis to the horror film, especially on a case-by-case basis (film by film, and perhaps cycle by cycle, and maybe even subgenre by subgenre) – for psychoanalytic analyses of selected horror films can be supported on the basis of our standard interpretive protocols, including historicist ones.

How many of the thousands of psychoanalytic interpretations of horror films meet those standards? Who knows? The prospect of doing the work necessary to determine that is beyond my resources. Indeed, the very thought of it is horrifying.

Notes

1   Because I have discussed the relevance of psychoanalysis to film theory at length elsewhere, here I will focus primarily on its relevance to interpretation. Consequently, the sentence above should be read as "Is psychoanalysis relevant to the *interpretation* of the horror film?"

2   The relevance of the surrounding culture and the cognitive stock of the audience to the retrieval of authorial intentions is that these factors are indicative of what the filmmaker intends to communicate for two reasons: (1) because the filmmaker is a similarly informed participant in that culture, and (2) because it is most plausible to assume that she means to exploit what she shares with viewers to secure audience uptake of her film. That is, the currency of certain ideas in a culture, or a significant segment thereof, is a fairly reliable indicator – where the film in question bears the stamp of said ideas – that the filmmaker intends to communicate them to her public (which is also her market).

3   Another constraint on psychoanalytic interpretations arises because psychoanalytic imagery often overlaps with imagery from other cultural sources. In a given film, imagery of a self divided between a bestial component and a saintly part may owe less to psychoanalysis and more to Christianity. Whether the appropriate hermeneutic framework in such a case is Christianity or psychoanalysis will depend

on the specific spin the film gives this imagery. That is, if it is to be defended on historicist grounds, a psychoanalytic interpretation requires as a pretext that there be some feature or features of the film that call upon its special resources rather than upon some other, perhaps more general, equally available cultural myth, like Christianity.

4 Evidence for this includes the program *Crossing Over* with John Edward. This program is so popular that it is crossing over itself from the Sci-Fi Channel to network televison.

5 Also, many viewers believe in aliens from outer space. If aliens are thought by Schneider to embody surmounted beliefs, then such viewers should not be horrified by extra-terrestrial monsters. But aren't the believers in life out there as horrified as the non-believers?

6 This problem also challenges Schneider on another front. He maintains that there is "realistic horror" – horror films whose antagonists are neither supernatural nor sci-fi beings, but ordinary psychos, like serial killers (such as Henry in the film that bears his name). But what beliefs are surmounted here since probably nearly everyone believes that there are sociopaths?

7 I say that this is a "default presupposition." By that I mean to signal that it can be overridden. A text may be at odds with what we know of human behavior. It may advance a palpably false, obsolete, or completely ungrounded view of human life or some aspect of it. At that point, we do not use what we know about human life in general to fill in the text. That is, our interpretations are constrained by the text; we do not normally, knowingly contradict it by projecting our own beliefs onto it, except cautiously in very special circumstances (as when the text is internally incoherent). Where a text contradicts our knowledge of human life, we typically attempt to reconstruct it from an insider point of view, appealing to what was believed about human life in the original context of its production or appealing to the *données* of the genre to which it belongs. Nevertheless, where the text is consistent with what we believe about human life and feeling, our default assumption is that we are warranted in using that knowledge to fill in the text.

References

Schneider, Steven Jay (2000) "Monsters as (Uncanny) Metaphors: Freud, Lakoff, and the Representation of Monstrosity in Cinematic Horror." In Alain Silver and James Ursini (eds.), *Horror Film Reader*. New York: Limelight Editions, pp. 167–91.

Žižek, Slavoj (1999) "The Undergrowth of Enjoyment: How Popular Culture Can Serve as an Introduction to Lacan." In *The Žižek Reader*, ed. Elizabeth Wright and Edmond Wright. Oxford: Blackwell.

Section III

Philosophy and Popular Film

10

Philosophical Insight, Emotion, and Popular Fiction

The Case of Sunset Boulevard

Men more frequently require to be reminded than instructed.

Samuel Johnson

Introduction

During the last decade, a veritable philosophical industry has arisen which posits an association between philosophy and mass culture. Three different publishers – Open Court, the University of Kentucky Press, and Wiley-Blackwell – sponsor series with the title Philosophy and ——, where the blank is filled in by some item of popular culture, like *The Lord of the Rings*, or *Lost*, or even baseball. But often the blank is filled in by the name of some movie or movie director. Similarly, Routledge, a subsidiary of Taylor-Francis, has initiated a series called Philosophers on Film in which a single motion picture, such as *The Third Man*, is interrogated by a handful of philosophers.

The ties between the pertinent pop culture example and philosophy can be various. In some cases, philosophers use an episode of a TV series, such as *The Twilight Zone*, to illustrate some philosophical position, like the coherence theory of truth, or to raise a philosophical question; for instance: does death harm the deceased? Using popular culture in this way, of course, is of great pedagogical value, since it exploits the student's interest in the example as a

"Philosophical Insight, Emotion, and Popular Fiction: The Case of *Sunset Boulevard*," in Noël Carroll and John Gibson (eds.), *Narrative, Emotion, and Insight* (University Park, PA: Penn State University Press, 2011), pp. 45–68.

device for seducing them to entertain, so to speak, philosophical issues that might otherwise try their patience. Call this the "spoonful of sugar" approach. However, in addition, some philosophers claim not only that popular culture can serve the Owl Minerva as a pedagogical tool, but that works of popular entertainment can *do* philosophy outright. That is, they hold that at least some popular fictions can produce philosophical knowledge.

Perhaps needless to say, the suggestion that any artifice of mass culture might afford philosophical insight has not been embraced by philosophers across the board. There are many skeptics. Some are broadly skeptical of the idea that *any* fiction, mass or otherwise, can deliver *any* sort of knowledge whatsoever, while others think that there is something about philosophical knowledge specifically that entails that popular fictions are incapable of providing it. In this essay, with reference to the movie *Sunset Boulevard*, I will argue that *some* popular narratives, including notably the aforesaid classic film by Billy Wilder, can promote philosophical insight, especially with respect to their intended audience, which is to say, the mass audience. That is, some mass fictions *do* philosophy in the arena of popular culture, where they encourage plain viewers, readers, and/or listeners to engage in what might be called popular philosophy.[1]

My case will be laid out in three parts. First I will introduce *Sunset Boulevard* and attempt to distill what I think is its philosophical content. In this section, I will also try show how the emotions, especially that of disgust, are enlisted to abet philosophical conviction. Then, in the ensuing section, I will consider objections to my conjecture that some popular narratives – in this case, *Sunset Boulevard* – can broker philosophical insight for their intended audience. That is, I will contend that the standard skeptical objections do not militate against the possibility of popular philosophy being propounded in popular narratives. Then this will be followed by a short summary.

Sunset Boulevard

Production background

Sunset Boulevard premiered in 1950 at the Radio City Music Hall in New York. It was released by Paramount Pictures. It was directed by Billy Wilder, who had won the Academy Award in 1945 for the motion picture *Lost Weekend*. Wilder was an important American film director by anyone's account. His masterpieces include, along with *Sunset Boulevard*, *Double Indemnity*, *Ace in the Hole*, *Stalag 17*, *Sabrina*, *The Seven Year Itch*, *Witness for the Prosecution*, *Some Like It Hot*, *The Apartment*, *The Fortune Cookie*, and *The Private Life of Sherlock Holmes*, among others. Wilder wrote *Sunset Boulevard* with his longtime collaborator Charles Brackett, although *Sunset Boulevard* was the last picture on which the two worked together. The film featured the silent film superstar Gloria Swanson as well as one of the major directors of that period, Erich von Stroheim, along with several other leading actors of the early twentieth century, including Buster Keaton. The iconic stature of these figures from yesteryear, as we'll see, is one of the major expressive strategies behind the articulation of the philosophical insight afforded by the film.

The film was a critical and a popular success. It garnered eleven Academy Award nominations, including Best Picture and Best Director, although it lost in most categories to *All About Eve*. Undoubtedly the face-off between these two films was somewhat ironic, since both are exposés of their respective milieus – Hollywood in the case of *Sunset Boulevard* and Broadway in the case of *All About Eve*. Nevertheless, Wilder and Brackett did not leave the award ceremonies empty-handed; they received the Oscar for best original screenplay.[2] For my money, *Sunset Boulevard* is clearly stronger than *All About Eve*, in part because it is superior in cinematic inventiveness. But, more importantly, *Sunset Boulevard* transcends being merely a show-business exposé. It is also a bracing example of popular philosophizing.

Brief synopsis

Sunset Boulevard begins with a shot of a curb with "Sunset Boulevard" stenciled across it. As police sirens blare, the camera pans upward and then begins to track down this famous Hollywood thoroughfare at a decidedly quickening pace. The credits start rolling by. In the background, we see police cars racing toward us and then veering into a driveway; and the voice-over narration begins.

The commentary is spoken by Joe Gillis, a Hollywood screenwriter, recently down on his luck, who is played by William Holden. Gillis is dead.[3] In one of the most memorable images in American cinema, we get a fisheye view from the bottom of the swimming pool of Gillis's body floating on the surface of the water.[4] Eventually the police will pull his body from the pool with garden tools; the overall impression of this imagery is of the body as meat.[5]

In Wilder's earlier film *Double Indemnity*, the story is narrated by a dying man, Walter Neff. In *Sunset Boulevard*, Wilder tops that, insofar as Gillis is a dead man – in effect, a ghost. This device, moreover, introduces us to the theme of morality that pervades the film.

In order to explain his untimely demise, Gillis returns us to a time roughly six months before his death. He was out of work. He had back rent due, and his car was about to be repossessed. In order to buy some time, Gillis lies to the repo men concerning the whereabouts of his vehicle. Desperate for money, Gillis approaches a producer with a project, he calls friends, and he button-holes his agent on a golf course, but all to no avail. Stopped at a traffic light at an intersection, Gillis decides to give up his Hollywood ambitions and return to Ohio. But at that moment, the repo men, in an oncoming traffic lane,

see him, and the chase is on. Gillis turns onto Sunset Boulevard with his creditors in hot pursuit. His tire blows out, and he veers into a driveway on the
10,000 block of Sunset Boulevard, thereby eluding his pursuers.

At first Gillis presumes that he has pulled into an abandoned estate. But it
is not abandoned – it is owned by Norma Desmond, a former movie star of
the highest echelon. As previously mentioned, she is played by Gloria Swanson,
herself one of the reigning film queens of the silent era. From offscreen, she
hails Gillis, mistaking him for the undertaker that she has summoned to bury
her pet monkey. When the camera locates her, she is sitting behind a bamboo
blind, her mirrored sunglasses highlighted; she looks like a creature in its lair.

Gillis goes into Norma's mansion and is sent upstairs by Norma's always
lurking butler, Max (played by Erich von Stroheim). There the confusion over
Gillis's identity unravels. However, before Gillis leaves, he recognizes Norma
Desmond as a famous movie star of the silent cinema. She takes offense at his
remark that she "used to be big" and replies, "I *am* big. It's the pictures that
got small."

They are off to a bad start, but when Norma learns that Gillis is a screenwriter,
she changes her tune. She quickly offers to hire him to help her edit a screenplay
that she's been working on for years – a version of the story of Salomé which she
hopes Cecil B. DeMille will direct and which, with her in the starring role, she is
confident will relaunch her movie career. Of course, the idea is preposterous,
since it is established that Norma is well past her youth. Nevertheless, the Salomé
project serves as a sign for the audience of the high degree of Norma's self-
delusion and of her veritable denial of the mortal aging process.

Since Gillis has no better prospects and since his creditors are on his heels,
he accepts the editing job. Ensconced in the lap of luxury, dressed (by Norma)
in the finest attire, and lavished with food and drink, Gillis plows through
Norma's script, which he confides to us is absolutely dreadful. But there is
nothing else on his horizon. So Gillis takes the line of least resistance and soon
is not only Norma's script doctor but her gigolo, lounging around the swimming pool she's had refitted for him and emptying the ashtrays of her guests,
"the waxworks" (Buster Keaton, H. B. Warner, and Anna Q. Nilsson) while
they play bridge with Norma.

Meanwhile, in a parallel development, a young studio script reader, Betty
Schaefer (played by Nancy Olson), has resurrected one of Gillis's earlier movie
proposals (or at least part of one) and has convinced Gillis to work with her
in order to make a go of it. Despite the fact that Betty is engaged to one of
Gillis's closest friends, Artie Green (played by a young and, for once, smiling
Jack Webb), a romance seems about to bud. But in short order Betty learns of
Gillis's affair with Norma, and Gillis, disgusted with himself, sends Betty back
to Artie, vowing to leave Norma. But then Norma, in a jealous rage, stops him
dead by putting a few bullets into his back. Gillis thus stumbles into her swimming pool, and we are back to where the story started.

The film concludes with the police ready to take Norma downtown, presumably to be booked. Norma is coaxed out her bedroom by her butler, Max, whom we earlier learnt was the famous silent film director Max von Mayerling (who, again, is played by von Stroheim, who was a major director during the silent era). Von Mayerling gets Norma to come down the stairs by pretending, with the help of some nearby newsreel cameramen, that shooting on her film *Salomé* is about to commence. The movie ends as Norma slithers toward the camera, as if to devour it, intoning one of the most frequently quoted lines from any film: "All right, Mr DeMille, I'm ready for my close-up."

Analysis

Sunset Boulevard belongs to the genre of what might be called the "Hollywood exposé." *The Bad and the Beautiful* falls into this category, as do various incarnations of *A Star is Born*. *Sunset Boulevard*, however, is arguably the finest example of this genre, not only for its virtually unflinching cynicism and corrosiveness, but also because of its imaginative cinematic and narrative design. Although Wilder is not usually regarded as a particularly visual director, it is through its imagery that *Sunset Boulevard* advances a great deal its criticism of Hollywood. In his youth, Wilder was a screenwriter in Berlin in the 1920s, and his grasp of German Expressionist symbolism is evident throughout *Sunset Boulevard*.

The Expressionist influence on *Sunset Boulevard* is perhaps most apparent in the horror-fiction iconography that pervades the film. One of Wilder's leading points is that Hollywood turns people into monsters, figuratively speaking. Norma Desmond, of course, is the leading example of this. That she is monstrous is literalized by Swanson in many ways.[6] She tightens the muscles in her hands in a fashion that makes them appear claw-like. Her strange, wire cigarette holder makes her hand appear gnarled, misshapen. She points her chin upward and clenches her teeth like a predator ready to clamp down upon its prey. Swanson also frequently growls her sentences. Her gaze is often steady, her eyes popped wide open and unblinking in a way that seems unnatural. And her turban suggests that she may share a haberdasher with the vampires from *Nosferatu* and *Bram Stoker's Dracula*,[7] where vampires themselves can be interpreted as horrific images of fantasies of immortality.

Moreover, the horror movie imagery of *Sunset Boulevard* extends into the architecture of the film. As the film script describes Norma Desmond's mansion, it is "mottled by the years, gloomy, forsaken, the little formal garden completely gone to seed" (Brackett, Wilder, and Marshman 1999: 23). Gillis compares the moldering building to Miss Havisham, one of Dickens's more Gothic creations. He thinks that it is an abandoned house, exactly the sort of place where monsters typically dwell. It is hard to resist the intimation that this is a haunted house, especially later when the wind blowing through the pipe organ emits the musical equivalent of a wheezing presence. Of course, the ghost is Norma.

That organ is played by Norma's butler, Max. His favorite piece of music appears to be Bach's Toccata and Fugue in D Minor, a favorite tune of mad scientists and opera phantoms in horror films (Staggs 2000: 142). Max himself has a limp, recalling the various crippled assistants of so many Doctors Frankenstein.

Wilder takes care to shoot the inside of the house in such a way as to emphasize not only its emptiness,[8] but also its largeness, a feature of so many of the castles and laboratories of horror films in the 1930s. Wilder shows us rats infesting the neglected swimming pool – rats being often-referenced correlates to the undead, notably vampires. And, of course, Norma is the kind of person we are apt to call metaphorically "a vampire," attempting to feed off of Gillis's youthfulness.

Gillis, somewhat ungraciously, labels Norma's friends, the former silent-film stars who are her bridge partners, "the waxworks," which was the title of a German horror film famous during Wilder's youth in Berlin. But perhaps the most extensive *hommage* to the horror film comes when Norma prepares for what she believes will be her return to the screen as Salome. In anticipation, as Gillis puts it, "an army of beauty experts invaded her house on Sunset Boulevard. She went through a merciless series of treatments, massages, sweat cabinets, mud baths, ice compresses, electric devices" (Brackett, Wilder, and Marshman 1999: 98). These are rendered via a montage sequence which critics have remarked resembles nothing so much as an experiment by a mad scientist in a horror film, undoubtedly due to the profusion of electrical equipment in a number of the shots. It is, indeed, a kind of creation scene à la Dr Frankenstein, and, as in the case of Frankenstein's experiment, it goes horribly awry. Norma emerges from this montage, not more beautiful, but rather grotesque, done up as she is in a chin rig that makes her face seem even more a frozen mask than before.

There are other horrific accents in the film. It rains quite a lot, as is often the case in the horror genre. There is the sardonically macabre dead monkey and then its burial in a child's casket, shot from a distance that makes it seem as though we are surreptitiously witnessing some unholy ritual from afar. And, of course, when Norma descends her staircase for her "close-up," she is demented, where insanity is another recurring trope of horror fiction.

Through these various cinematic strategies and more, Wilder gives cinematic substance to his theme – that Hollywood transforms people into monsters. As Arthur Danto might put it, these stylistic choices embody the meaning of *Sunset Boulevard*. In this respect, *Sunset Boulevard* is arguably the most cinematically accomplished Hollywood exposé. By primarily visual means, Wilder is able to figure Norma as monstrous and to elicit the kind of feelings of disgust toward her that we typically muster for the creatures in horror films. However, *Sunset Boulevard* is more than a Hollywood exposé; it transcends that subgenre and transmutes itself into a compelling instance of popular philosophy.[9]

What is the leading philosophical theme of *Sunset Boulevard*? The denial of mortality. The film begins with the image of death – the ghostwriter, Gillis, about to tell us about the folly of an aging movie star.[10] It is hard to resist the notion that the story is set on Sunset Boulevard because Norma has reached the "sunset" years of her life; surely her stardom "set" years before. She is, so to speak, "fading," but Norma is in denial. She thinks that she can return to the screen once more, although we are abundantly reassured that this is impossible.

The theme of aging is written all over the mansion, with its abandoned tennis courts and swimming pools. Decay is everywhere. The antique car mounted on blocks – the Isotta-Fraschini – is an unmistakable objective correlative for Norma, whose career is going nowhere and is as obsolete as the beached automobile.

Photography, which Bazin maintained "embalmed time,"[11] is an important element in the articulation of the theme of aging and its denial. Everywhere in the house there are photographs of Norma at the height of her celebrity, underscoring the contrast between the young Norma and her present self, a disparity which Norma consistently represses. That Norma is a movie star enables Wilder to foreground the theme of aging by showing us moving pictures of the youthful Norma (Gloria Swanson in *Queen Kelly)* and then cutting to Norma watching herself over twenty years later. Of course, moviegoers who were familiar with Swanson from the silent era could not fail to be struck by how her dewy good looks had fossilized (an impression heightened by Swanson's extremely stylized acting). Photography, including motion picture photography, is a time capsule. And all of those time capsules lying around in *Sunset Boulevard* bear resounding testimony to the fact that Norma, her delusions notwithstanding, is long past her prime.

Norma's aging is remarked upon in the narrative by the constant emphasis on her faded glory: the younger security guard at Paramount fails to recognize her; the studio wants her car, not her; DeMille comments that thirty million fans have abandoned her; the phony fan mail; and so on. Similarly, the subplot involving Betty Schaefer serves as a pointed foil to the relationship between Norma Desmond and Gillis. Both women are writing a script with him; both love Gillis; but one is young (it is established that Betty Schaefer is all of twenty-two), whereas DeMille's assistant says of Norma that "she must be a million years old."

In *Sunset Boulevard*, Hollywood celebrity stands to youth as obscurity stands to aging. Norma's refusal to acknowledge that her movie career is over is part and parcel of her refusal to acknowledge the passing of time. It is this, Gillis suggests, that accounts for her reclusiveness. To encounter the outside world would force her to recognize change – change in the world and change in herself. It would compel her to give up her conviction that "stars are ageless."

Given the homology between stardom and nonstardom, on the one hand, and youth and aging, on the other, the earlier equation between stardom and monstrosity takes on an additional and deeper significance: what is monstrous and unnatural about Norma Desmond is her resistance to accepting her age, as that refusal is epitomized by her obsession with playing Salomé. It is not her actual age that is monstrous, but her struggle against acquiescing to it. As Gillis says to her, "Norma, grow up. There's nothing tragic about being fifty – unless you try to be twenty-five." And, of course, in her desire to be Salomé, Norma is trying to be fourteen! Norma would prefer to descend into madness literally, as she does at the end of the film, rather than admit her time of life.

It is this denial of aging that makes Norma a grotesquerie in Wilder's eyes. This is what is monstrous about her. And ultimately it is the denial of mortality in this respect and its existential costs that colligates and unifies the disparate elements – narrative, visual, aural, and dramatic – that constitute *Sunset Boulevard.*

The disgust that Wilder mandates that we direct at Norma is rooted in her refusal to act her age – in her delusion that time has stood still and that she remains as fresh and desirable as she was before the movies learnt to talk. And undoubtedly a certain visceral recoil toward Norma is also exacerbated by the socially inculcated tendency that many viewers have which leads them to regard the erotic liaison between a younger man and a much older woman as unnatural (and "creepy," for that very reason).[12]

There are moments when we are briefly encouraged to sympathize with Norma, such as the scene on the set of *Samson and Delilah*. For a few minutes, Norma seems unguarded and vulnerable. But more often than not, her defenses are up and she behaves high-handedly, selfishly, ruthlessly. She is arrogant, cruel, and, most of all, vain. And it is her extreme vanity that shapes her demeanor in such a way that it turns her from a caricature into a monster.

Norma's story is extreme. She believes she can play the teenager Salomé. Indeed, she seems certain that she has remained the teenager she was when she first became a star. Undoubtedly, much of the uneasiness or discomfort we feel in response to that last shot of the film is energized by the palpable difference we sense between Norma as she is and the teenage Salomé she imagines she is playing.

However, upon reflection, thoughtful viewers, particularly those of us who are past middle age, are also apt to recognize something of Norma, if not in ourselves, then in certain of our acquaintances. For Norma's pathology is a recurring human trait writ large (as large as a major Hollywood motion picture production). It is the failure to acknowledge the aging process, and it is evident throughout our culture, in phenomena ranging from the so-called midlife crisis to our tendency to wear into old age the clothing of youth – e.g., faded blue jeans and athletic attire (jerseys, sweat-pants, sneakers, and so on). How often does one hear or even say oneself, "I don't feel *x*," where *x* takes the value of some number of years past what we call middle age. Although some may come close to rivaling Norma in their obsession with appearing youthful – whole industries are now predicated upon abetting this illusion – most pull back from the abyss of madness that engulfs Norma.

Nevertheless, Norma is a symbol of something more generic and is exaggerated for that very reason. Maybe her name is "Norma" because it is only one letter short of "normal." That is, Norma exemplifies a normal human tendency – the denial of aging – albeit in a way that is immensely magnified and symbolized by means of the imagery of Hollywood stardom.

In *Sunset Boulevard*, the narrative arc of a Hollywood career – from strutting center stage to being ushered offstage – and the delusions this risks, functions as an analog to the trajectory of a human life and the consequent pathologies that the human condition may invite; few readily accept being a has-been in either register. Furthermore, particularly in our own time, the obsession with Hollywood-type celebrity may even be a causal ingredient that helps account for the compulsion many seem to experience nowadays to appear as youthful as possible and to disguise, if not utterly suppress, their actual age. Admittedly, the degree of self-deception to which Norma is victim is far greater than ordinary. Yet her story nevertheless manages to hold a mirror up to the rest of us – although it is more of the nature of the kind of funhouse mirror that enlarges everything it reflects.

Often the task of philosophy is simply to coin new ideas and concepts. But, sometimes its office is to remind us of matters we know but of which we are perhaps only vaguely and inarticulately aware, if at all, or even is something we know, but actively ignore or repress. According to Wittgenstein, a leading function of philosophy is to enable us to understand what is in plain sight, although perhaps unrecognized; Stanley Cavell finds movies exemplary in their capacity to dramatize what is in front of our eyes and thereby to rediscover the philosophical insights we already know, but may not acknowledge.[13]

Our mortality with respect to the inexorable process of aging is one of those features of human existence of which we easily lose sight, conveniently forgetting and even repressing our awareness of this phenomenon as, in the heat of life, we press forward with our projects. The philosophical insight on offer in *Sunset Boulevard* vividly recalls for viewers this very central fact of human life. And *Sunset Boulevard* does this by revealing the desire to be ageless – Norma's notion of stardom – to be monstrous and unnatural, a rediscovery made all the more arresting and unforgettable for being underwritten by visceral feelings of disgust and horror.[14]

How can *Sunset Boulevard* be philosophical?

Objections

On the basis of my analysis of *Sunset Boulevard*, I have just asserted that *some* (in the sense of at least one) narrative, fiction film can do philosophy. Of course, I believe that more than one narrative, fiction film has this capacity. But a single case is enough to defeat the skeptics.

Nevertheless, I predict that the skeptics will not be satisfied merely by an interpretation of the sort I have just offered. Nor should they be. They will undoubtedly raise a series of objections. Three of the most likely ones are (1) *Sunset Boulevard* is not an example of philosophy, properly so-called, because even if it advances a philosophical theme, it does not demonstrate it; (2) the theme of the denial of mortality that has been associated with *Sunset Boulevard* is too banal to be deemed genuine philosophy; and (3) what possible *philosophical* purpose does the creation of an artistic object as elaborate as *Sunset* Boulevard serve? Surely Wilder's energies are actually being spent on something other than doing philosophy. In what follows, I will try to allay these anxieties in turn.

The No-Argument Argument

Even if we grant that *Sunset Boulevard* advances a philosophical theme – say, the existential necessity of acknowledging our mortality – the skeptic will observe that we do not have anything that amounts to doing philosophy. A fortune cookie, stuffed with a suitably sage Confucian adage, might propose something that sounds philosophical, but, sans argumentation, we would not say that it was doing philosophy. Why not? Because doing philosophy is not simply a matter of expressing some or another philosophical theme. Doing philosophy, properly so-called, requires supporting that theme with argument. To assert baldly and blandly that every one of my actions has been causally determined by antecedent events does not count as philosophy, unless and until that assertion figures as the conclusion of an argument – whether deductive, inductive, or abductive, and, as well, one that is preferably original. The skeptic will not countenance as philosophizing anything, if we cannot answer the challenge "Where's the argument?" But there doesn't appear to be any argument warning against the denial of aging in *Sunset Boulevard*. So, the skeptic surmises, the movie doesn't amount to a philosophical contribution.

Of course, it is not clear that the skeptic's demand for argumentation as an essential characteristic of philosophizing is uncontroversial. Nietzsche's aphorisms and Wittgenstein's puzzles are usually accepted as philosophy, although they typically come unaccompanied by argument. But, for the moment, let us grant the skeptic his premise and see whether we can still make out the case for *Sunset Boulevard* as a vehicle of philosophical insight.

The skeptic maintains that philosophy requires argumentation, but notes that there is no argument in evidence in *Sunset Boulevard*. One way in which to meet the skeptic's challenge here is to suggest that the skeptic is looking for the pertinent argumentation in the wrong place. Don't look to the voice-over narration for the argument. Nor do any of the characters articulate it. The argument lies elsewhere. Where? In the minds of the audience. *Sunset Boulevard* provides the material that the reflective viewer can and – in the ideal case – does use to reach the relevant philosophical insight on her own.

In this regard, *Sunset Boulevard*, like a number of other fictional narratives, is maieutic. That is, it draws the conviction from the audience about the human condition that it endorses as a midwife draws the infant-child from her mother. Here Billy Wilder stands in the lineage of Socrates, who educed geometry from the slave-boy in the *Meno* by asking him a series of pointed questions. Likewise, *Sunset Boulevard* confronts us with an unavoidable question, namely, what drives Norma Desmond deeper and deeper into delusion? Moreover, the narrative supplies us with ample material that clearly heads us in one direction: the realization that madness is the cost that Norma must pay for repressing her recognition of the temporality of human life, her desire that life be like a film image, eternally changeless, embalmed.

It is not the case that the only structure of legitimate philosophical argumentation must take the form of a progression from premises to conclusions. Rhetorical questions, as well, can function argumentatively, eliciting abductive leaps from listeners by introducing a selection of data whose implications gel when a strategically crafted question is posed. In such instances, the reasoning required to reach the conclusion is rehearsed by the audience. But the rhetorical question is no less an argumentative design just because it delegates the relevant reasoning to the listener. Indeed, the reasoning may seem all the more compelling to the listener because she appears to have reached it on her own.

What I want to propose is that narrative fictions such as *Sunset Boulevard* may function cognitively in a way that parallels the rhetorical question insofar as they can dispose viewers to reason, under their own steam, to the philosophical theme the fictional narrative itself is meant to embody.

Of course, *Sunset Boulevard* is not literally a question. It is rather the celluloid equivalent of a thought experiment, in this case a fictional narrative, designed to guide the audience to a definite conclusion, namely that the denial of mortal aging is self-destructive, risking a species of delusional thinking that may verge upon madness. *Sunset Boulevard* presents the viewer with a story that the spectator, on the basis of her own extracinematic experience, accepts as probable and from which she infers the lesson – the cautionary advice that Gillis offers to Norma about acting her age – which the spectator assesses to be credible, again on the basis of her own life experiences.[15]

Moreover, with respect to narrative fictions like *Sunset Boulevard*, it is not the case that spectators must reach such conclusions while in the thick of engaging with the story. They may also arrive at it afterwards in what Peter Kivy has felicitously called the *reflective afterlife* of the narrative fiction – that is, during an interval after the fiction has been absorbed when one contemplates its portents on one's own or in the company of others, immersed in lively conversation (Kivy 1997).

By locating the relevant argumentation or reasoning in the minds of the audience, we are also able to evade what might be thought of as the skeptic's dilemma. That dilemma goes like this: either the requisite argumentation is explicitly in the fictional narrative or it is not; if it is not in the fictional narrative, then the fictional narrative cannot be said to be doing philosophy, since doing philosophy demands argumentation; but, on the other hand, if the argument is explicitly stated in the narrative – either by some character or some authorial agency – then it is not by means of the narrative *as such* (by narrative means alone) that philosophy is being propounded; rather, philosophy is merely being parroted by some character or narrative agency that just happens to inhabit the narrative; the narrative could proceed as effectively, the skeptic insinuates, without said discursive interludes.

This dilemma, however, is averted by relocating the argument in the minds of the audience (as primed by the narrative *qua* thought experiment), since by being in the minds of the audience, the requirement that there be argument or reasoning is fulfilled in a way that is not liable to the charge that someone – some character or some narrative agency – is functioning rather like a ventriloquist's dummy in the world of the fictional narrative. Rather the narrative as such has been structured in such a way as to propone or to call forth the relevant reasoning in alert audience members.

One objection to relocating the required reasoning in the audience is that if we treat the narrative fiction in this way – as an elaborate thought experiment channeling viewers toward philosophical conclusions much in the fashion of a rhetorical question – then the fictional narrative must explicitly let the audience know about the exact dialectical context into which the narrative is intended to fit. Thought experiments, like rhetorical questions, occur in certain contexts. If the narrative fiction is to function as a proper thought experiment, the narrative must make its role in the pertinent debate perspicuous as well as elucidate the way in which it secures its intended point. Yet this would appear to reintroduce the threat of a dilemma. Either the narrative fiction does not unfurl its argument, in which case it has failed to specify its place in the relevant debate, or it does lay out its argument explicitly (by means of a character or a narrative agency), in which case it is not doing philosophy by means of narrative as such.

On the one hand, I am not convinced that the context in which a thought experiment figures always needs to be made explicit in the way the skeptic stipulates. In certain situations, where the participants in the debate know what is at stake – as at specialized sessions of the American Philosophical Association – a thought experiment may be voiced whose significance everyone in the room grasps, without its place in the debate needing to be spelt out in letter and verse. Indeed, informed listeners might find such an exercise pedantic. Moreover, in certain artistic milieus, especially in terms of various avant-garde movements, there may be overarching, animating questions – like what is art? or what is cinema? – of which virtually all informed spectators are aware and which, for that reason, do not require overt enunciation for uptake by prepared audiences of the relevance of the pertinent artistic thought experiments.

On the other hand, even if we accept the skeptic's contention that the dialectical context of any thought experiment that advances a philosophical thesis must be made explicit in order to count as *doing philosophy*, this challenge can be easily met with respect to *Sunset Boulevard*, while simultaneously avoiding the skeptic's dilemma. Even the most determined skeptic, Bruce Russell, allows that films can provide evidence for an informed audience to arrive at a philosophical conclusion (2009). He demands, however, that the fictional narrative at issue *also* specify the relevant dialectical context, which he appears to presume can only be done by itemizing its argumentative premises.

But this, maybe needless to say, he assumes, will mobilize the second wing of the skeptic's dilemma: it will necessitate outlining the premises of the argument by nonnarrative means (Russell 2009), thereby defeating the notion that fictional narratives as such (and notably movies) can provide philosophical insight. Yet this is logically fallacious. The possibility that the skeptic has overlooked is that the narrative may specify its dialectical context by merely stating its *conclusion* (rather than enumerating its premises) and then simply provide the audience with a compelling, emblematic example to support an inference that comports with their experience of the world and that matches the aforesaid conclusion.

And that is precisely what *Sunset Boulevard* does: as already mentioned, with respect to Norma Desmond, Joe Gillis explicitly states the pertinent thesis: "You're a woman of fifty. There's nothing tragic about being fifty – not unless you try to be twenty-five" (or, like Norma aspiring to play Salomé, a fourteen-year-old). The saga of *Sunset Boulevard* is then the thought experiment which inspires the audience to come to the conclusion on its own about the veracity of this philosophical thesis on the basis of their own experience of life outside the movies, and their own cogitations. The audience works out the relevant argument, in other words, without the reasoning being hammered home, step by step, on the soundtrack, either in the mouths of the characters or through voice-over narration.

The Banality Argument

The skeptic may grant, in response to the preceding section, that the reasoning, such as it is, necessary to substantiate the alleged philosophical insight in *Sunset Boulevard* is available through the ratiocination the film is most likely to engender in the prepared and alert viewer. However, the caveat here – "such as it is" – is key, just because the skeptic doubts that there is much reasoning at all involved in confirming the conclusion that I've attributed to the philosophizing in the film. Everyone grows old, and *everyone* knows this(!), the skeptic will bark. This isn't philosophy, the skeptic continues, it's common knowledge. This conclusion, if it can really be dignified by being labeled *a conclusion*, is too trivial to be glorified as an *insight*, philosophical or otherwise. It is, not to put too fine a point on it, banal.

Furthermore, in a caustic mood, our skeptic might add that all of the so-called knowledge purportedly retailed by our beloved fictional narratives is exactly of the same sort. Don't make snap judgments, recommends *Pride and Prejudice*. Well, yes. Yet that "discovery" is hardly on a par with Kant's Copernican Revolution. That which is applauded as Austen's philosophical acumen is, frankly, obvious. It's banal, whereas philosophical insight, properly so-called, is never banal. It is, perforce, original, defamiliarizing, unexpected, and/or unconventional.

Yet, once again, the problem here is that the skeptic presupposes too narrow a conception of philosophy. Philosophy may often be involved in the postulation of heretofore unimagined possibilities – monads, the phenomenal/noumenal distinction, and so on. That is certainly one office of philosophy. But, equally, another task of philosophy is to recall to mind features of human experience that, if known once, have been forgotten or are only dimly grasped or are ignored, neglected, and/or even repressed.

For example, central to the not unrelated philosophies of Kierkegaard and Heidegger is the observation that death is an inescapable fact of the human condition *and* that humans typically deny that death is a fact of life (of *Dasein*, as Heidegger would have it). "Terror, perdition, annihilation dwell next door to every man," Kierkegaard points out in *The Concept of Dread* (1957: 140); but most of us live in, as he says, "half-obscurity" about our existential plight (1954: 181; see also Becker 1973, esp. ch. 5). For Kierkegaard, this is our human birthright; as God casts Adam and Eve from the garden, He tells them, "Thou shalt surely die." And yet this is perhaps the hardest thing for us to get our minds around, as we immerse ourselves in our daily pursuits, no matter how insignificant.[16] Enmeshed in our daily affairs – that appointment for cleaning our teeth with the dentist, for example – we never allow to intrude on our behavior the thought of how unimportant this is given the absolute certainty of our ultimate demise. But how could we exist otherwise?

Heidegger is even more emphatic about our mortal tendency to deny mortality. He points out that "one *knows* about the certainty of death, and yet 'is' not authentically certain of one's own"; because "death is deferred to 'sometime later', and this is done by invoking the 'so-called' general opinion'.... Thus the 'they' covers up what is peculiar in death's certainty – *that it is possible at any moment*" (1962: 302). Kierkegaard and Heidegger are seminal philosophers precisely because they remind us of facts of the human condition which, although admittedly known, are readily forgotten. You might dismiss this as "prophetic philosophy," but it has been one of the tasks of philosophy since the get-go. Ancient philosophy was primarily concerned with how to live (and die) (Hadot 2000: 2009), and in this matter ancient philosophy is closer to what I am calling popular philosophy, the philosophy that primarily engages the layperson (as opposed to the academic).

Obviously, dwelling upon death could stultify action.[17] Why do anything if, in the larger scheme of things, dust is your final reward? So that thought needs be repressed. An important charge of philosophy is to compel us to remember that which we naturally suppress. This is connected to philosophy as a mode of living – which, in turn, is patently relevant to the mission of *popular* philosophy, as it was to ancient philosophy. Popular philosophy is not mainly for the graduate seminar room, where possible worlds await conquest. Popular philosophy is for places like the novel and the movie theater, wherein reminders of mortality have a definite rhetorical bite.

Narrative fiction is ideally suited to engage the populace in popular philosophizing. The insights about the denial of death found in Kierkegaard and Heidegger, for example, are energetically recalled to mind in *Exit the King* by Eugène Ionesco. In that play, the king, Berenger the First, is over four hundred years old. He is about to die. At one point it is predicted that he only has one hour, twenty-four minutes, and fifty seconds to live (putatively the remaining running time of the play). The "Exit" in the title, of course, refers to his death. Throughout the play, Berenger attempts to resist his destiny with various forms of specious reasoning, including the assertion that "kings ought to be immortal" (Ionesco 1967: 36). As he tries to talk his way out of dying, the audience recognizes in him their own – and, for that matter, everyone else's – constant refusal to confront their inexorable fate, including the possibility that we may no longer be here in one hour, twenty-four minutes, and fifty seconds. Wrapped up in our quotidian affairs, few prepare for the inevitable, but, as Berenger has done for over four hundred years, we thrust it out of mind.

That Berenger is so old, of course, emphasizes the tenacity of his denial. Moreover, his denial of his mortality is not unlike Norma Desmond's denial of her advancing age. Interestingly, Berenger's statement that "kings ought to be immortal" curiously echoes Norma's question "Stars are ageless, aren't they?" Both the play and the film not only call upon us to remember the unavoidable facts of our mortality, but also dispose us to recognize and acknowledge our indefatigable propensity to disavow the only guaranteed experiences to which flesh is heir. Indeed, death is even more inevitable than taxes. Furthermore, as argued earlier, we confirm these hypotheses on the basis of our own experience of ourselves and others by calling upon our familiarity with the world outside of fiction.

With respect to *Sunset Boulevard*, the skeptic is apt to charge that everyone knows that aging is inevitable and even that most are cognizant of our tendency to deny this by means of varying degrees of self-deception. Thus, since this is common knowledge, it is too banal to count as philosophy. Indeed, since this is so widely understood, saying that a narrative fiction like *Sunset Boulevard* enables us to "discover" it is ludicrous. There is no insight where the phenomena are in clear sight. And yet, however much we are inclined to agree that everyone knows the human realities that *Sunset Boulevard* dramatizes, we must also acknowledge that we conveniently forget them most of the time. The so-called facts of the matter are not truly in "clear sight." The skeptic is correct; *Sunset Boulevard* does not lead us to discover that which Norma has denied; but it does prompt us to *rediscover* what we already know, and one of the functions of philosophy, since its origins, has been to remind us of deep truths that we have repressed.

Furthermore, because these kinds of truths are so easily forgotten, it is the recurring task of philosophy to invent new devices and stratagems for recalling our attention to them. These include novel thought experiments of all sorts, including popular narrative fictions.

Reminding audiences of truths of the human condition we are disposed to suppress, albeit at our own peril, has been a function of the most significant narrative fiction since the beginning. *Oedipus Rex* concludes by advising, "Call no man happy until he is dead." In this, Sophocles is reminding audiences of one of the deepest insights of Greek philosophy, namely, that bad things can happen to good people. We have a tendency to become so involved in the details and projects of our lives that we forget how vulnerable we are to misfortune. We ignore the facts that disaster can befall us at any moment and that we won't know whether we have lived a happy life until once in the grave, we are out of harm's way. The role of tragedy is to remind us of truths that we tend to repress. It makes philosophy – particularly philosophy as it is related to the task of living – available to the populace. *Sunset Boulevard* stands in that tradition, recalling for us facts of life that, however mundane, are most frequently neglected, generally to our own peril.

The Excessive Elaboration Argument

As we have seen, *Sunset Boulevard* is a very complex artistic object, as is the case with many other supposedly philosophical narrative fictions. In fact, they are far more complicated than would appear to be necessary for the purpose of advancing the philosophical themes that they are alleged to communicate. Compared to the thought experiments one typically finds in standard philosophical discourse, these so-called thought experiments are very extravagant. This suggests that it is not the primary purpose of these narrative fictions – if it is their purpose at all – to present philosophy, popular or otherwise. With respect to *Sunset Boulevard*, the skeptic submits that it was designed to entertain, not to instruct. It is only the superego of people like me that motivates us to attempt to locate its value in terms of philosophical didacticism. Perhaps we feel the need to justify those hours at the movies when we should have been doing our homework.

Undoubtedly, the first thing to note in response to this argument is that it would not be a problem for the view (that narrative fictions can do philosophy in the manner indicated above) if this was not the only or even the primary purpose of the relevant fictions. Most fictions have multiple aims. That a narrative fiction may have more than one purpose is compatible with the assertion that philosophizing is one of them. Furthermore, it is not evident that entertainment and philosophical instruction must always be construed as opposites. Philosophical instruction can be entertaining by engaging the mind. Even thought experiments in professional philosophy journals often make a play for amusement.

But a deeper response to the excessive-elaboration objection rejects the charge that the kinds of narrative fictions that *Sunset Boulevard* represents are more complex than they need to be. Given the philosophical service that such a narrative is meant to perform, *Sunset Boulevard* has just the kind of structures required to discharge its function.

What is the function of *Sunset Boulevard?* Well, *one* function, *ex hypothesi*, is to impress spectators deeply with its insight into our tendency to deny our mortal finitude, particularly with respect to the passage of time. In order to drive that insight home forcefully, *Sunset Boulevard*, like most narrative fictions of the pertinent variety, recruits our emotions.[18] The supposedly over-elaborate structures that the skeptic maintains serve no philosophical function are precisely what are called for in order to enlist the spectator's emotions in the process of – let us call it – their philosophical education.

For example, earlier we stressed the subtle infusion of horror imagery throughout *Sunset Boulevard*. This, however, is not mere ornamentation for the sake of ornamentation. Its purpose is to direct our emotional appraisal of what Norma Desmond is doing. The recoil of horror that Norma Desmond elicits focuses our attention upon what is "against nature" in her behavior and marks it as monstrous. Because the emotions are essentially evaluative, we do not merely pick up an interesting anthropological fact about human nature from *Sunset Boulevard*, but instead one that is saturated with value. The aversion we feel for Norma not only shapes our assessment of her while viewing the film, but by being so emotionally arresting embeds the philosophical lesson to be garnered from *Sunset Boulevard* more deeply in spectators than would any prosaic statement of its theme.

Popular philosophy aspires to educe philosophical insight from broad audiences. In this endeavor, the emotions are a natural ally inasmuch as they serve not only to guide cognition and appraisal, but also to make a deep impression. Thus, much of the complexity of narrative fictions like *Sunset Boulevard* – which skeptics dismiss as irrelevant to their putative philosophical mission – functions to induce the kind of emotional engagement from audiences that facilitates achieving philosophical understanding and making it one's own.

One aspect of this is the development of rather detailed narratives, which emphasize the particularity of the events and persons recounted. This is important since our minds, including our emotions, have been adaptively calibrated by evolution as mechanisms responsive to our immediate and concrete surroundings. That is why popular philosophy relies so heavily upon very individualized stories. Likewise, fictional narratives like *Sunset Boulevard* cast characters and events in ways designed to trigger preordained emotional responses, like the revulsion we feel toward Norma Desmond, not simply to entertain us by provoking an affective rush, but in order to lead us to appreciate the significance of the events depicted in the proper evaluative light and to assure that that insight sinks in.

To a large extent, fictional narratives engage audiences emotionally by what I call criterial prefocusing (Carroll 1997). That is, the visceral appraisals that we call emotions track certain features of situations, the supposed perception of which triggers the state in question. For example, fear is the response to the perception of danger. In this regard, perceived danger is a criterion for the state of fear; perceived wrong is a criterion for anger; and so on. Fictioneers exploit the criteria of the emotions they mean to provoke by describing or depicting the events and persons in their stories in terms that saliently stress the pertinent emotional criteria – for instance, the piety of Aeneas is repeatedly underlined in order to secure our admiration for him. In this way, the fictioneer, so to speak, has predigested the story for us. He has prefocused our attention so that, in the largest number of cases, audiences shift into the intended emotional state smoothly and reliably.

A great many of the complex structures found in countless narrative fictions, especially popular ones, involve the emotional address of the story. This is true not only of popular fictions in general but also of those that promote philosophical insight. As we have already seen, the use of the emotion of horror – as criterially prefocused in a number of ways, including Swanson's performance – is central to *Sunset Boulevard*. It not only shapes our aversive response to what Norma Desmond is attempting to do but does so in a manner that is deeply memorable, indeed indelible. It helps us see her error in a way we are unlikely to forget. Thus, that which the skeptic is tempted to regard as structures so elaborate that they call into question whether *Sunset Boulevard* is really doing philosophy turn out to be just the kinds of designs that can foster popular philosophy.

Summary

In recent years, there has been a mounting interest in the relation between narrative fictions, especially popular narrative fictions such as movies, and philosophy. Some philosophers have maintained that such narratives can contribute to philosophical insight, while others have rejected this hypothesis. In this essay, I have identified one narrative, *Sunset Boulevard*, which I believe has a fair claim to the mantle of philosophy, albeit popular philosophy. I have identified its major philosophical theme as an exploration of the denial of mortal aging and the existential costs that entails, as exemplified in the story of Norma Desmond. I have also examined three arguments that skeptics might level against my claims on behalf of *Sunset Boulevard*. These include what I have called the no-argument argument, the banality argument, and the excessive-elaboration argument. The no-argument argument fails because it ignores the audience's share in producing the philosophical insight available through *Sunset Boulevard*. The banality argument falters because it overlooks philosophy's role as a discloser of hidden truths, known but repressed. And lastly, the excessive-elaboration argument stumbles because it underestimates the role of emotional engagement in the dissemination of popular philosophy, perhaps due to drawing too sharp a distinction between cognitive content and emotional content, an error to which we academic philosophers are frequently prone.

Notes

1   In this essay, I am concentrating on the possibility of popular fictions doing popular philosophy – philosophy for the masses. In other essays, I have defended the broader claims that fictions can convey knowledge and that artworks, including literary and audiovisual ones, can engender fairly sophisticated theoretical and/or philosophical knowledge. See Carroll (2006: 173–85; 2009; 2010a; 2010b). It is not that I have abandoned these broader claims but rather that I want in this essay to examine more closely the relationship of popular narratives to popular philosophy.

2   It also won Academy Awards for art direction and musical score.

3   When Gillis refers to himself as a "ghostwriter," the phrase takes on a second meaning; a verbal reference to ghosts also pops up when Gillis speaks of the "ghost of a tennis court."

4   One measure of the power of this image is that nearly fifty-nine years after the release of the film, it can serve as the source of an allusion in the installation piece *The Collectors* by Elmgreen and Dragset at the 2009 Venice Biennale.

5   Indeed, the fish-eye view of Gillis's body suggests visually that he may be something's next meal.

6   Indeed, Swanson referred to herself as a "sacred monster" in her memoirs. See Swanson (1980: 444–5).

7   The theme of Norma as vampire is developed at length in Lucy Fisher's excellent article "*Sunset Boulevard*: Fading Stars" (Fisher 1988). I have benefited from the many insights in Dr Fisher's essay. The idea is also broached by Haskell (1974: 246).

8   Where emptiness is an index of Norma's being alone, abandoned by her audience.

9   Here I want to emphasize that *Sunset Boulevard* is an example of *substantive* popular philosophy – which is my way of saying that it philosophizes about life, in contrast to many contemporary popular movies, which, if they aspire to philosophy or theory at all, are more often advancing general insight into the workings of motion pictures. For instance, Jim Jarmusch's *Limits of Control* explores the genre of the spy thriller, barring its devices, by suppressing crucial information in a way that enables the viewer to discover many of its recurring strategies, whereas in *Inglourious Basterds* Quentin Tarantino uses hyperbole and (inglorious?) exaggeration to limn the conventions of the war movie and the western (in fact, Tarantino's movie is the bastard child of these two genres). In this respect, both of these films are descendants of Jean-Luc Godard's *Made in U.S.A.*, which employs these strategies and more to expose the rhetoric of Hollywood filmmaking. We can assume that his title refers to *movies made in the USA*.

10   Indeed, the original scene in the movie, later dropped, involved Gillis talking to other corpses in the LA morgue. See Sikov (1999: 293, 301).

11   Bazin (2005: 60). It might be interesting to speculate that it is perhaps due to this "embalming effect" that Norma has been deluded into believing that, as she says, stars are ageless, since she appears ageless in the silent films of herself that she watches over and over again.

12   Swanson was only fifty at the time the film was made; her acting – including the stiffness that makes her seem like a living corpse – makes her seem much older. And, in any event, in the 1950s American audiences would have been even more likely to be conditioned to regard a relation like Norma's and Gillis's as disgusting.

13   Wittgenstein (1958: 42e); Cavell (2005: 190). The notion that narrative may recover knowledge is also developed by Gibson (2007, esp. ch. 3).

14   Indeed, stars, by Norma's definition, turn out to be unnatural, inhuman, and monstrous just because they are ageless, like vampires.

15   There should be no question about whether stories – including thought experiments couched as stories – can lead audiences to conclusions abductively. Think of Aesopian fables and then recall that not all of Aesop's fables came with the morals tacked onto them.

16   Indeed, it has been suggested that the brain has subconscious subroutines designed precisely to inhibit thoughts of our own mortality. For how effective could we be if, like some character from a Woody Allen film, we were constantly stricken by thoughts of our own mortality? See Carey (2009: D1).

17   As Aaron Smuts reminded me, Gilgamesh, in the epic that bears his name, undergoes an utter mental collapse when he realizes that he will die. Myths, like philosophy, remind us of verities we might prefer to forget.

18   Perhaps at this point some philosophers, in the tradition of Plato, will argue that by enlisting our emotions, *Sunset Boulevard* shows itself to be clearly not of the party of philosophy. For philosophy has no truck with the emotions. However, I think this is false. For instance, the emotions come into play when we consult our intuitions when confronting various thought experiments and counterexamples in moral and political philosophy, since those intuitions are rooted in our sentiments with respect to fairness, justice, obligation, and so forth. Ethics is not the only area

of philosophy where emotions have a legitimate role, but inasmuch as there is this one arena – indeed, an arena often germane to popular philosophy – we need not yield to the skeptic's claim that emotion has no place in philosophy.

References

Bazin, André (2005) "Cinematic Realism." In Thomas Wartenberg and Angela Curran (eds.), *The Philosophy of Film*. Oxford: Wiley-Blackwell.

Becker, Ernest (1973) *The Denial of Death*. New York: Free Press.

Brackett, Charles, Billy Wilder, and D. M. Marshman (1999) *Sunset Boulevard*. Berkeley and Los Angeles: University of California Press.

Carey, Benedict (2009) "Why the Imp in Your Brain Gets Out." Science Times, *New York Times*, July 7, D1.

Carroll, Noël (1997) "Art, Narrative, and Emotion." In Mette Hjort and Sue Laver (eds.), *Emotion and the Arts*, 190–211. Oxford: Oxford University Press.

Carroll, Noël (2006) "Philosophizing Through the Moving Image: The Case of *Serene Velocity*." *Journal of Aesthetics and Art Criticism* 64(1): 173–85.

Carroll, Noël(2009) "*Memento* and the Phenomenology of Comprehending Motion Picture Narratives." In Andrew Kania (ed.), *Memento*. London: Routledge.

Carroll, Noël (2010a) "Literary Realism, Recognition, and the Communication of Knowledge." In *Art in Three Dimensions*. Oxford: Oxford University Press.

Carroll, Noël (2010b) "The Wheel of Virtue." In *Art in Three Dimensions*. Oxford: Oxford University Press.

Cavell, Stanley (in conversation with Andrew Klevan) (2005) "What Becomes of Thinking on Film?" In Rupert Read and Jerry Goodenough (eds.), *Film as Philosophy: Essays on Cinema After Wittgenstein and Cavell*, 167–209. London: Palgrave Macmillan.

Fisher, Lucy (1988) "Sunset Boulevard: Fading Stars." In Janet Todd (ed.), *Women and Film*, 97–113. New York: Holmes and Meier.

Gibson, John (2007) *Fiction and the Weave of Life*. Oxford: Oxford University Press.

Hadot, Pierre (2000) *What Is Ancient Philosophy?* Cambridge, MA.: Harvard University Press.

Hadot, Pierre (2009) *The Present Alone Is Our Happiness*. Stanford: Stanford University Press.

Haskell, Molly (1974) *From Reverence to Rape: The Treatment of Women in the Movies*. Baltimore: Penguin Books.

Heidegger, Martin (1962) *Being and Time*, trans. John Macquarrie and Edward Robinson. New York: Harper and Row.

Ionesco, Eugène (1967) *Exit the King*. In *Exit the King, The Killer, and Macbett: Three Plays by Eugène Ionesco*, trans. Charles Marowitz and Donald Watson. New York: Grove Press.

Kierkegaard, Søren (1954) *The Sickness unto Death*, trans. Walter Lowrie. Garden City, NY: Anchor Editions.

Kierkegaard, Søren (1957) *The Concept of Dread*, trans. Walter Lowrie. Princeton: Princeton University Press.

Kivy, Peter (1997) "The Laboratory of Fictional Truth." In *Philosophies of Art: An Essay in Differences*, 121–39. Cambridge: Cambridge University Press.

Russell, Bruce (2009) The Limits of Film Again. Author Meets Critics Session, American Society for Aesthetics, Annual Meeting of the Pacific Division, Asilomar, California, April 15–17.

Sikov, Ed (1999) *On Sunset Boulevard: The Life and Times of Billy Wilder*. New York: Hyperion.

Staggs, Sam (2000) *Close-up on Sunset Boulevard: Billy Wilder, Nora Desmond, and the Dark Hollywood Dream*. New York: St Martin's Press.

Swanson, Gloria (1980) *Swanson on Swanson*. New York: Random House.

Wittgenstein, Ludwig (1958) *Philosophical Investigations I*, trans. Elizabeth Anscombe. London: Basil Blackwell.

11

Vertigo and the Pathologies of Romantic Love

Vertigo by Alfred Hitchcock appears to be one of those films that could not sustain a second look. Once one has had the opportunity to reflect upon its plot machinations – once one gets free of the emotional undertow of the hot-wired ending – you would think that all of its incredible improbabilities would leap out, making a second viewing, if not impossible, then, at least, risible.

Isn't the plot within the plot just too absurd, practically speaking? Gavin Elster's scheme is so clever it's dumb. So many things could have gone wrong (and, if it wasn't a film, they would have).

For example, if John "Scottie" Ferguson is such a good detective, what's the likelihood that he would not, sooner or later, have discovered the real Mrs Elster in her home away from town? Wouldn't a smart investigator – and the film assures us that Scottie is smart – do enough background sleuthing and interviewing to realize that there are one too many Madeleine Elsters? And how can Elster be so sure that Scottie will flee the scene of the crime, thereby allowing him and Judy Barton to slip away? Would a murderer really rest the entire success of his plot on the likelihood that Scottie would be overtaken by vertigo on the stairway? What if Scottie didn't look down? And, in any event, recall that Scottie almost makes it to the very top. One more flight and the jig would have been up for Elster and Judy. Surely Elster's plan is implausibly risky; it is way too baroque.

Nor are there only problems with the crime plot. Almost as soon as the film ends, inquiring minds want to know how Scottie ever got off that rooftop

"*Vertigo* and the Pathologies of Romantic Love," in David Baggett and William A. Drumin (eds.), *Hitchcock, and Philosophy* (Chicago: Open Court, 2007), pp. 101–13.

after his first bout of vertigo. And, with respect to the second story, one wonders, if Scottie and "Madeleine" were intimate in the first part of the film, how then does he fail to recognize that Judy feels the same, has the same beauty marks, freckles, and blemishes, kisses the same, smells the same, and so on, the second time around? *The New Yorker* called the film "far-fetched."[1]

Perhaps on an initial viewing of *Vertigo*, the amazing serendipity of it all is masked by the affective velocity of the narrative. But surely upon a second encounter with *Vertigo*, most viewers should be emotionally sober enough to find almost laughable the frictionless clicking into place of the various parts of this Rube Goldberg plot. And yet we don't. Many keep coming back for more, regarding *Vertigo* as among Hitchcock's greatest accomplishments, if not his greatest. It cannot be the rickety thriller plot that accounts for this acclaim. What does?

My suggestion is that what viewers find so compelling about *Vertigo* is not the mystery story, which is so patently contrived, but the love story. For the love story – or, more accurately, the love stories – provide the audience with the opportunity to engage in a carefully structured meditation on the nature of romantic love. Specifically, *Vertigo* enables the viewer to discover certain of the pathologies to which romantic love is *naturally prone*, given the sort of process romantic love is. *Vertigo* deserves its reputation less as a masterpiece of suspense and more as a contribution to the philosophy of love.

Aristotle, philosophy, and drama

In his *Poetics*, Aristotle observes that "poetry [drama] is something more philosophic and graver than history, since its statements are rather of the nature of universals, whereas those of history are singulars. By a universal statement I mean one as to what such and such a kind of man will probably or necessarily say or do, which is the aim of poetry."[2] In other words, according to Aristotle, drama (including literature and, for us, the motion picture) is not constrained to portray precisely what actually happens in all its detail; drama streamlines events (or event-types), pruning them of distracting clutter, in a way that makes their recurring patterns salient. Just as an overhead map provides us with a more legible picture of the way to our destination than is evident on the ground, drama may provide us with a clearer view into the dynamics of human affairs than that available first-hand from messy reality.

Of course, drama is more concrete than philosophy. Undoubtedly, this is one of the reasons why it is more accessible than philosophy; it engages emotion and judgment with vivid particulars (which is exactly what our pragmatic human mentality is most suited to deal with). But a drama is, at the same time, a concrete *universal*. For, it still trades in abstractions – character-types, for example, like Iago, who clarify certain human personality tendencies by being designed in such a way that any features are omitted from the portrayal of the character that might deter us from seeing him squarely as the *kind* of person who revels in evil for its own sake. Such characters are the epitome or paradigm of the human potentials they exemplify. They are ideal types.

But poetry not only supplies us with an inventory of possible human personality types and the schematics of their underlying syndromes; it also sketches the kinds of behavioral scenarios that are likely to evolve when certain character-types interact – when, for instance, two headstrong people, like Antigone and Creon, each convinced of their own rectitude, find themselves on opposite sides of an issue. (It's not pretty.)

Aristotle thought that drama could help us understand potential or probable courses of human events by illustrating (as ideal types) the kinds of people there are or can be, as well as the patterns of behavior that are likely to take shape when those kinds of people interact. Scottie and Judy are types of the sort Aristotle had in mind. And *Vertigo* is an exploration of how things are likely to go when these two types attempt to negotiate a relationship.

Obviously, *Vertigo* is primarily a love story. Effectively, the crime provides a pretext for the courtships. The amount of screen time that is lavished on the two love affairs is far greater than that allotted to the murder and its solution. Though *Vertigo* is typically classified as a suspense film, it is more accurately thought of as a romance. But it is not just the time spent on the two affairs that marks *Vertigo* as a love story. It is also the peculiar intensity of the passions involved, especially as they are annotated by the lush, often sentimentally charged musical score by Bernard Hermann. Though Hitchcock is typically acknowledged to be the master of suspense, his range is much greater. He is also an astute observer of amorous obsession, as many of his other films, including *Notorious, The Paradine Case*, and *Marnie*, attest. *Vertigo*, quite simply, is his most impressive treatment of the subject of the darker side of love.

Earlier it was alleged that *Vertigo* is a contribution to the philosophy of love. But how, it might be asked (in a skeptical tone of voice), can a narrative movie like this one contribute to the philosophy of anything? No generalizations are propounded and, in any event, even had they been uttered, without accompanying argumentation, some would maintain that they would scarcely count as genuine philosophy. And yet, in virtue of its structure, *Vertigo* is able to engage its audiences in thinking about love and to guide them forcefully to certain insights regarding its nature, including, most significantly, its inherent fault lines.

Vertigo does not stage this meditation outright after the fashion of a René Descartes. Rather, it presents the audience with a structure that elegantly prompts the viewer to think about love in both its brighter and its darker aspects. That structure, of course, is the "double" romance: the first putatively between Scottie and Madeleine, and then the ostensibly different one between Scottie and Judy Barton. By juxtaposing these two affairs sequentially, the film invites – even nudges – viewers to compare and contrast them. Though, perhaps needless to say, our assessment in this matter must be revisited by the conclusion of the film, nevertheless, as the film begins to unfold, we are introduced to something that at least initially appears to us as akin to a normal love relationship, which then we can later use to locate what is going horribly awry when Scottie meets Judy.

That is, by means of the parallel romances, *Vertigo* enlists the viewer as a co-creator in an analysis of love and its predictable malaises. The analysis of romantic love is not articulated in the film by a character nor announced from on high by a voice-over narrator. Rather the film presents us with two love stories whose convergences and divergences are so entwined that it is hard to imagine a thoughtful viewer who does not take up the invitation to compare and contrast the two scenarios for the purpose of making note of what is healthy and unwholesome about them.

The analysis of love and its pathologies available from *Vertigo* is worked out in the mind of the viewer. *Vertigo* neither performs the analysis itself nor does it offer any evidence for its conception of love. Rather, *Vertigo* maieutically draws the evidence and reasoning that supports its philosophy of love from the viewers, as Socrates educes geometry from the slave in the *Meno*. (The word "maieutic" comes from the Greek and pertains to the action of a midwife drawing an infant from the mother's body during birth. The word is also traditionally used to refer metaphorically to the process by which Socrates prompts insights from his interlocutors, such as Meno, who, by using their own resources, answer the questions and problems Socrates poses for them to solve.)

In *Vertigo*, the parallel-romance structure functions in a way comparable to a rhetorical or leading question. It elicits conclusions by recruiting the ratiocination and the standing beliefs of the audience to do the pertinent work of reasoning and analysis.

Love and fantasy

What is perhaps most striking to us about these parallel cases is that what is pathological in the second affair is also something that is present as a natural ingredient in the first affair, namely, fantasy. What *Vertigo* succeeds in illustrating so compellingly is that a natural, facilitating component of romantic love can also be the very thing that derails it. Fantasy can be the glue that cements lovers together or that which destroys the very possibility of genuine love.

Although it may strike you as fairly obvious that fantasy – such as Scottie's projection of his memory of Madeleine onto Judy – is a recipe for romantic disaster, it may seem bizarre to claim that fantasy has a rightful place in normal love. And yet it does in several different registers.[3] Most obviously, sexual fantasies energize the onset of infatuation and keep it going. Indeed, sexual fantasizing persists throughout most enduring love relationships.

But romantic love involves more than sexual fantasy. In the early stages of infatuation, whenever apart, the lovers dream of being back together again. Falling in love is essentially future-orientated; it involves the counterfactual anticipation of spending more time with the beloved and eventually of imagining a life together. So, romantic love is born in fantasy.

And once love blossoms, each lover must mobilize the imagination in order to picture what it is that will win the heart of the beloved and then he or she proceeds to act in accordance with that image. Courtship typically requires role playing from both parties. They must envision what will count as their "best behavior" in the eyes of their partner and then enact it. It is a matter of mutually reinforcing seduction in which both lovers imaginatively transform themselves – generally by expanding upon qualities they already presently possess or that are potentially readily within their reach. It is rare that a successful romantic relationship flourishes where the participants do not try – at least to some degree – to stoke the fantasies of each other.

Moreover, romantic love requires as a condition for its very existence a certain feat of imagination – that the lovers transcend their conception of themselves as absolutely discrete individuals and imagine themselves as one; that each of the lovers takes the interest of the beloved's to be his or her own. This involves an essential transformation of one's conception of oneself, a transformation that in large part requires going beyond what is factually given. The lovers must imagine that they are literally two parts of a larger whole.

But this is not the end of it. For, fantasy is also what enables the lovers to grow, both as a couple and as individuals. A feature of love, identified by writers like Stendhal, is the tendency of lovers to idealize the beloved.[4] Within bounds, this sort of fantasy is a very good thing. For, it encourages the beloved to live up to the idealization of the significant other. This is what the ancient Greeks, like Aristotle, thought was a virtue of certain forms of male-to-male love. The love of a virtuous partner provides an incentive to improve – to make oneself as attractive in every way as the beloved imagines one can be. Thus, if everything goes right in this process of mutual idealization, not only is each member of the couple enhanced, but the couple itself becomes something larger and greater.

Falling in love

As we first start following the budding relationship between Scottie and the woman we suppose to be Madeleine Elster, we are led to believe that, though "Madeleine" is troubled, the ensuing romance is a normal one – at least by

Hollywood standards. Fantasy, of what initially appears to be the benign sort, seems clearly at work. It is undoubtedly a mark of Hitchcock's genius that he is in large measure able to communicate this cinematically.

Idealization comes into play when Scottie first encounters "Madeleine" at Ernie's restaurant. Hitchcock has the actress Kim Novak, in profile, freeze in a portrait-like pose for Scottie's first close-up glimpse of her. Remember that this is Scottie's subjective point of view. To him, she appears to have the perfection of a work of art. Throughout the portion of the film where he is following her, he observes her sitting still, composed as if a statue (his Galatea). And she is expressly compared to a painting, namely the one of Carlotta Valdes. Seen from Scottie's perspective, "Madeleine" strikes us visually as a human artwork. This is one way that Hitchcock conveys that Scottie is coming to idealize her.

In one of the most famous moments early in the film, Scottie follows "Madeleine" into the somewhat drab, rear entrance of a building. When he peeks through the door that she has just closed behind her, there is a wondrous burst of color. She is in a florist's shop and there are bright flowers everywhere. The contrast with the muted palette in previous shots is striking. One feels that one has just been introduced to a new realm. What has been saliently marked is the exfoliation of Scottie's fantasy. The pronounced color, like that of the land of the Wizard of Oz, in the film of the same name, suggests that we are within Scottie's mind, privy to his subjectivity.

Hitchcock also conveys the feeling of fantasy by the way in which he orchestrates the sequences of Scottie tailing the fake Madeleine. The very activity of trailing someone is itself virtually obsessional. But, in addition, the gliding camera, the gliding cars, the absence of street noise, the rhythmic music, punctuated by silence, and the regular alternation of Scottie's point-of-view shots with long shots of "Madeleine's" car are mesmerizing, almost hypnotic. It is as if we are inside a trance. Indeed, the use of lighting, including mist, and color throughout give the film a dreamlike texture, where the trance and the dream, of course, belong, first and foremost, to Scottie.

After "Madeleine's" "attempted" suicide, the two speak and they begin to weave what seems to be a lovers' web of mutual fantasy. Scottie comes to regard "Madeleine's" welfare as his own. He begins to play the role of her "knight in shining armor."[5] He reaches beyond himself and becomes her designated "rescuer."[6] And "Madeleine's" mysteriously phrased, parting words to Scottie rehearse a lover's counterfactual wish for a future together; she says "I loved you and I wanted to go on loving you."

If fantasy appears to be a natural and even healthy part of romance as *Vertigo's* first love story unfolds, it is precisely what wrecks the second love affair. After Scottie is released from the hospital where he was treated for a mental breakdown following the death of Madeleine Elster, Scottie begins revisiting the places where he first encountered her. Standing outside the florist shop mentioned earlier, he chances to see Judy, a woman who despite her dark hair and somewhat vulgar demeanor bears a resemblance to the very blonde, regal "Mrs Elster." At this point in the film, neither Scottie nor the audience is aware that the reason for the similarity is that this *is* the woman Scottie fell in love with earlier. She was hired by the husband of the real Madeleine Elster to impersonate his wife in the elaborate murder plot alluded to previously.

Scottie follows Judy to her apartment and begins to woo her. He invites her to dinner. Despite the risk of being discovered as an accomplice to murder, Judy agrees to go out with Scottie. As she confesses in a letter she never gives to him, "I made the mistake of falling in love with you" and "I want you so to love me ... as I am myself." They have dinner – at Ernie's, of course. We know, as does Judy, that Scottie is still obsessed with "Madeleine," since we observe the way that his attention fastens upon a blonde woman in a grey suit who, from afar, vaguely resembles the alleged Mrs Elster.

Scottie wants to see Judy again. "I want to be with you as much as I can, Judy," he says to her as she sits in her apartment – a darkened silhouette (recalling his first close-up glimpse of "Madeleine"). At first, their love affair goes smoothly. They appear very happy simply being with each other – sight-seeing, strolling along a canal, and dancing together. He buys her flowers on the street.

But Scottie insists on buying Judy clothes. He describes with utter precision the kind of gray suit he is looking for to the manager at a fashionable women's clothing store. Needless to say, it is the kind of suit that "Madeleine" wore. Scottie's voice quavers with mounting frustration as he rejects outfit after outfit, until the one he wants is finally identified. It is an emotionally harrowing scene. Scottie's obsession is tangible. He reduces Judy to tears. She pleads "Couldn't you like me just the way I am?" but caves in to his will: "Well I'll wear the darn clothes, if you want me to, if you'll just like me." He also orders an evening dress, just like "Madeleine's," and wants it altered immediately.

His fixation does not abate with clothing; he wants Judy's hair dyed and coiffed like "Madeleine's," as well. Judy agrees conditionally: "If I let you change me, will it do it, if I do what you tell me, will you love me?"[7] In a final attempt at resistance, Judy does not pin her hair up as Madeleine did, but Scottie won't stop pleading. Judy relents and when she steps out of the bathroom, she looks exactly as she did when she feigned being Madeleine Elster. Hitchcock illuminates her in such a way that as she walks out of an overexposed patch of the image into an evenly lit portion she looks like a ghost being incarnated in flesh – an illusion coming to life.

At this point and in short order, the crime plot takes over again. Scottie figures out that Judy was the woman he thought was Mrs Elster and that she conspired with Mr Elster, who may have been Judy's lover, in the phony suicide. Scottie drags Judy to the scene of the crime – a bell tower in an old mission – where he wraps up the whodunit part of the story. The truth ruins their relationship, and, to make matters worse, Judy, "spooked" by a curious nun she appears to take to be Mrs Elster's ghost, falls to her death from the campanella.[8]

The second love story is far more compelling and even scarier than the crime story. As Scottie seeks to remake Judy in Madeleine's image, one can virtually sense that what he is doing is deeply wrong. It is antithetical to true love, because it involves a denial of the uniqueness and particularity of the beloved. A lover is not a type. That is why one's lover is always strictly irreplaceable. In refusing to see Judy in terms of who she actually is, Scottie turns their relationship into a perversion of love, in spite of the fact that Judy repeatedly and pointedly begs him to love her as she is.

Earlier, it was asserted that healthy love involves a degree of fantasy in the form of idealization. So the question here is: what is the difference between the sort of legitimate romantic fantasy we've called idealization and what Scottie is doing? Idealization, when it is healthy and productive, has a basis in reality – a basis in the real potential of the beloved. It acknowledges who the beloved is and values that, rather than treating the beloved as an instrument in the service of one's own needs. Scottie, in projecting his image of Madeleine on Judy, is blind to who Judy really is.

Though there is a fine line between these operations of fantasy, idealization in the good sense builds upon what can already be found either actually or potentially in the beloved. It enhances – but in a way that remains tied to reality – our view of our significant other. But the sort of fantasy that drives Scottie is blinding. He refuses to see Judy for who she is, despite her repeated appeals. Such a relationship is doomed. Perhaps we can interpret the violent ending of the film allegorically as the objective correlative of the destructive violence Scottie's fantasy has wreaked upon their love affair.

When Henry Higgins transforms Eliza Doolittle in *My Fair Lady*, one has the feeling that he is bringing out the best in her.[9] But Scottie is imposing something on Judy that she is not. He is more of a tyrant than a lover, and the palpable cruelty of what he is doing is constantly underscored by her recurring pleas that he love her as she is.[10] Unfortunately, Judy, though she understands too well that there is something profoundly flawed in her relationship with Scottie, cannot resist him. She becomes an enabler, facilitating the projective fantasy with which Scottie burdens her. She is thus participating in her own spiritual death as an individual with a claim to be loved for herself – a plight perhaps symbolized by her literal fall from the tower. Whereas "Madeleine Elster" was reputedly possessed by Carlotta in the first part of the film, Judy Barton is possessed by Scottie in the second part.[11]

Of course, the revelation of the murder plot impels us to reconsider the meaning of the first love story. Seen in retrospect, the theme of fantasy is even more evident, since Scottie is literally caught in an illusion fabricated by Gavin Elster and enacted by Judy. Ironically, Judy becomes her own worst rival by seducing Scottie so magnificently in the guise of Madeleine; her imaginative performance as Madeleine abets Scottie's creation of the distorting idealization that will foreclose the possibility of any lasting amorous relationship between them. For, the combination of an enabler like Madeleine/Judy and a projective fantasist like Scottie is as toxic as the relationship between an Antigone and a Creon – in both cases, catastrophe seems unavoidable when personality types like these come in contact.

Scottie seems to represent an especially unstable personality type. Through Midge, we derive the impression that he is wary of commitment. When he tells her that he is "still available," the look on Midge's face indicates disbelief, as though she thinks that he is deceiving himself. Scottie's vertigo, symbolically, may be a literalization of the notion that he is afraid of *falling in love*. And this anxiety, in turn, may help explain why he is prone to the kind of pathological projection that he inflicts upon Judy. It is his fear of engaging with another individual that prompts him to confect a surrogate fantasy in her stead. His "Pygmalion-complex" is a defense mechanism, a syndrome fending off romantic vertigo.[12]

If Scottie's behavior grows out of a resistance to love, Judy's self-destructive complicity with his fantasy arises from her need to be loved. But this is no way for her to realize her own hopes and desires, for it will not result in Scottie's loving *her*. So, to a certain extent, she is as delusional as he is.

Vertigo presents us with two recognizable character types. Let us call them the projector (the projective fantasist) and the enabler. And the film goes on to sketch with great clarity the predictable scenario that is apt to evolve when these two types come together and fuel each other's worst tendencies. Admittedly, the pathologies Scottie and Judy exemplify are pitched larger than life. They are far more perspicuous than the instances of these syndromes that one is likely to experience in the daily run of events. But it is a major function of drama to magnify and thereby clarify the patterns that shape human affairs, in order that we may be prepared to discern such regularities when they appear less diagrammatically in the flesh.

Knots

Drama, including cine-drama, has the power to reveal the probable patterns of human affairs that eventuate when certain character-types interact. Such drama is a kind of chemistry of the human heart that discloses which combinations of personalities are likely to be stable patterns and which are apt to be unstable patterns. Some of these patterns may take, among other things, the form of what the psychiatrist R. D. Laing called "knots" – situations where motives become so tangled that acting on them brings, through an almost inexorable albeit "crazy" logic, exactly the opposite result than the one you had hoped for.[13] That is precisely the sort of trap in which the enabler Judy has enmeshed herself by loving a projective fantasist such as Scottie. Moreover, it is a large part of the achievement of *Vertigo* that it is able to show us how this kind of knot – with its inevitably self-defeating "logic" – can be tied so neatly.

Undoubtedly there are readers who may argue that I have exaggerated *Vertigo's* contribution to the theory of love. Surely, some philosophers will say, the ill-suitedness of an enabler to a projector is no great discovery at all. Isn't it common knowledge?

Three things need to be said in response to this. First, when *Vertigo* premiered, we – especially the *we* of the general public – were far less sophisticated about the nature of love than we think we are now. Perhaps some or even many of us possess the understanding of certain aspects of love that *Vertigo* proffers because we have seen *Vertigo*. Second: philosophizing-through-the-movies is for the general public and not for the graduate seminar room of the research university. So *Vertigo* may in fact still be philosophically revelatory for its target audience. For, lastly, *Vertigo* may assist them in clarifying an insight into the ways of romantic love of which they were only dimly aware, if at all. That is, by means of *Vertigo*, Hitchcock lucidly demonstrates how fantasy, a natural part of romantic love, can become pathologically distorted by certain personality types to the point that love is destroyed.[14]

Notes

1   See the liner notes to *Vertigo: The Collector's Edition* from *The Alfred Hitchcock DVD Collection* (Universal City: Universal, 1996).

2   Aristotle, "Dramatic Imitation: From the *Poetics*," in George Dickie, Richard Sclafani, and Ronald Roblin (eds.), *Aesthetics: A Critical Anthology* (New York: St Martins Press, 1977), p. 214.

3   For an account of the role of fantasy in romantic love, see Robert Solomon, *About Love: Reinventing Romance for Our Times* (Lanham: Rowman and Littlefield, 1994), pp. 153–60.

4   Stendhal, *Love* (London: Penguin, 1975).

5   Minus Jung's commitment to archetypical men and women (the animus and the anima), the following quotation could serve as a partial summary of *Vertigo*: "Just as the animus projection of a woman can often pick on a man of real significance who is not recognized by the mass, and can actually help him to achieve his true destiny with her moral support, so a man can create for himself a *femme inspiratrice* by his anima projection. But more often it turns out to be an illusion with destructive consequences." See Carl Jung, "Marriage as a Psychological

Relationship," in Robert Solomon and Kathleen Higgins (eds.), *The Philosophy of (Erotic) Love* (Lawrence: University of Kansas Press, 1994), p. 187.

6   In the first half of the film, Scottie is led to believe that "Madeleine" is confused, often lost, helpless, and virtually without agency. He must take over. In a way, though with opposite effect, he acts in the same manner with the same beliefs with respect to Judy. He treats her as though she were without agency.

7   See Charles Barr, *Vertigo* (London: British Film Institute, 2002), p. 71.

8   Their relationship has been destroyed by the "ghost of Madeleine Elster."

9   Henry Higgins is working on behalf of Eliza's interests, if rather roughly, and Eliza knows it. Scottie, in a way that is inimical to genuine love, does not incorporate Judy's interests as his own (nor does he even seem to acknowledge that she has autonomous interests) and she, moreover, is in denial regarding Scottie's behavior.

10 In *The Second Sex* (New York: Knopf, 1952), Simone de Beauvoir discusses the ways in which the idealization of the husband by the wife can turn into a form of persecution for the former. In *Vertigo*, the man's idealization of the woman leads to her persecution.

11 One might argue that it is Gavin Elster who really "possesses" Judy in the first part of the film. For, not only is she probably a kept woman, but he takes/makes over her identity as well.

12 The expression "falling in love" suggests a loss of control. Scottie's romantic vertigo impels him to re-exert utter control over Judy by transforming her in accordance with his fantasy. See: Garrett Soden, *Falling: How Our Greatest Fear Became Our Greatest Thrill* (New York: Norton, 2003), p. 15. There is some evidence that those who literally fear falling are often averse to risks in other domains of life, including, perhaps, love. Fear of falling and fear of falling in love, that is, may in some cases be actually connected.

13 R. D. Laing, *Knots* (New York: Vintage, 1970).

14 I am not the only commentator to recognize *Vertigo* as an exploration of the ways in which the mechanisms of romantic idealization can lead to the denial of the otherness, the interests, and the autonomy of the putative love object. For a related, though more psychoanalytically inclined account, see Robin Wood, *Hitchcock's Films Revisited* (New York: Columbia University Press, 1989), p. 385 and also Barr, *Vertigo*, p. 78.

12

What Mr Creosote Knows about Laughter

And by his side rode loathsome Gluttony,
Deformed creature, on a filthie swyne:
His belly was up-blown with luxury,
And eke with fatnesse swollen were his eyne,
And like a Crane his necke was long and fyne,
With which he swallowed up excessive feast,
For want whereof poore people oft did pyne;
And all the way, most like a brutish bear,
He spued up his gorge, that all did him deteast.
…
In shape and life more like a monster, than a man.
Edmund Spenser, *The Faerie Queene*

Part VI: "The Autumn Years" of *Monty Python's The Meaning of Life* begins with a song about the glories of having a penis which is appreciated by all the audience in the cabaret, including the talking fish in an aquarium in the vicinity of the piano. The fish have the human faces of the Monty Python crew superimposed over their bodies and they call to mind something of the unsettling hybrid creatures found on hellish landscapes by Hieronymus Bosch, the fifteenth- and sixteenth-century Dutch artist. Their enjoyment of the ditty, however, quickly vanishes when they catch sight of the entrance of Mr Creosote into the restaurant. "Oh shit!" cries one of them as they whiz off-screen.

"What Mr Creosote Knows about Laughter," in Gary L. Hardcastle and George A. Reisch (eds.), *Monty Python and Philosophy* (Chicago: Open Court, 2006), pp. 25–35.

Minerva's Night Out: Philosophy, Pop Culture, and Moving Pictures, First Edition. Noël Carroll.
© 2013 Blackwell Publishing Ltd. Published 2013 by Blackwell Publishing Ltd.

Mr Creosote, a gargantuan figure, lumbers into the dining room. The music that accompanies his entry recalls the giant shark's in *Jaws*, and his belly is so ponderous it nearly scrapes the floor. His face, framed by muttonchops, is swollen to the point of swinishness. He is dressed in a tuxedo but his body is mis-shapen, more like a pyramid of wobbling flesh than a human form. As Creosote ambles to his table, he commands a flurry of attention from the sycophantic maitre d'. This is obviously a very, very good customer, one who could eat whole families under the exceedingly expensive tables of this lavish eatery.

Creosote is also a very churlish customer. He is consistently curt to the point of rudeness. When asked how he is faring, he says "Better" and pauses before completing his thought – "Better get a bucket." In other words, he never responds civilly, but only commands imperiously. When the aforesaid bucket is brought to him, he proceeds to vomit into it with the force of a fire hose in complete obliviousness to his surroundings and to the sensibilities of his fellow diners. He doesn't do this once but several times and then repeats the spectacle on the back of the cleaning woman who is trying to clean up the mess he is making. He shows no concern for anyone else; his inclinations are the only lights by which he steers. In every way, Creosote is crude, gruff, and utterly selfish.

Thus, his vomiting elicits no sympathy. He treats it as his privilege; he's paying for it; so he'll do whatever he wants. Creosote clearly, as a matter of course, stuffs himself to the point that his body cannot absorb the mass he ingests. He retches in order to gorge himself again. He is gluttony personified.

The maitre d' hands him a menu; he disgorges himself all over it. The servant has to wipe it off so that he can read it. Moreover, it should be added, this vomit looks pretty convincing. Even the most ardent Python fan is apt to feel a twinge of nausea coming on.

Hearing the specials, all delicacies of a diversity befitting the original Gargantua, Creosote orders the lot, mixed into a bucket with eggs on top, along with a double portion of *pâté*, six bottles of wine, two magnums of champagne and perhaps some ale. Pope Gregory the Great defined gluttony as eating too soon, too delicately, too expensively, too greedily, and too much. Creosote's nausea indicates he is not ready for his next meal; it is too soon. He eats expensive delicacies as if they were potato chips. And he eats too much; he eats the entire menu. It is no wonder that Michael Palin called this routine a "Gothic Extravaganza."[1] It is like an illustration of one of the Deadly Sins.

Creosote, reminding one of an image out of James Ensor, the nineteenth–twentieth-century Belgian expressionist, continues to vomit as he eats. Other customers are disgusted and start leaving to the visible chagrin of the maitre d'; some are heaving themselves. The maitre d' accidentally steps into Creosote's pail of vomit and Creosote erupts upon his leg, to the evident great annoyance of the maitre d'. The maitre d' is reaching the end of his tether. Finally, Creosote is finished, but the maitre d' willfully tempts him, even prods him, to take one more bite, just a bit of a thin wafer of mint, despite the fact that Creosote protests that he is absolutely full.

Almost immediately, that slice of mint does its vengeful work. Creosote literally explodes, issuing forth a tidal wave of vomit that splashes every comer of the dining room. In the center of this dripping mess, then, sits Creosote, his belly blown open so that one can see his rib cage; but his red, fist-like heart relentlessly continues pumping as it dangles under his chin. His eyes are open, his face still carrying that mask of impassive brutishness he has worn throughout the scene. The maitre d', overjoyed and very self-satisfied by the success of his revenge plot, gives Creosote the check.

To laugh, or to scream?

This scene, involving non-stop nausea and a graphically exploded body, sounds more horrific than comic. It, like so much of the humor of Monty Python, is on the dark side. The scene has few peers in the annals of motion picture comedy, save perhaps the pie-eating sequence in *Stand By Me*. But even that seems tame next to the spectacle of Mr Creosote's extravasation. The philosophical question it raises is: how is it possible to laugh at humor as black as this? Though it may seem paradoxical that mirth could issue from depicting a situation so gruesome and disgusting, perhaps this will not strike us as so strange when we recall how much humor – such as bathroom humor – revels in the repulsive. And yet there is nevertheless something perplexing about this scene. How can the gag function as a source of comic amusement for so many, rather than leaving them trembling in horror? Why is the sequence comic rather than horrific? This seems paradoxical. Since negotiating para-doxes is one of the charges of philosophy, answering that question is the aim of this chapter. And in the process, we wish to learn what Mr Creosote can teach us about laughter.

Let us agree from the outset that many people laugh at this scene; they find it comically amusing. This is not to deny that some also find it disgusting, and even unwatchable. And even those who enjoy the routine may experience moments during it when their stomach feels on the verge of revolting. Nevertheless, there are a significant number of people who find the scene on balance risible, and even continuously so – that is, they laugh all the way through. Our question is, How can they do so? How can anyone find the explosion of a human body to be comically amusing? If anything, the prospect is horrifying.

One way to make some headway with this problem is to think about what makes for horror, especially in mass culture.[2] In popular fictions, including literature and motion pictures, horror is typically focused upon a particular sort of object, namely, a monster – that is, a creature whose existence is unacknowledged by science and who, in addition, is dangerous and disgusting. For example, the Frankenstein monster is a scientific impossibility – electrifying dead flesh will fry it, not animate it – and the monster is disgusting, an impure being constructed of rotting, dismembered body parts. And perhaps most obviously, the monster is dangerous: it kidnaps, maims, and kills people.

Maybe we are tempted to think of the restaurant vomiting scene as horror rather than comedy because Creosote, it would appear, shares many of the attributes that characterize horror. For example, I expect that he is a physiological impossibility; even supposing that someone could reach his girth, it is unlikely that he would be able to move on his own power. Creosote is of a scale of obesity where the patient usually has to be moved by handlers. But Creosote is also beyond the ken of science, both in the manner of his explosion and, then, of his survival. People don't burst like that, balloons do; and if they did, they would not live to tell the tale. But one suspects that Creosote will have himself sewn up again in order to eat another day.

Moreover, Creosote, like Frankenstein's monster, is certainly disgusting. In the first instance, his behavior is disgusting. His constant vomiting presents a challenge to the strongest stomach. I think that were it not the case that film is odorless – that, thankfully, smell-o-rama has not yet been perfected – many viewers would be unable to hold onto their own dinners throughout this episode. Indeed, Creosote's name suggests a foul odor, inasmuch as it labels a colorless liquid, a pungent burning agent, that smells of smoked meat and tar. Creosote's incontinence, furthermore, functions metonymically in the same way in which the rats, spiders, and other vermin that inhabit the vampire's lair function – namely, as disgusting things designed to accentuate the abominableness of the thing to which they are attached or which they surround.

But it is not only what is connected to Creosote that is disgusting. Creosote himself is loathsome, an abomination. Undoubtedly, he is the sort of thing we call monstrous in ordinary language. Like the Frankenstein monster or the creatures in the *Alien* and *Predator* series, Creosote is physically repulsive. The thought of being hugged by Creosote is probably enough to make most of us squirm; and imagine what visualizing a kiss on the lips from him might do to your digestion. Once again, like the Frankenstein monster, the Alien, and the Predator, there is something viscerally revolting, unclean, and impure about Creosote.

It's the impurity of the monster in horror fictions that elicits the response of disgust from audiences. This impurity, in turn, is rooted in the ontology, or being, of horrific creatures. Such creatures are violations or problematizations of our standing cultural categories. For that reason they are abominations possessing a combination or collection of properties that our culture trains us to revile on contact. For instance, the Frankenstein monster violates the categorical distinction between life and death. It is both. It is a walking contradiction, as is Chucky, the puppet that kills, from the film *Child's Play*. The

Predator, a category violation if there ever was one, is part crab and part primate. The Blob defies our categories by not fitting into any of them; it is stuff out of control. The Amazing Colossal Man is horrifically repulsive because he is too colossal; he violates the criteria of what it is to be human in virtue of his scale. Creosote likewise is monstrous just because his figure seems to go beyond not only what is normal but even beyond what is humanly possible. He is a travesty of the human form; he is an affront to our norms of the human form. He strikes us as inhuman or nonhuman. But as a result of effectively claiming membership in that category – that is, in our species – he triggers an aversive response on our part.

Who's afraid of Mr Creosote?

Creosote is a monster and he incurs our disgust. So far the horror formula is realized. But two points need to be made. First, disgust, including disgust elicited by the violation of our standing norms and categories, does not belong solely to the domain of the genre of horror. It is, as noted earlier, also a natural ingredient of comedy. This, of course, should be extremely evident. Think of how much humor, especially juvenile humor, hinges on celebrating disgusting things – farts, feces, and slime. Insofar as mention of these things, which are themselves categorically interstitial (ambiguously both part of me and outside of me), is also a violation of the norms of propriety, they are staples of humor. Disgust, that is, belongs as much to comedy as to horror. But in order for a categorical violation to turn into an occasion for horror, something else must be added, namely, fear. So the second point to be addressed is whether the fear-condition for the elicitation of horror has been met in the Creosote sequence. For if it has not been, then we can start to explain why the Creosote scene is comic rather than horrific.

In horror fictions, the monster is fearsome and disgusting because it is dangerous and impure. Standardly, the monster in a horror fiction is not threatening to the audience. They know that they are encountering a fiction and that they can suffer no harm from the creatures that rule the page and the screen. Rather they feel fear for the humans in the fiction who are being stalked or otherwise imperiled by the monsters. Insofar as we feel concern for the plight of those fictional characters – that is, insofar as we anticipate that harm will befall them at the hands, talons, or other instruments of the monsters – the fear condition of the horror formula is activated.

However, when we turn to the scene with Mr Creosote, there is no fear factor. We do not fear for the other customers in the restaurant. They are in no great danger from Mr Creosote. They are unquestionably offended by him. This may garner some sympathy for them (or, it may not, if you regard them as insufferable swells deserving of being taken down a peg).

Yet it will not elicit fear on their behalf, since they are in no grievous danger, bodily or otherwise.

But perhaps Creosote is the human who should elicit our concern. After all, he's a person (ain't he got some rights?), and he does explode. And he is harmed by the machinations of the maitre d'. However, here Creosote shows us something about how comedy works. Creosote is not quite human. Not only is he too outsized. But he is utterly impervious to his repeated bouts of nausea – what human can take fits of retching in his stride the way Creosote does? – and he, of course, survives the massive explosion of his belly. In this, Creosote not only resembles the monster of horror fictions. He also resembles that staple of slapstick comedy, the clown.

The clown is not exactly human. With respect of our norms for the average human, the clown is either too fat or too tall, too thin or too short. His mouth is painted to appear exaggeratedly large and his eyes and head are often too small. He is a misproportioned human. Nor are his cognitive skills near the norm; generally he is too stupid. And his body can also take abuse that no actual person could. He can be hit on the head with a sledge hammer and suffer no more than a dizzy swoon where the rest of us would be hospitalized with a concussion. He takes falls with abandon and always pops up for another slam. It is as if his bones were made of rubber. Instead of breaking, they snap back into place.

It's because the clown is marked as so ontologically different from us – especially in terms of his imperviousness to bodily harm – that we have no fear for his life and limb. We can laugh at the way in which his body with its incongruities taunts our concept of the human, because the mayhem the clown engages is nonthreatening. We need not fear for the clown; nor, in the standard case, need we fear clowns. They are, for the most part, benign. Thus, though monstrous, clowns and the other denizens of slapstick incur no horror, since no genuine harm will result in or from their shenanigans.

Mr Creosote belongs to the same fantastic species as the clown. He is not precisely human, so we do not fear for him as we do for the characters in horror fictions. He is able to suffer through things that would incapacitate or destroy ordinary mortals, because he is marked as of a different ontological order. Because Creosote can neither harm nor can he be harmed, his monstrosity becomes an occasion for comic amusement rather than horror. This is one thing that Mr Creosote shows us about laughter.

It has been established experimentally that children will laugh when confronted with something incongruous – like a "funny face" – if the face is offered by someone with whom they are familiar, but they will cringe if it is presented by a stranger. This suggests that our responses to incongruities, anomalies, unexpected deviations from norms and standing categories will vary in terms of certain conditions. If the incongruity occurs in a context where it is threatening, it will dispose us toward a fearful response. This is perhaps the origin of the horror genre. On the other hand, if the context is one that is marked as non-threatening – where the prospect of harm and danger has been subtracted – the circumstances are ripe for comedy. The Mr Creosote scene illustrates this principle dramatically by getting as perilously close to the conditions that satisfy the horrific, but remaining on the side of amusement. In this it exemplifies a principle that makes much cruel humor possible: we need not fear for the victims of all the violence and malevolence done in darker shades of comedy, including slapstick, because they are not completely human. Punch and Judy can be beaten mercilessly but they will never come within an inch of their lives. Mr Creosote never suffers or dies. He is not precisely our kind of creature. Thus, we may laugh at him.

Just desserts

But this is not all that Mr Creosote tells us about laughter. It's true that in order to find a routine like his comically amusing we must not fear for him. And we do not, since he is not subject to human vulnerability. Instead we focus on his monstrous incongruity, his absurdity. But it's not just that we do not feel concern about Creosote because we know he cannot be harmed. We also are encouraged to form a positive animus against Creosote. We do not just laugh at the ontological incongruity of Creosote and what befalls him. Part of our laughter, even if it is not pure comic laughter, originates in our sense that Creosote gets what he deserves. Part of our laughter is vindictive or, at least, retributive. What has happened to Creosote, or so we are invited to suppose, is just. Though Creosote is not completely human, he is human enough to engender our scorn morally and to merit punishment. Moreover, we cannot help but think that his punishment fits his crime ever so appropriately. Think of how often we describe the aftermath of our own gluttonous escapades in terms of a feeling that we are about to explode. Creosote gets his just desserts, one might say. On the one hand, Creosote is a despicable character. He treats others with contempt, presumably because he thinks his evident wealth entitles him to do so. He spits upon servants with no sense of shame; they are beneath his selfish concern. He has no inkling of decorum and is insensitive to the existence of other people and their rightful claims. He is an egoist of stupendous proportions. And, of course, he has abused himself immensely. His vast bulk appears to be his own fault. It is the height of self-indulgence to eat so far past the point of satiation that one continues to press on while one is still egesting the surplus of one's last meal. Creosote has sown what he reaps. He has asked for what he has gotten. His own greedy appetite has backfired, so to speak. His explosion is poetic justice. The maitre d's retribution was warranted. To repeat, Creosote's predicament almost literally amounts to nothing more or less than his just desserts. The pun is intended by me, as it was also probably intended by the Pythons.

We laugh, but it is not precisely the laughter of comic amusement. It is the laughter that accompanies the apprehension that someone has "gotten what's coming to them." Thus, there should be no surprise that people laugh at the scene instead of being horrified by it. We are not repelled by the violence Creosote undergoes, in part because we believe that he has brought it upon himself; he invited it. Ours is the laughter of justice – the laughter that obtains when we perceive that the punishment suits the crime ever so neatly.

As already suggested, there is something medieval about the Creosote episode; indeed, a medieval theme runs throughout the film, including dungeons and the Grim Reaper (perhaps this is a result of taking up, and then dismissing, Roman Catholicism as a source of the meaning of life). In many ways, the scene is the modern equivalent of a morality play, an allegory of gluttony and its consequences. If you eat to the point where you feel like exploding, you will. The scene culminates in a visual pun or verbal image – that is, it literalizes the way we describe ourselves when we've overindulged at the table gluttonously. Creosote's *sentence* is the sentence "I've eaten so much that I'd burst if took another morsel." He does and he does. It is a punishment befitting Dante's *Inferno* or Kafka's "The Penal Colony" in its diabolical ingenuity and appropriateness. Indeed, it provokes laughter for being *so* appropriate, so well-deserved.

The laughter engendered by Creosote's predicament is, then, overdetermined. Part of it is rooted in incongruity – the absurdities of the scene presented in a context bereft of any perceived danger to human life and limb. But there is also another route to laughter here: the sense that justice is served, that the punishment matches the crime perfectly. Moreover, with respect to this second source of joy, Mr Creosote, I think, gives us additional insight into the springs of laughter. Much comedy, especially satire and even much of what is called black comedy, induces laughter because we feel that the objects of the indignities and violence suffered by its objects is deserved.[3] It is a different kind of laughter than the laughter prompted by an innocent pun. And it is our sense of justice that makes such comic genres possible. This too is something that Mr Creosote shows us about laughter.

Perhaps one thing that is so artistically effective about the Creosote episode is that it is able to weld these two sources of laughter so exquisitely. I suspect that it achieves this by the way in which the visual pun it articulates both comically amuses us with its absurdity – its violation of biological norms – while simultaneously satisfying our sense of justice in the most devilish manner. Like many medieval visions of hell, such as the punishments meted out in Dante's *Inferno*, the travails of Creosote mix horror and humor in a way that seems natural. Whether the scene has the same pedagogical intent is doubtful. But it is not a parody of such extravaganzas. Rather it taps into the same emotional well by being an updated version of them. Horrific imagery and humor are often interlaced. Mr Creosote shows us how these two ostensibly opposed elements can co-exist. They belong together because they both specialize in the incongruous and the impure – in violations of our standing cultural categories and norms. But the overall effect of these subversions of our cultural categories will not dispose us toward horror, unless they occur in the context of some clear and present danger. Where there is no danger to anything we would call human, there is no cause for horror, and there is an opening for laughter. That is Creosote. Moreover, Creosote is not just comically amusing for being a biological absurdity. He is also worthy of our derision for his sins (in his case, perhaps he is the sin itself personified). And this helps us to see that underlying the vitriol of humor is often a perception of justice.

Notes

1   The Pythons with Bob McCabe, *The Pythons: Autobiography by the Pythons* (New York: St Martin's Press, 2003), p. 326.
2   The ensuing account of horror derives from Noël Carroll, *The Philosophy of Horror* (New York: Routledge, 1990), especially the first chapter. For further background on comic amusement, see my article, "Humour," in Jerrold Levinson (ed.), *The Oxford Handbook of Aesthetics* (Oxford: Oxford University Press, 2003), pp. 344–65.
3   It may seem that this does not apply to a great deal of black comedy. In many instances the cruelties dealt in black humor do not appear to be directed at objects that morally deserve such punishment. Think of such genres of dark humor as dead baby jokes. However, in cases like this, the cruel humorist is encouraging us to direct our moral rancor not at the babies in the jokes, but at sentimental attitudes that usually accompany discourse about infants. It is that complacent sentimentality that the dark humorist thinks deserves a moral whack.

Similarly, the recurring mentally challenged "Gumby" characters in *Monty Python's Flying Circus* (see, for example, "Gumby Crooner" in Episode 9, "The Ant: An Introduction") seem to be basically an assault, by his own hand, on excessive sentimentality. It is not that Gumby deserves to be hit on the head with a brick, as he is; rather, the ethical energy underwriting the harsh laughter here is aimed at the sentimentalization of the mentally ill. The butt of the laughter lives off-screen, in a manner of speaking. It resides wherever pompous types congratulate themselves for caring for their "inferiors."

13

Memento and the Phenomenology of Comprehending Motion Picture Narration

Introduction

As is becoming increasingly apparent in the literature, Christopher Nolan's film *Memento* is replete with philosophical themes, including such topics as personal identity, truth, memory, knowledge (both of the self and of the external world), objectivity, free will versus determinism, retributive justice, and existential commitment.[1] Consequently, the film may be thought to broach questions of metaphysics, epistemology, and ethics. In this essay, I would also like to consider the philosophical contribution that *Memento* makes to aesthetics. For, although Andrew Kania has maintained that *Memento* does not address the ontology of art (Kania 2008) *and*, though this may be true under a very strict interpretation of that phrase, nevertheless, *Memento* does disclose to the thoughtful viewer certain insights about the dynamics of following a motion picture narrative. Thus, it may be construed as an instance of the philosophy of art, specifically the philosophy of motion pictures.

Nowadays, the issue of whether a motion picture can be said truly to do philosophy is a matter of pitched debate. Therefore, before dealing in detail with *Memento*, I will devote a section to explaining the sense in which I am claiming that *Memento* does philosophy, especially in terms of situating my conception of the way *Memento* does philosophy with respect to various skeptical arguments against the very possibility of movie-made philosophy. Next, I will attempt to locate *Memento* in a tradition of motion-picture

"*Memento* and the Phenomenology of Comprehending Motion Picture Narration," in Andrew Kania (ed.), *Memento* (London: Routledge, 2009), pp. 127–46.

production that attempts to meld popular genres with philosophical meditations. And then I will turn directly to *Memento* in order to show how it turns the film noir genre upside down in order to initiate the viewer into a phenomenological or introspective exploration of the experience of self-consciously constructing or co-constructing a narrative, thereby revealing to the viewer's reflective awareness a general aspect of the motion-picture experience that typically goes unnoticed and unacknowledged.

On the possibility of movie-made philosophy

During the last decade – undoubtedly prefigured and encouraged by the work of Stanley Cavell – anglophone philosophers have become keenly interested in the philosophical potential of the moving image. Anthologies abound in which rank-and-file philosophers attempt to distill the philosophical message to be found in this or that movie. Indeed, the very book in which this article was published is an example of this genre. And many of the articles in the journal *Film and Philosophy* are also in this vein.

Although many philosophers are interested in the relation between movies and philosophy, there is not a converging consensus about the nature of that relation. Some philosophers maintain that it is within the reach of the moving image to make contributions to philosophy that stand on all fours with the contributions made by card-carrying philosophers in journal articles and at academic conferences. Others argue that this is beyond the capability of the moving image. Such skeptics may concede that movies can illustrate philosophical ideas, motivate philosophical problems, suggest philosophical solutions, reframe problems, and possibly even present counterexamples to extant philosophical views. Nevertheless, the skeptics draw a line in the sand when it comes to the possibility of movies making philosophy – that is, of movies acting as vehicles for the creation and substantiation of original, positive philosophical theses. Since in this article I wish to claim that *Memento* has a positive philosophical contribution to offer, I must, therefore, first disarm the criticisms that are apt to be launched against a project like mine even before I get started.

Three recent arguments against movie-made philosophy have been advanced by Paisley Livingston (2006), Murray Smith (2006), and Bruce Russell (2005, 2008a, 2008b).[2] Livingston begins by introducing two conditions that he maintains must be met in order for any example to count as an instance of movie-made philosophy. The first condition requires that x is a specimen of movie-made philosophy only if it is a historically innovative philosophical proposal, rather than simply an illustration of a pre-existing position. It must not be parasitic on previous philosophical discourse; it must be independent. Thus, Rossellini's *Blaise Pascal* (1972) does not count as movie-made philosophy, since the actor playing Pascal is only repeating what Pascal already said. Ditto Derek Jarman's *Wittgenstein* (1993).

In addition to this independence requirement, Livingston also demands that a candidate for the title of movie-made philosophy be articulated exclusively by cinematic means. Consequently, a cinematic recording of a contemporary philosopher, such as Bob Solomon, sharing his thoughts with the camera on the philosophy of the emotions – as he does in one of The Great Courses, produced by The Teaching Company – falls short of movie-made philosophy just because the mode of presentation does not really exploit features, like montage, that are putatively exclusive to the moving image. Rather Solomon basically communicates his philosophy to listeners in the conventional way by lecturing.

With these two criteria in hand, Livingston presents the proponent of movie-made philosophy with what he regards as the dilemma of paraphrase. It goes like this: Either the motion picture articulates a philosophical thesis that can be put into words – that can be paraphrased – or it doesn't. If it doesn't, then there is no call to suppose that it has propounded philosophy, either innovative or otherwise; the possibility of movie-made philosophy cannot be based upon something ineffable. On the other hand, if it can be put into words, Livingston maintains that this will run afoul of both the independence requirement and the demand for cinematic exclusivity. It will conflict with the cinematic exclusivity condition because, if it requires a paraphrase in order to be identified as a piece of philosophy, then this particular piece of philosophy has not been forged exclusively by cinematic means alone. It needs language to finish the job. Moreover, if the case in question requires, as it undoubtedly will, a paraphrase that must make reference to existing philosophical debates, then the candidate will not be altogether epistemically innovative. Thus, it will violate the independence requirement.

Murray Smith does not argue that there are things philosophy can do but movies can't. Both can, for instance, concoct thought experiments. However, the two practices fashion their thought experiments for different purposes. The philosopher hatches his in order to motivate a distinction or to pose a counterexample. The movie maker presents hers, first and foremost, for the sake of art. These differing purposes – that we might call, roughly and only provisionally, the *cognitive* and the *artistic* – shape the design of the thought experiments, issued from these different precincts. Ostensibly the philosophical thought experiment will aspire to clarity, whereas the artistic thought experiment will aim for ambiguity, insofar as ambiguity is a value of art. Moreover, this commitment to ambiguity will cashier the candidate movie from the order of philosophy, since however virtuous ambiguity is in the realm of art, it is a disqualifying factor when it comes to philosophy.

Bruce Russell explicitly identifies doing philosophy with explicit argumentation and explanation. Like Livingston, he would deny that a motion picture containing explicit argumentation and explanation would count as *movie-made* philosophy, since, he surmises, if a movie has a philosopher, or actor playing a philosopher, reciting an argument or an explanation outright, then it is not the movie making the philosophy, but the monologue. That is, language and not cinema gets the credit here.

I do not find the meta-philosophical assumptions upon which the preceding skeptical arguments rest to be ultimately decisive. Livingston's requirement that movie-made philosophy be created solely through cinematic means is not finally compelling. One problem here is isolating exclusively cinematic means. A feature of film, like montage, is shared with video, photography, and even the novel, as in the case of John Dos Passos. With respect to *Memento*, I will be arguing that it affords the reflective viewer insight into the processes of narrative comprehension through the way in which the film manipulates its narrative structure. Narrative structure, of course, is not exclusive to cinema. But I see no reason to deny that *Memento* makes a contribution to the thought-ful viewer's understanding of the way in which the structure of the movie narrative recruits her in the co-construction of the story.

Moreover, if I understand Livingston's worries about why paraphrasing the view of the movie compromises its status as independent philosophy, then I think that Livingston has set the bar for original philosophizing way too high.[3] He seems to think that if the paraphrase draws on pre-existing philo-sophical discussions, which it is. indeed highly likely to do, then that shows that the movie is not truly independent. But I think that a standard this draconian would disallow most of what we are ordinarily ready to call philosophy. There aren't that many brand new positions. There are generally new arguments, new examples, and nuanced qualifications of already existing positions. Indeed, an absolutely independent philosophical thesis – one detached from pre-existing philosophical discourse – might just be too inde-pendent for any of us to grasp.[4]

Smith's argument on the basis of ambiguity is not conclusive because at best he is dealing with tendencies. Perhaps much philosophy, or, more accurately, most philosophy in a certain tradition, goes in for clarity. But sometimes a philosopher, especially one like Nietzsche, Kierkegaard, or Philip Kapleau, from a non-analytic tradition (or Wittgenstein from the analytic tradition), may have a motive for shrouding their thought experiments in ambiguity, while the thought experiments of some artists, such as George Orwell, serve his artistic purposes by being blazingly clear.

Bruce Russell maintains that philosophy requires explicit argumentation and/or explanation. If a thought experiment is presented, for example, its author has to accompany it with an explanation of how it works. I find it strange that Russell holds this position on thought experiments, since he agrees that motion pictures can provide counterexamples without auxiliary explana-tion, and, of course, many thought experiments are counterexamples.[5] Moreover, I am not convinced that movie-made thought experiments must always be attached to explicit explanations, because I'm not persuaded that the thought experiments union-certified philosophers bandy about always need to be explained. The context in which the example is offered may be enough to drive the point home, as may happen in the discussion period after the presentation of a philosophical lecture to informed listeners. The context may be so pregnant and the thought experiment so deft that everyone gets it on contact.

Since I am not swayed by any of the preceding skeptical considerations against the prospects of movie-made philosophy, I will outline, without embarrassment, what philosophy I believe can be found in *Memento*. However, even if these arguments had hit their target more accurately, I still believe that I could make the case for movie-made philosophy in *Memento*. For it seems that the preceding arguments against movie-made philosophy presuppose, either directly or indirectly, that the primary vehicle of philosophy must be language. But perhaps that presumption is up for grabs. Maybe audiences can be led to philosophical insights by having their experiences shaped and directed in certain ways.[6] They may come to a philosophical conclusion on the basis of their acquaintance with the phenomenon in question through their own experience, as that experience has been molded in order to facilitate the recognition of the processes upon which the experience rests.

Call this appeal to the audience's experience of an artwork for the purposes of casting reflection upon how the artwork works on the audience a matter of *phenomenological address*. It is my contention that *Memento* offers philosophical insight to reflective viewers by means of its phenomenological address to the audience. Moreover, since the structures of phenomenological address need not be strictly linguistic and may remain inexplicit, the movie-made philosophy that comes by way of phenomenological address is not threatened by the kinds of skeptical concerns rehearsed in this section.

Memento and the Art Cinema

Memento belongs to the popular cinema. It is an example of the well-entrenched genre of the film noir. Thus, it may seem strange to assert that it possesses a philosophical dimension. Motion pictures with philosophical pretensions, it might be thought, are native to the avant-garde and the "Art Cinema," not the mainstream, commercial cinema.[7]

However, it is a mistake to suppose that the popular cinema, the avant-garde cinema, and the Art Cinema are utterly insulated from each other. Since the days of the silent film, the avant-garde has poached popular forms for its own purposes. Sergei Eisenstein not only used circus techniques in his early masterpieces, but the style of editing that he perfected – along with Kuleshov, Pudovkin, and others – was rooted in the editing techniques of the American popular film, especially as those had been popularized by D. W. Griffith. And the found-footage films of cineastes such as Bruce Conner, Ken Jacobs, and Jim Hoberman often employ clips from popular movies.

Nor is the connection between popular film and the avant-garde a one-way street. Lewis Milestone re-appropriated Soviet montage in his *All Quiet on the Western Front* (1930), Walt Disney adapted Igor Stravinsky's *Rite of Spring* for *Fantasia* (1940), and Alfred Hitchcock hired Salvador Dali to do the dream scenes in *Spellbound* (1945). Moreover, further examples of these crossovers can be multiplied in both directions. For example, French New Wave directors, such as Jean-Luc Godard, enlisted American genre motifs for his modernist agenda in works from *Breathless* to *Alphaville*. Interestingly, for our purposes, many of these references to Hollywood movies were often allusions to American crime films, including films noirs. Perhaps emboldened by the example of Godard, some directors in the mainstream cinema began to help themselves to the techniques of the emerging Art Cinema of the sixties. In a number of cases, mainstream cinema began to be "Europeanized" in terms of the use of complex, nonlinear narrative structures and editing.

Richard Lester is an early example of this tendency, his experiments culminating with *Petulia* (1968). Other examples include Nicholas Roeg's *Don't Look Now* (1973) and *Bad Timing* (1980), John Boorman's *Point Blank* (1967), and some of the films of Arthur Penn and Mike Nichols. These movies, and others, imported some of the more venturesome narrative and editing experiments of the Art Cinema into popular genres, such as the crime movie (*Point Blank*) and the horror film (*Don't Look Now*). *Memento* is in the lineage of this tendency – that is, by now, a tradition – in popular cinema, a tradition that seeks to assimilate avant-garde developments into the mainstream.

However, in *Memento*, Christopher Nolan has not only dragooned the sort of experimental narrative structure more common to the Art Cinema and the avant-garde. He has also made one of the great projects of the avant-garde and the Art Cinema his own. The project, broadly speaking, is that of reflexive critique – the recurring modernist commitment to disclosing the conditions of possibility of the various art forms by reflecting upon exemplary instances thereof (for example, to reflect upon the conditions of painting by means of paintings, upon sculpture by means of sculpture, and so forth).[8] Moreover, the specific critique that *Memento* initiates involves an exploration of the way in which audiences follow and comprehend movie narratives and render said structures intelligible to themselves.

Memento pursues this theme by addressing audiences phenomenologically, that is, by problematizing their *experience* of the movie in ways that reveal something *essential* about following a movie narrative in general. *Memento* presents viewers with a work from a familiar genre, the film noir, but in an unfamiliar (or de-familiarized) way. This puts pressure on the audience to negotiate the film with a heightened consciousness of what they are doing. The audience, in other words, is encouraged, even nudged, toward adopting an apperceptive stance toward their own sense-making activities with respect to the narrative structure of *Memento*. And this, in turn, enables the thoughtful spectator to notice what is common between his or her experience of *Memento* and his or her less reflective encounters with the general run of movie narratives.[9]

In this regard, *Memento* recalls a classic film of the European Art Cinema, namely Alain Resnais's *Last Year at Marienbad* (1961).[10] In the course of that motion picture, the elusive, repetitive, inconclusive narrative structure constantly frustrates our desire to understand what is going on in the storyworld of the film. In this, it manages to make us aware of the degree to which our comprehension of narratives is organized around formulating tacit questions that we then expect the story to go on to answer. *Marienbad* provokes this insight by generating a plethora of questions – for example, did the couple meet the year before at Marienbad? – but then refrains from answering any of them. Likewise, in the tradition of Resnais's film, the narrative structure of *Memento* challenges spectators to make sense of it and, in the process, to observe introspectively the way in which they manage to accomplish this feat.

Memento and narrative comprehension

Memento is the story of Leonard Shelby, a one-time insurance investigator, who, in the course of a burglary of his home, is battered on the head by a thief with the result that Leonard is stricken by anterograde amnesia, a condition involving chronic memory loss. Leonard's memory can only hold onto things for ten to fifteen minutes. One of the most intriguing aspects of the film involves the ways in which Leonard attempts to make up for this deficit by tattooing vital information on his own body, writing notes and Post-its to himself, and taking and annotating Polaroid photographs of the people and places that are important to his ongoing concerns.[11]

Foremost among those concerns is revenge. Leonard believes that during the burglary, his wife was murdered by a thief who escaped the scene of the crime and in whom the police are not interested, since they are not convinced this thief ever existed. It is even suggested that Leonard may have invented this thief in order to cover up his own skullduggery. Nevertheless, Leonard is certain of the thief's existence and is committed to tracking this man down and inflicting retribution. This quest is what gives meaning to Leonard's life. In this, he is aided by a former policeman, John "Teddy" Gammell, who, while assisting Leonard, also appears to use him for his own purposes involving drug-trafficking, as does the major female character in the story – a barmaid called Natalie.

Throughout the main story – the story of Leonard's revenge quest – there are flashbacks to Leonard's life with his wife, to the burglary, and to a parallel story of another case of anterograde amnesia – the story, told by Leonard, of one Sammy Jankis. This story sheds light on Leonard's condition and, it is suggested, may even be Leonard's own story projected upon the imaginary Sammy.

The action in *Memento* begins as the credits roll. We see a Polaroid photo of a blood-spattered wall. Gradually the Polaroid fades out of focus, alerting us to the fact that the scene is being shown in reverse, thus introducing the viewer to the signature stylistic variation in the movie – that the story is being told backwards. The opening scene of *Memento* is the last episode in the chain of events that comprise the particular segment of Leonard's life that is being recounted.

What we come to realize is that Leonard has just killed John "Teddy" Gammell (or "Teddy," for short). Ostensibly, Leonard has come to believe that Teddy is the person who killed his wife, although Teddy has just told Leonard that he, Leonard, killed the man who did that long ago. Indeed, Teddy has given Leonard a Polaroid showing an exultant, bloodied Leonard, which Teddy says was taken when Leonard nailed his wife's murderer.

But that does not deter Leonard from starting up the search again and again, this time concluding with the execution of Teddy. Does this happen because Leonard has simply forgotten that he has already exacted his retribution, or is it because Leonard realizes that it is only in virtue of an ongoing revenge quest that he has something to organize his life around and, in that way, to give it meaning?

Actually, by the end of the chain of events the story recounts, it seems to be a bit of both. It appears that Leonard, exploiting his own memory deficits and his memory prompts, is able to leave enough phony "clues" to himself to frame Teddy as his wife's murderer. That is, Leonard stage-manages his own situation in such a way that he is able to deceive himself, while simultaneously remaining unaware of what he's done. He sets Teddy up for the kill, thus removing the only person who, if he is telling the truth, can bring Leonard's quest to a halt. Yet with Teddy out of the way, Leonard is free to embark upon his mission of vengeance once more – killing one victim after another and then forgetting about it – thereby bringing unity and meaning to his existence.[12]

Memento was not the first story to be told backwards. Precedents include Harold Pinter's play *Betrayal* (1983), Martin Amis's novel *Time's Arrow* (1991), and an episode of *Seinfeld*. And subsequent to *Memento*, the French film, *Irreversible* (2002), another revenge quest, hit the screen. Although these works all employ backwards narration, each appears to do so for its own purposes. For example, *Betrayal* deploys the structure to underscore the reversal of fortune recounted in the play; the narration begins at the end of a love affair that it traces back to the beginning, where, ironically enough, the play itself ends happily. *Seinfeld* plays the structure for laughs, whereas *Irreversible* uses it to conjure up an aura of utter implacability.

In *Memento*, the backwards narration has more than one function. The one most commented upon is that it puts the viewer in a position somewhat like

Leonard's. Due to his condition, Leonard has no memory of what has immediately preceded the present moment on screen. Similarly, the audience does not know what has just happened prior to the moment before us, since we haven't seen it yet. So we are being dropped into situations *in medias res*, which is, of course, the condition of Leonard's life.[13]

Of course, our experience is not exactly Leonard's plight, since at some point we are able to gain a semblance of a whole story, which will always lie beyond Leonard's ken. Nevertheless, the backwards narration is a very effective expressive device for communicating to viewers a taste of what Leonard is experiencing.

Again, our relation to the chain of events does not precisely mirror Leonard's insofar as he will never be able to reconstruct the big picture out of the puzzling fragments, whereas, since we are still in possession of our short-term memories and can convert them into long-term memories, we will be able, by the end of the film, to assemble a coherent story out of the pieces. And this is connected to a second function of the backwards narrative – what we might call its "meta-narrative function" in contrast to its function as an expressive means for conveying so effectively Leonard's bewilderment.

By telling the story backwards, *Memento* forces the audience to make sense of the narrative with heightened self-awareness.[14] The process of following the story becomes conscious and deliberate. We have to think overtly about what we are doing. We have to construct the story and, while we are putting it together, we need to stand back, figuratively speaking, to make sure we are tying up the loose ends. That is, we have to observe ourselves assembling the events of Leonard's life into a coherent story. And in the course of self-consciously configuring the narrative in this way, the reflective viewer ideally will arrive at certain discoveries *about* narration and narrative comprehension.

Of course, it is not the case that the spectator only constructs or co-constructs a movie narrative when the story is told backwards. The audience is always involved in constructing what happened in the storyworld from the movie narration, even when the story is told forwards.[15] But by narrating events backwards, the makers of *Memento* have made the execution of this process difficult, thereby forcing us to take a close look at it or, as the Russian Formalists liked to say, smashing the glass armor that surrounds the narrative structure in a way that requires that we take notice of it. The meta-narrative function of the backwards storytelling in *Memento* is, in other words, to afford the opportunity for the thoughtful spectator to gain certain insights regarding narrative – both in terms of its structure and its comprehension.

The most basic of those insights, of course, is that there is a distinction between the order in which events are told or shown in a narrative and the order in which those events follow each other in the storyworld. The difference between these two event orders is drawn by means of distinctions such as *story* versus *discourse*, or *histoire* versus *récit*, or *fabula* versus *syuzhet*, where the second term in each couplet refers to the event-order of the telling of the tale and the first refers to the order of events as they transpired in the pertinent world, whether fictional, merely possible, or the one we inhabit. Admittedly, this is a very basic idea, but it is one of those things that "everybody knows," yet which, at the same time, is fundamental, indeed, essential to the nature of narrative, however easily forgotten, and, therefore, always worthy of a vivid reminder.

The second insight that is likely to dawn on the thoughtful viewer has to do with the relationship between – to adopt one of the previous dichotomies – the story and the discourse. By means of the backwards narration in *Memento*, we realize by introspectively observing our experience and engagement with the film that we are involved in a constant process of constructing the story out of the discourse. This is part of what it is to follow any movie narrative. But with most movies this process flies, so to say, under the radar screen. That is, we are unaware with most movie narratives of our contribution to the narrative.

Memento not only makes us conscious of our participation in the co-construction of the narrative, however, it also alerts us to the way in which we follow the story by foregrounding – through its temporally reversed structure – the process by which we assemble a story out of the discourse. That is, the third insight that *Memento* affords the interested viewer is the opportunity to scrutinize the nature of the relationship between its story and its discourse – its storyworld and its telling – and *Memento* enables us to exploit that insight in order to reflect upon our commerce with more straightforwardly composed narratives.

But what exactly does this third insight come to? What precisely does the spectator do as she watches *Memento* progress – or, perhaps more aptly, regress? Primarily, I submit that we ask questions. The most obvious questions are: Who, and even more importantly, why was the man killed in the opening sequence? These are what we may call the movie's "presiding macro-questions." Moreover, a moment's reflection will reveal to the self-conscious viewer that most movies have presiding macro-questions and that we use them to unify our experiences of them. For example, we surmise that the movie is over when its presiding macro-question or questions have been answered; when the featured lovers kiss and make up, we realize that the film is on the brink of declaring "The End."

Yet it is not only presiding macro-questions that spectators use to organize their experience of following the story. Smaller questions – what we may call micro-questions – glue our attention to the screen in the expectation that they will be answered. In fact, we employ these questions to modulate our attention – that is, we stay on the lookout for answers to them.

For example, an early scene of *Memento* finds Leonard in the restroom of a restaurant. When he exits, the maître d' hands him an envelope and tells

Leonard that he left it on the table. "Why was Leonard in the restaurant?" we ask ourselves. In a subsequent scene, Leonard enters the same restaurant, where he meets Natalie, who gives him the envelope containing compromising information about Teddy. Everything falls into place. Our question has been answered.

Other questions include: Why is Leonard in the bathroom holding a bottle of scotch, although he doesn't feel drunk? Why is Leonard running through the trailer park? Why is Leonard in Natalie's bed? Why is Natalie so nasty to Leonard upon first meeting him?

When we follow most movie narratives, the questions that we deploy to organize and direct our attention and to render ongoing events intelligible remain tacit. But the backwards narration of *Memento* forces them out into the open. We formulate them explicitly in our minds. We become aware that there is something we want to know and we process the film with an eye to finding it.

If with most movies, our attention is driven by questions about what happens next, *Memento* bids us to ask, "What happened earlier?" Moreover, since this is an unfamiliar way of having the story served up, it brings to the fore what is generally tacit: the fact that we are tracking the narrative with certain questions in mind.

There is no doubt that *Memento* is a challenging film to follow, more challenging, in fact, than *Irreversible*, another revenge quest that is told backwards. Perhaps the reason for this is that *Memento* is not only narrated in reverse, but also because Leonard may be being deceived – being given false information – by other characters such as Teddy, Natalie, and the hotel clerk, as well as himself. This, plus the manner in which the story is conveyed temporally, makes the movie difficult to cognize, and that provocation compels the viewer to reconstruct the story self-consciously, thereby, in the process, acquiring phenomenological access to one's response to the vast majority of movie narratives.[16]

Of course, it is no accident that our approach to most movie narratives involves question formation. For it is a long-known principle of plot engineering that this is one of the most effective ways of holding onto the audience's attention. With reference to playwriting, David Hume wrote, "Had you any intention to move a person extremely by the narration of an event, the best method of encreasing its effect would be artfully to delay informing him of it, and first to excite his curiosity and impatience before you let him into the secret" (Hume 1985: 221). What Hume here labels "the secret," I am now calling an answer to a question.

The vast number of movie narratives are erotetic – they motivate our continued interest, and structure and guide our attention by a network of questions and answers (Carroll 2008). Curiosity, as Hume argues, keeps us in our seats. Although it is uncertain how many people in Hollywood are familiar with Hume's essay, there is no question that the town understands Hume's method. For example, several screenwriting manuals recommend that plots be built upon the question/answer model. Dona Cooper advises "To create eagerness in the audience, the screenwriter intentionally plants questions in the viewers' minds – almost like leaving a trail of bread crumbs in the forest," while Michael Hauge writes, "When you open your screenplay, you want to create a question in the mind of your reader so that he will stick around (emotionally) to find out the answer" (both quoted in Keating 2008).[17]

Moreover, though Christopher Nolan may not have read Hume, Hauge, Cooper, or any other commentator on plot structure, he designed *Memento* with an awareness of the importance of the question/answer format. He says of the screenplay, "I think that it's very important that we have answers to those questions. And that's how it's always been constructed. [The screenplay] is not deliberately contradictory. We were very deliberate in the plotting, and the answers to those questions" (quoted in Mottram 2002: 179).[18]

Thus, *Memento*, by means of a structure that in some ways is not typical of Hollywood plotting, not only affords the conscientious viewer insights into the nature of our experience of typical movie narratives; it also, by way of illuminating the structure of that experience, makes it possible for the spectator to grasp the way in which such plots are generally designed – in terms of questions and answers – to facilitate our understanding of the story and to hold onto our interest in it. It is no accident that we call such stories "gripping."

The meta-narrative function of *Memento* involves enabling viewers to reflect upon the ways in which they both experience and process movie narratives, which, in turn, abets insight into the fundamental structure of typical movie narratives. By engendering awareness of the operation of the erotetic design of *Memento*, the audience is able to extrapolate what it has learned from *Memento*, and apply it, on the basis of their own experience, to the sorts of movies it is more accustomed to consume. In this way *Memento*, in virtue of its phenomenological address to its audience, fosters the discovery of essential features of a certain type of movie narration and, thereby, makes a contribution to the philosophy of the motion picture.

Concluding remarks

In this essay, I have argued that *Memento* makes a contribution to the philosophy of art, specifically to the philosophy of motion pictures. By means of phenomenological address, it encourages thoughtful audience members to reflect upon their experience of the film in such a way that they are suggestively led to certain philosophical insights about the nature of a typical species of movie narrative and the comprehension thereof. That is, by manipulating our cognition of it, *Memento* sends the audience in a certain direction of thinking where one may derive a novel idea or, at least, the recognition of standardly neglected, essential features of movie narration and comprehension. *Memento*, in other words, is the occasion for an *apprise de conscience*, one that has been carefully guided by the structure of the motion picture. Through *Memento* the reflective viewer can acquire philosophical insight because of the way in which Nolan has modified and defamiliarized the moviegoer's experience.

By locating the philosophical work that *Memento* gets done, I have attempted to evade skeptical objections to movie-made philosophy that are rooted in the prejudice that philosophy must in all cases be linguistic. In addition, I contend, one might draw philosophy from others maieutically by orchestrating their experience in such a way that they are led to certain philosophical insights, especially about the experiences in question and the conditions that give rise to them.

Nevertheless, I suspect the skeptics will not be placated by this maneuver. On the one hand, they are likely to charge that the philosophical insights I attribute to *Memento* are not original to that field. Some are at least as old as Hume. So the philosophical insights allegedly available from *Memento* do not meet the criterion of originality, discussed earlier, which is put forth by Livingston and Russell. On the other hand, it may be argued that *Memento* does not literally offer us philosophical insights. That is, the alleged insights are not, strictly speaking, provided *inside* the movie.

With respect to the latter objection, I agree that the insights I have catalogued are not in the motion picture itself. They emerge from the experience of the interested spectator as he or she reflects upon their experience of the movie. But I see no reason here to discount *Memento*'s philosophical stature. Leading folks to come to a philosophical conclusion seems to me to deserve the title of doing philosophy. Aren't we doing philosophy when by asking carefully chosen questions or making pregnant observations we point our students and non-philosopher friends in the direction of an insight that they work through on their own? Consider such luminaries as Socrates and Wittgenstein.

Surely, we can advance a philosophical thesis by asking a series of rhetorical questions. The answer is not literally contained in the rhetorical question, but the rhetorical question may function as a philosophical argument nonetheless, even if it needs to be completed in the minds of our interlocutors.

Likewise, simply posing situations in a pointed manner may provoke philosophy from listeners or viewers. And that is exactly what I contend *Memento* does. Against the argument that the philosophy in *Memento* isn't original enough, it is important, as I mentioned earlier, not to go overboard on the requirement that the philosophical thesis in question be absolutely original, since most of what we regard as philosophy usually involves incremental variations that sit on a continuum with past philosophical inquiry. Certainly, it counts as doing philosophy if one is able to come up with a new way of framing an old question and/or substantiating one's answer to it. And, in this way, it seems that *Memento* merits being classified as a contribution to philosophy.

Of course, the skeptic may reply that the so-called "insights" that I've culled from *Memento* are too banal to deserve being labeled "philosophy." The problem here is not that these supposed insights fall short of absolute originality. Rather, they are such hackneyed commonplaces that they lack any claim to originality whatsoever. For instance, consider the claim that the viewer learns that she is involved in co-constructing the work. How trivial can you get? What narratologist doesn't know that?

I think that this objection overlooks the venue for which movie-made philosophy is intended. It is not primarily made for working philosophers. There aren't enough of us to support the production costs of even a modest motion picture, let alone to guarantee profits. Movie-made philosophizing, like the movies that house it, is directed at the mass of non-professionals. It reminds them of things that they might have forgotten or neglected or it leads them to insights that are novel for them. That movie plots are driven by a network of questions and answers may be old news to the philosopher of narrative, but it may crystallize a new and exciting idea in the mind of the plain movie-goer. That is, relative to its theater of operations, the insights delivered by *Memento* are original enough to its audience, rather than banal.

Furthermore, returning to our earlier observation, *Memento* would appear to have a legitimate claim to finding a new way to draw the pertinent philosophical insights out of thoughtful viewers, even if those insights are not totally new philosophically. For, once again, it is not the case that doing philosophy is something that only transpires between academics in accordance with the protocols of their journals. We also philosophize with our students and our friends, and we are engaged in philosophy if we are able to produce a compelling new example that will draw a new idea from them by prompting and guiding their reflection on the case at hand. And in this way, too, *Memento* is worthy of being regarded as a contribution to philosophy.

Notes

1   For an excellent survey of the philosophical themes in *Memento*, see Kania (2008).
2   These skeptical arguments on the philosophical limitations on cinema have been addressed critically by Aaron Smuts (2008) and by Thomas Wartenberg (2008). I have profited immensely from their remarks on this issue.
3   Livingston emphasizes the kind of originality he does because he presupposes that if a movie can be said to do philosophy, the philosophy must be articulated by the movie maker. This overlooks the possibility that the philosophical insight may be located in the viewer's uptake of the motion picture, albeit under the guidance of

the cineaste. This insight, in turn, may be original to the target audience, even if it is not something altogether novel in the established universe of philosophical discourse. Later I will be arguing that Christopher Nolan manages to impart philosophy through *Memento* by enabling reflective spectators to acquire theoretical insight as a result of the way in which he, Nolan, has structured his film.

4 Points in this paragraph have been made by Wartenberg (2008) and Smuts (2008).

5 This observation has also been made by Wartenberg (2008).

6 Furthermore, this seems highly likely since people are able to derive philosophical insight through experiences that haven't been designed to bring these about. Think of all the philosophy that has sprung from the phenomena of visual illusions.

7 For an account of the Art Cinema, see David Bordwell (1985, 2008).

8 My point here is not that self-critique is the exclusive property of the Art Cinema and the avant-garde, but rather that Nolan belongs to a tradition within the mainstream cinema that also dabbles in reflexivity. Evidence that Nolan is trafficking in reflexivity can be found in the analogy he draws between Leonard and motion picture directors (Mottram 2002: 173).

9 *Memento* not only comments on movie narration in general, but also specifically on the genre of film noir. Films noirs are, of course, often about memory, a theme that *Memento* reworks in a most unexpected way. Often film noir uses memory in order to articulate themes of fatalism and/or guilt. In *Memento*, the theme of guilt emerges when the possibility of Leonard's guilt – on more counts than one – is raised.

10 The reflexive interrogation of the motion picture experience and/or the essence of the motion picture were often the explicit topics of the avant-garde cinema movements of the sixties and seventies, especially in the United States and Great Britain. In this regard, there is an interesting correspondence between *Memento* and *Zorns Lemma* (1970) by Hollis Frampton. Both films can be thought of as confronting the audience with memory tests for the purpose of indicating the indispensable operation of memory for processing motion pictures.

11 Perhaps the title *Memento* can be interpreted as referring to these mementos.

12 It may be thought that without Teddy, Leonard will be unable to function – that killing Teddy, in other words, will undermine his "quest." On the one hand, whether in fact this would be so in the world of the fiction is irrelevant to what Leonard appears to believe and act upon. But, on the other hand, Leonard may very well be able to get along without Teddy. After all, he is able to dispatch Teddy pretty effectively. And he has his dossier. Moreover, there may be more handlers where Teddy came from – for instance, maybe Natalie.

13 Another parallel between Leonard's condition and that of the audience member is that many of the sequences in the main line of the story (that is, the story excluding the embedded flashbacks) approximate the length of Leonard's ability to remember. Like Leonard, we are plunged into a present time slice of a certain unnaturally delimited duration with no memory of what preceded it.

14 Responding to *Memento* is not like responding to something like a crossword puzzle, where responding to a crossword puzzle does not typically force us to

self-consciously reflect upon the way in which we solve the pertinent problem. For *Memento* is of a different order of difficulty. Usually a crossword puzzle tells you the question that you need to answer. With *Memento*, you need to figure out and formulate the questions relevant to tracking the story as well as the answers. The viewer has to review her hypotheses and her strategies for picking out and putting together clues. Our false starts and revisions brings the process of our making sense out of the movie to the forefront of our consciousness. Sometimes something like this may occur with a crossword puzzle as when we realize that we're dealing with a trick clue. But *Memento* is tricked out thus through and through.

15   See Bordwell (1985: 48–62, 156–204).

16   It might be argued that *Memento* is so uncharacteristically difficult that it cannot reveal much about our ordinary experience of processing narrative movies. But, on the one hand, *Memento* is not that difficult to follow. Surely it's no *Finnegans Wake*. And, on the other hand, what we observe ourselves doing in response to *Memento* – framing questions, tracking answers – can be readily observed in response to more mundanely structured movies. Just stop a motion picture at what screenwriters call "the turning point" and the audience's tacit questions will well up and be voiced loudly.

17   Keating (2008) also quotes Dona Cooper advising: "You guide and focus your viewers' attention by the way you give and withhold information. Viewers can then experience a sense of satisfaction when they finally get the *answer* for which they've been searching" (emphasis added).

18   Actually, there may be some evidence that Nolan is familiar with the textbook theories of movie narration and that he intends to draw our attention to the principles behind them. As Mottram points out, *Memento* has the conventional Hollywood three-act structure with what is called "the twist" occurring precisely where it should – namely, as the second act turns into the third (Mottram 2002: 173). There is also evidence from the rest of Nolan's oeuvre. The very title of Nolan's first feature, *Following* (1998), surely refers not only to the characters' voyeuristic pursuits, but also the viewer's attempt to reconstruct the fragmented story. *The Prestige* (2006) begins with Christian Bale's character inquiring slyly, "Are you watching closely?"

References

Bordwell, D. (1985) *Narration in the Fiction Film*. Madison: University of Wisconsin Press.

Bordwell, D.(2008) *The Poetics of Cinema*. London: Routledge.

Carroll, N. (2008) "Narrative Closure," in P. Livingston and C. Plantinga (eds.), *The Routledge Companion to Philosophy and Film*. London: Routledge, pp. 207–16.

Hume, D. (1985) "Of Tragedy," in *Collected Essays*, ed. E.F. Miller. Indianapolis, IN: Liberty Classics, pp. 216–25.

Kania, A. (2008) "*Memento*," in P. Livingston and C. Plantinga (eds.), *The Routledge Companion to Philosophy and Film*. London: Routledge, pp. 650–60.

Keating, P. (2008) "Plot Points, Macro-questions and Emotional Curves: Three Ways to Think about Screenplay Structure." Presented at the annual conference of the Society for the Cognitive Study of the Moving Image, Madison, WI.

Livingston, P. (2006) "Theses on Cinema as Philosophy." Journal of Aesthetics and Art Criticism 64: 11–18.

Mottram, J. (2002) *The Making of 'Memento'*. London: Faber and Faber.

Russell, B. (2005) "The Philosophical Limits of Film," in N. Carroll and J. Choi (eds.), *Philosophy of Film and Motion Pictures: An Anthology*. Oxford: Blackwell.

Russell, B. (2008a) "Film's Limits: The Sequel." Film and Philosophy 12: 1–16.

Russell, B. (2008b) "Replies to Carroll and Wartenberg." Film and Philosophy 12: 35–40.

Smith, M. (2006) "Film Art, Argument, and Ambiguity." Journal of Aesthetics and Art Criticism 64: 33–42.

Smuts, A. (2008) "Film as Philosophy: The Bold Thesis." Presented at the Eastern Division Meeting of the American Society for Aesthetics, Philadelphia, PA.

Wartenberg, T. (2008) "On the Possibility of Cinematic Philosophy." Presented at the annual conference of the Society for the Cognitive Study of the Moving Image, Madison, WI.

Further reading

Livingston, P. (2005) "Narrative," in B. Gaut and D. M. Lopes (eds.), *The Routledge Companion to Aesthetics*, 2nd edn, London: Routledge, pp. 359–69. (An accessible introduction to some central issues in narrative theory.)

Wartenberg, T. (2007) *Thinking on Screen: Film as Philosophy*. London: Routledge. (A defense of the idea that film can "do philosophy," including several case studies.)

Section IV

Philosophy and Popular TV

14

Tales of Dread in *The Twilight Zone*
A Contribution to Narratology

Introduction

There are several different sorts of story-types among the episodes of *The Twilight Zone*. Although most are dramas, there are also a number of comedies, including "Mr Dingle the Strong," "Mr Bevis," "The Whole Truth," "Once Upon a Time," "Showdown with Rance McGrew," "Hocus-Pocus and Frisby," "Cavender is Coming," "I Dream of Genie," and "The Bard," among others. Likewise political allegories appear with regularity in the series; some examples are "The Monsters Are Due on Maple Street," "The Obsolete Man," "The Shelter," "The Quality of Mercy," "The Mirror," "The Gift," "He's Alive!," "Number Twelve Looks Just like You," and "I am the Night – Color Me Black." Nevertheless, the story-type that seems to appear most often is that which we may call the Tale of Dread.

As will emerge in what follows, I define a Tale of Dread as: (1) a narrative fantasy; (2) about an event in which a character is punished; (3) in a manner that is appropriate (the punishment fits the crime); and (4) mordantly humorous (for example, often ironic). I call these stories *Tales of Dread* because they mandate that audiences entertain paranoid or anxious imaginings – specifically that the universe is governed by an all knowing and controlling intelligence that metes out justice with diabolical wit.

Although the Tale of Dread recurs frequently in *The Twilight Zone*, the Tale of Dread is not unique to *The Twilight Zone*. It appeared as soon as popular authors

"Tales of Dread in *The Twilight Zone*: A Contribution to Narratology," in Noël Carroll and Lester Hunt (eds.), *Philosophy in "The Twilight Zone"* (Oxford: Wiley-Blackwell, 2009), pp. 26–38.

Minerva's Night Out: Philosophy, Pop Culture, and Moving Pictures, First Edition. Noël Carroll.

began to mine supernatural themes for inspiration. For instance, "The Black Cat," by Edgar Allan Poe, is a Tale of Dread. After hanging one black cat, the narrator acquires another almost identical-looking one, which develops strange white markings around its neck that gradually take the shape of a scar as caused by a noose. Later, the second cat preternaturally divulges the place where the narrator has hidden the body of his wife whom he had axed to death only days earlier. Though it is never said outright that the second cat is the first cat reincarnated or a ghost thereof, it is difficult to resist the thought that the action of the second cat is connected to the violence done to the first cat as a sort of cosmic revenge.

Tales of Dread, of course, predate pulp fiction. For example, Aristotle tells the story of the statue of Mitys in Argos, which falls upon the murderer of Mitys who traveled to Argos to evade apprehension and punishment for his crime only to be crushed by an image of his victim. Although this tale makes no explicit reference to a causal relation between the murder and the death of the murderer, readers have a strong feeling that there is a kind of magical linkage between the two events. Again, the universe itself appears to be enacting its own species of retribution.

Tales of Dread often appear next to horror stories in periodicals, short-story compilations, and anthology-type TV series, such as *Tales from the Darkside*.[1] Like horror stories, Tales of Dread may use either supernatural fancies or science-fiction inventions to induce the anxiety in which they specialize. That is certainly the case with respect to *The Twilight Zone*.

In this chapter, while making reference to episodes of *The Twilight Zone*, I will attempt to elucidate Tales of Dread. I will try to explain not only what they are but the way in which they elicit the sensation of dread that it is their function to engender, while also indicating the ways in which they both resemble and contrast with horror stories.

Tales of dread: some examples from *The Twilight Zone*

Tales of Dread, it seems to me, are the most frequently recurring kind of story in *The Twilight Zone*. Here are few examples. There are many more where these came from.

"Judgment Night": Carl Lanser, a German, does not know how it has come about that he is on ship called the *S.S. Queen of Glasgow*. But he is sure that the boat is going to be attacked by a Nazi submarine. And lo and behold, a U-boat does crest through the waves at 1:15 a.m., and Lanser, through a pair of binoculars, sees himself on the deck of the warship. He is the captain of the submersible and he orders that the *Glasgow* be torpedoed and that the survivors, including Lanser-the-passenger, be gunned down.

The episode concludes: "The *S.S, Queen of Glasgow*, heading for New York, and the time is 1942. For one man, it is always 1942 – and this man will ride the ghost of that ship every night for eternity. This is what is meant by paying the fiddler. This is the come-uppance awaiting every man when the ledger of his life is opened and examined, the tally made, and then the reward or the penalty paid. And in the case of Carl Lanser, the former Kapitan Lieutenant, Navy of the Third Reich, this is the penalty. This is the *justice* meted out. This is judgment night in the Twilight Zone."[2]

Another example from the first season is "The Four of Us Are Dying". Arch Hammer has the ability to reconfigure himself, including his face, at will. A rather seedy lowlife, Hammer uses this talent for ill, seducing a woman and then inveigling money from a gangster. But when the gangster catches on, Hammer evades him by assuming the look of a boxer whose picture he sees on a poster. However, the father of the boxer runs into Hammer and, mistaking Hammer for his son, shoots him for the disgrace the boxer caused his family. Just desserts? Karma? We have the strong impression that Arch Hammer is being punished by the universe for the misuse of the gift it had bequeathed him.

Tales of Dread not only occur regularly in the first season of *The Twilight Zone*. For instance, in the third season, there is installment entitled "Four O'Clock". Oliver Crangle is a McCarthyite type, engrossed in tracking down and unmasking mercilessly those whom he takes to be suspect. He is presented as an altogether vile and despicable human being. Although it is never explained how he intends to pull this off, we learn that he plans to shrink all those he deems evil to a height of no more than two feet tall. This way, he reasons, they will be readily detectable. The mass reduction is scheduled for four o'clock. But when four o'clock rolls around, only Oliver Crangle has been downsized.[3]

As the voice-over narration observes: "At four o'clock, an evil man made his bed and lay in it, a pot called the kettle black, a stone thrower broke the windows of his own glass house. You look for this one under 'F' for fanatic and 'J' for *justice* – in the Twilight Zone."[4]

Thus as is often the case in Tales of Dread, Crangle, like Arch Hammer, is undone, ironically enough, by his own design, or, as Shakespeare puts it in *Hamlet*: "For 'tis the sport to have the engineer/Hoist with his own petard."[5]

The nature and function of Tales of Dread

Tales of Dread obviously fall under the broad category of poetic justice – a phrase introduced by Thomas Rymer in 1678 in his *The Tragedies of the Last Age Considered*. Basically, poetic justice is the notion that, when it comes to literary works, evil doers must be punished for their misdeeds. That is, virtue and vice must both receive their due. What goes around, comes around.

Of course, the notion captured by the phrase "poetic justice" predates Rymer. It is perhaps first suggested by Aristotle who points out in his *Poetics* that if a virtuous person is destroyed, tragedy will misfire, for rather than eliciting pity from the audience-members, they will respond with outrage at this cosmic miscarriage of justice. Poetic justice is also a concept beloved by censors, such as the Hays Office, which scrutinized Hollywood scripts in order to make sure that no transgression – from sexual promiscuity to murder – went un-penalized by the last reel of the film.

We may think of the structural requirement that no wrong go un-chastised as the basic or ground-level version of the idea of poetic justice. It is the demand that there be justice-*in*-poetry (in literature, in fictions), especially in terms of evil being castigated. But there is a related, yet more complex and richer, notion of poetic justice as well. It is that of *poetic* justice, by which I mean that the punishment have a symbolic dimension – that it almost allegorically *fits* the crime. Evil is not only punished, but there is something appropriate or symbolic about it. The punishment, in a manner of speaking, *says* something about the crime.

So many of the penalties in Dante's work belong in this category. In the *Inferno*, for example, as its translator John Ciardi points out, the Opportunists have to "race round and round pursuing a wavering banner that runs forever before them in the dirty air .... As they sinned, so are they punished."[6] Likewise, in *Purgatory*, the wrathful are enfolded in a foul-smellling cloud of smoke. Ciardi notes "As wrath is a corrosive state of the spirit, so smoke stings and smarts. As wrath obscures the true light of God, so the smoke plunges all into darkness."[7]

The word often used to describe these images of punishment in Dante is "contrapasso" which simply means "retribution" or a "return punishment," an idea that can be traced to Aristotle's *Nicomachean Ethics*. However, in Dante's usage, the punishments are more than that. They also amount to poetic reflections upon the offenses of the damned.

Of course, this variety of poetic justice is not restricted to the Renaissance. A classic twentieth-century example of it occurs in Proust's letters where the garrulous Madame Strauss is said to eventually suffer cancer of the jaw. Here, the coincidence between Madame Strauss's characterological flaw and her affliction appears so arrestingly fitting that one entertains the thought that Fate had a hand in it, albeit Fate with a somewhat diabolical, if not perverse and mocking, sense of humor. Indeed, often with respect to Tales of Dread, poetic justice takes the form of an ironic twist of fate, in which a character's actions lead precisely to the opposite outcome that he or she intended. The narrative trajectory of the Tale of Dread, that is, resembles what Hegel would catalogue under the rubric of the Cunning of Reason.

In *The Twilight Zone*, poetic justice can be the result of overt supernatural agency, as in "The Chaser" (which involves a love potion), or by explicitly elaborated, science-fiction means as in "Execution" (which employs a time machine). But even where fantasy elements like these are not overtly incorporated into the plot, a supernatural agency always seems *covertly* at large.

In "I Shot an Arrow in the Air", for example, the character, Corey, thinking his rocket ship has landed on an asteroid, kills a fellow astronaut in order to increase his own share of food and water; but soon after the murder, Corey discovers that his space ship has actually fallen back to Earth – near Reno, Nevada – where he will have to pay for his cowardly crimes. The commentary calls it a "*Practical joke* played by Mother Nature and a combination of *improbable* events".[8] That is, even though, on the face of it, this set of events might be explicable naturalistically, it strikes the viewer as if the universe – here identified as Mother Nature – has set Corey up, in order to reveal his true and corrupt inner nature, and then has taken him down. Ironically, the actions he undertakes to save himself damn him.

Whether or not Tales of Dread explicitly invoke magical or science fiction elements, they nevertheless impress us – as they weave their web of poetic justice – as trafficking in the supernatural at their deepest structural level of organization. For they involve coincidences and vastly improbable events that defy – or, at least, virtually defy – explanation in terms of mundane causal regularities and nomological principles. Moreover, these events are invested with so much apparent significance – they are so replete with *poetic* justice – that the forces governing the fictional world would appear to have no counterparts in ordinary experience. And this, in turn, prompts us to hypothesize that they are the product of some mysterious, controlling agency. The universe appears as if authored, and events seem to manifest a powerful, diabolical intelligence in operation, guiding the way in which circumstances unfold. That is, it is as if the universe "intends" to trick its "victims."

Of course, most narratives, in fact, yield the impression of an organizing intelligence; most involve some unlikely events and coincidences. If there weren't something unusual about them, most stories might not be worth telling. Gregory Currie and Jon Jureidini call this feature of narrative hyper-connectedness "overcoherent thinking."[9] However, naturalistic or realistic narratives generally attempt to downplay or, at least, draw attention away from their artifactuality.

Tales of Dread, on the other hand, revel in their "overcoherence" and they use it as a means to encourage the audience to abandon reliance upon the regularities that we depend upon to make sense of the world in which we live and, instead, invite us to infer the operation of a different order of causation – a kind of moral causation rather than physical causation.[10]

Whereas the authors of many realistic or naturalistic narratives strive to deflect attention away from themselves, the creator of the Tale of Dread aspires to elicit the uncanny feeling or apprehension that the world represented in the fiction is itself authored – that is, governed ontologically by a presiding intelligence. With its blatant, even shameless, emphasis upon the improbability of its events and its coincidences – not to mention the way in which these occurrences are charged with poetico-moral and often ironic significance – the Tale of Dread is a hypotrophic narrative, a narrative, in other words, of an extremely high degree of overt narrativity.

The Tale of Dread resembles nothing so much as a schizophrenic or paranoid delusion with its presumption of a mysterious and powerful agency that has special knowledge and control over the character or characters upon whom the story is focused. If characters in the Tales of Dread in *The Twilight Zone* often seem on the verge of madness, then that may be because the situations in which they find themselves are structured after the fashion of a schizophrenic worldview. Tales of Dread are expressive of paranoid thinking – expressive of a paranoid frame of mind.[11] Perhaps part of the attraction/fascination of Tales of Dread and of series like *The Twilight Zone* has to do with the way in which they acknowledge the paranoid – or the paranoid tendencies – in each of us.

Of course, the primary function of the Tale of Dread is to provoke a shudder of fear, apprehension or anxiety. The Tale of Dread succeeds in this by inducing us to entertain the thought of or to imagine a world governed by a mysterious and powerful but *diabolical* intelligence. That intelligence is diabolical in two senses. Just as the devil in the Old Testament was an agent of Yahweh's justice, so the agency that rules the Twilight Zone is dedicated to righting wrongs. Of course, it rights these wrongs in a poetical fashion, which is to say that it frequently punishes the wicked by means of tellingly appropriate, darkly humorous, or ironic twists of fate, as when the U-boat commander torpedoes himself for eternity. Just as the devil is often a trickster, turning into nightmares by means of punning interpretations the wishes of those who broker their souls to him,[12] so the Twilight Zone itself, as an agent, tempts or seduces and entraps wicked humans like Corey and then, in jest-like fashion, hoists them upon their own petards.[13]

Here I want to stress that I take the analogy between Tales of Dread and stories of demonic tricksters (including genies) quite seriously. Consider two of the episodes of *The Twilight Zone* that involve devils: "A Nice Place to Visit" and "Of Late I Think of Cliffordville". In the first, a hood named Rocky Valentine dies. He thinks he has gone heaven. An angelic-looking figure (he's dressed in white), Mr Pip, indulges Rocky's every sordid appetite. When eventually and predictably Rocky is sated, he wants to check out the "Other Place," to which Pip replies with, shall we say, diabolical pleasure that "This is the other place." In the Tale of Dread, on the other hand, the devil as an explicit character in the fiction is subtracted out and the Twilight Zone itself, animistically construed, takes on his function.

In "Of Late I Think of Cliffordville", the demon – one Miss Devlin – offers Mr Feathersmith, an unscrupulous millionaire, the opportunity to return into the past to his home town, Cliffordville, on condition that he turns over all his fortune, save $1,400, to Satan. Miss Devlin does not bargain for Feathersmith's soul, since he's already lost it. Feathersmith jumps at the opportunity, since he believes that he can parlay this $1,400 into an even greater fortune than his present one by purchasing land in Cliffordville that he knows contains oil. Unfortunately for Feathersmith, the land is not yet accessible to drilling at the time he buys it and, flat-broke, Feathersmith finds himself marooned in 1910.

However, Miss Devlin reappears and offers Feathersmith a chance to take a magical train back to the present for a price; but in order to secure the train ticket, the now penniless Feathersmith has to sell the land he has just purchased. Thus, he returns to the present a poor man, his greediness facilitating his seduction by the devil in a manner that results in Feathersmith destroying himself in a cruelly ironic way, but a manner that warrants a devilish chuckle.[14] Here, the devil is meting out justice in this life and is rubbing Featherstone's face in it in a particularly taunting fashion.

In most of the installments in *The Twilight Zone*, there is no devil figure.[15] For in those episodes involving Tales of Dread, the Twilight Zone itself performs the function of Miss Devlin.[16]

The correlation between the Twilight Zone and the devil suggests the way in which the Tale of Dread is able to discharge its central purpose – to engender dread, anxiety, or fear. In his *Poetics*, Aristotle notes that tragedies are able to stir fear in the breasts of viewers because the viewers recognize that insofar as the tragic hero is like them – that is to say, not a saint – the kind of unforeseeable calamity that befalls an Oedipus might befall them too. Tragedy, according to Aristotle, instills fear because it brings viewers face to face with the fact that they are fortune's pawns. At any moment, disaster may overwhelm one. Thus, realizing that they are like the tragic victim, tragedy strikes fear in the hearts of the audience – fear for themselves.

The Tale of Dread also provokes fear in audiences, for in entertaining the thought that the universe is governed by forces that have complete knowledge of and complete power over us, we surmise that there is, or, at least, there may sometime be – especially if the temptation is great – some wickedness on our part that will rouse these forces against us.

Perhaps needless to say, the Tale of Dread is different from Greek tragedy, as theorized by Aristotle. In a way, it is less profound. What Aristotle took to be central to tragedy and crucial to the fear that it arouses is that tragic occurrences can lay low people who have done nothing to deserve their own destruction. In other words, tragedy reminds us that bad things can happen to good people (or, at least, non-bad people). That is, it makes us aware of what Martha Nussbaum has called the *fragility of goodness*. The Tale of Dread, on the other hand, reassures us that bad things will happen to bad people. But since almost all of us feel guilty about something or recognize that we are capable of being led into temptation, the thought that the universe is being policed so effectively can evoke a premonition or palpable tremor of apprehension in us.

However, fear and anxiety are forms of distress. Thus, as with the case of horror stories, Tales of Dread raise the question of why we would subject ourselves to something like *The Twilight Zone*, if it is designed to cause unease in us. That is, there is a paradox in the offing here, namely: unease is something that we avoid, but *The Twilight Zone* has done nicely over time. It enjoyed five seasons on air, is often re-run, is available on DVD, and it has won a cult following substantial enough to warrant an anthology like the one you presently hold in your hands. Clearly, people are not avoiding *The Twilight Zone*; rather they seek it out, because it gives them pleasure. But dread, fear, and anxiety are not pleasureable; they are unpleasant states of mind and body. So, if a characteristic aim of Tales of Dread is to induce dread, then how can folks derive pleasure from them?

The answer, I think, lies in the fact that, even if Tales of Dread exact some quotient of displeasure in terms of apprehension, that is more than compensated for by the pleasure we derive from such stories. And that pleasure is connected to the diabolical character of the universe in Tales of Dread. In the case of *The Twilight Zone*, the Twilight Zone itself is demonic, an agent of justice with a sense of ironic wit. To the extent that we realize that all flesh, including our own, is weak, that stimulates a palpitation of fear in us.

But, on the other hand, most of us realize that we are not *that* bad – not bad enough for the universe itself to pay much attention us – and, anyway, even really bad people underestimate or rationalize away their wickedness. Thus, most of us are glad to entertain the thought that it is in the nature of things – in this case, the Twilight Zone – that wrongs will be righted.[17] That is, poetic justice appeals to our sense of justice, even though it does not match up with the implementation of justice in the world that we inhabit.

The Tale of Dread is gratifying because it mandates us to imagine a state of affairs where Ideal Justice prevails – not in the world as we know it, but in a Twilight Zone. And the satisfaction which that thought occasions outweighs the displeasure that comes with the passing fear that we might be on the Twilight Zone's hit-list.[18]

Horror fictions and tales of dread: a brief note

Earlier I noted that Tales of Dread are often featured alongside of horror stories in anthologies with titles like *Great Tales of Terror and the Supernatural*.[19] Likewise, there are horror stories, like "To Serve Man", next to the Tales of Dread in *The Twilight Zone*. An interesting question is why we find these stories seem to belong together. One factor, perhaps the most obvious, is that both rely upon imagining story-worlds that go beyond what is recognized as natural by contemporary science. Both horror stories and Tales of Dread deploy either magic or science fiction to concoct possibilities that exceed the boundaries accepted by the hard sciences.

However, horror stories have a feature that Tales of Dread lack, namely monsters including supernatural ones like vampires, aliens from outer space, spiders larger than houses due to their exposure to radiation, and so on.[20] And yet Tales of Dread seem to belong to the same family as the horror story. Why?

One suggestion, based upon the previous section of this chapter, might be that Tales of Dread invite an almost animistic way of regarding the universe. The Twilight Zone itself is a facet of the universe, Nemesis as the Greeks would have called her, the goddess of retribution. The Twilight Zone is a sort of being, a diabolical agency enforcing cosmic justice with a mordant sense of humor. Although there is no monster in evidence in the Tale of Dread, properly so-called, there is something like a monster, specifically the universe as a kind of controlling, retributive intelligence like Nemesis. Since this being is not physically manifest, as most of the monsters in horror fictions are, the Tale of Dread does not elicit the feelings of disgust that horror stories do on the basis of the anomalous biologies of the creatures that populate them.

Nor is the fear that the Tale of Dread invites precisely like that of horror stories. With horror stories, we fear for the characters beset by monsters. But in Tales of Dread, we momentarily fear for ourselves as the thought occurs to us that the imagined, vengeful universe in such fictions might have cause to get on our case. Thus, we feel apprehension. The Tale of Dread is premonitory, whereas the horror story confronts us with a clear and present danger. The Tale of Dread leaves a lingering feeling of uncanniness, while the horror most often attacks us frontally.

Nevertheless, the Tale of Dread is kin to the horror story, for like horror fictions, it contains a fantastic being – a cosmic force for poetic justice – which, in the case before us, goes by the name of the Twilight Zone.

Notes

1   TV shows of this sort appeared very early in the history of the medium, including series like *Tales of Tomorrow* and *Lights Out.*

2   Quoted from Marc Scott Zicree (ed.), *The Twilight Zone Companion*, 2nd edn (Los Angeles: Silman-James Press, 1992), p. 51 (emphasis added).

3   "Last Night of a Jockey" is the inverse of this. Prompted by the spirit of evil in him, a jockey who thinks he has just been cashiered, wishes to be big – literally big. But once his wish is granted, it turns out that the decision against him has been reversed. The relation between stories like "Four O'Clock" and "Last Night of a Jockey" is an interesting one. In "Last Night of a Jockey", there is a demonic figure in the form of an internal voice that lays the trap for the jockey's downfall, whereas, in "Four O'Clock," it is the Twilight Zone itself that does the devil's work. We will

have more to say about this parallel relation between Tales of Dread and stories with demons in them later in this chapter.

4 Quoted from Zicree (ed.), *The Twilight Zone Companion*, pp. 275–6 (emphasis added). Often the commentaries at the beginning and ending of *The Twilight Zone* recall those of programs like *One Step Beyond* and *The Inner Sanctum* where hosts like John Nuland prefigure the role Rod Serling plays in his series.

5 The episode "The Little People" is also a Tale of Dread. See Aaron Smuts's discussion of it in "'The Little People': Power and the Worshipable" in Noël Carroll, and Lester Hunt (eds.), *Philosophy in 'The Twilight Zone'* (Oxford: Wiley-Blackwell, 2009), pp. 155–70.

6 John Ciardi, Headnote, *The Inferno* by Dante, trans. Ciardi (New York: New American Library, 1954), p. 91.

7 John Ciardi, Headnote, *Purgatorio* (New York: New American Library, 1961), p. 170.

8 Quoted from Zicree (ed.), *The Twilight Zone Companion*, p. 98 (emphasis added).

9 Gregory Currie and Jon Jureidini, "Narrative and Coherence," *Mind and Language* 19(4) 2004: 407–427. Throughout this chapter, I have benefited from their article as well as from Currie and Jureidini's earlier article "Art and Delusion," *The Monist* 86(4) (2003): 556–578.

10 In this, the conclusion of a Tale of Dread resembles the punchline of a joke. It encourages the audience to hypothesize an explanation for what has just been recounted, albeit a hypothesis that goes against good sense. On punchlines, see Noël Carroll, "On Jokes," in *Beyond Aesthetics* (Cambridge: Cambridge University Press, 2000).

11 See: David Shapiro, *Neurotic Styles* (New York: Harper Torchbooks, 1965), especially ch. 3.

12 Stories like this give meaning to the expression "the devil's in the details." For, when the contract for the soul of the human character is drawn up, there is virtually always a loophole in the details through which the devil turns the victim's wishes against himself.

13 Often, in stories that have demonic figures in them the devils appear to be practical jokers, especially in terms of the way in which the devils manage willfully to misinterpret or mislead the humans who traffic with them. In this regard, it is particularly interesting that the Twilight Zone itself is portrayed as a practical joker in "I Shot an Arrow in the Air". Again, as in "Four O'Clock," it is the Twilight Zone that performs a function parallel to that of demonic figures in meting out poetic justice.

14 Tales of Dread involve reversals of fortune on the part of the pertinent characters. However, this should not be confused with stories that involve reversals of the audience's expectations, even though these too involve an ironic punch. In *The Twilight Zone*, episodes that involve the subversion of the audience's expectations include "Third Planet from the Sun," "Eye of the Beholder," "Invaders," "Midnight Sun," and "Probe 7 – Over and Out." These contrast with Tales of Dread, since Tales of Dread usually fulfill our expectations. These exercises in ironic reversals of the viewers's expectation in *The Twilight Zone* seem undertaken thematically, in the main, in order to defamiliarize our earthly condition.

The episodes I've just listed all belong to the kind of story said to have snapper or surprise endings or to conclude with O. Henry twists. In his article in this volume, Carl Plantinga calls these endings *frame shifters*. See Carl Plantinga, "Frame Shifters: Surprise Endings, and Spectator Imagination in *The Twilight Zone*," in Carroll and Hunt (eds.), *Philosophy in 'The Twilight Zone'*, pp. 39–57.

15   One episode that lies halfway between Tales of Dread and stories with the devil in them is "Nick of Time". For here the audience is not sure whether the fortune-telling machine (with the bobble-headed devil on top) is itself a demonic agency or whether it is merely a snare set for unwary humans by the diabolical Twilight Zone. This episode is discussed by Carl Plantinga, "Frame Shifters: Surprise Endings and the Spectator Imagination in *The Twilight Zone*," and by Aeon Skoble, "Rationality and Choice in 'Nick of Time'," in Carroll and Hunt (eds.), *Philosophy in 'The Twilight Zone'*, pp. 147–154.

16   It should be noted that, in addition to Tales of Dread, there are also what might be called Tales of Redemption in *The Twilight Zone*. These are cases – like "The Last Flight" and "Night of the Meek," where the universe gives the protagonist a second chance. Interestingly, Tales of Redemption are paralleled by stories with angelic intermediaries – like "Mr Denton on Doomsday" and "A Passage for a Trumpet" – just as Tales of Dread are paralleled by stories with diabolical figures.

17   Moreover, perhaps the fear that the Tale of Dread instills may be required in part to deliver the pleasure we take in imagining such a justice-driven universe insofar as the fear we feel may phenomenologically reinforce our transitory feeling that a vigilant universe is on the lookout for evil-doing everywhere, including in our very own hearts.

18   Also, the fear component in our response to the Tale of Dread may not be altogether displeasureable. For an account of the satisfaction that may accompany the fear that supernatural stories engender, see Noël Carroll, "The Fear of Fear Itself: The Philosophy of Halloween," in Richard Greene and K. Silem Mohammad (eds.), *The Undead and Philosophy* (La Salle, IL: Open Court, 2006), pp. 223–36.

19   Herbert E. Wise and Phyllis Fraser (eds.), *Great Tales of Terror and the Supernatural* (New York: Modern Library, 1944, 1972).

20   This view is defended in Noël Carroll, *The Philosophy of Horror, or Paradoxes of the Heart* (New York: Routledge, 1990).

15

Sympathy for Soprano

Sympathy for the devil

The marriage of *The Untouchables* with the sit-com, of violent action with the soap-opera, and pornography with domesticity, *The Sopranos* seems to be a strange brew, appealing to high-end critics and popular audiences alike. But much of this apparent paradox disappears when one realizes that the hair-pin mood shifting – from mirth to mayhem and from parody to rage – admired by the highbrow clientele is a matter of shuffling rapidly between genres – such as the gangster film and crime show, the sitcom, the soap-opera, the family drama, and soft-core pornography – already familiar to the general audience and beloved by them. *The Sopranos* has taken the family theme of *The Godfather* and split it in two, augmenting the literal kinship side of the analogy and adapting it to enshrined TV formats: TV does the natural family so well, because it is the family that is its coveted audience, one to whose narcissistic inclinations it congenially caters with the sit-com and the soap-opera. Juxtaposing mundane family life with life in the "crime family," while enabling the two terms of the comparison to inform each other in insightful (sometimes comic, and sometimes unsettling) ways, also relieves the banality of everyday family life with a dash of excitement, much in the manner that an evening of crime shows leavens the routine of actual family existence either after or even during dinner.

"Sympathy for the Devil," in Richard Greene and Peter Vernezze (eds.), *The Sopranos and Philosophy* (Chicago: Open Court, 2004), pp. 121–36.

However, even if *The Sopranos* is not as altogether bizarre as it may appear at first blush, it possesses some stubbornly anomalous features that invite philosophical reflection. Perhaps the strangest of these is what we might call "sympathy for Soprano" – that is, the pro-attitude that most viewers, including the most law-abiding, bear toward the central figure of the show, the mobster-boss, Tony Soprano. What is, of course, strange about this response is that most viewers would feel anything but care and concern for Tony Soprano's real-life counterpart; indeed, many would feel moral revulsion. Nevertheless, many – perhaps most – of us do appear to care for the fictional Tony Soprano, whereas we would loathe an actual person just like him. Does this make any sense? How is it possible?

Maybe needless to say, the preceding paradox is not unique to *The Sopranos*. It's an instance of a broader paradox that is sometimes called "sympathy for the devil." The problem is basically how a viewer can be sympathetic (care for, or have a pro-attitude) toward a fictional character whose real-world counterpart she would abhor totally? Using Tony Soprano as our particular specimen of the devil, let us consider why, maybe to our own surprise, we may find ourselves on his side.

Perhaps the best way to begin to appreciate this mystery is to remind ourselves of Tony Soprano's many crimes. He is the head of a New Jersey crime family that traffics in drugs, prostitution, extortion, usury, money laundering, murder, bribery, theft, suborning witnesses, pornography, and crimes of which I don't even know the names; he contributes to the corruption of policemen, assemblymen, clergymen, unions, and various businesses, large and small. Nor is it the case that Tony Soprano is merely a distant CEO, presiding over all this criminality from afar. He is a hands-on gangster, relishing, as he acknowledges more than once to his psychiatrist, the adrenaline rush of violence, the "thrill" of beating a man to death with his bare hands, or running down a welcher with a car. Tony, at one point, is on the verge of suffocating his mother with a pillow, and he is prepared to kill his own uncle.

Nor are his transgressions only legal in nature. He is a tireless philanderer and adulterer. He is an inveterate liar, dishonest to his family, doctor, friends, and lovers, not to mention to enemies and the law. He is a man of large appetites; he is closely acquainted with virtually every vice and, at one time or another, seems to indulge each one excessively, sometimes in turn and sometimes in tandem. He is a man that most of us would give a wide berth if ever he came anywhere near our neighborhood. Few of us would hesitate for a moment to condemn the real-life Tony Soprano. If we read of his death in a gang war, we would not shed a tear; if we learnt that he was imprisoned and that they threw away the key, we would cheer.

But that is how we would react, if Tony Soprano were an inhabitant of the actual world. As a denizen of the fictional world, called *The Sopranos*, however, he somehow engenders our sympathy (understood as "care"), or, if that is too strong a word here, he at least elicits from us a pro-attitude. Yet how can this be?

It was fascination

An initial response to this apparent paradox is to say that it is just that – merely "apparent." In fact, it might be said, we do not really have a pro-attitude toward Tony Soprano. Admittedly we do feel something toward Tony – indeed, we feel something rather strongly – but it is not sympathy. Instead it is fascination. Tony is this bizarre amalgam of the ordinary and the exotic. He is a family man beleaguered by everyday trials of the sort that one might encounter in a sit-com, or a soap-opera, or, to a certain extent, in one's daily life. There are disciplinary problems with the kids, arguments with aging relatives, household squabbles of every sort, bickering over the family finances, sicknesses, troublesome in-laws, issues concerning the children's education, and so on. But Tony Soprano is no ordinary family man; his business is in an underworld of violence and forbidden desires which he rules, often with great brutality. He has a Good Housekeeping suburban dream house, but his office is in a dingy strip joint, the Bada-Bing!

The disconnect between his unexceptional family life and his exceptional professional life is nothing short of staggering. Among other things, his family life seems absolutely contemporary and conventional, whereas his professional life appears to be both a throwback to a bygone era and extraordinary in its transgressiveness. These two opposed life-worlds clash audibly.

Tony and his cronies sit around planning murders, robberies, and scams, but they also gossip about ailments like the hypochondriacs with whom we are all familiar, use the current psychobabble, and speak about stolen property like consumers parroting advertising copy. They obviously read the same magazines and catalogues that everyone else does, but when they talk to each other about it in their New Jersey cadences, it seems so strange coming from their mouths. Undoubtedly, this is realistic. Actual gangsters are probably not as aphoristic as Don Corleone. But it is nevertheless jarring to hear every day consumer-speak issuing from the lips of these thugs. And in almost every way, Tony Soprano himself is an oxymoron: a ruthless Mafia chieftain with a soft spot in his heart for ducks.

In addition, there is Tony's psychiatric treatment. The sessions with his doctor, Jennifer Melfi, are dazzling. The layers of intentional dissembling, unconscious self-deception, understatement, knots, hypocrisy, and misdescription that Tony puts in motion are consistently engrossing; one is constantly comparing what he says and what he is aware of with his actual situation (as we know it). Both in terms of his strikingly bifurcated and oxymoronic life and his labyrinthian mental gymnastics – often the result of depression but also sometimes of simple guile – Tony Soprano is an undeniably fascinating character – one whose doings frequently strike us with their unprecedented juxtapositions of elements and their continuing potential to take us by surprise.

For these sorts of reasons, we are interested in Tony Soprano; we keep coming back for more. But it would be a mistake, it may be argued, to regard this kind of interest as a matter of caring for Tony Soprano. It is more like being bewitched by him. We can't take our eyes off him, because he so amazes us. But amazement and fascination do not add up to a pro-attitude, since we can be transfixed by what we find despicable.

However, even though it is true that we are fascinated by Tony Soprano – often for the reasons just given – it does not seem quite so easy to dispel the paradox that concerns us. For there are a number of oxymoronic characters in *The Sopranos* who also wear symptoms of denial on their sleeves but who, however fascinating for those reasons, do not mobilize in us the kind of pro-attitudes that Tony does.

Consider Richie Aprile. A devotee of yoga, this self-consciously short gunsel with a Napoleon-complex is at the same time sociopathic in his brutality, repeatedly running over his former associate Beansie with his SUV to the point where Beansie is paralyzed for life. Richie can show as much barely explicable rage as Tony, and his occasionally New Age lingo sits uneasily with his sado-masochistic sex games with Tony's sister Janice. Given his curious alchemy of attributes, Richie is as riveting as Tony. But surely no one has a pro-attitude toward Richie Aprile. The series mandates quite the opposite stance toward him and, for probably everyone, it is an assignment we discharge effortlessly.

Fascination and caring are distinct. Even if we are fascinated by Tony Soprano, that does not preclude that we also have a pro-attitude toward him. Acknowledging how very arresting for us he is does not make the fact that we also care for him disappear, since there are equally "thought-provoking" anomalies populating the world of *The Sopranos* for whom we have no sympathy.

Wish fulfillment

One way of trying to explain the pro-attitude we bear toward Tony might be to argue that he fulfills our darkest wishes. Tony is Rabelaisian in his self-control: he eats, fucks, drinks, and smokes whatever he pleases. He permits his rage to flow in torrents. He beats the Jersey assemblyman, Zellman, who is on his payroll, with his belt because the politician is having an affair with Irina Peltsin, one of Tony's former *goombas*. Vengeance is his and he metes out his own version of justice unconstrained by anyone. In her dream, Melfi associates Tony with a huge panting dog – a rottweiler. Often Tony seems to be nothing short of a personification, in the lineage of King Ubu, of the unbridled id. Moreover, he seems to be able to get away with the worst crimes and misdemeanors – at least with regard to civil society.

Given all this, one might speculate that Tony represents the symbolic realization of deep repressed fantasies, especially for the males in the audience. They wish to be as unrestrained as Tony. Insofar as he enacts their dreams, they give him a pass. That is the basis of our pro-attitude toward Tony. Our sympathy for Soprano is nothing but our egoistical love of our own egoism. We have a pro-attitude toward Tony because he actualizes, albeit fictionally, the sort of abandon we want for ourselves – the capacity to pursue our desires unshackled and, in large measure, unpunished.

However, this is an unpromising strategy for explaining our pro-attitudes to Tony Soprano. The reason for this is of a piece with our preceding objection to the fascination hypothesis: there are many characters in the world of *The Sopranos* who behave as wantonly as Tony does, if not more so, but we do not regard them positively in any way, whereas we do Tony. Ralph Cifereto, the psychopath who inherits the mantel of Richie Aprile, is at least as incontinent at Tony. Yet we never feel inclined in his behalf. He is always menacing. His humor is generally more mean-spirited than funny. Like Tony, he denies himself nothing. But when he beats his pregnant girlfriend Tracee to death, the audience hates him. Sinning, at least when Ralph does it, is not a way to our hearts. We are consistently supposed to regard him with disdain, distrust, and disapproval and we readily do so. Ralph is as clear-cut an image as Tony of the dark forces of the psyche. Nevertheless, no normal viewer has an inkling of sympathy for Ralph. Therefore, our pro-attitude toward Tony cannot be explained simply on the grounds of his transgressiveness.

Identification

Undoubtedly, the notion that Tony might function as a wish-fulfillment fantasy may call to mind the different but related idea that we have a pro-attitude toward him because we *identify* with him. Insofar as Tony is a figure of what one wishes to become, one is, by definition, not *yet* identical to him. Tony must be different from us in order to satisfy our wishes. But, it might be suggested, our link with Tony is not based on the grounds of what we wish to become, but on the grounds of what we already are.

Especially in terms of the quotidian side of Tony's existence, many of us can recognize our own lives in Tony's – broken water heaters, rebellious or otherwise misbehaving children, querulous elderly relatives, marital tensions, annoying extended family members and overbearing in-laws, and so forth. Like many of us, Tony finds himself – to his chagrin – in a world where the rules he grew up with are rapidly changing. Many of his complaints – for example, about his children's schools or about the self-indulgence of the me-generation – may be our complaints. On the basis of these and other points of tangency between ourselves and Tony, it might be argued that we identify with him – regard ourselves, in some sense, as identical to him. And if we identify with him, then, it could be observed, our pro-attitude toward Tony would follow fairly straightforwardly from our own partiality to ourselves.

Understood one way, the suggestion that we identify with Tony Soprano is patently absurd. For however many similarities there are between any audience member and Tony, no one of them is literally *identical* with him, nor, and this is perhaps more important, do any of them take themselves to be strictly identical with him – often, for example, we are *appalled* at those of Tony's very actions that *thrill* him.

Moreover, to suppose oneself to be identical with Tony would be to court paradox: if I thought myself Tony Soprano, then that would imply that I could meet myself (Noël Carroll); but I know it is logically impossible to meet oneself. So identification cannot explain the pro-attitude we bring to Tony because strict identification seems an inadmissible state of mind.[1]

But maybe when people claim that they identify with Tony Soprano and other fictional beings they are thinking of something less than strict identification. They do not take themselves to be identical with such characters in every way, but only in some ways. They do not imagine themselves being Tony Soprano but only as sometimes feeling or desiring as he does. This imaginative state is aspectual.[2] When Tony desires revenge, we imagine ourselves into his situation and likewise desire revenge; when he wishes to kill his mother, we take on his murderous rage; when he is exasperated by Gloria Trillo's temper tantrums, we are too. As well, we find Jackie Junior's incredible stupidity as frustrating as Tony does; we merge our frustration and his. And insofar as we imagine our feelings and Tony's to be the same, we are as disposed to regard his feelings as positively as we regard our own. And this, of course, adds up finally to a pro-attitude toward Tony.

Though this version of the notion of identification appears less problematic than its predecessor, I am not convinced that it is plausible. It too has unhappy consequences. If I imagine feeling what Tony feels, then if Tony imagines becoming infatuated with someone, say Valentina La Paz, then I should imagine becoming infatuated with her. But then wouldn't I be jealous of Tony and wish his affair ill? Yet I don't. So it cannot be the case that I am imagining having the same feelings as Tony Soprano. In point of fact, I would argue that what I feel is quite differently than what Tony feels. The object of his emotional state is Valentina, whereas the objects of my state, I conjecture, are Tony and Valentina, neither of whom I am infatuated with and both of whom I wish well.

Nor is infatuation the only feeling state where the aspectual conception of identification goes haywire. If Tony desires a certain "business" account then

I should want it too. But that would make us competitors and I should desire that my rival's efforts come a-cropper. However, I don't. Furthermore, if I possessed Tony's particular desire for revenge, then shouldn't I resent it when he, rather than I, gets to wreak violence on its object? But that is not how most of the fans of *The Sopranos* feel; indeed, we might suspect anyone who reacted to Tony in these ways to be someone with a screw loose. So this model of our responses to Tony is not adequate.

Audiences cannot be identifying with Tony where identification is understood as aspectually imagining themselves to have the same feelings and motivations as Tony does. And if they cannot be identifying with Tony, since the very process would appear to have dubious implications, identification cannot explain our pro-attitude toward Soprano.

Of course, it may be charged that we are taking the notion of identification too literally. But if it is not intended to model our relations to the emotions and desires of characters, what identities are at issue here? Surely if the process is called identification, there must be some dimension of congruence. And one would think that the likeliest vein of correlation would be in terms of shared desires, feelings, motivations, and emotions. But, as we've seen, in a number of significant cases, postulating identification along these lines has unacceptable results.

Perhaps it will be said that, however strange it sounds, identification has nothing to do with identity. Maybe all people mean by saying that they identify with a character is that they care for him. Though I doubt that people actually have so weak a notion in mind, if this is really all identification means, then it will not help us account for why we bring a pro-attitude toward Tony, since, on this interpretation, saying people identify with him alleges no more than that they have a pro-attitude toward him. That is, under such a watered down construal, identification would have no explanatory power for our purposes; it would merely be a way of redescribing what already mystifies us.

Paradox solved

Though I have argued that we do not identify with Tony Soprano (or, for that matter, any other fictional character), it is evident that we do have some kind of affinity for him. In order to avoid the untoward implications of the concept of identification, let us say we are *allied* to Tony Soprano. This, of course, does not explain why we have a pro-attitude toward him. However, it may suggest a way of working out such an explanation. Let us ask why we would find Tony Soprano to be an appropriate ally? Why might we form an alliance with him? If we can answer these questions, then maybe we will be in a position to explain our pro-attitude toward him.

Talking about forming an alliance with Tony may sound weird. What lawful citizen in their right mind would contemplate being in league with Tony? Well probably no one, if we are speaking of the real world counterpart of Tony. But the alliance we strike is not with an actual gang lord, but with the fictional Tony Soprano, an inhabitant of a very unique fictional world. Moreover, when we look at the moral structure of that fictional world, it seems to me that Tony is the most likely candidate or, at least, one of the likeliest candidates for an alliance, given the entire available array of characters as they are portrayed in the series. Nor is he the most suitable ally because he is putatively just the strongest or the smartest character. He also has a fair claim to being the most moral or, at least, no less moral than the other significant figures in the series.

This is not to say that Tony is moral, but only that within the relational structure of the fictional world of *The Sopranos*, he has an equally strong or stronger claim to morality than any of the other major players to whom we are extensively exposed.[3] Compared to the other mobsters, especially to the more maniacal ones (like Ralph, Richie, Paulie, Furio), Tony seems *relatively* less volatile and sadistic, and more judicious and prosocial. Within the bounds of the Mafia code, he appears to be the fairest gangster (not absolutely fair, but relatively fair) and he has a capacity for compassion (albeit obviously not fully developed).

Furthermore, the law is not represented as a positive moral counterweight. Virtually all the Jersey policemen (save one) whom we encounter are corrupt – on the take – as is the state assemblyman. The FBI are not outright venal, but the side of them that we observe is not morally unambiguous. We do not see them protecting the weak and the innocent. We see them trying to blackmail felons like Adriana La Cerva and "Big Pussy" Bonpensiero into spying on their friends and loved ones; and we watch them planting a listening device in Tony's home. Rather than witnessing the FBI engaged in heroic activities, we find them involved in these more unseemly or shady subterfuges which are apt to strike many as possibly questionable intrusions into the private sphere, if not illegal then intuitively immoral and perhaps verging on abuses of power. They are, in other words, cast in a light that makes them seem at least somewhat compromised and unscrupulous, and which, in any event, is not offset by showing them to be forthright representatives of justice.

Other representatives of moral authority also appear tarnished. Black civil rights leaders are revealed to be in cahoots with the mob, betraying their own people (something Tony would never do). The Catholic priests whom we encounter are hypocrites, willingly feeding at the Mafia trough. Indeed, hypocrisy of one sort or another is the characteristic that marks most of the "civilians" who receive appreciable air time in *The Sopranos*. Furthermore, many of those who bear the brunt of Tony's ire have brought it upon themselves – Davey Scatino by gambling beyond his means, despite Tony's warnings, and Shlomo Teittleman by trying to renege on his deal with Tony.

In important instances, Tony is more sinned against than sinning: no one deserves a mother as manipulative and as poisonous as Livia, whose namesake is a scheming character from *I, Claudius*.[4] Tony's sister Janice has inherited all of her mother's malefic low cunning and, if she does not cause as much damage as Tony, that is only because her theater of operations is much smaller. One senses that in Tony's position, she would be far more dangerous. Nor is Tony his uncle Junior's moral inferior; it is Junior who initiates plots against Tony's life, not vice-versa. In some respects, though Tony would be the last to cop this plea, Tony is a victim and, although this hardly exculpates him, it does shift a modicum of weight onto his side of the moral scales. Of course, Tony should know better and the fact that he inherited his criminal role does not exonerate him, but it does garner him some slight measure of mitigation.

In addition, Tony does possess some positive moral characteristics. He is loyal to friends and family, including his nephew whom he forcibly enrolls into a detox program. Tony makes a serious effort at being a good parent and he plans for a better life for his children, one free of any taint of the mob. He does play by certain rules; even if those rules are those of a criminal society, Tony is nevertheless undeniably conscientious. He has a sense of justice, not in the legal sense, but in the sense of trying to give people their due within the bounds of the peculiar code to which he is sworn. And Tony agonizes over the various conflicting loyalties that pull him in opposite directions. In short, Tony has some virtues that we may unblushingly refer to as moral in addition to a number of nonmoral virtues such as brute power, raw tactical intelligence, and a quick wit.

In the world of *The Sopranos*, Tony is far from the worst character.[5] Of course, there are characters of whom we know too little to compare to Tony morally and others who do not elicit comparison because they are too secondary to the plot, like Tony's sister Barbara. But, for the most part, when we situate Tony Soprano on the field of the pertinent cast of characters in the series, he turns out to be one of the most savory, morally speaking. This is not to deny that Tony Soprano is morally defective, but only to suggest that among an array of ethically challenged characters, he is one of the least deplorable.

There is a joke, a shortened variation of which Hesh tells at the party after Livia's funeral, which illustrates Tony's moral standing in the world of *The Sopranos*. The full version goes like this:

> Because the town has no rabbi of its own, its citizens hire one from another village to officiate at Moshe's last rites. At the end of the service, the rabbi says, "Since I am not from this village, I can say little about this man's life. So I would like someone from this shettl to tell us something now about Moshe's good works." This is followed by a resounding silence. The rabbi repeats his request

with no results. Finally he says: "I don't think you understand; we are not leaving here until someone says something good about Moshe." Eventually an old man stands up and offers the following: "I knew his brother; he was worse."

This, I submit, is how Tony figures in the moral economy of *The Sopranos*. Of most of the relevant characters in this fictional universe, they are worse or no better than Tony Soprano.

Furthermore, this provides us with our grounds for our willingness to ally ourselves with Tony. In most situations, it is pragmatically urgent for us to ally ourselves with the people whom we assess to be the most moral. This is a simple matter of prudence. The people we estimate to be the most moral are the ones who are the safest to interact with, the most trustworthy, and the most reliable. Alliance with the most moral agents available, in effect, is an insurance policy of sorts. They are our best bet for securing reciprocal relations of exchange[6] and fair treatment. Tony is not a moral man in any absolute sense, but inasmuch as most of the other characters in *The Sopranos* are worse, Tony is a natural candidate for solidarity.[7] Thus the pro-attitude that we extend to Tony Soprano is a result of the fact that we are allied to him. And we are allied to him because in the fictional world of *The Sopranos* alternative alliances would either be worse morally or irrelevant. This is not to say that we are not appalled by features of Tony, like his racism, or by many of his actions, including the murders he perpetrates. But in a world of moral midgets, insofar as he is the closest approximation of probity we find, we ally ourselves with him.

It might appear contradictory that we can muster a pro-attitude for the fictional character Tony Soprano, whereas we would not be similarly disposed toward his real world counterpart. That is, we seem to be staring at the following inconsistency:

1. Audiences have a pro-attitude toward the fictional Tony Soprano.
2. In terms of every pertinent moral property, the fictional Tony Soprano is identical to a real-life Tony Soprano.
3. Audiences would morally abhor a real-life counterpart of Tony Soprano (that is, by definition, they would not bear a pro-attitude toward him).

Nevertheless, the contradiction that looms in this triad of propositions is avoided once we realize that the second proposition above is false. It is not the case that Tony Soprano and his real-life counterpart are morally the same in every respect because relative to the fictional world of *The Sopranos* Tony is more morally palatable than his real-world counterpart would be, since the real world has much more morality in it than what we find in *The Sopranos*.

For example, the actual police, FBI, civil rights leadership, and so on are more ethically upright than what is pictured in *The Sopranos*. A Tony

Soprano would not occupy the same relative position morally in the real world that he stakes out in the fiction. In the fiction, a fallen world if there ever was one, Tony is the best of the worst, and, thus, a natural ally for the viewer who has scant other options to negotiate. That is the basis of our pro-attitude toward him. However, an actual Tony Soprano would not present us with the same bargain, given the difference between the actual world and *The Sopranos*. The divergence of contexts entails that it is not the case that our two Tonys are identical in every respect morally. Thus, there is no inconsistency in bearing a pro-attitude to the fictional Soprano, while finding an actual Soprano to be morally despicable. That is, sympathy for the Soprano in the fiction is compatible with antipathy for an actual gangster with all the same intrinsic properties.

A remaining problem

Though we have answered the question of how it is possible for us to have a pro-attitude toward the fictional Tony Soprano, our answer may have provoked another question: is it morally permissible for the creators of *The Sopranos* to produce a fiction that elicits our alliance with a creature like Tony? Isn't it simply immoral to do this? Perhaps one might suspect this on the grounds that eliciting a pro-attitude toward Tony is likely to have some carry-over effect upon our judgments of real-life miscreants.

I don't think this anxiety is serious. First of all, even with respect to *The Sopranos*, our pro-attitude toward Tony is highly circumscribed. Though allied with him on various fronts, our allegiance is not unconditional. We are still repelled by a great many of the things he says and does. Our capacity for sympathy for Tony is limited. Our appreciation of his relative merits in his fallen world does not impair our capability to be morally outraged by many of his criminal behaviors and ethically deficient attitudes, such as his racism and sexism. Thus, there is little cause to fear some slippage from our assessment of the fictional Soprano to our judgments of real-world criminals. As indicated by our disapproving reactions to the fictional Tony, *The Sopranos* leaves our capacity for moral indignation generally intact.

Nor do I think that it is problematic that *The Sopranos* exercises our talent for calculating the most morally optimal alliances possible in ethically murky situations. Certainly it is not a moral deficit that we have such a mechanism at our disposal; it enables us to navigate all those situations in life that compel us to make the best morally of a bad set of choices. That *The Sopranos* engages this ethically beneficial capacity in a way that may sharpen it cannot count as morally reprehensible.

In all likelihood, there are some who are prepared to charge that by encouraging audience-alliances with Tony Soprano the television program invites viewers to emulate his actions – the bad ones as well as whatever good ones there might be. *The Sopranos* should be condemned morally, then, because it will have immoral consequences in the form of nefarious copy-cat behavior. But, of course, no one is really in a position to substantiate this hypothesis. My own suspicion is that people will only be likely to replicate onscreen behaviors that they already regard to be morally permissible. Normal viewers will not reproduce what they believe is immoral behavior just because they see it on television. That which audiences are disposed to imitate from fictions, I conjecture, is only what they already judge to be acceptable ethically. Therefore, *if* anyone ever imitates Tony's immoral behavior, I reckon that they were already morally corrupt before the show and not that *The Sopranos* corrupted them.

And finally, on the positive side of the ledger, it may be argued that the sympathy we have for Soprano contributes to the very salutary moral message that the series promotes. In an interview with Peter Bogdanovich, David Chase, the creator of *The Sopranos*, suggests, alluding to something that the character Octave says in Renoir's *Rules of the Game*, that a major theme of the program is that "the problem is that everyone has his reasons."[8] That is, everyone has justifications and/or explanations for their actions which legitimatize them – at least in the minds of the agents in question. But it is precisely our proclivity to see ourselves as always in the right that makes human life so full of strife and resistant to conflict resolution.

Through the ingenious psychoanalytic sessions with Melfi and by narrating the world of *The Sopranos* primarily in terms of a point of view convergent with Tony's, Chase shows us that Tony has *his* reasons, reasons made especially pressing to us in the process of our allying ourselves with him. But, of course, it is just because Tony can have what he takes to be self-justifying reasons that enables him to persist in his evil ways. That is the very problem that *The Sopranos* discloses. By eliciting our sympathy for Tony, Chase reminds us how obdurate a problem this really is. Chase casts this issue in relief by strategically punctuating the show with outrageous behaviors and views on Tony's part that shake us from our sympathy for him and from our inclination toward his point of view, thus alerting us to the danger that sympathetic understanding may risk moral misunderstanding.

In a manner of speaking, David Chase is committed to questioning the commonplace coined by Alexander Chase that "to understand is to forgive, even oneself." *The Sopranos*, most notably with respect to Tony, presents us with situations that we understand, but ultimately should not forgive nor allow Tony to forgive, nor do we forgive with regard to many of Tony's crimes and attitudes. But inasmuch as we frequently find ourselves allied with Tony, often preferring Tony's reasons and assessments relative to other characters, we see how slippery the moral slope can become and how easy it may be to lose one's footing. Or, to change metaphors, by taking note of the pro-attitudes Tony elicits from us we may come to appreciate how subtly our moral compass can be demagnetized. Thus, by inciting us to care for Soprano, David Chase makes vivid our realization of the moral threat of rationalization.

Notes

1   For objections to the notion of strict identification, see Richard Wollheim, *The Thread of Life* (Cambridge, MA: Harvard University Press, 1984); and Noël Carroll, *The Philosophy of Horror* (New York: Routledge, 1990).

2   The idea of aspectual identification is developed by Berys Gaut in his "Identification and Emotion in Narrative Film," in Carl Plantinga and Gregg M. Smith (eds.), *Passionate Views: Film, Cognition, and Emotion* (Baltimore: Johns Hopkins University Press, 1999), pp. 200–16.

3   The importance of the relative moral standing of characters in eliciting audience affiliation was introduced in my "Toward a Theory of Film Suspense" which is anthologized in Noël Carroll, *Theorizing the Moving Image* (Cambridge: Cambridge University Press, 1996). The approach is also developed in Murray Smith, "Gangsters, Cannibals, Aesthetes, or Apparently Perverse Allegiances," in Plantinga and Smith (eds.), *Passionate Views*, pp. 217–238.

4   "Appendix B," in David Lavery (ed.), *This Thing of Ours: Investigating the Sopranos* (New York: Columbia University Press, 2002), p. 245.

5   Our moral estimation of Tony Soprano also benefits from what we might call the "out of sight, out of mind" phenomenon. That is, we are not shown many of the long-term repercussions of Tony's criminal activities and, as a result, do not figure them into our moral calculus. We do not see how his calling-card scam might have effectively taken food off the table of an immigrant family with undernourished children. This phenomenon, of course, is related to the fact that much of the program is narrated from Tony's point of view in the sense that he too is oblivious to a great deal of the destruction that his actions ultimately engender.

6   On the importance of reciprocal exchange for relations with non-kin, see Robert A. Hinde, *Why Good Is Good: The Sources of Morality* (New York: Routledge, 2002), pp. 72–94.

7   Of course, it might be said that there are other major characters who are not so compromised morally as Tony, such as his wife Carmela and Melfi. Carmela is a tricky case, since she is also evidently an accomplice of Tony's and somewhat of a hypocrite, but, in any event, both Carmela and Melfi are themselves allies of Tony's and, consequently, our putative alliance with them would not conflict with our alliance with Tony.

8   Peter Bogdanovich, "Interview with David Chase," *The Sopranos: The First Season* (HBO Home Video, 2001), DVD Disc 4. For an exact quotation of what is said in *Rules of the Game*, see Octave's remarks on p. 53 of the Classic Film Scripts edition of *Rules of the Game: A Film by Jean Renoir*, trans. John McGrath and Maureen Teitelbaum (New York: Simon and Schuster, 1970).

16

Consuming Passion

Sex and the City

Shop till you drop. It's a Moral Imperative.
Vancouver Sun, December 26, 2005

I. Introduction

Carrie Bradshaw, the central character in the television series *Sex and the City*, is a journalist.[1] She has a weekly newspaper column in which she muses about the sex lives of thirty-somethings in New York City in particular, though presumably with implications for contemporary urban dating everywhere. Ostensibly each weekly installment of the show is an audio-visual rendition of her column, frequently rounded off with a summary observation or even a moral.

The character of Carrie Bradshaw is loosely modeled on the actual writer Candace Bushnell from whose column the program derives its title, though not its plot-lines. Broadly speaking, the genre that Bradshaw and Bushnell ply falls under the heading of *advice*. Often Carrie will pose an explicit question about sexual mores or strategy on the voice-over soundtrack which question then the rest of the show may then be taken to address and/or attempt to answer. The advice Carrie has to offer concerns how to live – specifically, how to conduct one's sexual life. In this respect, Carrie is quite clearly a practical ethicist or moral advisor. Thus, it is not too fanciful to interpret the TV program as communicating, via the medium of motion pictures, advice about how to live one's life.

"Consuming Passion: *Sex and the City*," *Revue internationale de philosophie* 64(254) (2010): 525–46.

Episodes typically begin with Carrie working on her column. As she speaks, the question or problem she intends to tackle this week often simultaneously flashes on the screen of her computer. Then the episode moves from the essayistic mode into narrative, though sometimes, in concert with the voice-over narration, the words from her column interrupt the flow of the imagery.

Carrie has three friends: Samantha, Miranda, and Charlotte. They may discuss the issue that interests Carrie while sharing a meal; the question that initiates the series in the opening episode (entitled "Sex and the City"), for example, is whether women can and/or should have sex like men – that is, sex without emotional entanglements. Subplots – involving the experiences of Carrie and/or one or more of her friends – then evolve, illustrating various attitudes or perspectives that could be taken toward the presiding theme. "Valley of the Twenty-Something Guys," for instance, develops two vignettes about the downside of dating younger men. Like a great deal of practical ethics as featured in newspapers, *Sex and the City* approaches its issues of conduct anecdotally rather than argumentatively.

Though primarily comedic, *Sex and the City* has serious elements as well. In the course of the series, Charlotte experiences a traumatic divorce; Samantha is stricken with cancer; Miranda's mother-in-law has Alzheimer's; and Carrie's great loves, in contrast to those of her friends, all go down in flames. Still, the program never despairs; it radiates that upbeat "There'll always be a tomorrow" point of view. Nor is the counsel it brokers ever particularly heavy-handed, since the multiple story-line approach that it has toward its animating questions from program to program works against the suggestion that one size fits all.

Nevertheless, despite its light touch and undeniable entertainment value, the show – no less than the fictional newspaper column that supplies its pretext – still functions as a source of information about sex in the city, sometimes by way of sharing observations, sometimes by offering model behaviors, and sometimes by articulating advice outright. Though it proposes its ethics genially – indeed, its irresistibly appealing geniality itself is something that needs to be discussed – it is still in the business of essentially recommending conduct. It is no accident that Carrie writes an advice column – and, for that reason, the program needs to be interrogated in terms of the kind of life it advocates.

At this point, the casual viewer might complain – the kind of life that *Sex and the City* ultimately backs is one dedicated to the search for enduring love, where that is regarded as a real possibility (as witnessed by the way that things turn out for Miranda, Charlotte, and for a time even Samantha). Why does that need to be *interrogated*? Surely, it can be said, that that is an altogether morally wholesome, if not utterly platitudinous, life-plan to exhort. But, I shall argue, that the kind of life that *Sex and the City* showcases is more complicated than the preceding thumbnail sketch allows, even though that sketch is generally accurate as far as it goes. But, if one probes a bit further, it becomes evident that beneath the affirmation of the possibility of enduring love, the program is, as well, a celebration of consumerism – a way of life that has come to dominate much of so-called developed world and which, in addition, inspires much of the developing world.[2]

I will attempt to substantiate this claim by discussing in depth an episode from the fourth season of *Sex and the City*, entitled "A *Vogue* Idea," which aired on the cable channel HBO on February 2, 2002. However, before looking closely at "A *Vogue* Idea," I need to clarify what I mean by "consumerism" and to explain why I think that it is ethically problematic.

II. Consumerism

Consumerism as a way of life for significant portions of the populations in the economically developed countries of the North Atlantic and elsewhere, including Japan and the Asian Tigers, became an increasingly familiar phenomenon toward the end of the third quarter of the twentieth century. As more economies, such as China and India, join this group of advantaged nations genuine questions arise about whether or not the Earth possesses enough resources to sustain this kind of lifestyle globally.

Very roughly speaking, the notion of *consumerism* marks a gradual transition from an economy principally devoted to industrial production to one with a growing emphasis upon mass consumption – of industrially produced items, of course, but also increasingly of services, such as fast food.[3] It seems fair to hypothesize that this transition first became most evident in the United States, beginning in the first part of the twentieth century.

A seminal moment was undoubtedly Henry Ford's introduction of the Model T, an automobile that he wanted to put within the reach of the purchasing power of the workers who labored in his plants. Ford realized the absolute necessity of creating a pool of buyers for his products, if his market, and, thereby, his business/profit margins were to expand. As an industrialist his innovation was to figure out how to make cars cheaply. As an economist his discovery, which was possibly even more momentous, was to turn ordinary folk into consumers and, consequently, to create a sustainable mass market.

Ford made his product available – on easy terms – to very sizable numbers of people across the economic spectrum. One thing that is very crucial here was not only that an affordable automobile had been designed, but also that the *desire* to own such a vehicle was created – a desire whose realization became not impracticable for an impressive proportion of families in the United States. Soon everyone had to have one. Other businesses followed suit. Everything from ready-made clothing to labor-saving devices, like washing machines, began to be widely marketed, as they say, "on reasonable terms." Installment payments, for example, were introduced. And consumerism was off and running.

Now, of course, people have to acquire things to live. Consumption, understood in the most basic way, is a necessary part of human life. Yet, when I refer to "consumerism" in this article, I am not referring to the consumption of our daily bread or the purchasing of coats, *simpliciter*, in order to protect ourselves from the elements. What is fundamental to *consumerism*, as I am using the term, and, as I think as most other commentators use it, is that, *consumerism*, properly so called, involves the acquisition of goods and services that, relative to the society in question, do not count as bare necessities. The objects of consumerism, in this strict sense, do not satisfy basic needs – such as nutrition pure and simple – so much as they satisfy cultivated needs and desires, often ones inculcated by the very entrepreneurs who market the goods and services in question.

Needs are what we require in order to survive and to sustain a modicum of well being. Our needs include biological ones, as well as material, social, cultural, and psychological ones. In contrast to our needs, we may speak of our desires – in this sense, what we want, but don't necessarily need. Consumer society tends to promote the impression that the objects of desire – accosting us on every side by means of the mass media – are actually things we *need*. Moreover, this is often achieved by making consumers think that the products on offer can be ingredients in the construction of the kind of person we want to become. As Robert G. Dunn puts it, consumer society "attempts to *conflate* need, want, and desire, all of which tend to merge in a whole complex of subjective feelings and meanings surrounding the commodity."[4]

Colloquially, the objects of consumerism are "extras" – stuff above the utter baseline equipment standard for living in the pertinent culture. Frequently, we are encouraged to crave this stuff because it is associated with lifestyles that strike us as attractive. We want the stuff, in other words, because we think it will grant us entry into the lifestyle we covet.

For example, though a TV may be said to be a normal accoutrement to adult life in contemporary America, a plasma screen TV is not. But the desire for such a TV is precisely the sort of hankering the electronics industry wants to engender in *consumers*. Creating desire is as important as creating new products to be desired. That is, perhaps predictably, why the advertising industry grows apace with the rise of mass consumerism. For, advertising abets the spread of consumerism across a widening variety of products as well as across an expanding diversity of peoples (otherwise known as *customers*).

Consumerism is a way of organizing society. Members of that society are invited to see themselves reflected in their purchases. I shop, therefore, I am. I buy my slacks at the Gap; therefore, I'm cool. By associating commodities with self-esteem, consumerism, as a system, keeps the markets expanding.

The economic transformation from a culture that emphasizes production – with industrial production being the leading component – into a culture that is progressively dependent upon ever accelerating mass consumption, in order to keep afloat, brings with it a change in the personality type suited to living and serving the emerging society in question. That is, in order to operate effectively a consumer culture requires a new kind of person – specifically, people with a different repertoire of traits and attitudes than found in the earlier culture. Whereas in the era of the industrial revolution, deferred gratification was the order of the day for the majority, as material abundance became more widely available, leisure and the possibility of the protracted pursuit of personal preferences – also known as *happiness* in the relevant social formation – was democratized.[5] Moreover, the pursuit of happiness – of self-fulfillment or self-realization through the acquisition of products – was increasingly promoted by advertising, not to mention peer pressure, and further facilitated by continuing innovations in credit availability – from "easy" installment plans to charge cards. Whereas once restraint was the order of the day, impulsiveness rules the consumer society.[6]

The expansion of the emerging economy, in other words, came to depend more and more upon enticing citizens into an endless spiral of buying. The consumer society is about desire – about inducing desires for all sorts of things heretofore unimagined, like suntans in the middle of winter in Alaska. In order to convince people to step onto this treadmill of desire, buying gets represented not only as a mode of gratification, but of personal expression, satisfaction, and fulfillment. Buying this beer manifests one's manliness; using that hair conditioner supposedly releases your inner silkiness. Sometimes people are encouraged to buy things just because it is *fun*, and, in addition, its purchase signifies that you are a fun *kinda* guy.

Consumerism is a form of life that echoes Arthur Schopenhauer's metaphysical vision perfectly. Driven by unending desire, the consumer society is a perpetual motion machine – always churning, always expanding. First, the desire for this brand of sneaker (sorry, *running shoe*) is implanted across the whole population; everyone just has to have a pair. But next year, another style of footwear is in vogue, and now everyone wants to have that. No one can keep up with the consumer market.[7] As soon as one desire is satisfied, another one is instilled. Consumerism is not about fulfilling our desires; ultimately it is about arousing them.[8] And if things get boring, a trip to the department store can always stir things up. Passing time, walking down the aisles, bombarded by titillating sensations on every side, cravings excite us almost automatically and languor disappears.

Consumerism can be called a *lifestyle* in two senses. First, it can become a way that one spends large amounts of one's time and energy, and, moreover, a way of spending time that is encouraged by numerous, redundant channels of blandishment (from commercials to peer pressure). As a result, for many an afternoon at the mall is itself a form of entertainment. Consumption is frequently presented as being pleasurable in and of itself as well as being a means to pleasure. Call it shopping as amusement.

But second, consumerism is also connected to the idea of a lifestyle insofar as it is presented, if only implicitly, as a way of constructing a life, of shaping oneself as a certain type of personality, notably through buying. Through advertising, and other mass media imagery – including motion pictures, cinematic and televisual – certain products are associated with, loosely speaking, identities or modes of being in the world. So, with your credit card, you are free to purchase things – from soft drinks to vacations – that have images of various (usually putatively enviable) personality profiles attached to them. For example, buy a Porsche and become a ladies' man; buy a van and be a provident and responsible dad. Or, this toothpaste will make you bright and vivacious in a way that men find bewitching.

In the consumerist society, people are encouraged to use products as resources in the construction of a sense of self; items are associated with images and narratives of enviable ways of being in the world; consumers are tempted to believe that they can acquire those associated modes of being by simply buying the products in question. As Richard Eliot says: "Consumption as a social practice is a dynamic and relatively autonomous process which involves the construction of a sense of self through the accumulation of cultural and social capital."[9] That is, through consumption, consumers attempt to construct a self-image not only for others, but for themselves.[10]

Consumerism thrives on a kind of magical thinking – that you could purchase a life by buying something linked, often only imaginatively, to it: as if drinking a Cosmopolitan, for a while the cocktail of choice in *Sex in the City*, could, for instance, make you cosmopolitan.

III. Ethics and the evils of consumerism

Even supposing that consumerism, as just described, is a lifestyle recommended by *Sex and the City*, we still need to be explain why it is an ethically questionable lifestyle, if we intend to chastize *Sex and the City* for advocating it. So what's morally wrong with consumerism? It turns out that consumerism is ethically challenged in several different respects.

Perhaps, the first and most obvious moral problem with consumerism is its global unfairness. People in developed countries spend large amounts of money on different brands of bottled water that are barely discriminable from ordinary tap water, but which promise to imbue consumers with an aura of Gallic or other sorts of sophistication, while, at the same time, people all over the world are suffering from a lack of clean drinking water. If the bottled water connoisseurs contributed the money they spent on packaged H_2O to an international clean water fund, everyone would have healthy, potable sustenance. Thus, consumerism contributes to global inequality.

But consumerism also undermines political understanding. Consumerism insinuates that you are *free* to be whatever you wish (so long as you can pay for it, if only on credit). Consumerism thus involves a curious displacement of certain political ideals. The pursuit of happiness is translated into – indeed, reduced to – the pursuit of gratification, operationalized as the pursuit and then purchase of certain desired material objects and/or services. Unfortunately, happiness is finally unattainable, since there is always something else to buy.

Similarly, freedom in the political realm is devalued or marginalized; instead, people measure their freedom in terms of buying power. If the avowed ideal of the immigrant to the United States was once the "freedom to become anything," where that was understood in terms of social aspiration – for example, that the child of a refugee could become a cabinet member – now that freedom has been shrunken by the advertising industry to the opportunity to become a really sporty guy by drinking Gatorade or something else that is virtually indistinguishable.

In the constitution according to consumerism, freedom of choice becomes the freedom to choose between a dazzling array of generally only marginally differentiated breakfast cereals, coffees, hamburger vendors, patent medicines, motor vehicles, airlines, ready-made pizzas, lingerie, slacks, and so forth where the greatest number of these choices are linked associatively with mass-produced fantasies (typically immensely flattering ones) about the kind of person who would make such choices (buy Levi jeans and become a rugged cowboy; buy a Jeep SUV and become the Master of All Outdoors; buy almost anything and become a *winner*). The right to choose your life – our birthright – gets transmogrified into the prerogative to purchase a product that has been antecedently trademarked with the imagery of a particular lifestyle. You pays your money, you gets your identity/personality. "Freedom" is just another word for something else to buy.

Historically, according to John Kenneth Galbraith in his *The Affluent Society*, the creation of consumer-based middle class led to the eradication of working-class solidarity, because, as David Brown suggests, labor was undermined as "the individual worker traded his ability to affect social change for entrance into the middle-class consumer state."[11] That is, consumerism abets a tendency toward individualistic social solipsism, thereby undercutting the likelihood of concerted political action with others.

From the perspective of philosophical ethics, then, consumerism can be criticized from several perspectives. The first, and, undoubtedly the most obvious, is the way in which consumerism misallocates or unfairly distributes resources. While people in consumerist societies – that is, economies driven to a great extent by essentially contrived desires – are paying for ointments and even more expensive and exotic treatments for the removal of unsightly body hair, others in poorer nations are suffering from malnutrition.

Second, political philosophers, especially Western Marxists, have argued that consumerism saps the citizenry's eagerness to participate in democracy; instead of attending town meetings, most would rather visit the mall. Furthermore, some theorists suggest that by providing a surfeit of consumer goods, a populace awash with transitory pleasures is too besotted to notice the machinations of the powers that be and, anyway, happy shoppers are too preoccupied by being on the lookout for the next best bargain to see that anything is amiss. Consumerism, on this view, is a way of distracting attention from serious public deliberation about questions of justice and equity.

And once again from the viewpoint of political philosophy, there is also the serious worry that consumerism contaminates the electoral process. Candidates are "sold" like bug sprays and toilet deodorizers; slogans, sound-bites, and images replace anything remotely like policy discourse and political debate. Political parties spend vast amounts of money to curry for their clients the same kind of gut reactions to which ad men hawking shampoo aspire to pander. Candidates are not weighed in terms of issues, but in virtue of associated lifestyles and staged identities/personalities. This guy is projected as comfortable, a "good old boy"; that guy is too "French."

As this example from political life indicates, consumerism is a worldview that colonizes the web of human relations beyond the marketplace. Students think of themselves as consumers and make demands upon their professors on the grounds that they are paying good money for their education. Thus, they should be allowed to search their e-mails during lectures. And, as we shall see with respect to *Sex and the City* even love relationships may start to be treated as shopping – not just sleeping – around.

So far, these critical observations concerning consumerism fall into the realm of social ethics. They take note of the way in which consumerism has bad consequences for the national body politic in particular and the world community at large. But consumerism also raises questions of personal or individual ethics. That is, consumerism may not only involve harm to others; it may, in addition, involve harm to oneself.

The issue here may not be immediately apparent to many anglophone ethicists who throughout the twentieth century have been particularly preoccupied with determining which specific kinds of actions – in accordance with which moral criteria – are good or bad. But with consumerism, it is generally not that any particular act is especially evil. Probably most consumer purchases considered individually are neither here nor their on the great moral calculus. It is rather that one of the most significant ethical problems that consumerism raises may be with the kind of person consumerism encourages one to become.

For, consumerism can seduce people into living an impoverished form of life. Despite the imagery of self-fulfillment, consumerism may promote a squandering of opportunities. We spend thousands on the sporting goods piled in our closets, promising to start a new exercise regime next week. But though "next week" never arrives, we deceive ourselves that we are doing something by way of improving our health insofar as we have purchased the image of those "abs of steel" that we saw on TV when we reached for the credit card next to the telephone. Though promising the good life, consumerism serves up a much diminished life, a life enmeshed in fantasies.

Though questions of the good life and of happiness, properly so called – including the kind of character and virtues required to live it – were the primary focus of ethics for classical philosophers like Socrates, Plato, Aristotle, the Stoics, Epicureans, Skeptics, and so forth, moral philosophers in the twentieth century, especially in the English-speaking world, have shied away from the topic, preferring to batten upon the question of the moral status of acts rather than lives. In earlier decades, some Anglo-American philosophers dismissed the phrase "the meaning of life" as oxymoronic, though that sort of austerity has slackened in recent years. Yet even now, there is still wariness among anglophone philosophers about evaluating desirable life patterns – a practice they suspect by calling it perfectionism or even paternalism.

Thus, the proposition – that consumerism trades in counterfeit lifestyles – is not an ethical problem that contemporary analytic ethicists are readily prepared to confront. However, any discussion of consumerism will not only have to consider the degree to which this social system causes harms to others (including the community construed as a corporate entity) – something which admittedly contemporary ethical theory is well suited to calibrate; we will also need to consider the harm that consumerism disposes people to perpetrate against themselves by opting mindlessly for the pursuit of externally manipulated gratifications.

Indeed, at the very least, consumerism involves people in a self-inflicted form of self-deception, inasmuch as consumerism involves buying into the assumption that, paradoxically enough, by purchasing mass market commodities available to anyone who can pay for them, you can recreate yourself as a unique individual.[12] Call this the contradiction of consumerism: the illusion that you can define yourself as a person by means of the acquisition of products to which everyone has access. Arguably, to submit to such an illusion is to base one's sense of self – one's life – on a lie. And yet, many of us living in a consumer society, at least to some extent, diminish ourselves in this way.

IV. Consumerism and the mass media

The mass media is central to the lifestyle imagery that stokes consumerism. It produces and disseminates most of it. This is nowhere more apparent than in the advertisements – some to which I've already alluded several times – which advertisements feed the broadcast and print media that, with a wall of images, envelope virtually anyone awake and alive in the modern world. Of course, it is no accident that consumerism and the advertising industry have flourished in tandem. They are, as they say, made for each other. Mass consumerism needs desires of all sorts in order to thrive; and advertising specializes in awakening desire. You don't have to be a rocket scientist to figure that out.

However, it may be less obvious that the media excites consumerism not only through advertisements; the mass media also promotes consumerism through many of the programs that the aforesaid advertisements frame. Of course, there are entire television stations that are all advertisements, like the Shopping Channel. And a number of other late night TV networks in the United States turn over substantial blocks of time to paid programming dedicated to selling exercise regimes, strategies for success in business, etc. And, as well, almost every cooking show, in various ways, is inviting the viewer to spend more time and money in the kitchen. How-to shows remind you of the wonderful tools you have not got. Talk shows typically feature segments on new products and styles (where the word *fun* gets tossed around a lot). And even though these phenomena are not technically advertisements, they function as such, as do the style and travel sections of newspapers and magazines. So much of the information provided in these putatively factual reports essentially concerns what to buy next. Indeed, the line between reporting and publicity begins to blur. People talk about "infotainment," when, in fact, what we might call "ad-infotainment" is probably more extensive.

The preceding examples, of course, all occur in what is usually categorized as belonging in the nonfiction precincts of the mass media. But the consumerist lifestyle is not only flaunted in ads and nonfiction programming. It is also built into certain mass media fictions. That is, some fictions are themselves celebrations of and de facto recommendations for consumerism.

An intimation of this was already grasped after the World War I when American motion pictures began to flood the international movie market. Many countries, like Great Britain, attempted to limit and to control the distribution of American movies within their borders by means of quota systems. But these quotas were not only established in order to protect native film industries. It was also realized that American fiction films were, in effect, advertising American products. Those who erected the quota systems feared that their countrymen would see the snazzy, silver plated cigarette lighters – not to mention the Fords – and want them. Likewise, apart from any product in particular, many movies from the States – especially those set in contemporary times, showcased the emerging *American* lifestyle of conspicuous consumption.

Movie-star celebrities, of course, have become heroes of consumption – whole "information" industries have arisen documenting and chronicling how they spend their money, where they go, what they possess, where they live and on what scale, and so forth. These stars, in turn, have become, according to Juliet Schor, the targets of what might be called upwards emulation.[13]

But even more than the lives of movie stars, the movies they make, particularly those of urban life in the fast lane, function like imaginary "department store" catalogues. If you see it in the movies or on TV, you might think that you would like to have it too, or maybe even need it or, at least, something like it.[14] The movies, later followed by TV, often function as consumer training grounds. Nor is this only something that happened in the distant "unsophisticated" past, as I hope that our discussion of *Sex and the City* will establish.

V. *Sex and the City*

As already indicated, *Sex and the City*, the television show, features four women, living in Manhattan and ranging in age from their early thirties to their early forties. They are Carrie, the journalist who is the fictional narrator of each episode and the central character in the series; Miranda, a lawyer; Samantha, a publicist; and Charlotte, a sometime gallery employee and museum docent. These women eat together and party together. Each of Carrie's friends can be taken to represent a facet of an ideally whole person: Miranda is the mind (practical and prudent); Samantha is the body (insatiably carnal, rippling with pheromones); and Charlotte is the heart (she's the sentimental one). Carrie's existential task, it would appear, is to fuse these aspects into one personality.

When these women gather, as they often do for lunch, they usually discuss men, typically processing the question or questions of the week that vex Carrie's column from their different viewpoints.[15] Does one's relationship with one's father predestine one's relations with other men for the rest of your life? And what about anal sex?

The women are very close friends – steadfast and mutually supportive. They are funny and smart, and, of course, pretty and fashionable. But it is undoubtedly the warmth generated by their camaraderie that is the most attractive thing about them. It is hard not admire the bond between them. They are so *simpatico* in every sense of the word. The actresses portraying them do a terrific job of ensemble acting. Like other TV shows, such as *Cheers*, *Friends*, *Entourage*, and even *Seinfeld* in its way, *Sex and the City* nurtures, among other things, a yearning to belong to a community as tight and as charming as the Fabulous Foursome.

It pays to repeat that these women are professionals: a journalist, a lawyer, and public relations/press agent – even Charlotte's occupation requires a background, and probably even a degree, in art history. But when they meet to talk – as they do once or twice an episode at some upscale eatery – what do they talk about? Men, clothes, accessories, and the newest restaurants and nightclubs. They are – with the exception of Miranda – always dressed in patently high style and they are magnificently coiffed. Whereas Samantha and

Charlotte are infallibly dressed to the nines, Carrie's outfits are more exper-imental and idiosyncratic – although we are clearly meant to appreciate that, in fact, she is in the avant-garde of taste-making. In fact, in one episode, she is even enlisted as a model. Gay men – presented within the show as possessed of exquisite taste – frequently make appearances, generally in order to endorse the style of Carrie and her friends.

Brands, like Manolo Blahniks (shoes), mentioned in the first show and referred to constantly throughout the series, are spoken of like household names and often in awe (albeit with a pronounced ironic accent, although one perhaps betrayed by its obsessive recurrence). Often the brand-name of Carrie's outfits are cited – that's a Roberto Cavelli in "The Good Fight," should you want to know. And, moreover, the labels that are not mentioned are nevertheless shown.

A recurring motif of the series is that Carrie loves shoes. In one episode ("Ring a Ding Ding") it suddenly dawns on her why she doesn't have enough money in the bank to purchase her apartment: in just the last few years, she has spent $40,000 on shoes – 100 pairs at $400 a piece. Needless to say, the issue of shoes comes up often in the show. Watching regularly, you could learn the hottest new items to buy – not only Manolo Blahniks, but Christian Louboutins and others.

Yet, even more significantly, you might get infected by Carrie's enthusiasm – she seems to enjoy shopping for shoes so very much – that you might be inspired to become her kind of foot fetishist yourself. After all, wouldn't it be so cool? And anyway, it would give you something to do, as would all the club hopping and restaurant cruising featured in the series. If nothing else, these ladies are champions of the New York consumer experience. They are role models; even if it is not feasible to buy what they buy, they reaffirm the central-ity of consumption to living as a single.

As the ladies sit down to eat in "Ring a Ding Ding," the episode immedi-ately preceding the episode "A *Vogue* Idea," they observe, with unrepressed glee, that Richard Wright, Samantha's boyfriend, has just given her "*the* Chanel wallet." That night, Samantha opens another gift; and, as she exclaims "Le Petite Coquette!" Richard announces that he'll pour them some Cristal. We then learn that Samantha's gorgeous body comes to her by way of Pilates. We even get the dope on the engagement ring that Charlotte gives to Carrie in order to buy her apartment; it's from Tiffany's, the diamond is 2.7 carats, and it has a platinum mount. The saleslady at the jewelry market reassures Charlotte and us that it is *very* expensive.[16]

At this point, it might seem as though I've become obsessed with product placement and that I've wandered away from the point of the show – which is about sex in the city. Why don't I talk about that? And indeed, most of the series is devoted to courtship; consequently, there is a lot of dating or in Samantha's case, of just hooking up. But it would be a mistake to think that dating and consumption are not intimately connected, since sex in the city and consumerism are entwined, both externally, and, as we will argue, internally as well.

With respect to the external relation, simply remember that dating is the fuel that runs substantial parts of the consumer businesses in large cities. To whom are all those fancy bars, lounges, bistros, restaurants, and clubs catering to, if not to the dating classes? It is misleading to think of consumerism simply in terms of material things. Services are objects of consumption as well – including meals, music, and shows. But in terms of the material stuff, who do you imagine is buying all those sexy outfits (and shoes), flowers, candies, fine wines, and for what reason?[17] During its initial run, *Sex and the City* provided eager viewers – women and men of various sexual preferences – with fashion bulletins from the dating front. Take notice: Carrie has shifted from ordering Cosmopolitans to Dirty Martinis.

It is no accident that *Sex and the City* is so enmeshed with consumerism. For in being about dating, it is unavoidably about consuming in the city; without dating, the economy of Manhattan would take a major hit.

Yet dating seems related to consumerism not only economically. There is a psychological or internal relationship as well. Just as one searches for the brand of jeans that suits one best, so dating has become a matter of shopping around – shopping around for a mate. One tries on partners as one might try on the most up market shoes for the most comely fit. Just as there is comparison shopping, the array of male types "displayed" on *Sex and the City* suggests that there is comparison dating. In "A *Vogue* Idea," Carrie jokes that men are the new accessories, a *bon mot* that she had already made in an earlier episode in the first season. And, though this thought is advanced ironically, it does seem to reflect how the women in this story-world frequently gossip about their once and future boyfriends.

Contemporary dating, as limned by *Sex and the City*, also resembles consumerism psychologically insofar as the current dating game has the real potential to become endless. One craves a new piece of apparel and buys it. But pretty soon, as Jean-Jacques Rousseau predicts, we notice a different item of dress on another. We compare ours to hers competitively and often find ours wanting. We need to buy something better. But there is always something better to buy, especially as we egg ourselves onwards by competitively comparing ourselves to others.

Just as there is buying upwards, there is dating upwards (and even marrying upwards, as we know from the phenomenon of "trophy" brides). That is, what happens with apparel can also happen with lovers. Is this the right one? There is always one more date beckoning from the horizon. Like the consumption of designer clothing, there is always another date to try on. In this way, consumerism with respect to things paves the way for consumerism with people. As noted earlier, consumerism as a worldview invades every other area of life, including modern romance. That is perhaps the dark, scarcely acknowledged, underside of *Sex and the City*.[18]

So just as consumerism may infect the political system, it can also invade the domain of intimate personal relations. The parade of male acquaintances parallels the parade of products in *Sex and the City*, and the exchange of affections is often correlated with the exchange of coveted ciphers of conspicuous consumption, as in the aforesaid case of Samantha and Richard.

Granted, by the end of the last season of the show, three of the four women are living in what seem to be settled relationships. Only Carrie remains unattached. But remember she is *the* heroine, and she is presented as headed into her future bravely and alone – *heroically*, the fiction signals – to what...? A life composed of more dating, shoes, nightclubs, and so forth. It's a hard life, but, from the perspective of the series, it's a noble one – someone's got to do it. The search for the right man – for the right fit – is like the search for the right shoe: relentless.

Certainly consumerism is the wrong model for intimate relations. Such relationships require commitment – something with which Carrie has problems – in a way that yesterday's fashions do not. But even apart from the portrayal of courtship in *Sex and the City*, the series warrants moral scrutiny for its celebration of conspicuous consumption in its handling of acquiring things

VI. "A *Vogue* idea"

At the end of the episode entitled "All that Glitters," Charlotte's apartment is photographed for a spread in the magazine *Home and Gardens*. We learn that this is a magazine that Charlotte read as a child and that she used in order to fantasize about her own future. Being featured on the pages of *Home and Gardens* is a "dream come true" for Charlotte. Furthermore, we are told that Charlotte's juniors will be looking at Charlotte as Charlotte looked at the layouts of her youth – as a patent of desire, as a blueprint for life in the "happily ever after."

Then, in "A *Vogue* Idea" we learn about the magazine of Carrie's dreams – *Vogue*, a journal of current fashion whose very masthead advertises that it specializes in what is, well, in vogue. As the episode opens, Carrie informs us that she has just been hired by "the most relevant and provocative magazine on the news stands today – at least to me – *Vogue*, also known as Mecca ..." Though there is a discernible pinch of self-irony in this description, Carrie is also quite serious in her devotion to *Vogue*. We learned in an earlier episode that sometimes, when she first arrived in New York City, Carrie skipped meals so as to afford a copy of *Vogue*.

Carrie has outfitted herself with a new hair-do and a perfectly tailored, grey pin-striped suit in order to approach this citadel of taste; as she walks down the corridor to *Vogue*'s central offices, she passes the line-up of legendary *Vogue* covers which decorate the walls like a row of portraits of national heroes or legendary forebears. If *Vogue* is a mecca, as Carrie says, then it is a mecca for shoppers. As you might imagine, the place positively reeks with *haute couture*.

The central plot line involves Carrie's new job at *Vogue*. Her first article has not won the heart of her new editor, Enid. Another editor, Julian, takes Carrie under his wing and tries to help her to fit in. Later, we learn his interest in Carrie is anything but avuncular.

There are also two subplots. One involves a baby-shower that Charlotte arranges for Miranda; the other, Samantha's birthday present for her boy-friend Richard. As you might predict, the *Vogue*-plot-line affords ample opportunity for product placement and branding. Within the first few min-utes, the names of Oscar de la Renta, Chanel, and Dior are intoned with the kind of respect others might reserve for Darwin, Pasteur, and Einstein. Later, Versace and, of course, Manolo Blahnik are cited positively, while Tom Ford's line is dissed off-handedly. Moreover, the fact that the business of *Vogue* is pushing product is made quite explicit. At lunch, Carrie shows her friends a photograph of a Marc Jacobs "ultra-modern" notebook that Carrie is sup-posed to plug in her next column.

It is true that putatively the central issue in Carrie's story in this episode revolves the question of the influence of the relation of fathers and daughters upon women's subsequent relations with men. However, that theme is set against a parade of fashion items which are treated as almost "natural" objects of desire – asked how she celebrates after finishing an article, Carrie says by buying shoes and purses. How else?

The baby-shower subplot also involves a great deal of consumption, though this time the subject is baby paraphernalia. Again, there is a dramatic side here, concerning Miranda's anxieties about being a good mother and Charlotte's wish for a child of her own. But the subplot is also a lesson in what you need to buy in preparation for a newborn. Various learning toys are men-tioned, along with cribs, strollers, and breast pumps. As Carrie and Samantha talk to each other at the shower, they pass baby clothes to nearby women. We learn that the hot present of the season is a birthday "cake" made of diapers, with lotion, bottles, and a receiving blanket packed inside. There is wrapping paper all around.

One gift, a silver Tiffany rattle, reminds Charlotte of her own thwarted desire to be a mother and sends her to her bedroom in despair. But the setting for Charlotte's crisis is an array of conspicuously displayed consumer goods. Call it melodrama laced with shopping tips.

The third plotline concerns a gift for Richard's birthday. Samantha wants to buy him something. But Richard is a very wealthy hotel magnate – a good-looking version of Donald Trump. In short, he is the man who has everything.

He wants to skip the celebration of his birthday; however, Samantha presses him to ask for something.

In response, he requests a night of three-way sex with a beautiful young waitress named Alexa. On the one hand, this plot line does not seem to feature consumerism, save for the obviously expensive clothing that people wear and take off, and their surroundings, especially the restaurant where Alexa works. But, on the other hand, this subplot belies the internal connection between consumerism and sex that persists just below the surface in this series: after all, in this episode, a person, Alexa, albeit quite willingly, is being treated as a gift, a ravishing young thing, ripe for exchange, ready to be consumed.

This, moreover, occurs within the narrative context where Carrie has written an article in which she declares men to be the upcoming fall accessories. According to her, "A Prada dress should always be worn with an investment banker." She also suggests that men are like the new black and she says of her editor Julian that he is the perfect dinner accessory. This metaphor is one that occurs as early as the first season of *Sex and the City*. It is, of course, presented as a joke, and yet, all told, the turnover rate of men in the series probably is close to the number of shoes in Carrie's closet. That is, sex in the city seems linked to consumerism and is sometimes figuratively equated with it.

And even if the connection in the series between courtship and consumerism does not strike you as being as suggested as I have urged, the endorsement of conspicuous consumption with regard to things in "A *Vogue* Idea" is unmistakable. Though pervasive in the background of the shower subplot, consumerism forcefully dominates the foreground of Carrie's story. After Carrie finally finishes her article and confides to Julian that upon completing an assignment she rewards herself by buying shoes and purses, Julian suggests that they visit the *Vogue* accessory closet, a storehouse of the items that designers have sent to the magazine in order to be photographed.

As the door opens, the camera, motivated from Carrie's point of view, lovingly pans over clothes, shoes, bags and so on. Carrie squeals "Oh God! It's too good." Julian remarks that she is like a kid in a couture candy store, and the camera keeps panning over what looks like cornucopia of women's wear.

Carrie lights upon a pair of shoes. She can barely contain herself; she gasps "Do you what these are? Manolo Blahnik Mary Janes. I thought these were an urban shoe legend," adding that they are made of authentic patent leather. The scene then becomes slightly more serious when Carrie discovers what Julian really has on his mind (sex, perhaps needless to say).[19] But the orgy of fashionable consumer goods and the unswerving representation of Carrie's unabashed lust for them are never for a moment called into question.

The episode ends with the conceit of Carrie the columnist explicitly giving her audience some advice about the need in life to accessorize (improvise) with what you've got. Implicitly, she has also endorsed the consumer lifestyle as a smart, fun, and enviable mode of being. Why don't you try it on?[20]

VII. Lighten up

Readers who have seen the episode "A *Vogue* Idea" are likely to find the preceding analysis of it somewhat exasperating. I suspect that they will contend that my take is far too dour. Although the episode has serious moments, they will correctly point out that the installment is mostly comic. They will complain that I have not paid enough attention to the blatant irony in the episode.

The narrator, Carrie, lets us know from the get-go that she realizes her obsession with fashion is way over the top and an appropriate object of self-ridicule. She says she believes *Vogue* to be "relevant and provocative" in an obvious gesture of self-mockery. Every time she pronounces *Vogue*, her voice drops in order to underline the exaggerated importance invested in it by the people who work there. And her enthusiasm in the *Vogue* accessory closet has a playful, self-parodic edge to it. Carrie makes fun of her own consumerism; she recognizes that there is something silly about it and she invites viewers to laugh along with her at her own expense. So, why go on as if we are dealing with a naive unself-aware endorsement of consumerism of the sort one might find in a used-car commercial. Lighten up – get a life – laugh along with *Sex and the City* at the obsessive consumerism of the swinging single *modus vivendi*.

Of course, there is no doubt that there is this comic dimension to *Sex and the City*. However, it is evident that the fun Carrie pokes at her own mania for fashion is not intended to warn viewers away from the lure of consumerism. There is not, as in *The Devil Wears Prada*, a discernible parting of the ways with the fashion business. Nor does the humor in *Sex and the City* have a sharp edge of social satire. As indicated earlier, it is genial – a form of self-joshing. It functions to pass Carrie's consumerism off as a delightful foible – a harmless idiosyncrasy, one of which she is aware and which she acknowledges is a slightly absurd, and worth a chuckle. If it is a flaw, it is not a serious one – it is just a charming eccentricity.

When it comes to consumerism, Carrie Bradshaw exhibits a sophisticated form of akrasia (or, weakness of will). She knows that there is something wrong about her shopping compulsion – after all, she learns that she's blown $40,000 on shoes – but she neutralizes the implications of this tendency by diminishing it with humor, just as an alcoholic might attempt to avoid facing up to the ramifications of his habit by joking about it. The strategy here is sophisticated, because rather than denying altogether the character flaw that you know afflicts you, one acknowledges it, however only as a somewhat comic quirk, worthy of a smile, but nothing more.

In this way, Carrie exemplifies an evasive tactic that is quite common in the culture of consumerism. How often does one hear people pass off their consumer excesses as a bit of self-confessed craziness? "It's nuts, I know, but I couldn't resist buying another Mont Blanc." Needless to say, Carrie Bradshaw did not invent this way of managing her consumerism. But by employing it with such endearing and amiable wit, she reinforces the technique for viewers. Consumerism itself gets transformed into an occasion for light entertainment. Carrie not only exemplifies consumerism, but in effect suggests a way of living with it through self-effacing humor.

Amusement at one's ethical failings can be a kind of moral evasion. Self-joshing in the form of self-deprecating laughter may be a technique for not honestly appraising one's own behavior. It is a strategy for diminishing the importance of one's transgressions. This strategy already exists in contemporary consumer society as witnessed by popular catch phrases like "retail therapy" and "When the going gets tough, the tough go shopping." Carrie Bradshaw not only adds new modes of expression to that repertoire, but, in addition, makes them appear charming.

If consumerism is often a species of akrasia (something that many of us indulge though we also know it to be in some sense is wrong, if only because it is obviously wasteful in so many different ways), then it is not simply a matter of individual moral pathology. For, the conditions that facilitate consumerism and the denial thereof are sustained by political and economic arrangements; consumerism is a social pathology.[21]

Foremost among the institutions that promote this pathology in capitalist societies are the mass media: the television fictions, movies, songs, magazines, advertisements, and so forth that present riveting and reigning models of desirability and success.[22] *Sex and the City* is clearly part of that system. It is noteworthy not only because it subtly projects consumerism as a given in the good life in the city. In episodes like "A *Vogue* Idea" it also suggests the way in which self-deprecating humor can palliate a bad conscience about our consumer manias.

VIII. Summary

Consumerism is a significant, though often unacknowledged, ethical issue for the lives of many people in economically advantaged nations. It is a system that enables modern economies to expand. But it does so with moral costs which are both social and individual. An important engine driving mass consumption is the mass media, not only in terms of clearcut devices like advertisements, but also through many of its dramatic presentations. So many television programs, like *Dallas, Dynasty, Knots Landing*, and so on, are as thoroughly spectacles of conspicuous consumption as are the game shows that lavish prizes on their contestants.

But dramatic fictions are not the only vehicles for encouraging imitation in the promotion of consumerism. As illustrated by the episode "A *Vogue* Idea" from the series *Sex in the City*, a comedy can also be an effective vehicle for showing consumerism in a most beguiling light. Indeed, comedy may be especially disarming in this regard. For in showing audiences how to laugh at and shrug off their consumerist enthusiasms, a comedy can inspire viewers to give themselves a pass, morally speaking, on their way to the store.

Notes

1   *Sex and the City* is a television program that originally aired on Home Box Office (HBO). It began on Feb. 2, 1998 and ran for six seasons, ending in 2004. It now appears in bowdlerized versions on other networks. A movie version of the show, called *Sex and the City*, appeared in 2008 and another, *Sex and the City 2*, in 2010. This essay is primarily concerned with the television program, although some remarks refer to the 2008 motion picture.

2   In the 2008 movie, Carrie identifies her topic as "the two Ls: labels and love." See Anthony Lane, "Carrie," *New Yorker* (June 9 and 16, 2008), 112–14.

3   See Benjamin R. Barber, *Consumed: How Markets Corrupt Children, Infantilize Adults and Swallow Citizens Whole* (New York: W. W. Norton, 2007). Barber contends that consumerism is a capitalist survival strategy – one which allows the economy to continue to expand by creating, as Marx would put it, new "needs" (pp. 45, 48).

4   Robert G. Dunn, *Identifying Consumption: Subjects and Objects in a Consumer Society* (Philadelphia: Temple University Press, 2008), p. 12.

5   On the demise of deferred gratification, see Barber, *Consumed*, pp. 38–45.

6   See James Davison Hunter, *The Death of Character* (New York: Basic Books, 2000), esp. ch. 1.

7   Barber, *Consumed*, pp. 114–115.

8   Z. Bauman, *Liquid Life* (Cambridge: Polity), p. 92.

9   Richard Elliott, "Making Up People: Consumption as a Symbolic Vocabulary," in Karin M. Ekström and Helene Brembeck (eds.), *Elusive Consumption* (New York: Berg, 2004), p. 133.

10   Colin Campbell, "I Shop Therefore I Know that I Am: The Metaphysical Basis of Modern Consumerism," in Ekström and Brembeck (eds.) *Elusive Consumption*, pp. 38–39.

11   David Brown, "The Dialectic of Consumption: Materialism and Social Control in American History" in Gabriel R. Ricci and Paul Gottfried (eds.), *Culture and Consumption* (New Brunswick, NJ: Transaction Publishers, 2000), p. 8.

12   Z. Bauman, *Consuming Life* (Cambridge: Polity), p. 15.

13   Dennis Soron, "The Politics of Consumption: An Interview with Juliet Schor," *Aurora Online*. At http://aurora.icaap.org/index.php/aurora/article/view/13/24, accessed Mar. 26, 2013. See also Juliet Schor, *Born to Buy* (New York: Scribner's, 2004).

14   This tendency in response to mass media in general is further exploited by what is called "product placement" – the placing of the advertiser's product in the world of the fiction – which practice is increasing in both cinema and TV at present. Whereas

in the past, we would be accustomed to seeing a gangster drinking a generic can of beer, now we see him drinking the brand of the program's sponsor.

15   It has been said that programs like *Sex and the City* and *Desperate Housewives* provide an answer to Freud's question of what women what: lots of sex with lots of sexual partners and the opportunity to talk about it with confidants.

16   In the 2008 movie of *Sex and the City*, Carrie is about to be married. Trying on wedding gowns, she says she has met "new friends like Vera Wang and Carolina Herrera and Christian Lacroix, Lanven and Dior."

17   "Dating," *n + 1*, 3 (Fall, 2005), pp. 4–5.

18   I am not the only one to detect an analogy between shopping and romance in *Sex and the City*. Of the movie, Owen Gleiberman notes "High on their pink drinks and showpiece handbags, literally high on their designer heels (*and on the prospect of turning the search for a mate into another form of shopping*), they embraced the right to be cosmetic, acquisitive, and – yes! – superficial." Indeed, perhaps Carrie admits as much when she says that her bailiwick is labels and love. See Owen Gleiberman, "Is It True Love?" *Entertainment Weekly* 995/996 (June 6, 2008), pp. 96–97 (emphasis added).

19   Julian's attempt to use high-end fashion items as a prelude to sex once again reinforces the connection between sex and consumerism that pervades the show.

20   On a highly speculative note, it is interesting to observe that Sarah Jessica Parker, the actress playing Carrie Bradshaw, has what is often said to be impossible – a body like the doll Barbie. Inasmuch as Barbie is what is called a fashion doll, a patent of what is in which serves, so to speak, as a training grounds for young women, perhaps Carrie Bradshaw is tantamount to a Bardie doll for grown-ups – a model ready to be imitated.

21   See Amelie Oksenberg Rorty, "Political Sources of Emotions: Greed and Anger," Midwest Studies in Philosophy 22 (1998), pp. 22–43.

22   Rorty, "Political Sources of Emotions," p. 28.

Section V

Philosophy on Broadway

17

Art and Friendship

Yasmina Reza's play *Art* is about one man, Serge, who buys a painting, and the reactions of his friends, Marc and Yvan, to his purchase.[1] Marc's response is quite volcanic; for him, Serge's purchase of the painting threatens to wreck their friendship. Yvan tries to mediate the disaffection between Serge and Marc, often at the cost of redirecting their hostilities at himself.

As the play opens, Marc addresses the audience directly. He says:

> My friend Serge has bought a painting. It's a canvas about five foot by four: white. The background is white and if you screw up your eyes, you can make out some fine white diagonal lines.
>
> Serge is one of my oldest friends.
>
> He's done very well for himself, he's a dermatologist and he's keen on art.
>
> On Monday, I went to see the painting; Serge had actually got hold of it on the Saturday, but he's been lusting after it for several months.
>
> This white painting with white lines.[2]

This prelude explicitly connects the two major themes of the play – art and friendship (Serge is one of Marc's oldest friends), and the relation thereof. After this brief exposition, then, there is a flashback to the scene where Marc first sees Serge's painting, a painting by Antrios, a famous artist. At first Marc reacts warily, tentatively, but, in almost no time at all, he denounces the painting as shit, despite its whiteness. Marc tries to pass off his vituperation as humor and invites Serge to laugh along with him. But Serge finds nothing

"*Art* and Friendship," *Philosophy and Literature* 26(1) (2002): 199–206.

funny about the situation, which deteriorates throughout the play as everyone's nerves fray and angers mount.

The action of the play raises an immediate question. Why is Marc's reaction to the painting by Antrios so intense, so violent? Why would a painting endanger a friendship? Why do Marc and Serge seem to be willing to split apart after fifteen years over a matter of taste? Can't they just agree to disagree and leave it at that?

But Marc, at least, cannot. He says, "It's a complete mystery to me, Serge buying this painting. It's unsettled me, it's filled me with some undefinable unease." And that undefinable unease is enough to motivate Marc to attack Serge and Yvan savagely to the point where the friendship among them seems no longer possible. But what is the nature of this undefinable unease and what does its existence tell us about the relation of art to friendship?

Marc and Serge obviously see the painting very differently. Marc keeps referring to the Antrios as white, prompting Serge to correct him – pointing out that it has diagonals as well as bits of various other colors in it. Perhaps this is author Yasmina Reza's way of signaling that Serge, so to speak, sees something in the painting – sees that there's something to it – whereas for Marc, it's a blank, it's empty, it's nothing, it's worthless. Marc continues to be amazed that Serge has paid two hundred thousand francs for the painting. But it's not the money, as such, that bothers Marc; it is what the money symbolizes: that Serge sees something worthy in that which Marc finds worthless. And this threatens their friendship. Why?

One of the earliest conceptions of friendship in Western thought is Aristotle's notion of what he calls the friendship of character or character friendship. This is not the only type of friendship there is – there are also friendships based on such things as expediency – but, for Aristotle, character friendship is the highest sort. This is the type of friendship that obtains between equals – people of equal virtue and excellence.

Now you might think that people who are virtuous and excellent already should have little need of friends. They already have it all.[3] But Aristotle suggests that without friends – friends who are our equals – we have no way of objectively assessing our own qualities – no objective measure of assessing whether or not we are virtuous or excellent. Genuine self-knowledge requires an outside viewpoint to validate it. From the inside, we all seem virtuous to ourselves. But how can we see how things really stand with us?

Aristotle's answer is ingenious in its simplicity: look at your friends. See what kind of people they are. They will reflect your character. Your character will be like their character. They are what Aristotle calls "other selves" and what we, by way of the Romans, call "alter egos." The character and values of such alter egos will mirror your character and values. You would not be friends of the relevant sort, if they did not.

Thus, you will find out who you are by looking at who they are. This is why our parents always warned us against hanging out with the wrong crowd. Who our friends are indicates who we are. They show us, as well as others, including our parents, what we value, not only in the sense that we value our friends, but also in the sense that we are friends with them because we share the same values. Moreover, who our friends are is an important ingredient of who we are, since, just as we use a mirror to correct the part in our hair or the knot in our tie, we use our friends to shape our behavior. Our friends are "mirror selves" as well as being "other selves." Friendship of the highest sort, then, according to Aristotle, is vital to our conception of ourselves – to the apprehension and construction of our character.

Now if we suppose that the friendship between Marc and Serge is of this sort, then it is easier to understand the violence of Marc's response. Serge's incomprehensible appreciation, from Marc's point of view, of the painting implies that Serge and Marc are not alter egos, and this, of course, threatens Marc's and then Serge's sense of who they are.

Yvan, who functions throughout the play as a kind of jester or Shakespearean buffoon, has told his psychoanalyst, Finkelzohn, about the dispute between Marc and Serge. And the analyst has summarized the predicament paradoxically but with comic pointedness by suggesting this conundrum: "If ... I am who I am because you're who you are, and if you're who you are because I'm who I am, then I'm not who I am and you're not who you are ..." Or to frame the idea by means of Aristotle's metaphor, the mirror relationship between Marc and Serge has been shattered. Moreover, since, at least once, Marc refers to the disputed painting as a picture, and since the association between pictures and mirrors is as longstanding as Plato, maybe we should interpret Serge's painting as a mirror that is no longer operating properly vis-à-vis Marc and Serge.

Marc tries to understand Serge's expressed fondness for the painting. But he can only come up with cynical explanations for Serge's behavior. Serge, Marc protests, is only feigning appreciation for the painting in order to enhance his upward social mobility. Serge bought the painting, Marc hypothesizes, as an investment in what Pierre Bourdieu calls social capital. Serge wants to enter a more elite circle of acquaintances, which is also why, Marc further alleges, Serge uses the pretentious but unfathomable word "deconstruction."

This is an interpretation of Serge's behavior that Marc can at least understand, even if it does not please him. But ultimately, I think, we come to see that Marc himself does not accept this cynical rationalization. The rift goes deeper. Marc realizes that Serge is moved by the painting – that there is something in Serge that is not in Marc – and this is what disturbs him. This is what threatens his sense of who he is.

But how, you might ask, can a mere painting do all this? How could an artwork come between friends in this way? It seems almost unthinkable. One can understand that a deep disjunction in values – over something like, say, the Israeli–Palestinian conflict – could destroy a friendship. But it appears unimaginable that a difference in taste could cause such a parting of the ways. But it is perhaps Yasmina Reza's staging of this possibility that is her greatest philosophical insight, an insight, furthermore, that sheds light on the neglected or, at least, under-theorized relation of art and friendship.[4]

Philosophers of art tend to think of our relation to art in two ways: in terms of the relation of the individual to the artwork or in terms of art in relation to society as a whole. The first relation is atomistic: how does the artwork affect the experience of the individual audience member in contemplative isolation from everyone else? The second area of concern asks about the consequences of art, or certain types of art, for society at large. If the art is too violent, will society be more violent; if it is too sensational, will it contract our attention spans; and so on. Call the atomistic approach the small-range focus and the societal approach the big-range focus. Both of these perspectives are important – indeed, indispensable. However, there is, additionally, a medium-range focus which is also integral to our daily commerce with art, but which is almost never discussed.

Often when we attend a play, a concert, or a movie, we do it with friends; likewise we read novels, and exchange our opinions with each other over dinner or coffee or drinks. Art is not just a personal affair, nor is it only a force in society writ large. It is also a medium through which we forge our small-scale, face-to-face, everyday relations with others. Sharing experiences of art with others on a face-to-face basis is a way in which we explore and discover one another – discover one another's sensibility and temperament.

Art, of course, is not the only medium through which we do this. Food, sports, fashion, humor, and politics are serviceable in similar ways. But though art may not be the only way or the unique way in which we explore each other, initiating this sort of exploration of each other's sensibility, temperament, and taste is one of the central functions of art, and probably not only in our time and our culture. Art, in short, is, among other things, a vehicle by which we may discover and construct an intimate community – by which we cultivate (a pregnant metaphor here) a circle of friends. This is especially true for those for whom art – rather than, say, sports – is a primary source of socializing. For them, art functions as a kind of social cement.

Naturally, when we discuss art among our intimate circle of confreres, we do not always agree. We may differ about whether something is good, bad, or indifferent. Nevertheless, we must share certain values in common even for meaningful disagreement to proceed. Otherwise, there is simply an utter breakdown in communication. If I fail to appreciate Frank Sinatra, amity may still prevail. But if I regard all singing as shit, as Marc might say, and you come to believe that I am sincere, you will gradually come to realize that I am very unlike you in some very deep way and, to that extent, a stranger to you.

You may come to suspect that I have a screw loose. But, at the very least, you cannot continue to value me as your "other self."

Sharing our tastes in art with others is sometimes a condition, sometimes a cause, and sometimes a combination of both in the process of cultivating our friendships with others. This is a mundane fact, readily confirmed at the intermission of every play. Just look around the lobby. But though the phenomenon is mundane and neglected, it is still a fact. What Yasmina Reza has done in *Art* is to bring this fact out into the open, where we can begin to scrutinize it and its ramifications.

Admittedly, the case she imagines is an extreme one. Her thought experiment is exaggerated and streamlined to make a point. But inasmuch as the situation she sketches strikes us as a psychologically plausible one, it reveals sources of value, motivation, and importance with respect to our traffic with art which, though often as ignored by us as a fish ignores water, structure our ordinary experiences of art. Art is not only social in the sense that it shapes society at large, albeit often in mysterious ways; it is also social in the sense that it has a role in the formation and enrichment of friendship; it is a locus of intimacy. Sharing taste and sharing our lives, to the extent that we do, typically go hand in hand. That is, taste in art and taste in friends are not randomly related.

Marc is in a panic over Serge's love of his painting by Antrios, because Marc cannot feel what Serge feels. Their sensibilities, then, are profoundly different. Marc can only respond to this disappearance of his other self – which he naturally experiences as existentially self-undermining – with hostility. Serge, on the other hand, is brought to a comparable predicament, since Marc's hostility shows him that Marc lacks the capacity to be moved in the deep way that abstract art can move him. It is as if Serge just discovered that the person he regarded as his alter ego has no feeling whatsoever for music. How close could you be to such a person? Could you be their lover?

The part of Serge that resonates to the painting is deep in his being; it is unpremeditated and barely cognitive; it is his sensibility. Sensibility is one of the most important things that friends share – a foundation, often, for everything else. Art, in turn, is standardly something expressly designed to engage our sensibilities. So when art divides us, it indicates a deviation in our sensibilities which, in the kind of extremely rarefied case that Yasmina Reza proposes, can have the potential to turn friends into strangers, or even embittered enemies in the wake of unrequited friendship. And though the case that she imagines is undoubtedly hyperbolic, it arguably tracks the joints of many friendships, especially those where shared sensibilities are of the utmost importance.

Throughout the play, Reza attempts dramatically to advance this theme of the concomitant breakdown of friendship and common sensibility by what, in effect, is a running analogy between art and humor. Notice how often the characters accuse each other of having lost their sense of humor. Whether people can laugh together for the right reasons becomes a constant test of whether they have changed for the worse and/or for whether they ever really had anything in common to begin with. The characters interrogate each other's laughter in terms of whether it is contemptuous or open-hearted and mutual – for example, Serge cannot laugh along with Marc at the Antrios, because Marc's laughter is dismissive and superior, whereas he will laugh with Yvan in shared astonishment at his own *l'amour fou* in paying so exorbitantly for an artwork.

Humor, of course, requires something shared – often called a sense of humor – which in many ways resembles taste. Laughter among friends is a pleasure, and one of the pleasures of friendship is the opportunity to share laughter. At the same time, laughter reveals something about who we are – our beliefs, attitudes, and emotions – and, for that reason, we are often only willing to be so open about our sensibilities around friends. We don't joke with the Pope, though we may tell jokes about the Pope to friends – to friends rather than to strangers, since we usually have no idea about their attitudes about religion. For these reasons, humor is a special ceremony among friends. And when friendships deteriorate, the feeling of a shared sense of humor often begins to dissipate proportionately. We no longer laugh together or laugh in the same way at the same things. Our former friend's sense of humor starts to seem cruder or, at least, more peculiar to us.

Reza charts the tension between Marc, Serge, and Yvan not only through their attitudes toward the painting by Antrios, but through parallel disconnects in their senses of humor. At one point, there is even a minor disagreement at a lower order of taste – Marc thinks the food at the Lyonnaise restaurant is fatty; Serge does not. And Serge reports his instinctual, almost chemical aversion to Marc's lover Paula. It is as though once their heretofore apparently shared sensibility unravels over the painting, the fabric of their entire friendship begins to tatter.

If Marc and Serge are to sustain their friendship, they must in some way re-establish a shared sensibility. Marc must come to see something of value in Serge's painting. And this, of course, happens, though through a very odd chain of events.

In order to show that he cares for the friendship, Serge encourages Marc to efface it with a felt-tip pen. Marc draws a man skiing down a slope on the white field. Later, together, they clean the painting, erasing the skier. However, now, Marc, the anti-modernist, anti-abstractionist, can see something in the painting: a man disappearing in a blinding blizzard as he skies down a whitened snowscape. Just as Arthur Danto suggests that one might see a pure red painting as pharaoh's army at the moment that the Red Sea engulfed it, Marc has transfigured Antrios's abstraction into a representation. Speaking figuratively, friendship has prompted Marc to see something in a new light, to find value where Serge does, though not exactly in the way that Serge does,[5] and this makes possible a renewal in their friendship, underscoring the potential of art not only to confirm the existence of friendship, but the potential of friendship to expand the excellence – in this case of the sensibility – of the other self.[6]

Yasmina Reza's *Art* belongs to the theater of ideas. Specifically, it is a contribution to philosophy – to the philosophy of friendship, to the philosophy of art, and to the intersection thereof. The highly contrived, though psychologically plausible confrontation, between Marc and Serge, affords an occasion to ponder the nature and dynamics of friendship by showing one, credibly, in the process of dissolution and prodding us to infer why this is happening. At the same time, it limns the importance of art to friendship, certainly one of the most overlooked facets of the importance of art to human life in general. The play discloses something neglected about the value of art in ordinary life by means of an extraordinary case – one whose very possibility disposes us to reconceive certain ordinary experiences with new and deeper understanding. In this, *Art* provides much to think and to talk about after the play, let us hope, with friends.

Notes

1   Yasmina Reza, *Art*, trans. Christopher Hampton (London: Faber and Faber, 1996).
2   That Serge is a dermatologist may be a joke about his having a predilection for surfaces.
3   This is a view that Epicurus attributed to Stilbo. See Seneca, "On Philosophy and Friendship: Epistle IX," in Michael Pakaluk (ed.), *Other Selves: Philosophers on Friendship* (Indianapolis: Hackett, 1991), p. 119.
4   One philosopher who has not neglected the relation of art and friendship is Ted Cohen. This interpretation of *Art* is deeply indebted to his penetrating investigations of, among other things, taste and humor. I doubt this essay could have been written had I not had the benefit of Ted Cohen's powerful insights on these matters.
5   Since where Serge sees modernist abstraction, Marc sees imitation, though imitation pushing at the envelope.
6   One philosopher, explicitly mentioned in the text of the play, is Seneca, who, like Aristotle, saw part of the value of friendship in its capacity to spur one on to greater excellence. It is just this sort of transformation, I conjecture, that Serge exhibits in the final lines of the play.

18

Martin McDonagh's *The Pillowman,* or The Justification of Literature

Since 1996, with the premiere of his play *The Beauty Queen of Leenane*, Martin McDonagh has emerged as one of the most powerful young voices in the English-speaking theater world.

The Pillowman is his most philosophical work.[1] It is a meta-theatrical exercise that obliquely addresses the question of whether theater (and, by extension, literature) can be justified in anything that it says. Or, instead, are some things out of bounds, perhaps sometimes warranting regulation?

In Book III of his *Republic*, Plato opens his attack upon poetry with a series of arguments that we may anachronistically call "the bad role model arguments." Plato is worried that if the gods, demi-gods, and heroes are portrayed in certain ways, they will encourage the young guardians – upon whose education Socrates is discoursing – to emulate them. Portrayals of conflict among the gods, for example, may favorably dispose the future rulers of the state toward civil war. The lamentations of heroes, such as Achilles in Hades bewailing his fate, might incline warrior-guardians toward self-pity and fear of death – hardly the sort of martial virtues befitting the Republic's auxiliaries. And so on. By means of these arguments and others, Plato ultimately proposes to banish the poets from the good city.

Although we are no longer worried about the same issues that made Plato anxious – we don't care if grown men cry – arguments of the bad-role model variety are still with us. Whereas Plato opined that poetry might make soldiers too soft-hearted and even cowardly, some today fear that the bad role

"Martin McDonagh's *The Pillowman*, or The Justification of Literature," *Philosophy and Literature* 35(1) (2011): 168–81.

models on page, stage, and screen will encourage violent behavior and/or sexual misconduct. Indeed, many fear that violence in the various media will encourage imitation. For that reason, they argue that such media should be regulated, if not outright censored. Even the less puritanically minded among us may complain that the violence and sex in the mass media drag the general level of the culture downwards.

Insofar as his works can be quite brutal,[2] the fictional representation of violence is a topic of abiding interest for Martin McDonagh. In *The Pillowman*, he explores the issue of whether it is justifiable or not, and he leaves the question disturbingly open.

The central character in *The Pillowman* is a writer named Katurian. Actually, his full name is Katurian, Katurian, Katurian, and he lives in Kamenice, which is governed by a fictional totalitarian regime. The emphasis on *K*s here, of course, leads one to think of the hero K in Kafka's *The Trial*.[3] Like K, Katurian is initially interrogated about a crime that is not defined by the police. We do not know of what he stands accused. Because he is blindfolded and because torture is threatened, we reckon that he is suffering at the hands of a police state, a supposition later confirmed by the play. We quickly learn that he is a writer, although he supports himself by working in an abattoir, and the fact that Katurian is an author encourages us to conjecture, as does Katurian himself, that he is in jail because of something politically incorrect that he has written. Thus, the issue of censorship is introduced almost immediately. And, undoubtedly, most liberal viewers will automatically sympathize with Katurian, virtually by reflex, since liberals tend to plump for the writer whenever there is a confrontation between art and the state.

Initially, these sympathies seem warranted. Katurian does not appear to be a writer concerned with politics in any overt way. He writes very short stories – abbreviated, suggestive fairy tales, recalling, somewhat, Kafka's parables. Katurian protests that he only cares about storytelling; he has no larger themes to broadcast. He says, "The *only* duty of a storyteller is to tell a story ... [T]hat's what I do, I tell stories. No axe to grind, no anything to grind. No social anything whatsoever." That is, he claims to be in it only for the art – the art for its own sake. So the audience is prone to give Katurian a pass, if only on the grounds of formalism.

So, we side with Katurian at first. We anticipate that the police interrogators, Tupolski and Ariel, will produce some trumped-up, misinterpretation of one of Katurian's fairy tales in order to represent it as subversive. But, in the first of many reversals, we realize that McDonagh has set us up. As the interrogation proceeds, we learn that Katurian's stories tend to have a recurring and very morbid theme – violence against children, including infanticide – and, furthermore, that some of these stories precisely mirror recent, actual, vicious child-killings. In one case, a little girl dies as the result of being forced to swallow little figures made of apples with razor blades inside them. In another case, a young Jewish boy bleeds to death after the toes on one of his feet have been hacked off. Karturian, it turns out, is not under suspicion due to some alleged, ideological deviation, but for possible complicity in very palpable offenses against young children. His stories, it appears, may have either served as the blueprints for these atrocities or they were written later in such detail that they seem as though they could only be the work of accessory to the crime, if only after the fact.

Katurian's story "The Three Gibbet Crossroads" tells of a poor little boy who shares his meager sandwich with a stranger driving a cart full of vermin. In "reward," the driver cuts off the boy's toes on one of his feet with a meat cleaver and then leaves the village of Hamelin behind. Since we infer that the mysterious cartman is none other than the Pied Piper of Hamelin, his wounding of the boy, perversely enough, saves the child's life, since, once crippled, the boy cannot keep up with the other children of Hamelin as they dance to their deaths. Thus, one could even read Katurian's story as endorsing the parting of the boy's toes from his body. Or, at least, it seems that someone did. So, even if Katurian is not directly to blame, he may be guilty of inciting some impressionable person to murder and mayhem, a prospect that should be worrisome to any community, totalitarian or otherwise.[4]

Although Katurian protests that he just writes stories, the evidence mounts against him. By the end of Act I, Scene 1, the police have discovered a child's toes hidden in the home that Katurian shares with his apparently mentally retarded brother, Michal. In addition, Katurian's interrogators further inform him that Michal has confessed to the crimes, although they do not believe that Michal could have carried them off by himself, since they surmise that he's not smart enough. They suspect that Katurian had a hand in it. At this point, the audience is unsure what to believe, although most have probably suspended their initial, reflex sympathy for Katurian. For now what is at stake is not some vague political issue, but the most heinous of crimes imaginable, the torture and murder of children.

Act I, Scene 2 is a flashback which is narrated by Katurian and simultaneously enacted by characters identified as the Mother and the Father, along with children whom we come to recognize retrospectively as Katurian and Michal. Katurian recites this flashback in a way that is highly reminiscent of his fairy tales – down to beginning the flashback with the formula: "Once upon a time ..." Katurian's writing and the play itself begin to merge into a stylistic unity,[5] implying that in whatever ways Katurian's parables are accountable, so too is McDonagh's play. And like Katurian's parables, McDonagh's play also trades in child abuse. So if Katurian is, so to speak, on trial, then so is McDonagh.

Although the story recounted in this flashback is not immediately marked as Katurian's own, what, in effect, Katurian reveals is the source of his macabre imagination. The Father and the Mother have two boys. They decide to nurture literary genius in one of them. They give him paints and books, pens and paper, and they encourage him to write. He produces short stories, fairy tales, and little novels, some of which are quite good. But getting him to write is only half of their plan. They also have very definite ideas about the kind of thing he should write.

To that end, they design what Katurian calls "an experiment." Every evening, in a room adjacent to Katurian's bedroom, they torture another child with drills and electrical devices. Nightly, Katurian hears the muffled cries of the gagged child next door. As a result, and in accordance with his parents' intentions, Katurian's stories got "darker and darker. They got better and better, due to all the love and encouragement, as is often the case, but they get darker and darker, due to the constant sound of child torture, as is also often the case." Thus, it is as if Katurian's parents are scientifically testing the ancient, enduring "theory" that art arises from suffering (and, perhaps, that great art emerges from great suffering).

On his fourteenth birthday, Katurian receives a note from the tortured child explaining the parents' "artistic" experiment. It is signed "Your brother." When Katurian confronts them, the parents manage to explain everything away by means of a scam. Later, however, Katurian ventures into the room next door, where he finds what appears to be the corpse of a 14-year-old boy whose body is broken and burned. Ironically, Katurian also finds a story by his dead brother which is better than anything Katurian has ever produced.

Then suddenly, miraculously, the corpse sits upright; Katurian's brother is alive, although he is extremely brain-damaged because of the incessant torture he's suffered. In retribution, Katurian suffocates his parents with a pillow. Given the particulars of the story, the murder of the parents would appear well deserved in requital for inflicting – in the most callous and coldhearted way – seven years of unrelenting abuse upon Michal.

Act 2, Scene 1 returns us to Katurian and Michal in the present. Michal is in jail. Katurian is thrust into Michal's cell, where Michal reassures Katurian that he is innocent, although he admits to confessing his guilt to the interrogators so as to avoid torture. Katurian believes Michal and begins concocting an elaborate conspiracy theory, explaining the ways in which the police are attempting to frame him. He even starts to compose it in his characteristic fable-style, thereby once again merging McDonagh's plot with Katurian's prose. But Katurian breaks off the narration, complaining that he lacks a pen to finish it properly. Shortly after, Michal asks Katurian to tell him a story. The story Michal requests is "The Pillowman," the story from which the play derives its title.

The eponymous Pillowman is nine feet tall and is made of pink pillows, including his round head which features a smiley-face smile and eyes made of buttons. The Pillowman has to look soft and nonthreatening because he works with children. Basically, the Pillowman visits suicides during their last moments. He returns them to their childhood, to the time just before their lives began to take the turn for the worse that will eventuate in their desire for death. The Pillowman explains all of the horrible things which await them in later life and attempts to convince them to kill themselves while they are still happy, thus averting an inevitable life of pain and suffering. The Pillowman helps them to stage their suicides so that they look like accidents – for instance, by telling them when to dart out from between parked cars and into busy traffic. This way the parents of the suicides do not blame themselves for the death of their children.

Basically, it is the Pillowman's doleful task to sway children to take their own lives. Finally, however, the Pillowman becomes so depressed by his work that he decides to do no more than one last job. Yet upon arriving at his destination, he discovers that his client this time is none other than himself as a child. True to his decision, he then persuades his child-self to douse himself with gasoline and to set himself aflame. As the pillow-child burns up, the adult Pillowman starts to fade away, but not before he hears the screams of all those suicides who, because he never grew up, suffer the disappointment and despair from which he tried to save them. That is, the children the Pillowman was able to persuade to destroy themselves have returned to their miserable lives. In effect, "The Pillowman" represents the killing of children – or, at least, assisting in their suicides – as a form of mercy killing.

Michal loves this story and says that he thinks the Pillowman, although, in effect, a child-killer went to heaven. Perhaps, then, it is no surprise that in short order Michal tells Katurian that he did the killings for which they have been incarcerated. He says that he identifies with the Pillowman. Katurian asks Michal, "What did you do it for?" Michal answers, "You know. Because you told me to." Katurian denies anything of the sort. Playing on the ambiguity of the word "tell," Michal argues, "And I wouldn't have done anything if you hadn't told me, so don't act all innocent. Every story you tell me, something, something horrible happens to someone" and "all the things I did to all the kids I got from stories you wrote and read out to me."

Through the exchanges between Michal and Katurian, McDonagh raises the question of the causal efficacy of literature, along with the related issue of authorial culpability. If, like Katurian, one writes works of grisly violence, does one share in the responsibility for that violence, if only indirectly? Katurian argues that he is not responsible for the interpretations that readers make of his work, especially readers of limited intelligence, like Michal. But Michal suggests the author's complicity by observing, "you've just spent twenty minutes *telling* me a story about a bloke, his main thing in life is to get a bunch of little kids to, at minimum, set themselves on fire … And he's the hero!" (emphasis added). That is, since he makes his morbid stories so intriguing and alluring, with their offbeat imagery and neat plot turns,

Katurian should not be surprised that they will appeal to the darker instincts of some audiences.[6]

Katurian and Michal carry on the debate, with Michal asserting that some stories have the power "to make people go out and kill kids." That, of course, is far too extravagant. But McDonagh does seem open to the possibility that there is something suspicious about a person who writes obsessively about violence and imbues it with the sort of narrative elegance that Katurian does. Katurian tells Michal the story of "The Little Green Pig" in order to prove that not all of his stories involve physical pain and suffering (although this one does involve the psychological persecution of a piglet – the taunting of a green one for not being pink). The story puts Michal to sleep. Then Katurian, presumably in order to save Michal from future torture, suffocates him with a pillow, as he did to his parents. Again, murder is figured as mercy killing.[7]

Katurian confesses to killing his brother and his parents and abetting Michal in the deaths of the two murdered children. He also warns the police that there may be a third murder underway at that moment, based on Michal's fascination with the story "The Little Jesus" (in which a young girl's foster parents force her to re-enact the passion of the Christ because of her identification with Jesus). Katurian feigns his involvement in Michal's crimes in order to persuade the policemen, both of whom reveal that they had been assaulted as children, not to destroy his manuscripts after they execute him. Death is inevitable for Katurian, but he clings to the writer's hope that his stories will immortalize him.

Hooded, with around 10 seconds left to live, Katurian imagines his last story. The Pillowman appears to Michal just before his parents begin their ruthless experiment. He describes to Michal all of the terrible things that will befall him and encourages the boy to kill himself. But Michal balks at the idea. He reasons that if he dies, Katurian will never write the stories that he, Michal, loves so well. He tells the Pillowman, "I think we should probably just keep things the way they are, then, with me being tortured and him hearing and all of that business, 'cos I think I'm going to really like my brother's stories. I'm going to really like them."

Here, something like the pleasure to be had from stories putatively justifies, for Michal at least, the abuse he underwent. And probably, in Michal's mind, that pleasure also justifies the child killings that he perpetrated supposedly under their influence, although even if Michal might be entitled to endure his own torture in exchange for the literary pleasure he anticipates, he is hardly in a position to justify the deaths of those children on the basis of the delight he derives from Katurian's stories.[8] That is, whatever rewarding experience Michal ultimately derives from Katurian's stories cannot be compensation for the lives of two other children. Michal may have the right to condone his own suffering as a child, but he has no authority to exact suffering and death from other children.

In *The Pillowman*, McDonagh seems to be asking, if literature inspires harm, can the gratification it affords ever be enough to justify it – can literary pleasure ever cancel out the wrongs that may be incurred in the pursuit of the potential delights of literature? Here the challenge is relevant to all of us who enjoy stories that at least risk dark consequences in the world outside of our fictions, including, if not specific acts, only the general degradation of our culture.

Michal appears to think the violence is a fair trade for the pleasure of stories. Ultimately, however, Katurian does not. This is signaled narratively by his intention to end his last story with their being destroyed by the police. He doesn't believe they are worth the horrors in which they are implicated. But before Katurian gets to work out that ending, he is executed. Tupolski had said Katurian had 10 seconds to live, but, arbitrarily, he shoots him after six seconds, thereby leaving Katurian's story unfinished in the world of the fiction. And instead of Katurian's stories being incinerated, as they would have been had his story been completed as he intended, they are filed away in his dossier by the ambiguously named Ariel[9] at the end of McDonagh's play where one day they might yet again inspire someone like Michal.

Thus, in terms of what happens in the narrative, Michal, in a manner of speaking, gets the last word. Horrible things in the world can be justified by the aesthetic pleasures to which they are connected. Katurian intends to deny this narratively by attempting to imagine that his stories are destroyed. But McDonagh saves them at the last minute. Does McDonagh, then, belong to the party of Michal?

In *The Pillowman*, it is given that stories may give rise to violence against children, as well as being the product of said violence. Indeed, even where such stories do not have dire consequences, they nevertheless are suspect inasmuch as they encourage our voyeuristic desires to be regaled with sadistic tales, *grand guignols*. That is, stories can be ethically compromised in several directions, often grievously so. And this, in turn, prompts us to ask whether stories that are linked to evil can be justified. Indeed, should their existence be tolerated?

Michal, in refusing to assent to the Pillowman's suggestion that he kill himself, votes for the continued existence of Katurian's stories (and, by extension, of literature), no matter how deeply implicated in immorality they may be in various ways. The reason he gives is that he will like these stories. In other words, they will give him pleasure or, in the idiom of the eighteenth century, they are beautiful. And this beauty makes the suffering and death connected with them acceptable.

Of course, as Arthur Danto points out, "it is through beauty that we vest death with meaning, as in funeral ceremonies with flowers and music and fine ceremonial words."[10] And, the same is true of suffering, as is evident in all those stunning religious paintings of Christian martyrs. Historically, beauty was enlisted to accent positively something that was presupposed to be antecedently worthy – the life of the dearly beloved departed or the suffering and death of a saint. But Michal thinks of beauty as valuable for its own sake, irrespective of its relations to other things, including evil, and, thereby, unworthy things, such as his own suffering and presumably the suffering and death that he inflicted upon at least two innocent children.[11] And Michal appears, in one sense, to get literally the final say on the matter in the play, since Katurian's exquisite stories survive destruction, despite his apparent last wish that they be destroyed for the terrible things they will cause or, at least, in which they will be implicated. So, in this way, it does seem that McDonagh sides with Michal.

But McDonagh is a playwright who specializes in setting up and then overturning audience expectations. Recall how he uses the totalitarian conceit in the opening of *The Pillowman*, only to complicate it. Remember how, later, he first has Michal convincingly deny the killings, only to confess shortly afterwards. In *The Beauty Queen of Leenane*, McDonagh leads us to believe that Mary Polan has gone off with Ray Dooley, but then reveals that this was only her fantasy. In *The Cripple of Inishmaan*, the playwright encourages us to believe that Cripple Billy will finally get his modicum of joy on a walk with Helen that promises at least "not much kissing and groping." But as soon as he is alone on stage, he coughs up blood and we know that he is doomed. In *A Skull in Connemara*, we are convinced that Mairtin Hanlon desecrated Mrs Dowd's grave, but then, in a surprising turn of events, we learn that the culprit was really his brother, Tom Hanlon. In short, engendering expectations and then subverting them, is McDonagh's signature strategy.[12] In a layering of reversals, scenes spin on a dime from warm and sensitive to vicious. They are by turns brutal then tender, and comic; then tragic and comic again. McDonagh is the master of the abrupt about-face. His specialty is pulling the rug from beneath the audience's feet (or seats).

Consider what Joan FitzPatrick Dean says of the end of *The Cripple of Inishmaan*:

> The end of *The Cripple* perhaps best exemplifies McDonagh's rollercoaster reversals. In the last two scenes, the audiences and the characters are given to believe variously that Billy has died of tuberculosis in Hollywood; that Billy did not die in Hollywood, but returns because he loves Inishmaan and its people; that Billy failed in Hollywood; that Billy has TB; that Billy's parents killed themselves to pay for the insurance benefit for his care; that Billy's parents tried to drown Bill but that Johnnypateemike rescued him and paid his medical expenses; that Billy is going to drown himself; that Billy and Helen will go walking. Despite Billy's tuberculosis and imminent death, *The Cripple* ends at this moment, perhaps the happiest in the play.[13]

Exactly this sort of lightning peripeteia marks the conclusion of *The Pillowman*. In the story that Katurian imagines seconds before he dies, he means to override Michal's response to the Pillowman's rhetoric; he intends to dream that his writings are destroyed. Yet just before he can think that thought, a bullet suddenly crushes his brain. What did Katurian want to say by this narrative gesture that he never got to make – at least literally, in his own voice? Perhaps that beauty – or aesthetic experience parsed in terms of pleasure – can never justify the suffering that it emerges from and/or gives incentive to.

The Pillowman reminds one of the philosophical problem of evil. How can an omnipotent God allow evil in the world? Often the answer is in terms of what the sufferance of evil will allow to obtain, which might otherwise be unattainable. For example, evil may be the price for free will. Or for beautiful moral gestures, such as self-sacrifice. Likewise, Michal suggests, suffering and death, even the suffering and death of children, may be the cost of the existence of Katurian's nearly perfect stories.[14] And by rejecting the Pillowman's appeals, Michal shows that that is a price he is willing to pay.

Katurian, on the other hand, wills that his stories be destroyed. Presumably, in the last analysis, he does not consider literary achievement in the form of beautiful stories and/or the pleasure they instill in audiences, as important enough to risk encouraging evil. And perhaps Katurian also worries that if one function of beauty is to console, as Danto suggests, then there may be something wrong with the way in which beauty is mobilized in his presentations of the violence to and abuse of children insofar any move toward reconciling us to such crimes is itself morally questionable. That is, if beauty has a rhetorical function, it should not be an accomplice to evil, either by inciting evil or even just by reconciling us to it.[15]

However, it is unclear that McDonagh endorses Katurian's view, since McDonagh has one more peripeteia up his sleeve. Instead of burning Katurian's stories, the policeman, Ariel, inexplicably places them in Katurian's file. The last words of the play follow: remarking upon Ariel's behavior, it is said "A fact [the depositing of the stories in the dossier] which would have ruined the writer's fashionably downbeat ending, but was somehow … somehow … more in keeping with the spirit of the thing." So, even if Katurian intended to end his story in a manner that suggests that the immoral risks with which some stories flirt cannot be justified by the beauty they sustain, McDonagh ends *his* story – the aforesaid *thing* – in a way that would have met with Michal's approval.

In short, during the closing moments of *The Pillowman*, McDonagh stakes out conflicting viewpoints on the relationship between literary beauty and evil. On the one hand, literary beauty is regarded as a tolerable exchange for evil in cases where beauty conciliates us toward it or even inspires it. On the other hand, by willing that his stories be destroyed, Katurian, the writer, signals that beauty is no excuse or compensation for evil and, perhaps, that censoring (destroying) stories that function like his is warranted. Nevertheless, it is difficult to say confidently which position McDonagh favors, since they come so quickly upon the heels of each other, cancelling each other out at the velocity of a ping-pong volley.

This, of course, forces the reflective viewer to wonder where McDonagh stands which, in turn, calls for an interpretation from us. But McDonagh has left indications of his intentions of roughly equal weight on both sides of the argument. As a result, if one favors one position over the other, the likelihood is that your own position on the issue, rather than the text of the play, is what is guiding you to your conclusion.[16] Moreover, once that comes to pass, one is prompted to reflect on the pertinent debates – indeed, to stage them inwardly, rehearsing the strengths and weaknesses of both sides in the court of the mind. That is, McDonagh quite ingeniously deploys his peripeties in order to provoke an inward philosophical meditation from thoughtful viewers.

In other words, by deploying his characteristic stylistic strategy of reversal, McDonagh strives to compel philosophy from his audience. By piling up contradictory (or, at least, conflicting) theses in such short order in the closing moments of *The Pillowman* – by thrusting them at the audience at a dizzying pace – McDonagh engenders the sort of confusion about the author's point of view that mandates an interpretation. And the project of interpretation, in this case, excites the viewer to engage in philosophy.

For, inasmuch as an interpretations that stays within the bounds of a "close reading" of *The Pillowman* cannot resolve the apparent "antinomy" with which McDonagh confronts us, we must try to stage the debate on our own in the "theater" of our minds. Whether such stories are justifiable or not becomes our responsibility to determine.

The Pillowman is a play about storytelling and playwrighting as relentlessly as Almodóvar's recent *Broken Embraces* is about filmmaking. Moreover, McDonagh ties his own practice to Katurin's through a number of strategies, including the way in which Katurin's stories tend to blend seamlessly into McDonagh's prose. Thus, as we judge Katurin, so should we judge McDonagh. Like Katurian, McDonagh specializes in entertaining violence, gratifying the audience's taste for atavistic bloodlust, itself a morally questionable enterprise, contributing as it does to a brutal culture in which carnage sells,[17] while also willingly risking the emulation of impressionable audiences, if only by folks as "damaged" as Michal.

The Pillowman is set in some unidentified locale, suggesting allegorical import. Its moral, in other words, will apply anywhere. This is one way in which McDonagh's ambition is philosophical. But, in addition, his subject is probably the most ancient question in the philosophy of literature – the issue of the justification of literature. This topic is relevant to McDonagh especially due to the extreme violence in which his plays traffic and the way in which he portrays it. At times, it is so excessive that it becomes comic; it generates laughter rather than revulsion, recalling the farcical mood of Tarantino's *Pulp Fiction*. But can such callous laughter at human suffering really be morally acceptable?[18]

At other times, as exemplified by Katurin's seemingly naive and uninflected stories in *The Pillowman*, McDonagh's representation of violence achieves a high level of literary beauty with their fable-like structures – their just-so narrative rhythms with everything falling neatly into place. But is such beauty enough to justify their existence, given the potentially dangerous power of literature, and its frequent association with evil across several dimensions?

These are questions raised across the totality of McDonagh's oeuvre so far. *The Pillowman* not only presents us with McDonagh's most wildly dysfunctional family up to now, but it also affords us his most recent reflection upon his own practice to date. It is a kind of summing up – an interim report.

However, rather than straightforwardly offering viewers a conclusion, it lures us into the discussion. By deploying one of his characteristic lightening reversals at the end of the play, he leaves the thoughtful viewer in a quandary about the author's viewpoint on the justification of fictional violence. This, in turn, beckons us to interpret the play in order to excavate McDonagh's position. But the text underdetermines our sense of McDonagh's conviction in these matters. Like so many Socratic dialogues, it leaves us to wrestle with the matter philosophically on our own, which seems particularly appropriate, since we have just enjoyed roughly two hours of aesthetic fascination in the process of dwelling upon the representation a series of events most vile.

After all, there would be no *Grand Guignol* without us.[19]

Notes

1   Martin McDonagh, *The Pillowman* (London: Faber and Faber, 2003). For another critical discussion of the play, see Brian Cliff, "*The Pillowman*: A New Story to Tell," in Richard Rankin Russell (ed.), *Martin McDonagh: A Casebook* (London: Routledge, 2007), pp. 138–48.

2   In *The Beauty Queen of Leenane*, there is a matricide; in *The Lonesome West*, there is a fratricide and two suicides; in *A Skull in Connemara*, there is an attempted murder and possibly a wife-killing. In *The Cripple of* Inishmaan, there is an attempted infanticide. Out of eight characters in *The Lieutenant of Inishmore*, five are killed, along with two cats and of the remaining three characters, two are likely to be killed by the third. Moreover, McDonagh's films are scarcely less gruesome. In his Academy Award winning short *Six Shooter*, there is a matricide, a suicide, an attempted suicide, a lethal gun battle between the police, and a raving psychopath, and the assassination of a rabbit, as well as the natural deaths of one child and one wife. In *In Bruges*, two assassins are killed by a third, who then kills himself; a priest also dies, along with a child and someone mistaken for a child. These body counts might not strike viewers of movies like *2012*

as very high, but one needs to keep in mind that the casts of characters in McDonagh's fictions are very small, so these numbers are, proportionally speaking, astronomical.

3   Also, that Katurin lives in Kamenice suggests a location somewhere in Central Eastern Europe – another association with Kafka – since "Kamenice" is a recurring Slavonic place-name. See Werner Hubner, "From Leenane to Kamenice: The Dehibernicising of Martin McDonagh," in Christopher Houswitsch (ed.), *Literary Views on Post-Wall Europe* (Trier: WVT, 2005), pp. 283–93; and Patrick Lonergan, "Commentary," in Martin McDonagh, *The Lieutenant of Inishmore* (London: Methuen, 2001), p. xxiii.

4   One reason to regard *The Pillowman* as a reflection by McDonagh on his own practice is that the story "The Three Gibbet Crossroads" is based on something that McDonagh wrote when he was 16. See Fintan O'Toole, "A Mind in Connemara: The Savage World of Martin McDonagh," *New Yorker* (March 6, 2006), pp. 40–7. Indeed, all of Katurian's stories come from treatments he developed for short films thereby suggesting some sort of identification between Katurian the storyteller and McDonagh, whose initials, like Katurian's, are made up of successive consonants – KKK and MM. See Joan FitzPatrick Dean, "Martin McDonagh's Stagecraft," in Russell (ed.), *Martin McDonagh: A Casebook*, p. 35.

5   This merger of the play and Katurian's story is further enhanced by the fact that it is not just read aloud but is also played out on stage by actors, thereby investing it with the same degree of bodily presence as the play in which it is contained.

6   McDonagh is famous for having said in a newspaper interview that "I don't think that Martin Scorsese can be held responsible because John Hinckley saw *Taxi Driver* many times and became obsessed with Jodie Foster." Some suggest that *The Pillowman* repeats the same sentiment – that Katurian can't be blamed for what Michal did, and, by extension, McDonagh can't be held accountable for whatever "inspiration" some intellectually challenged viewer might find in the violence of McDonagh's fictions. But I think that this interpretation is too hasty. McDonagh's approach seems much more complex and subtle in *The Pillowman* than it is in that interview. At the level of the narrative, Katurian's fiction is more closely tied to the precise details of the murders than Scorsese's is tied to the Hinckley case; whereas, symbolically, Michal is represented as Katurian's brother and is intimately connected to Katurian's distinctive imaginative style. Thus, I suspect that in *The Pillowman* McDonagh is giving more dialectical weight to the possibility that an author may be more liable for censure for producing entertaining violence than he was admitting in the article in the *Los Angeles Times*. See Patrick Pacheco, "Laughing Matters," *Los Angeles Times* (May 22, 2005), E24; See also José Lanters, "The Identity Politics of Martin McDonagh," in Russell (ed.), *Martin McDonagh: A Casebook*, p. 11.

7   Also, since this is the second time that Katurian has killed with a pillow, it is difficult to resist the suggestion that he, too, is some sort of "pillowman." Perhaps his message – as embodied in his stories – is that life is just too horrible to bear.

8   Here one thinks of Ivan's argument in *The Brothers Karamazov*: "Listen! If all must suffer to pay for the eternal harmony, what have the children to do with it; tell me, please. It is beyond comprehension why they should suffer. And why they

should pay for the harmony." Ivan's point is that since the children have done no wrong, their suffering is unjust even if it serves the purposes of cosmic harmony. Likewise Michal's victims cannot be fairly expected to contribute to paying the price for literary beauty.

9   Is he Shakespeare's Ariel or Milton's, or, given the aura of political violence in the play, Ariel Sharon (Charon)? See José Lanters, "The Identity Politics of Martin McDonagh," p. 13.

10 Arthur Danto, *The Abuse of Beauty* (LaSalle, IL: Open Court, 2003), p. 137.

11 Michal must think that literary beauty is valuable for its own sake, since the suffering Katurian's stories are related to are unworthy. In fact, just because the relevant events are unworthy, the rhetoric of beauty is misused in commemorating them.

12 In *The Lieutenant of Inishmore*, the cat whose purported death has initiated all the onstage carnage saunters into view just before the curtain falls, while *Be-handing in Spokane* ends with the main character realizing that he had recovered his lost hand untold be-handings before.

13 Joan FitzPatrick Dean, "Martin Mcdonagh's Stagecraft," in Russell (ed.), *Martin McDonagh: A Casebook*, p. 37.

14 By the way, it is often said that if one means to talk of some allegedly splendid literary work that some character has produced in a work of literature, it is always better never to present it, since anything you present is likely to disappoint. Katurian's stories are an exception to this rule. They are simply mesmerizing.

15 Or perhaps just acclimatizing us to it, as the incessant reinvention of violence of the mass media normalizes or anestheticizes us to it.

16 Perhaps this intended to be a subtle comment upon all thematic interpretation. Maybe it is all what Gadamer would call "application."

17 See Laura Eldred, "Martin McDonagh and the Contemporary Gothic," in Russell (ed.), *Martin McDonagh: A Casebook*, p. 124.

18 On comedy in McDonagh, see Maria Doyle, "Breaking Bodies: The Presence of Violence on Martin McDonagh's Stage," in Russell (ed.), *Martin McDonagh: A Casebook*, pp. 92–110.

19 In this regard, it is interesting to compare *The Pillowman* with Michael Haneke's film *Funny Games* (both versions – 1997, 2008).

Section VI

Philosophy across Popular Culture

19

The Fear of Fear Itself

The Philosophy of Halloween

Halloween: the festival of the wandering undead

Halloween is the night of the living dead. In all likelihood, the festival originated in Ireland where it was celebrated on November 1, Samhain, which
was, for the ancient Celts, the first day of winter, the season of death.

According to legend, on Samhain, the souls of all those who had died in the
previous year gather from hither and yon to enter the otherworld. The living
would put out food, drink, and other offerings to placate the traveling souls
of the dead, perhaps to expiate any wrongs that they had done to them.
Bonfires were lit and recently harvested food was fed to the flames as a
sacrifice.

This should sound somewhat familiar to you. For it is very probable that
the practice of going from door to door dressed as skeletons, vampires, zombies, ghosts, mummies, ghouls, Frankenstein's monster, and other assorted living dead in the expectation of receiving candy, money, and the like is a
re-enactment of the itinerary of the wandering Undead on Samhain.

Catholic missionaries penetrated Ireland in the fifth century, entering into
competition with the indigenous Druidic religion of the Celts. But rather than
attempting to stamp out Samhain entirely, they appropriated it. In accordance
with a strategy developed by Pope Gregory the Great, Catholic missionaries
melded their myths with the local ones. In this way, pagan fertility imagery,
like painted eggs and rabbits, was dragooned into the iconography of Easter,

"The Fear of Fear Itself: The Philosophy of Halloween," in Richard Greene and K. Silem Mohammad
(eds.), *Zombies, Vampires, and Philosophy* (Chicago: Open Court, 2010), pp. 223–35.

and pre-Christian symbols, like the Germanic *Tannenbaum*, were re-identified as trees of special significance to Jesus. In Ireland, Samhain became All Saints' Day – the day in which all those saints without feast days of their own were honored – and the day after that – November 2 – became All Souls' Day, a day, like Samhain, dedicated to all of the souls of the departed. Though now in Catholic vestments, these days were still marked as belonging to death and winter as clearly as Easter is associated with spring and rebirth.

Halloween, of course, is the day before All Saints' Day. Saints, needless to say are hallowed. So, "Halloween," in other words, is "All Hallows' Eve," or more archaically, "All Hallows' Even," which was shortened to "Halloween."

The Catholic missionaries also re-described the gods of the Druids as demons, devils, fairies, goblins, and monsters, and their priests and devotees as witches and wizards. Their kingdom was identified as the underworld. So, on Samhain, that enchanted moment on the seam between two seasons, the gates of hell are opened not only to receive the wandering dead but also, in the process, to loose onto the world the denizens of the domain of death, including devils, demons of every monstrous shape, and witches, not to mention the prisoners of the underworld – ghosts and other Undead in every manner of degeneration from the horrifically mutilated, fraying, and decaying to bone-dry skeletons. This is, of course, a cast of characters whom you already know, even if you never heard of Samhain. In their trail, evil and chaos reigns.

This superstitious belief then was given embodiment by mummers and maskers who, dressed like the minions of hell, go from door to door exacting tribute. For whenever the Undead appear, they typically want something from the living. When the Irish emigrated to America, they brought this custom with them, and they came in such large numbers that it became a national theme. As I recall the Halloweens of my youth, it is easy to re-imagine them as visions of hellish chaos – with piles of autumn leaves burning in the twilight, and clusters of witches and skeletons and ghosts scurrying madly in every direction, driven by too much sugar.

The predominant imagery of Halloween revolves around death. The most traditional costumes allude to the wandering dead – ghosts, ghouls, skeletons, and so forth. The devil, of course, is the lord of the dead and witches are his missionaries. Since they are often members in good standing in the league of the living dead, many movie monsters are naturals – or, perhaps more aptly, supernaturals – for Halloween masking, including the Mummy, Dracula, Frankenstein's monster, zombies, and so on. Likewise, any demon from *Buffy the Vampire Slayer*, especially perhaps from the episode devoted to Halloween, is ripe for masquing.

In fact all manner of monsters can inspire Halloween mumming – even those who hail from outer space – since they would fit into the Christian redefinition of the Halloween universe as demons, soldiers of Satan's armies of hell. Of course, not every costume on Halloween is monstrous. But what is nevertheless very striking is that so many of the most frequently recurring ones are connected to the realm of the Undead in one way or another. Over three-fourths of the Halloween outfits and masks at my local costume shop were of monsters, most of them of the Undead variety.

Halloween decorations also invoke death imagery. The Jack-o'-lantern refers to an Undead trickster – a blacksmith named Jack – who, having been exiled from both heaven and hell – wanders the world, some say with his head in his hand. Dummies – sometimes scarecrows, perhaps to ward off carrion feeders – are often set up or hung from porches, and they are joined by effigies of witches, ghosts, corpses, and, more recently, movie monsters. Mock spider webs, replete with rubber arachnids, imitate the interiors of crypts, while various vegetables, like cobs of corn, are hung on doorways. Often these vegetables are already in a state of deterioration, reminding onlookers that they were mowed down in the recent harvest. Leaves, already in the colors of autumn decay, are everywhere, whether intentionally or not. And, of course, there are cut-outs of Halloween figures like witches and ghosts plastered on windows, blackboards, and the like.

Nowadays, many of these decorations are store-bought, rather than homemade. And the entertainment industry uses this celebration of death as a marketing ploy. Horror movies, like the recent remake of *The Fog*, a ghost story, are released around Halloween, as was John Carpenter's classic *Halloween*, in order to exploit the seasonal taste for death. You'll recall that Michael Myers becomes one of the Undead in the course of that film. For similar reasons, the DVD of George Romero's *Land of the Dead*, a zombie thriller, was released on October 18, 2005, so as to give everyone who desired a copy time to buy one in order to horrify themselves and their friends on Halloween night.

And, of course, broadcast television literally goes into its vaults to exhume a veritable bestiary of the Undead for the weeks approaching Halloween night. Starting at noon of October 23, 2005, the American Movie Channel ran a solid week of horror films. Obviously, the programmers at this station were quite confident that there are, at any given moment at this time of year, a sufficient number of viewers eager to have the bejesus scared out of them to warrant a non-stop fright fest.

Though AMC – and, of course, the Science Fiction Channel – may be the most extreme examples here, other stations feature an upsurge of horror fictions during this season. It is, for example, a perfect occasion for marathon re-screenings of *The Twilight Zone* and *Outer Limits*. Nor was it an accident that Showtime chose the beginning of the 2005 Halloween weekend to premiere its new series *Masters of Horror*. For on and around Halloween has come to be the time of year when people gather before their flickering hearth not to tell ghost stories, but to watch them.

And finally, another frequently observed trend is that Halloween is becoming more and more of an adult holiday – an opportunity for masquerade parties, where the traditional costumes of the Undead are never far from sight. The fancier parties may even have TV monitors scattered about, re-running favorite monster movies continuously.

The paradox of halloween

A great deal of what I've just said is not news to most of you. Except for the bits about the history of Samhain, the rest is widely known and very familiar. But – and this is where this chapter really begins – it is so familiar that I think we lose sight of the fact that this is all very peculiar, even paradoxical. Many derive some strange kind of pleasure or satisfaction from the horror films that bombard them during this season. Indeed, they seek them out. They revel in spectacles of corpses and decomposing bodies.

But how many among them would jump at the opportunity to spend the afternoon in the city morgue viewing dead and decaying bodies, and, even if they did, would they derive the same sort of satisfaction they get from the horror movies? If some of those stiffs could be re-animated, would they be willing to dance with them? The Undead in reality would be pretty revolting, not entertaining.

Moreover, the paradox extends beyond the motion pictures customarily marketed around this time of year. It pertains to Halloween itself. For, the strange pleasure or satisfaction that we take in these movies prefigures the larger mystery of how we can enjoy Halloween. For, Halloween is about death, perhaps the most fearful aspect of human life. According to the philosopher Martin Heidegger (1889–1976), it's the source of *Angst* so deep that most of us spend our lives denying the inevitable fact of death. Rather than face it, we turn ourselves into social robots.

And yet on Halloween, we appear to embrace death's imagery. Many thrill at the prospect of the representatives of death wreaking evil and mayhem in our popular entertainments, and we derive a strange satisfaction from our fellow citizens wandering the streets in the make-up of the Undead. Of course, not all this imagery is, so to speak, "straight." Much of it is parodic, from *Abbott and Costello Meet the Mummy* to the capering skeletons in Halloween parades. In 2005, Tim Burton's *Corpse Bride* and Wallace and Gromit's *The Curse of the Were-Rabbit* arrived just in time to satirize the myths of Halloween horror. But isn't it just as anomalous that we should laugh at mortality as that we should find any satisfaction in being, as we say, "scared to death"? These are the paradoxes of Halloween that philosophy needs to address.

Needless to say, this is not an issue that most schools of philosophy have broached. However, since many of the traditional figures of Halloween are associated with the kinds of creatures who haunt nightmares, and since psychoanalysis has advanced hypotheses about the significance of these figures in our dreams, psychoanalysis is an obvious place to look for suggestions about our attraction to imagery of the evil dead which, one would think, should repulse us. One book that would appear to be especially pertinent is *On the Nightmare* by Ernest Jones,[1] perhaps best known as Freud's biographer and the person responsible for bringing Freud to England in his flight from the Nazis.

A psychoanalytic solution

Jones's book employs Freudian analysis in order to plumb the symbolic portent and structure of such nightmarish figures of medieval lore as the vampire, the devil, the witch, and so forth. Since many of these imaginary beings correspond to the recurring figures of Halloween, some may be tempted to adapt Jones's analysis of the relevant dreams to the costumes and entertainments of October 31.

Jones's account, moreover, seems initially promising, if only because it has the right structure. For he appreciates that the fantastical beings that concern us are simultaneously attractive and repellant. As a hard-line Freudian, Jones is committed to the notion that all dreams involve wish-fulfillment. However, many wishes are for things forbidden. So dreams driven by forbidden desires putatively camouflage their objects in symbolism – often symbolism that makes the objects appear to be anything but desirable – indeed, sometimes symbolism that transfigures the objects of desire into something loathsome. It's as if the dreamer is saying to his psychic censor "I can't be desiring this, because I find it so repulsive."

That is, the selfsame item may be both the subject of a wish and of an inhibition. The inhibition component takes the form of negative imagery or affect. The function of the dreamwork, including the nightmare, is to construct situations that, in a manner of speaking, forge a compromise between our wishes and our inhibitions.

Jones writes:

> The reason why the object seen in a nightmare is frightful or hideous is simply that the representation of the underlying wish is not permitted in its naked form so that the dream is a compromise of the wish on the one hand and on the other of the intense fear belonging to the inhibition. (p. 78)

For example, on Jones's analysis, the vampires of lore have two essential characteristics: they are Undead revenants and they subsist on the blood of the living, which they extract orally. According to the vampire legends that serve as the basis for Jones's investigations – and as opposed to the way in which the vampire is represented in contemporary popular culture – vampires first return from the dead to visit their relatives and to feast upon them. This imagery, Jones hypothesizes, can be interpreted initially as the wish, on the part of the living, for the dearly departed relative to return from the dead. But the alleged loved one is a horrific figure. Specifically, what is fearful about the revenant is bloodsucking, something that Jones associates with sexuality and seduction. Moreover, since the revenant is a relative, the sexuality in question is incestuous. So the wish that underwrites the symbol of the vampire is a wish for incest. However, this wish is simultaneously inhibited by the dream-work inasmuch as the vampire is represented as an abominable and dangerous predator.

That is, the forbidden desire for an incestuous liaison with a dead relative is transformed, by a process of denial, into something very different – a vicious attack. Attraction and love for the relative is alchemized into fear and disgust. Instead of yielding lips, the living quarry imagines himself or herself to be penetrated by merciless fangs. The humans portray themselves as passive victims and the Undead as aggressors. It's the vampire who is the active agent, not its prey. This supposedly allows the pretended victim to consummate, in the dream, a sexual, indeed an incestuous, relation with the vampire without blame. For, in this scenario the mortal must be innocent, since she is being ruthlessly savaged. The sexuality here, on Jones's account, is primarily regressive, a blend of the sucking and biting characteristic of the oral stage of psychosexual development. But all this nuzzling can be indulged without guilt, since it has been reconfigured as an unwanted onslaught.

Jones then goes on to analyze the iconography of other fantastic beings, many of whom are the staples of our popular entertainments, including Halloween. Given his Freudianism, in case after case he discovers that the imagery masks sexual wishes. The horrific imagery functions to deflect the sanctions of the psychic censor, also known as the super-ego. For the wish is disguised as its negation, namely as fear and disgust, and delight masquerades as aversion. In the case of the nightmare, the dreamer putatively cannot be charged with sexual transgression, because she is having the attentions of the vampire, the ghost, the ghoul, and so forth forced upon her. As anyone can see, she is not enjoying herself; she is being violated. Her predominant feeling is ostensibly not pleasure, but horror, though, according to Jones, this horror is actually the price that she has to pay for pleasure that comes from the dreamland gratification of her sexual desires.

In favor of Jones's hypothesis is the fact that sexual themes are germane to some of the figures that concern us. Often witches are first encountered as beautiful young maidens, only to reveal their horrific aspect the morning after. And Dracula is usually depicted as a handsome seducer, though not when he sports his Nosferatu look. Satan is a seducer too, but not a carnal one. Some of these monsters abduct women; maybe that is supposed to insinuate rape. Perhaps all the rough-house to which these nightmare figures subject their victims belies the childhood confusion over sexual congress and violence of the sort that Freud maintains occurs when children witness the primal scene.

Furthermore, with special reference to Halloween, the notion that all these figures are fundamentally transgressive fits with the ritual suspension or carnivalesque inversion of the rules on the holiday. For, like April 1st, Halloween is an evening when tricks are permitted, as well as being a time when excessive eating and drinking is the order of the day (or night). One might also say that Halloween is a period when a major ontological role-reversal occurs: the living "become" the dead.

But there are also problems with expanding Jones's hypothesis to cover Halloween. Some of the figures at the intersection of the nightmare, Halloween, and popular culture may have explicit sexual connotations, but just as many do not. Skeletons, on the face of it, are not sexy. The suavely attired Count Dracula may be alluring, but the case is less convincing with zombies, ghouls, milky wraiths, and creatures or demons from outer space like the Predator and the Alien from the film series bearing those names.

The psychoanalyst may reply that these examples are beside the point, since, according to Jones, the sexual significance of these figures is concealed by design. It is precisely the fact that these creatures strike us as the opposite of sexually inviting that enables them to trick the censorious super-ego into admitting them into the bedroom. The advantage of this "black means white" mode of interpretation is that it can account for from whence the pleasure or satisfaction comes with regard to this otherwise vile imagery. However, it does require the presupposition that these fantastical beings *always* stand for a wish, indeed a sexual wish, often one connected to the putatively universal desire for incest, and that the horror that accompanies exposure to these figures is only ever a diversionary tactic cloaking a deeper source of satisfaction.

And yet, might it not be the case that sometimes a zombie is just a zombie, and being devoured by one is simply cannibalism? That is, might it not be that frequently we are just horrified by our Halloween entertainments? When the leprous revenants in the re-make of *The Fog* pummel Mayor Malone into the cemetery to the sound of startling claps of thunder, my blood runs cold, which is not a tingle of sexual arousal. Nor does it seem plausible to speculate that I have any incestuous inclinations toward these ghosts, since they are not my relatives. Likewise, as Moonface drills out the eyes of his victim in "Incident on and off a Mountain Road" (the first installment of the aforesaid *Masters of Horror*), I am squirming, but not with pleasure. Isn't it possible that I am just horrified by the spectacle?

It may be alleged that I am merely in a state of self-deception here. My ego, along with my super-ego, has been duped; only my id knows and it's not talking. Moreover, if I say that I'm simply horrified by the spectacle, how are we to explain the satisfaction that I take in it? But again, notice that this explanation comes with an expensive theoretical price-tag.

One has to presume an awful lot of hypothetical states, laws, and processes, including a universal desire for incest, the reducibility of all the pertinent desires to sexual desire, the idea that all such fancies are wish-fulfillment fantasies, the mechanics of repression, the homuncular behaviors of the different parts of the psyche, indeed, the supposition that the psyche is partitioned in this way, the existence of the unconscious, and so on. In short, one must accept large portions of psychoanalytic theory in order to get this hypothesis off the ground, including the idea that we are always in a mental state of disavowal regarding what is really happening to us as we consume horror fictions.

This is a very elaborate – some might unsympathetically say "Rube-Goldberg-like" – explanatory apparatus. Would not a simpler model be far more compelling? For example, might not the notion that we are literally terrified by the appropriate moments in *The Fog* be a better account of what is going on, especially if we could say how that terror can be satisfying without resorting to the complex paraphernalia of psychoanalytic theory? All things being equal, a more economical explanation of the phenomenon should make us less confident of the more byzantine psychoanalytic account. So let us see if we can find one.

The meta-fear of fear

We can start to evolve an alternative explanation to the psychoanalytic one by focusing on part of the phenomenon before us in order to see what the part can tell us about the whole. So let's ask: what is it about the popular entertainments, like horror movies and television programs, that seem to yield pleasure or satisfaction at the same time that they are designed to raise negative emotions – emotions of fear and disgust?[2] It is perhaps useful here to recall the primary audiences for such entertainments – adolescent and young men, though, in recent decades, more young women are joining their ranks. What is it that they might derive from horror spectacles?

The adolescent male viewers – who often tramp to the cineplex in groups – are engaged in a rite of passage. Speaking as one who enacted this ritual himself, they wish to demonstrate to themselves and to their peers that they can endure spectacles of substantial amounts of violence, carnage, filth, and impurity. They come to the theater with a certain fear of their own fear, namely that their feelings may swing out of control when subjected to particularly gruesome stimulation. For the adolescent horror aficionado, Franklin Roosevelt's aphorism – that the only thing we have to fear is fear itself – might be amended to say "we, untested as we are, are very afraid of being afraid." Exposure to the horror spectacle, then, confirms that the viewer will not lose it, at least in the culturally controlled situation of the movie theater where the viewer has been insulated from genuine danger by the ontologies of fiction and the screen.

Adolescence is a time, at least in our culture, when one is especially prone to anxiety about one's emotions This is true not only of fear but of anger, love, desire, and so forth. The fear is that one will be unable to handle one's emotions – that they will take control of us with untoward consequences. With the changes in our bodies, attendant to adolescence, our emotions and desires begin to seem mysterious to us. We develop a nagging fear of what might occur under their aegis.

A large part of that fear is that we are entering an emotional terrain that is, as of yet unknown, a *terra incognita.* Various aspects of adolescent popular culture enable us to explore that country to a limited degree and to become familiar with it in such a way that we no longer feel utterly "out of it" and helpless with respect to our affects. Perhaps electronic shooter-games enable us to play with rage in this manner. It is my hypothesis that horror fictions, especially audio-visual ones, allow us to test our own fear factor. Its power over the viewer – at least to the extent that that power rests upon the fact that our emotional dispositions are frighteningly obscure for being untried – can be reduced by giving our fear a reassuring trial run.[3]

One objection to this is that an adaptive account like this overlooks the obvious. We are never going to encounter vampires, ghosts, ghouls, Undead skeletons, and the like, so the fears we test at horror screenings are not really relevant to the experience of any kind of fear-producing situation that we are going to encounter in life. What we see in horror fictions are scientifically impossible events; they are not the right sort of things to test our authority over our feelings.

Nevertheless, the imagery of the Undead does combine many elements of legitimate anxiety. First, there is the prospect of death. Halloween spectacles of the Undead invite us to confront the fact of death itself. The Undead, moreover, are often in some pronounced state of decay or deterioration. This too is a fact of life that horror fictions bring to the fore. The impurity of the zombie is connected to an automatic fear of corpses that most of us feel, while the misshapen and twisted bodies of many Halloween horrors are exaggerations of actual abnormalities that may affront us in the real world. Likewise the aggressiveness and ferocity of many fantastic beings have real world parallels. The war of the worlds, in the film of the same name, is a form of intergalactic genocide.

So one source of satisfaction to be drawn from typical Halloween horrors is a kind of control or mastery that some can derive from experiencing fear close up. This is not to say that horror fictions inoculate us against fear, but rather that they can alleviate the meta-fear of fear by permitting us to explore the first-order level of fear itself. Extrapolating, then, from the satisfaction that can be found in typical Halloween entertainments to the holiday itself, I speculate that the festival itself, with its convergent horrific iconography of the living dead, is a cultural platform that invites experimentation with the negative emotions that surround death and deterioration for the purpose of palliating the fear of fear.

That the holiday is primarily an affair for the young and for adolescents may be offered as corollary support for this hypothesis, since they are probably especially prone to fear of the emotions. Halloween is a social occasion that affords the opportunity to educate youth in the process of emotional management. It is a folk remedy for the fear of fear whose medium is primarily the iconography of the Undead. Nor is it without efficacy for us oldsters who feel death approaching as our bodies ourselves show signs of decay.

Another piece of corollary, albeit informal, evidence for my hypothesis has to do with a feature of Halloween to which many of you may feel I have not yet paid sufficient attention. As mentioned earlier, much Halloween iconography, including that of the Undead, is offered in a parodic spirit. *Scream* is just as likely to be shown on Halloween night as is *The Curse of Frankenstein*. Halloween parades of the Undead and campy imitations of Bela Lugosi belong to the holiday as much as the imagery designed to make onlookers cringe.[4] This is probably especially true of adult masquerade parties.

Halloween levity may, at first blush, appear to contradict my hypothesis about the function of the holiday to mitigate the meta-fear of fear by means of inducing fear. However, as is well known, humor is a widely acknowledged device that is used by people in professions, like medicine, mental health, the military, and law enforcement, which professions bring them into close contact with death, injury, decay, and malevolent behavior. These professionals use laughter – what the philosopher Henri Bergson called the anaesthesis of the heart – in order to control their emotional reactions in such a way that they can get on with their work. That is, laughter too is a well known means of emotional control. That laughter and horror exist side by side on Halloween may be the result of their sharing the same basic function for revelers: both contribute to enhance their feelings of self-control with respect to the emotions, most notably fear and disgust.

The conjecture that Halloween iconography of the Undead – both media-made and handmade – imparts satisfaction and pleasure due to the alleviation of our fear of fear and, thereby, to emotional control, is in competition with better-known explanations like psychoanalysis. But the fear-of-fear hypothesis is not only simpler than its psychoanalytic rival. Its leading assumption – that many of us, at least at certain times in our lives, are prone to the fear of fear – is readily confirmed introspectively, whereas much of the psychoanalytic account relies upon the existence of operations and entities that defy direct confirmation. To its dialectical advantage, then, the fear-of-fear hypothesis of the pleasure taken in the Halloween iconography of the Undead is more economical both with respect to the number and complexity of the concepts and operations it presupposes as well as being simpler in terms of the kinds of observations that contribute to its confirmation.

Fear itself may not be the only thing that frightens us on Halloween; but it is one of them.[5]

Notes

1   Ernest Jones, *On the Nightmare* (New York: Liveright, 1951).
2   For an account of horror that relates it to the arousal of the emotion of fear and disgust, see Noël Carroll, *The Philosophy of Horror* (New York: Routledge, 1990).
3   The idea that many entertainments are a means of enabling emotional management, especially for children, is explored at length by Gerard Jones in his *Killing Monsters* (New York: Basic Books, 2002).
4   On the connection between laughing and screaming, see my "Horror and Humor" in my book *Beyond Aesthetics* (Cambridge: Cambridge University Press, 2001).
5   This chapter's background information on Halloween comes from Jack Santino (ed.) *Halloween* (Knoxville: University of Tennessee Press, 1994); Jack Santino, "Halloween in America: Contemporary Customs and Performances," *Western Folklore* 42 (1983): 1–20; Jack Santino, "The Folk Assemblage of Autumn: Tradition and Creativity in Halloween Folk Art," in John Michael Vlach and Simon Bronner (eds.), *Folk Art and Art Worlds* (Ann Arbor: UMI Research Press, 1986), pp. 151–69.

20

The Grotesque Today

Preliminary Notes toward a Taxonomy

Growing up in the 1950s and early 1960s with a taste for the grotesque, I remember being constantly on the lookout for some way to sate my craving for the monstrous. One had to be ever vigilant, I recall. New horror films were hardly a weekly affair, and, when they were released, they did not always reach my local theater on Long Island, nor, when they did arrive, did they stay long. One had to move fast. Likewise you had to be very attentive to the racks in the local stationery stores, if you hoped to secure the relevant magazines, comic books, and paperbacks that would arrive only sporadically. A lot of us were on the same quest; it took dedication to score. Often I had to satisfy myself by turning to the pictures of hell in my Baltimore Catechism.

But, of course, as the saying goes: "Kids today have it easy." Presently the grotesque proliferates in mass culture at a rate almost as accelerated as pod people in a small town. Just as it was once claimed that "the sun never sets on the British Empire," it can be said now, I conjecture, that without much effort, one could, given the composition of contemporary mass culture, find something to quench one's thirst for the grotesque every hour on the hour every day of the week.

If that seems exaggerated, start by thinking about what is available (in the United States) on television on a fairly regular basis: *The X-Files, Earth 2, Star Trek* (many generations), *Stargate, Farscape, Buffy the Vampire Slayer, Tales from the Crypt, Millennium, Brimstone, Alien Nation, Babylon 5, Friday the 13th, The Legacy, Dark Angel,* reruns of *The Twilight Zone, Dark Shadows,*

"The Grotesque Today: Preliminary Notes toward a Taxonomy," in Frances S. Connelly (ed.), *Modern Art and the Grotesque* (Cambridge: Cambridge University Press, 2003), pp. 291–311.

Tales from the Darkside; and fantastic beings also frequently populate *Hercules, Xena, Warrior Princess*, and *Sinbad*, not to mention their appearance on shows about superheroes, both live-action and animated, like *Gargoyles*. In addition, for very young children, there are cartoon series like *Pokemon* that nurture a liking for such creatures while undoubtedly muting their most fearsome aspects, which is a strategy also exploited by Disney.

Moreover, television obviously relies on the movie industry for much of its staple product. And there television finds a treasury of classic and not-so-classic horror and sci-fi films – including films that went directly from the editing table onto video. Television, both network and cable, screens these films at such a pace that an insomniac can usually find something of this sort to watch nightly. And, in any case, if you can't, then you can routinely look to Direct-TV, which typically has at least one, if not more, offerings for the aficionado of fantastic beings. Or there is always the video rental store, where the sections devoted to horror and science fiction are among the largest. And, if all else fails, you can even go to an actual movie theater where horror, science fiction, and related genres are released at a steady pace.

Perhaps needless to say, television and film are not the only outlets for contemporary grotesquerie. The iconography of a great many video games is grotesque, even often horrific, inhabited by fantastic beings of every imaginable physiognomy. And the print media abound with novels and anthologies of horror and science fiction, frequently comingled, not to mention sword-and-sorcery adventures – that is, the sort of serial fantasy novels, like *Krondor: Tear of the Gods*, that are everpresent on bestseller lists.

Stephen King's serialized, on-line horror novel *The Plant*, now temporarily on hold, was certainly one of the most discussed publishing events of the year 2000. And, of course, since that time, King has served up in hardcover no less than three entries that have all made their way to the charts. Further, for those more reverentially minded horror fans, there is the apocalyptic series of novels by Tim LaHaye and Jerry B. Jenkins of which the popular *The Mark* is the eighth installment.

Comic books, the largest number of which appear to specialize in grotesquerie, are available everywhere. Moreover, even the so-called legitimate theater has realized that fantastic beings sell, as the profits from musicals such as *Jekyll and Hyde, Beauty and the Beast*, and, arguably, *The Lion King* attest.

So far I have primarily been inventorying what might be thought of as the dark side of the grotesque in popular culture. But a taste for the grotesque is also pervasively evident in the success of comedies that indulge it lavishly. So many cartoon series, including *The Simpsons, South Park*, and *Futurama*, make monstrosity their metier. It seems that nearly every episode of *South Park* introduces a fantastic being – Barbra Streisand as virtually the twin sister of mechno-Godzilla, or Satan and his minions, or assorted space aliens – while *The Simpsons* not only presents horror parodies in its Halloween specials – including the "Treehouse of Horror" series – but explores it weekly, inasmuch as Homer is himself grotesque, a being of Rabelaisian appetites whose unaccountable adversarial relationship with his own brain and his elastic capacities for bodily mutation make him stupendously and comically a biological anomaly. And aliens and other monsters also figure throughout the series, both in many of the prologues that open each episode and even in many of the stories themselves.

Perhaps it is the freedom for imaginative invention that the cartoon genre affords through drawing that predisposes animators toward the grotesque. Similarly, advances in special effects technologies and makeup contribute to the avalanche of photographically based grotesquerie we find on our television and movie screens. Nor is this inclination toward the grotesque to be found only in animated cartoons; it served as the motivation for a great many of the panels in Gary Larson's late lamented, syndicated *Far Side* comics.

Comic grotesquerie is not only limited to cartoons, of course. From *Beetlejuice* to *Little Nicky* and Ron Howard's *The Grinch*, horror and comedy meld in the photographic cinema, while science fiction and the comic grotesque mix in parodic films like *Galaxy Quest* – just as they do in television skits on *Saturday Night Live*, perhaps most famously those featuring "The Coneheads." One could go on. But it seems clear that from a merely statistical point of view, the grotesque is one of the leading formats of mass art today. Had I been transported from my youth to the present in a time machine, surely I would have believed that I had died and gone to heaven, though a heaven that looks more like hell.

Nor is the contemporary eminence of the grotesque simply a quantitative matter. Another difference between the 1950s and the present has to do with the prestige of the monstrous. It is no longer a marginal concern of the culture. It has gone mainstream. That is not to say that there are not still many cheap, poorly crafted and ineptly executed grotesqueries in the marketplace, but rather that the grotesque can also be found on the A list of mass culture. Film directors such as Tim Burton, who specializes in stories of fantastic beings like Edward Scissorhands, and Steven Spielberg, no stranger to the grotesque, can be counted unblushingly among our leading cinéastes.

The grotesque is so much a part of our common cultural idiom that recently the armed services released an advertisement to cineplexes across the country featuring a potential recruit doing battle with a gigantic monster straight out of a computer game. And you know that when the military catches on, we're talking *really* mainstream.

But the grotesque belongs not only to the mass audience. Grotesque iconography is a recurring motif of gallery postmodernists, such as Cindy Sherman, and it can provide a mythic source of commentary for ambitious reflexive films such as *Gods and Monsters* and *Shadow of a Vampire*. Considering all this evidence – which could be augmented readily – few, I think, could deny that our era is marked by a pronounced taste for the grotesque. Notice that I said "for the grotesque," rather than "for horror." For admittedly, horror simpliciter is somewhat on the wane from its heyday in the 1970s and 1980s. However, once one realizes that the grotesque is not restricted to horror, but also cuts across genres, notably comic ones, the grotesque still seems omnipresent. Thus it appears timely to address it theoretically.

Hearing my suggestion – that the present period is marked by an obsession with grotesque imagery – is apt to elicit the guarded response: "It all depends on what you count as grotesque." Whether you agree that the grotesque is as pervasive as I allege rests on how we intend to characterize it. So it is imperative to answer the question "What is the grotesque?" Nor is this an easy question to answer, since, though, like obscenity, we may all think we know the grotesque when we see it, it has proven difficult to say exactly what is meant by this concept.

Despite the fact that the term only came into existence in the late fifteenth century as a way of describing certain ornamental frescoes involving composite fusions of animal, vegetable, and human forms (recently excavated in the Golden Palace of Nero), the phenomena named by the Italian word *grotteschi* were obviously of long-standing vintage, already evident not only in Nero's time, but in earlier classical periods through figures such as satyrs, centaurs, and the Minotaur.[1] Moreover, hybrid creatures of this sort can also be found transculturally and transhistorically from time immemorial.

However, the label "the grotesque" sheds little light on the concept that defines this phenomenon, for the term is virtually stipulative. The Italian word from which it derives merely alludes to the locale of the designs in question which were believed to be located in a grotto or cave, since the excavation site was beneath street level.[2] Thus, the term "grotesque" or, in Italian, *grottesco* – meaning something like "from the grotto" – says little more than where the relevant images, named this way first, came from, and not what defines them as a class.

Complicating matters is the fact that what appears to count as falling under the label of the grotesque changes over time. Some authors use the term as an evaluative concept: neoclassical commentators use it as a term of abuse, whereas romantics and postromantics are often likely to use it as a term of praise. But even where the concept is used descriptively, it is subject to wide variation.

According to Philip Thomson, eighteenth- and nineteenth-century aestheticians, for example, tended to associate the grotesque with the ludicrous and the burlesque, whereas twentieth-century critics emphasize its horrific elements.[3] On the face of it, this seems to render the category paradoxical, virtually teetering on unintelligibility, since, at least initially, the comic and the horrific appear to be opposite affects. One way, of course, to negotiate this apparent contradiction is to bite the bullet and declare that the very point of the grotesque is to celebrate this instability or ambivalence through images that at once engender laughter and disgust, comic amusement and horror.[4] And though this seems right about some of the imagery we call grotesque, it does not appear to be on the money about all of it. This conception of the grotesque – that it is necessarily horrific and comic simultaneously – is too exclusive, since it discounts as grotesque candidate images that are only horrific or only comic, as well as examples to be discussed that are neither comic, horrific, nor a combination thereof.

Similarly, theories of the grotesque that regard it as essentially allegorical – allegories of the nature of art, or of figuration,[5] or of human life[6] – are also too narrow. Though examples of allegories of each of these kinds, using the grotesque as a vehicle, can be found, there are also simple grotesque caricatures – predicated on amusing – that have nothing of larger significance to say. Thus Wolfgang Kayser's famous attempt to define the nature of the grotesque as our world estranged, a play with absurdity, that attempts to invoke and subdue the demonic aspects of the world[7] is at once too grand and selective, overlooking the existence of grotesque political cartoons – including gigantic, robotic Al Gores – that are merely vernacular expressions of partisan vituperation. Commentators like Kayser, it seems to me, are attempting to characterize the grotesque in terms of its singular metaphysical significance. But surely there is no single metaphysical significance that can be attributed to every instance of the grotesque.

If one thing is agreed upon by historians of the grotesque, it is that the concept appears unstable, referring to a wide gamut of material ranging from mythological figures like griffins and basilisks, to perhaps pagan residues like gargoyles, to the imagery of Bosch, Bruegel, Dürer, Goya, Doré, and innumerable caricaturists, to writers such as Rabelais, Swift, Hoffman, Poe, and Kafka, to the surrealists, and, if I am right, to countless producers of contemporary mass art. Is there any way to find unity in such an unruly concept? Or is the concept of the grotesque so heterogeneous that it is itself grotesque?

One problem with many previous accounts of the grotesque, as such, is that they attempt to identify the entire compass of the grotesque in virtue of a single function: to elicit simultaneously comic amusement and horror, or to allegorize the nature of art or the human condition. These are unquestionably functions that the grotesque can perform, but they are not the only ones. Nor is it evident that there is some single function that the grotesque performs. Sometimes it may be used to satirize, sometimes it may be used to communicate religious doctrine, sometimes to engage the eye decoratively, and so on. Thus a more fruitful strategy might be to define the grotesque in a way that does not rely essentially on functions.

A structural account is an alternative to functional accounts. The hypothesis that I would like to explore is that the *genus* of the grotesque can be characterized structurally. Then, after we have a structural account of the grotesque at our disposal, we may go on to characterize functionally certain of the *species* that comprise the grotesque. In this light, the comic and horrific grotesque are functionally defined species of the genus of the grotesque, where the genus, in turn, is defined structurally.

The figures from Nero's villa that were first tagged with the label "grotesque" were fusion figures, including griffins and what might be called plant-boys – humans from the waist up and foliage from the waist down. This feature of combining elements from different biological or ontological orders in a single composite being is shared, as well, by such paradigmatic examples of the grotesque as the fusion of ears with a knife in the Hell panel of Bosch's *Garden of Earthly Delights* and the bat bewinged scribe in Goya's *Against the Public Welfare*. These images serve different functions: the first is ornamental, the second illustrates religious doctrine, and the third is social satire. Nor do they elicit the same effect: the first playfully delights the eye, the second terrifies, and the third promotes a cruel, dark, indignant humor. But they are structurally similar in that they all mix distinct biological or ontological categories. They each arrest and fix our attention for this reason, as does Gregor Samsa. Perhaps it is this tendency toward mixing categories that makes the grotesque such a serviceable vehicle for conveying visual metaphors.

One trope of the grotesque, then, is the combinatory or fusion figure. The yoking together of categories generally thought to be otherwise exclusive is the basis of the monstrosity in this type of grotesquerie. Moreover, the ways of combining said figures come in two major forms. Instances of nonconverging categories can be combined in space, yielding biological and/or ontological hybrids, like the plant-boys; or the categories can alternate or metamorphose in time, like shape-changers. Either strategy or a combination of the two will result in a grotesque figure. Indeed, the grotesque can combine many categories to the extent that the virtually formless result strikes one as effectively uncategorizable.

Of course, not all paradigmatic grotesques are combinatory figures. Gargantua and the Brobdingnagians are very large, but they are undeniably human in all their parts. Yet they are still monstrous, still grotesque. So, what do giants have in common with fusion figures such that we are disposed to group them in the same category? Perhaps this much: they are all violations of our standing categories or concepts; they are subversions of our common expectations of the natural and ontological order. Fusion figures cross categories that we think are distinct; the giants are too big – they exceed the norm or standard with respect to the size of human beings. Fusion figures and giants are both anomalous, though anomalous in different ways. The fusion figure instantiates categories that we think should preclude each other. The giant instantiates the category of the human (or of some other species) excessively, going beyond the limits of what we think possible.

It is interesting to note that we are more prone to call the very large grotesque rather than the exceedingly small. One exception to this may appear to be the fact that dwarves figure widely in the traditional iconography of the grotesque. But maybe that is because their heads are disproportionately large, given our normative concepts of human shape. Moreover, considering the saliency of dwarves in the tradition, we should add a disproportion of parts to the standing concepts of fusion, formlessness, and gigantism as recurring strategies of the grotesque.

All these features, furthermore, can be comprehended by the same structural principle: that something is an instance of the grotesque only if it is a being that violates our standing or common biological and ontological concepts and norms. That is, the grotesque subverts our categorical expectations concerning the natural and ontological order. Fusion, disproportion, formlessness, and gigantism are the most frequently recurring ways of realizing this structural principle.

It should be noted that I have explicitly limited the grotesque to beings, by which I mean things perceived to be animate, which would include science fiction robots. However, buildings (unless they have biomorphic elements, as some of Bosch's do) and arguments, I suspect, can only be called grotesque by metaphorical extension. To call a plot that combines anomalous events grotesque is also a metaphor. These, of course, may be particularly apt and informative metaphors. I am not militating against them. I am only claiming that they are just not literally instances of the grotesque.

Likewise, I have restricted the notion of the grotesque to violations of our biological and ontological categories. What I am trying to exclude here – as a defining feature of the grotesque – are violations of moral concepts. Tony Soprano is not a grotesque, strictly speaking, even though he mixes moral and emotional characteristics in dissonant and exaggerated ways. If one calls him grotesque, that is using the concept metaphorically. I would not deny that calling Tony Soprano morally and emotionally grotesque provides a revealing and effective description of him. I am only denying that he literally falls into the same class of images that gargoyles do.

Of course, the grotesque is often coupled with immorality. Most frequently, it is associated with evil. This is understandable for several reasons. In general, whatever falls outside our standing concepts is potentially dangerous, threatening, or harmful to us. It is a short step from regarding something as potentially harmful to us to regarding it as evil. Perhaps this is why we are prone to invest the normative dimensions of our biological and ontological concepts with such pronounced moral energy. The grotesque and the monstrous are natural vehicles for portraying evil because the anomalous typically, though, as we will see, not always, suggests a threat, and we tend to regard threats as evil. That is why it seems so apt that monsters in horror films do evil things; their usually violent nature is an objective correlative of the cognitive threat they portend. And it is the association with evil that motivates us to portray political adversaries as grotesques.

Morality and grotesquerie, then, stand in interesting relations. However, immorality is not a fundamental ingredient in the grotesque. Many grotesque figures signify immorality. But many are amoral and some are even moral. Immorality is not a defining characteristic of the grotesque, even if it is often a recurring feature. Rather, the grotesque, I propose, is defined by a structural principle that omits reference to morality; something is grotesque only if it is an image, whether verbal or visual, of an animate being that violates our standing biological or ontological concepts and expectations. That is, the concept of the grotesque is the concept that comprehends violations of concepts of a certain sort – those that pertain to the biological and ontological criteria that determine membership in our categories of animate being.

The core criteria that define the genus of the grotesque are structural. However, we can use this core concept to chart several of the major species of the grotesque and their relations to each other by observing how the structure that defines the genus of the grotesque enables the grotesque to discharge its leading functions. Of course, as we have already seen, the grotesque can perform many functions. I cannot hope to canvass all of them. Instead I will focus on the function of the grotesque to elicit certain affective states, namely, horror, comic amusement, and awe.

I am concentrating on these states for three reasons. First, they are undeniably the recurring affects that most grotesqueries aim fundamentally to produce. Second, even if instances of the grotesque have broader aims, like allegory or satire, securing these sorts of affective responses generally contributes to those larger purposes; thus, the function of eliciting these emotions may have some claim to being foundational for the grotesque. And third, and perhaps most important, these emotional responses have interesting family relations with each other and with the core structure of the grotesque. Thus, in elucidating these relations, we may begin to disclose the internal coherence of the category of the grotesque.

Supposing that the basic form of address of the grotesque is emotional, we can organize our discussion of the emotive functions of the grotesque by asking what it is about the core structure of the grotesque that enables it to promote the recurring emotions of horror, comic amusement, and awe so frequently associated with it. However, before that can be done, something needs to be said about the emotions.

In ordinary language, the emotions are frequently identified as feelings: visceral feelings, like an accelerated heart rate, or phenomenological feelings, such as tension and relief. And certainly the emotions involve feelings like these. However, the emotions are not just a matter of brute feelings, like pain. They possess cognitive elements as well.

One way to see this is to recall that emotions are directed at objects – people, events, and so on. When I am angry, I am not simply in a certain feeling state, as when my head pounds with a migraine. I am angry *at* someone or something. Pain is a feeling state, pure and simple. When I am in pain, the pain is not directed at anything outside me. But emotions are different. When I am angry, my mental state is directed at some object, say the bastard who just cut me off in traffic.

Being cut off puts me in a feeling state, such as being hot under the collar. But unlike pain, the feeling state of anger involves something more than a brute physical feeling; rather, it is directed at something I take to be outside of me. But what is this "something more" that anger possesses but that pain does not? A cognitive dimension. When I am angry or in any other garden-variety emotional state, I cognize the object that my mental state is directed at in a certain way. Indeed, it is the fact that I cognize the object of my emotional state in the way I do that causes me to have the visceral and phenomenological feelings that attend my overall state.

So garden-variety emotions comprise, at least, cognitions, on the one hand, and visceral and/or phenomenological feelings, on the other hand. Moreover, these elements are related causally: the cognitive elements or cognitions cause the relevant feelings. But what is the nature of these cognitions? When I am angry at the driver who has just cut me off, I see him in a certain way; I see him as someone who has wronged me. Seeing him as someone who has wronged me makes me hot under the collar. That is, I subsume his activity under the category or concept of wrongness and that "makes my blood boil" (that's why I'm hot under the collar). The type of cognition that is relevant to engendering my overall emotional state of anger is a matter of subsuming the particular object of my mental state under a concept.

This tells us that emotions are not utterly irrational. They involve the application of criteria of appropriateness to the particular objects that provoke the emotions in question. To be angry involves cognizing the object of my overall mental state in terms of certain criteria of appropriateness, such as perceived wrongness or offensiveness. All things being equal, we will call an emotional episode anger only if it issues from a cognition that comprehends its object as satisfying the criteria of wrongness or offense.

Turning from anger, then, to the kinds of emotions associated with the grotesque, we can use this model of the emotions in order to determine what it is about the grotesque, structurally defined, that enables it to support the kinds of cognitions appropriate respectively to horror, comic amusement, and awe. These are different emotional states; they have different criteria of appropriateness. How is it possible, then, that the grotesque can function to promote such divergent mental states?

Let us begin with horror, perhaps the emotion now most frequently associated with the grotesque.[8] Horror, of course, involves an element of fear. The composite demon figures that fill Bosch's various hells are usually malevolent, torturing sinners, for example. They are dangerous; they mean to do harm to humankind. This is also standard in contemporary horror fictions where, typically, the monsters present a clear and present danger to human life. But horror involves more than fearsomeness. We find many a movie gunman fearsome, but it does not seem right to regard them as horrific, save metaphorically. Again, the prospect of a Tony Soprano is frightening, but not, strictly speaking, horrifying. So, what needs to be added to fear in order to add up to horror?

In his recent novel, *In Hollow Houses*, Gary A. Braunbeck describes a monster. He says it resembles a glass ape, since it is almost simian-shaped, and its epidermis is gelatinous. It is dangerous; it is a killer; it absorbs people. But it is not merely frightening, as this description indicates:

> It stood at least eight feet tall and a yard wide. Like the *Invisible Man*, its skin was almost completely transparent, only there were no internal organs that could be seen. Instead the interior was filled with a grotesque, roiling form of primordial soup. Bits of bone and skull, wet, shredded tissue, large pieces of lungs and intestines, free floating hands and eyes, tags of flesh that were once the skin of a face before its owner had been opened up to die, [and] then be absorbed. The cloudy liquid in which these pieces floated glowed like radioactive waste. Once, as the liquid flowed around, Kirkwood could have sworn that one of the faces was trying to form words: *Help me.*

To be sure, this creature is frightening; it feeds on people. But it is more than that. It is also repulsive. It is not the sort of thing you would want to touch, a fact that Braunbeck emphasizes by analogizing its innards to radioactive waste. The description is also apt to make you queasy; one imagines that seeing such a being would be nauseating. It is designed to make one's flesh crawl. In addition to being frightening, then, it is also disgusting. Here, the emotion elicited involves two elements: fear and disgust. Moreover, this pattern is fairly generalizable across horrific imagery, from Bosch to George Romero. Horror, then, extrapolating from such cases, appears to be at least a compound emotion, a combination of fear and disgust.[9]

In order to count as the emotion of fear, the object of the emotion must satisfy the criterion of harmfulness. Horrific grotesques, both historical and contemporary, satisfy that criterion, but it is hard to see how fearsomeness alone is to be connected directly to the core structure of the grotesque, since, as noted above, many things may be fearful – a terrorist, for example, threatening to explode a bus – without being grotesque. However, here it pays to attend to the second component of horror, namely disgust. For the criterion of disgust is impurity, and impurity can be related to the core structure of the grotesque in a fairly straightforward manner.

That which is impure correlates with the violation of our standing categories in various ways. Things like blood, fecal waste, mucus, vomit, and pieces of flesh are treated as impurities because they are ambiguous or interstitial between categorical distinctions such as me/not me, living/dead, and inside/outside. Likewise, things that combine contradictory cultural categories are impure; this is probably why many recoiled from bearded ladies in circuses of the past. A standing cultural category can also be problematized by confronting incomplete instances of it (such as amputees) or disproportionately misshapen instances (like dwarves) or excessive ones (such as giants). Moreover, stuff that escapes categorization altogether, like sludge or sewage, is apt to be regarded as impure and disturbing, in part because it resists being readily subsumed under any entrenched cultural category.

Inasmuch as impurity depends on the same kinds of features as the grotesque, structurally defined, it is not surprising that the grotesque can function to elicit horror. For in virtue of categorical problematization, the grotesque and horror share a necessary condition. However, as noted previously, not all grotesques are horrific. For a grotesque to count as horrific, it must also be fearsome.

The notion that horror is a compound emotion, the criteria requiring that an instance be both harmful and impure, has several advantages. On the one hand, it accounts for why the grotesque can function as a vehicle for horror, as it so often does, in light of the supposition that the impurity condition for horror can be readily implemented by the core structure of the grotesque. On the other hand, this definition of horror also does a very good job of tracking paradigmatic cases of the horrific grotesque, both historical and contemporary. The horned demon figures of yesteryear are generally pictured as composite, categorically contradictory figures, often fusing features of different genera and species: rams, humans, and reptiles, for example. And, of course, since these are demons, their antipathy to humanity makes them, by definition, harmful.

Similarly, the bestiary of contemporary horror fiction is virtually an operationalization of the conditions for impurity sketched above. Shape-shifters are contradictory beings, amalgamating different species in a single being, like the "twisted king" in the movie *The Cell*, who in his last manifestation is a man with the scaly golden scalp of a snake. The very popular cyborg monsters of contemporary horror fiction, of course, mix flesh and machine. In *Dreamcatcher*, Stephen King describes Mr Gray, the alien, as a mushroom with a high IQ, thereby anomalously fusing the vegetable and the intelligent in a way that violates categorical distinctions.

Vampires, in turn, are also interstitial beings, anomalously crossing the categories of living and dead, as are zombies, Frankenstein monsters, and perhaps cyborgs as well. Maybe part of what is so creepy about monster robots in general is that they are ambiguously animate and inanimate, mind and metal. Similarly, the intelligent bugs in *Starship Troopers* are, from the perspective of our conceptual scheme, category errors.

Headless horsemen, of course, transgress our category of the human by being incomplete – to put it mildly – while giant spiders, mosquitoes, scorpions, and giant you-name-its violate the norms of our categories by dint of their scale, as do disproportionate beings, like the Hunchback of Notre Dame. Formless creatures, such as sentient, mind-altering vapors, such as those emitted by the planet in *Solaris*, not only affront standing concepts by being interstitial, but also by being amorphous – too insubstantial to be categorized.

But even if our account of horror explains how it is possible for the grotesque to be horrific, and even if it zeroes in on the pertinent variables of the horrific grotesque (both historical and contemporary), this account raises a troublesome question as well: Why is it that not everything that realizes the structural principle of the grotesque – and which, for that reason, one would expect to count as impure – evokes horror? This is an important question, but one that I think we can answer by recalling that horror is a compound of *fear* and disgust.

However, it is important to note that this is not a simple compound, but a complex one. That is, exposure to the conceptually anomalous in isolation may not raise disgust and horror. Yet when the conceptually anomalous is conjoined with fear, the element of conceptual anomaly becomes fearsome in its own right. The fearsome component in horrific imagery acts like a chemical agent and releases a dormant property, impurity, in the object of conceptual anomaly. Or, in other words, the fear transforms the anomaly into an impurity in the manner of a catalyst.

A monster that tears people limb from limb is dangerous; it will induce fear. But if it is also conceptually anomalous – a dead, broken thing, moldering, but somehow alive – its lethal potential, what we might call its first-order fearsomeness, will cast its anomaly in a new light – yielding a second-order or emergent fearsomeness, a sense that the monster is impure, that to touch it or be touched by it would be loathsome, because, broadly speaking, it is toxic.

For obvious reasons I call this process toxification. Grotesques, both historical and contemporary, that are horrific raise both fear and disgust because the first-order fearsomeness of a given monstrous anomaly invests it with a second-order or emergent fearsomeness – specifically, that it is toxic or impure.[10] This perception, then, elicits disgust, since disgust is primarily an evolutionary safeguard for avoiding the poisonous, the noxious, and the contagious by spitting or vomiting it out if we ingest it, by closing down our nasal passages if we smell it, or by cringing or wiping it away violently from our bodies if we touch it.

But, of course, we do not always respond to the grotesque with horror. Both with respect to the historical grotesque and, as we have seen, the contemporary grotesque, our response is often laughter. That the grotesque is allied with comic amusement should be evident from its long association with caricature, parody, and satire. Indeed, contemporary cartoon parodies, like *The Far Side*, often allude to the very monsters that are designed to horrify us in their "serious" manifestation in the movies. This, then, raises two related questions: how is it possible that the grotesque, structurally defined, can promote humor, and why, if the comic grotesque mobilizes the core structures of the grotesque, does it not provoke horror? Let us address these questions one at a time.

How is it possible for the grotesque, characterized structurally, to be capable of supporting comic amusement? Comic amusement, like horror, is an emotional state. As such it is criterially governed. According to the most promising theory of humor we have, in order to be counted as an episode of comic amusement, the amusement must be directed at a particular – a saying, a joke, a plot, a pun, a character, a situation, a gesture, a drawing, a song, and so on – that is perceived to be incongruous. That is, something is amusing only if it can be subsumed under the category of perceived incongruity. Perhaps for self-evident reasons, this is called the incongruity theory of humor; it is probably the most heavily subscribed theoretical approach to humor today.

Consider this joke: "What do Winnie the Pooh and Alexander the Great have in common? They share the same middle name." According to the incongruity theory of humor, a large part of the amusement here rests on the fact that the answer to the question is incongruous; quite literally, it is a category mistake or an absurdity to count the "the" in these cases as a middle name. It is a classificatory error; it is a confusion of the sort that we would expect from the infamous moron of the jokes named in his honor.

Admittedly, defining incongruity or the relevant form of absurdity required by this theory satisfactorily in a fashion that would accommodate every instance of humor, while not being overly inclusive, is still a persistent challenge for incongruity theorists of humor.[11] However, it is clear that one of the main sources of the incongruities that promote mirth are ones that violate, transgress, problematize, or jam our standing categories, in the way that the proposal of "the" as a middle name does in the preceding joke. Likewise, an image of a diminutive Buster Keaton in a football outfit that is too large for him strikes us as funny, because it violates our concept of an all-American gridiron hero. And the very movements of the fowl in *Chicken Run* are amusing because these creatures behave like human beings, thereby mixing species known to be categorically distinct.

The domain of humor is broader than that of the grotesque. The grotesque pertains, first and foremost, to animate beings, whereas the objects of humor are not restricted to animate beings, but can include funny sayings, jokes, maxims and the like, which make no direct reference to animate things. Yet humor and the grotesque can overlap, as they do in the case of certain caricatures, just because grotesqueries are incongruous conceptually. That is, the grotesque can serve as the basis for certain kinds of incongruous humor

because these overlapping conceptual domains share an overlapping condition: conceptual anomaly.[12]

Clowns, for example, are grotesque because they are improbable representations of the human; their features are wildly exaggerated and misshapen,
while their biological and cognitive capacities are humanly anomalous. They
can be dropped from heights or beaned with bricks without bodily damage,
just as their intelligence is usually subhuman. And yet they are also humorous
just because the core structures of the grotesque, committed as they are to
subverting our standing concepts, can serve as a source of the kind of incongruity that yields laughter.

Likewise, as we have already noted, the very monsters that frighten and
disgust us in movies can amuse us in other contexts.[13] The horrific grotesque
can be easily transformed into the comic grotesque. But how is this possible?

In the *South Park* episode entitled "Trapper Keeper," Eric Cartman acquires
a Dawson's Creek Trapper Keeper, a sort of laptop entertainment center,
game-boy, and personal computing system all in one. This device, we learn
from a robot from the future, à la *Terminator*, is destined to take over the
world as it incorporates into itself everything it meets, including humans –
notably Cartman – as well as plants and other computing systems. As it grows
in size, it becomes a large, formless, fleshy mass, sprouting both tentacles *and*
wires in glorious interstitiality. But instead of eliciting primarily disgust, it
prompts laughter. Nor is this conjunction of the monstrous and the comic
something new. Medieval grotesqueries, for instance of devil figures, are often
comic, a tradition also evinced by the visions of hell and its satanic majesty in
South Park: Bigger, Longer & Uncut. But though such examples of the comic
grotesque are well precedented historically, they still force us to ask why we
laugh at grotesque figures that, at least in theory, one might suppose, should
make us recoil with fear and disgust.

Here, it is useful to note that incongruity is, at best, only a necessary condition for comic amusement. Obviously, not all encounters with incongruity
amuse. Confronted by an incongruity, we may be disturbed or frightened. When
a child sees a caregiver pull a funny face, she chuckles; but when a stranger does
likewise, the child is more likely to cry. Incongruity alone does not promote
laughter. The incongruity must appear in a context where it is unthreatening
before it can be enjoyed. A grotesquerie can serve as a vehicle for comic amusement, then, but only if it occurs in a context that is unthreatening.

Yet why do we take Cartman's Trapper Keeper's attempt at world conquest
to be unthreatening, since similar quests by so many movie monsters are a
source of high anxiety? Why are the grotesqueries in *South Park* comic, but
those of *The X-Files* usually horrific?

When we respond with fear to horror fictions, we do not fear for our own
lives. We fear for the characters besieged by grotesque monsters. We care for
them, if only because they are human beings. Moreover, the narrator of a horror

fiction dwells at length upon their suffering and death. But in "Trapper Keeper," the characters supposedly endangered by the monster are palpably not really human. And, more importantly, the comic narrator does not dwell, or invite us to dwell, on the mutilation and death of the victims of creatures like the Trapper Keeper. Comedy is strikingly amoral in this regard; it deflects our attention from the harm and the human cost of the mayhem it retails. A joke may involve death and destruction. But if someone is blown apart in a joke, the narration quickly glosses over it.[14] If the damage done to the character's body or its repercussions for his family were explored, the joke would be destroyed. Contrariwise, horror fictions are highly moral in the sense that concern for human harm is in the forefront of the narration.

Moreover, if our earlier discussion of toxification is correct, then, if there is no element of fear accompanying the grotesque, there will be no disgust, and, therefore, no horror. Insofar as the comic narrator banishes the apprehension of harm from his story, he banishes fear, and, if he subtracts fear from the equation, a grotesque that might otherwise strike us as impure and horrifying will instead appear merely incongruous and amusing.

Thus, the grotesque, structurally defined, can serve as a vehicle of comic amusement, because its conceptual anomaly can function as a source of incongruity. The comic grotesque does not horrify, on the other hand, because by downplaying or even altogether erasing the issue of harm in the presentation, the relevant conceptual anomaly does not provoke a sense of horror, since instead of impurity, what remains is merely an incongruity to be enjoyed in a way that, ideally, invites laughter.

Within a single narrative work, the same grotesque figure can be presented as alternatively horrific or comic, depending upon whether, in context, the fear card is played or not. Beetlejuice, in the film of the same name, for example, is sometimes scary and sometimes ridiculous. In certain earlier portions of the film, he is a buffoon, explicitly attired like a clown, and a source of laughter. This is because he appears to be unthreatening. However, in the final sequence, he becomes horrifying, since, by that time, we appreciate how very dangerous he is. One feature of many contemporary films is a penchant for shifting emotional timbres like this, moving from horror to comedy or vice-versa, often using the same grotesque figure as a pivot. The idea, it seems, is to send the audience from the theater both laughing and screaming. This is possible, I suggest, just because the grotesque, defined in terms of conceptual anomaly, can go either way, depending upon whether the variable of fear is mobilized or not. And, furthermore, if the artform is narrative, the fear component can be turned on and off sequentially.

So far I have been discussing the grotesque primarily in terms of horror and comedy. These are certainly the major forms it takes today in mass culture. But there is at least one more use of the structure of the grotesque that warrants examination – the grotesque as a vehicle for awe or wonder.

Consider our introduction to the dinosaurs in *Jurassic Park*. We are perhaps prepped for it by the stunning natural vistas visible from the helicopter on the approach to the island. We see scenes of enthralling beauty – the expanse of the island and the cascading waterfall – that are apt to elicit a sense of wonder at nature. Then the characters board a jeep. Ellie begins complaining that the foliage on the island shouldn't be there. As she speaks, there is a cut to Grant; the camera moves in as his face evinces puzzlement; the music on the soundtrack signals mystery.[15] He strains to see more clearly; he takes his hat off. In the next shot, Grant stands up in the jeep, and removes his sunglasses. We know from his behavior that he's seen something that he can't quite believe. He needs to see more clearly still.

Ellie continues dithering on about the plant life on the island. On a cut, Grant reaches back and turns her head toward what he is seeing. Her mouth literally falls open. The next cut, motivated by a deep off-screen bellow, shows us what she has seen – what has caused her jaw to drop: a brachiosaur with a 30-foot neck, munching on a treetop. The camera tilts up the dinosaur's body vertiginously – the expanse of the beast surpasses our wildest expectations. The music becomes processional, solemn, and triumphant. In ensuing shots, Ellie and Grant walk underneath the brachiosaur, emphasizing its enormous scale. Grant, the world-renowned paleontologist, is reduced to childlike naivety and joy; it is both comic and exhilarating when he says, happy but baffled: "It's a dinosaur."

Several shots follow, registering more flabbergasted reactions to the brachiosaur, while Hammond, the owner of the island, explains more of its wonders, concluding by saying "Welcome to Jurassic Park," a cue for a choir to enter the soundtrack, making the moment almost religious, if not celestial.[16] Then the camera closes in on Grant again, his mouth opening as he sees something else startling. There is a cut to a stately, peaceable panorama of different families of dinosaurs moving in herds. Ellie is so awestruck that she is hyperventilating, while Grant is visibly reeling – almost literally knocked off his feet. Again the choir underscores this as virtually a mystical experience.

This carefully edited sequence, comprising 23 shots, is predicated on eliciting awe or wonder from the audience. It employs a variety of devices in order to do this. The editing, of course, composes a narrative of gradual revelation, amply supported by the acting, which behaviorally exemplifies curiosity, then astonishment and joy. Director Spielberg also emphasizes the unexpected scale of the brachiosaur by means of very extreme low-angle shots and long shots that underline the size of the dinosaur in contrast to the puny humans in front of it. This use of mammoth, unexpected scale is a strategy for inducing wonder that was already in place in Spielberg's repertoire at least since the appearance of the awesome, unexpectedly large, mother ship in *Close Encounters of the Third Kind*.

As well, the music by John Williams plays an important role in the sequence. It moves from engendering mystery to taking the form of a processional, the kind of music played at a coronation or a graduation. These musical allusions connect with the plot nicely. The music crowns the brachiosaur as majestic, while Grant "graduates" in a stroke, so to speak, from being a student of dead creatures to live ones. The addition of the choir, then, editorializes the moment as miraculous.

Narration, editing, character-gesture, scale, and the musical commentary all function concinnitously to elicit the emotion of awe in the spectator. But it is important to note that the object of that awe is a grotesque being, a dinosaur, the kind of being that, by definition, is extinct.[17] A contemporary dinosaur is a category mistake from the point of view of contemporary science. How can such a creature so large exist in an atmosphere like ours whose oxygen content is so much lower than that of its natural habitat? It is a mystery; it is a wonder.

In other scenes of *Jurassic Park*, the dinosaurs will strike us as horrific – the raptors and the T-rex – and, at moments, even comic – as when Nedry first meets up with the initially silly-looking dilophosaurus. But our initial, full-scale introduction to the brachiosaur is swathed in awe. Undoubtedly, our reaction is encouraged, in part, by the astonished reactions of observers, like Ellie and Grant. However, the cinematic structures here also provide redundant channels of information. One suspects that even without the character reactions, the narrative, editing, composition, and music might have induced awe in the audience. But the question is, Why is the reaction to these grotesqueries awe, rather than horror or comic amusement, as it is in other portions of the film?

The emotive criteria of horror are the harmful and the impure. The criterion for comic amusement includes perceived incongruity sans threat. The appropriate criterion of awe is the miraculous, where, following St Augustine, we may define the miraculous as "A portent [that] is not contrary to nature, but contrary to our knowledge of nature."[18] Obviously, the grotesque, structurally defined, is capable of serving as a vehicle for awe, just because the governing structural principle of the grotesque is the violation of our standing concepts and categories, our expectations concerning the natural and ontological order. Whereas the horrific grotesque implements that governing principle in terms of the impure and the comic grotesque by means of the incongruous, the awesome grotesque traffics in the miraculous.

The miraculous defies our conception of nature. As Adam Smith notes, wonder arises when an object "refuses to be grouped … with any set of objects."[19] This may occur when something violates our standing categories. Christianity exploits such imagery by, for example, affirming the existence of a god who is also a man – an omnipotent god who is also, strangely enough, a victim and whose mother is, unaccountably, a virgin.[20]

The miraculous is mysterious, inexplicable, baffling, unexpected, astonishing, and impossible. Yet, the experience of awe is not just one of curiosity: it is also appreciative. The awesome engenders an appreciative stance; the object of awe commands our rapt attention. It is an object-absorbed experience that combines our sense of its unlikelihood with an acceptance of it, no matter how much it deviates from our standing biological and ontological categories. Though a disturbing discontinuity with our ordinary scheme of things, the object of awe is embraced and affirmed, and this is accompanied by a feeling of exultation and expansion in both mind and body. Our mind seems to expand as we dwell on the diversity of the phenomenal world, while our body takes in the air needed to replace the breath that has just been taken away.[21]

Inasmuch as the grotesque, structurally defined, can serve as the sort of categorical violation that counts as miraculous, it can convey awe. In the recent Japanese animated film *Princess Mononoke*, the forest spirit is at once both grotesque and an object of awe. The creature is a hybrid, both in terms of being a fusion figure and a metamorph. It is a metamorph in that it changes from the Night Walker to the forest god at sunrise. Moreover, in both these incarnations, it is a fusion figure. The forest spirit has the body of a large stag, but also the benevolent face of a human that possesses the Buddha-esque quality of Sam Jaffe's grand lama in *Lost Horizon*; when it walks, it speeds up the vegetative process – plants spin to life and die in its path. It is the lord of life and death, forces it brings into play inexplicably as far as the characters in the fiction can understand. It also walks on water, to emphasize its supernatural status.

Furthermore, at sunset it metamorphoses into the Night Walker, another anomalous fusion figure whose face resembles that of a beaver, but whose translucent body, though that of a colossal humanoid, has the serrated though gelid fins of a dragon. This grotesque, anomalous figure, as well, is intended to incarnate the paradoxical forces of life and death, which the forest spirit bequeaths inexplicably.

The use of the miraculous grotesque occurs frequently in animated films, especially in Japanese *animé*, like *Princess Mononoke*, as well as in the portrayals of beneficent or innocent aliens in live-action movies. However, the question still persists as to why these grotesqueries do not strike us as horrific or comic.

The most likely reason they do not engender horror is that they are not associated with fear. In *Jurassic Park*, the brachiosaur is oblivious to the humans. It is not a predator, nor does it act aggressively. As long as the humans do not get underfoot, they are safe. Likewise, the forest god in *Princess Mononoke* is characterized as benign and even gentle; its touch is so light it even walks on water. Thus, in such cases, the toxification process does not take hold with respect to the creatures' conceptual anomaly.

But why doesn't the brachiosaur provoke comic amusement? Comic amusement, like horrific disgust, involves an element of rejection. We want to expel the disgusting from our bodies. Laughter, too, is a gesture of expulsion.[22] Even though comic amusement involves taking pleasure in the absurd, we resist it bodily, casting it out, so to speak, in bursts of laughter – bursts of breath expelled away from us. The absurdity of humor sneaks up on us and takes us in, as we fall for the incongruous, often surprising, but additionally compelling logic within the punch line of a good joke. But we also signal our awareness of the incredibility of the joke by laughing, a gesture of expulsion that establishes our distance from the absurdity.

Awe is different. Awe carries with it acceptance. The intake of breath not only probably enhances our sense of euphoria and exultation physically, but is also symptomatic of our willingness to take the absurdity into ourselves, to incorporate it, to accept it. The object of awe is not something that disposes us to flight, or even to the unthreatened rejection found in the response to absurdities of comic amusement. Awe invites acceptance of the absurd.[23]

How this invitation is extended may differ from case to case. Often the object of awe is presented in fictions as ultimately benevolent, as in *Princess Mononoke*. But awe need not only correlate with an intimation of the divine or the numinous. In *Jurassic Park*, the brachiosaur is unaware of, rather than favorably disposed toward, human life. However, the element of acceptance is still crucial to our response. For in *Jurassic Park* our acceptance is based on the *givenness* of the dinosaur; that is, in Spielberg's fictional world, as in the real world, it is presumed that "seeing is believing" is a reliable epistemic maxim, in the absence of evidence to the contrary.

The object of awe is the miraculous – a perceived violation of natural order – that is, something taken to be unthreatening, inexplicable, and yet, for all that, accepted. The grotesque can serve as an object of awe rather than comic humor, if its transgression of our categorical frameworks is accepted – if only imaginatively within the parameters of a fiction – rather than rejected. The grotesque functions to promote awe, instead of horror, where the monstrous engenders neither an attitude of expulsion nor the disposition either to fight or flee in response to the prospect of harm to oneself or others.

The elicitation of horror, comic amusement, and awe are the leading functions of the grotesque today.[24] The grotesque is able to support these seemingly disparate functions because structurally it is rooted in the violation, transgression, or jamming of our standing concepts and categories. With horror, categorical anomaly takes the form of impurity; with comic amusement, the form of incongruity; and with awe, that of the miraculous.

Given this preliminary taxonomy of the grotesque today, it is tempting to ask why we currently seem so obsessed with horror, humor, and awe. The easy answer, one I've flirted with myself is that we live at a time when our standing categories appear buffeted from every direction. But though that is the easy answer, I am starting to distrust it, since the grotesque is always with us. If our allegedly postmodern era is a moment of radical conceptual change, surely the Dark Ages were not. Nevertheless, the grotesque flourished as extravagantly in the Middle Ages as it does today.

My own suspicion is that the marked taste for the grotesque nowadays may have more to do with the expanding market for leisure than with reflecting the spirit of the age. For the grotesque provides a ready source of intense emotion and novelty. Almost by definition, it is a departure from the ordinary and, therefore, a natural target for development as the entertainment industry expands exponentially. That is, there may be so much more grotesquerie available today than there was in the 1950s just because the entertainment industry has grown so dramatically in tandem with the accelerating pursuit of leisure. This suggestion, needless to say, needs further argument and refinement. But that, of course, would require another essay.[25]

Notes

1 For useful histories of the concept of the grotesque, see Wolfgang Kayser, *The Grotesque in Art and Literature*, trans. Ulrich Weisstein (Bloomington: Indiana University Press, 1963); Philip Thomson, *The Grotesque* (London: Methuen, 1972); Geoffrey Galt Harpham, *On the Grotesque: Strategies of Contradiction in Art and Literature* (Princeton: Princeton University Press, 1982); and Frances S. Connelly, "Grotesque," in Michael Kelly (ed.), *Encyclopedia of Aesthetics* (New York: Oxford University Press, 1998).

2 Connelly, "Grotesque," 339.

3 Thomson, *The Grotesque*, 13–14.

4 Thomson suggests this move on page 27. On the other hand, Thomson's definition of the grotesque as "the unresolved clash of incompatibles and work and response" (27) seems far too broad. Contradictory arguments, though unfortunate, are not grotesque. Moreover, Thomson's formula is either too exclusive – can't some grotesqueries appear resolved? – or too vague (what exactly does *unresolved* mean?).

5 Harpham seems to favor an interpretation of the grotesque as implicitly representing allegories of art and/or figuration in his *On the Grotesque*.

6 See Kayser, *The Grotesque in Art and Literature*.

7 Wolfgang Kayser, "An Attempt to Define the Nature of the Grotesque," in *The Grotesque in Art and Literature*, 179–89.

8 An extended analysis of horror may be found in Noël Carroll, *The Philosophy of Horror* (New York: Routledge, 1990).

9 This hypothesis is defended at greater length in Carroll, *The Philosophy of Horror*, ch. 1.

10 Perhaps one reason why the very small, though anomalous, do not typically raise horror is that, since the very small do not usually conjure up a sense of danger, the toxification process does not take hold. Predictable exceptions would obtain, however, where the very small have some special, harm-producing power or where a great many – often swarming – very small things are massed together with harmful intent.

11 See Noël Carroll, "Humor," in Jerrold Levinson (ed.), *The Oxford Handbook of Aesthetics* (Oxford: Oxford University Press, 2003).

12   See Noël Carroll, "Horror and Humor," *Journal of Aesthetics and Art Criticism* 57(2) (1999): 145–60.

13   Perhaps these creatures are doubly incongruous. They are not simply anomalous beings. But, in addition, these monsters, when reduced to harmless butts of humor, become more laughable still, since they *also* violate the concept of horrific monsters once their fearsomeness is taken away from them.

14   The recurring death of Kenny in *South Park* is quite intriguing in this regard. I suspect that it is able to function comically because it is turned into a highly absurd, running joke.

15   My comments on the music in *Jurassic Park* have benefitted immensely from discussions with my brother Hugh Carroll III.

16   At points, Grant whispers, underscoring the church-like atmosphere.

17   Some have questioned my categorization of the dinosaur as grotesque. I have claimed it to be so on the basis of its status as an impossible being. But I also think that its visual resemblance to gargoyles and dragons, classically grotesque beings, also supports this categorization. Moreover, the particular dinosaur in *Jurassic Park*, in virtue of the size of its neck, looks grotesque. It strikes one – even one familiar with representations of dinosaurs – as being excessively long (something Spielberg is at pains to emphasize cinematically). Thus, it counts as a case of the structural grotesque in terms of its disproportion of parts. I'm not claiming that such a creature didn't have a neck that long, but only that it strikes the average viewer (the nonspecialist) as inordinately long – contrary to our expectations.

18   Augustine, *The City of God* (New York: Modern Library, 1950), vol. 21, 8.

19   Adam Smith, "History of Astronomy," in *Essays on Philosophical Subjects*, ed. I. S. Ross (Indianapolis: Liberty Classics, 1982), 39.

20   Contradiction is also a recurring feature of mystical language dedicated to the expression of awe.

21   This paragraph has benefitted from R. W. Hepburn's essay "Wonder" in his collection *Wonder and Other Essays* (Edinburgh: Edinburgh University Press, 1984), 131–54.

22   Indeed, it has been suggested that laughter is an aborted fear-response.

23   Here it is useful to think of acceptance in terms of nonresistance, both morally and intellectually. With horrific monsters we are prone to adopt the stance of moral resistance; with jokes, we evince a kind of intellectual resistance, signaled by a laugh. But with awe, we are nonresistant.

24   I do not say that these are the only functions of the grotesque today. There is at least one more that I am aware of. I call this the "surrealistic grotesque," for want of a better name. This use of the grotesque involves the presentation of the relevant sort of image without any attempt to elicit an affective response. The surrealistic grotesque is presented affectlessly or dispassionately. Some of Magritte's paintings are like this. The anomalous is displayed as given and inexplicable, but no emotional response is engaged. This use of the grotesque differs from horror, humor, and awe inasmuch as they all command an affective response, whereas what I am calling the surrealistic grotesque does not draw emotions from us. It casts the stubbornly anomalous in a cold light.

My use of the notion of surrealism here does not, I admit, correspond to all of the artifacts produced by the historical surrealists. My usage is stipulative, referring only to the affectless grotesque. Moreover, it is probably because the surrealistic grotesque (or whatever we wind up calling it) does not elicit intense emotional responses that we do not find many examples of it in the domain of contemporary mass art. Rather, it is more common in avant-garde venues.

Another form of the grotesque that I have not discussed in this essay is the decorative grotesque. I have avoided comment on it, since it does not appear to be a major function of the grotesque today. However, I would like to make one observation about its apparently paradoxical nature.

Why don't decorative grotesques excite horror, humor, or awe? Perhaps because the decorative grotesque works its anomalous figures into a pattern, thus imbuing them with an overall or collective sense of order, despite the fact that individually, each grotesque figure in the pattern is an offense to order. Maybe an important part of the pleasure with respect to the decorative grotesque has to do with precisely this tension between order and abnormality.

25 This essay was written in the idiom of the cognitive theory of the emotions. At present I am more in favor of a hybrid approach to the emotions of the sort found in my essay "Movies, the Moral Emotions, and Sympathy," which appears as Chapter 5 of this volume.

21

Andy Kaufman and the Philosophy of Interpretation

I. Introduction

With respect to art, a current issue in the philosophy of interpretation – the issue to be addressed in this paper – is the debate between actual intentionalists and hypothetical intentionalists.[1] Insofar as both sorts of intentionalists *are* intentionalists, these two positions are ranged against anti-intentionalism – the view, influential since the 1940s – that maintains that considerations of authorial intentions for the purposes of interpretation are strictly irrelevant or inadmissible.[2] Actual intentionalism and hypothetical intentionalism, in contrast, allow a role for authorial intentions (or something like authorial intentions – namely, hypotheses about authorial intentions) in the interpretation of artworks.[3]

For anti-intentionalists, focusing primarily on the meaning of literary texts, the meaning of a work is determinable solely by reference to public resources, such as the conventions of language, including grammar and dictionary meanings, and, as well, the history and conventions of literature. From their perspective, reference to the meanings of the text intended by the author is not only extraneous – since it draws attention away from the text itself – but also logically inappropriate – since the text means what it says and cannot be made to say something else simply in virtue of an author's intention to mean otherwise.

Though formidable, these objections are not decisive. Against the anti-intentionalist's anxiety that concerns for authorial intention divert attention

"Andy Kaufman and the Philosophy of Interpretation," in Michael Krausz (ed.), *Is There a Single Right Interpretation?* (University Park, PA: Penn State University Press, 2002), pp. 319–44.

away from its proper object – the text itself – intentionalists can respond that holding the author's intentions to be relevant can enrich our interpretations of texts. That is, consideration of authorial intentions can redirect our reading of a text, enabling us to understand better the structural and semantic choices in the text and, thereby, enlivening our appreciation thereof.

Nor do the intentionalists agree that texts can be interpreted solely by means of attention to the conventions and history of language and literature – without reference to authorial intentions. The case of irony, for example, shows that in order to interpret a text as a complex utterance, one needs to identify the author's intention in presenting the text in a concrete context. For irony can obtain in texts bereft of conventional linguistic or literary markers. Moreover, the case of irony exemplifies a feature of utterances in general, namely: that utterances are connected to the utterer's intentions. Thus, it is not logically inappropriate to refer to authorial intentions in the process of interpreting the texts when they are construed, as they should be, as the utterances of historically situated individuals.

Of course, the anti-intentionalists are correct in arguing that an author cannot make a word sequence mean just anything by simply willing it. One cannot make the word "purple" mean "orange" merely by intending it to be so. Consequently, we cannot interpret "purple" in the text in question by noting that the author says he intended it to mean "orange."

However, sophisticated intentionalists need not be committed to the notion that a text means simply whatever its author intends. Rather, the sophisticated intentionalist only maintains that authorial intentions are relevant to the interpretation of the meaning of texts where the intended meaning of the text is compatible with and/or supportable by what the author has written in terms of the conventions and histories of language and literature.[4] Thus, where the conventional meanings available in the text are open to more than one interpretation, the intentionalist sides with the interpretation that accords with the author's intention (or our best hypotheses of authorial intent). And when and if there is only one interpretation of the text, the intentionalist presumes, as we do in ordinary conversation, that that mirrors the author's intention. (Of course, where it is discovered that the author had some meaning in mind that is utterly incompatible with and/or unsupportable by what is written, the intentionalist agrees that the author has failed to realize his or her intention in the text).

Though sophisticated intentionalists have the means to address the leading objections of anti-intentionalists, they are nevertheless not in complete agreement among themselves. They are divided into at least two camps: actual intentionalists and hypothetical intentionalists. Roughly, the actual intentionalists contend that the authorial intentions that are relevant to the interpretations of artworks are the actual intentions of the pertinent artists.[5] In contrast, hypothetical intentionalists claim that what is relevant for interpretation is merely our best-warranted hypotheses concerning the intentions of actual authors.

In this paper, I examine the debate between actual intentionalists and hypothetical intentionalists by taking a look at an extended case study: the comedy of Andy Kaufman. I argue that the best interpretation (the one that today most would agree is the correct interpretation) of one of the most important phases of Kaufman's career (his wrestling performances) can only be reached through actual intentionalism – and by ignoring what the hypothetical intentionalist argues are the special considerations of our interpretative practices with regard to literature, artworks, and the like. However, before explaining how Andy Kaufman represents an exemplary problem for hypothetical intentionalism, more needs to be said about what is involved in actual intentionalism, hypothetical intentionalism, and the dispute between them.

II. Actual Intentionalism

The variant of actual intentionalism that concerns me may be called "modest actual intentionalism." It should be understood to contrast with might be called "extreme actual intentionalism."[6] Extreme actual intentionalism is the view that actual authorial intentions fully determine the meaning and, therefore, the interpretation of artworks, such as literary texts. Extreme actual intentionalism is committed to the view that the text means what its author intends it to mean. Therefore, extreme actual intentionalism entails that if, by writing "purple" in the text, the author intends "orange," then "orange" is always what his inscription means.

The modest actual intentionalist avoids this counterintuitive commitment by denying that authorial intention fully determines meaning. Instead, authorial intentions are relevant to interpretation where the authorial intentions at issue are compatible with and/or supportable by what has been written – if we are speaking of literary texts – in accordance with the conventions and histories of language and literature. Where the author intends "orange" by writing "purple" and there is no ground for suspecting irony, the author fails in his intention instead of changing the meaning of his utterance of "purple." At the same time, where a text is open to several interpretations, the modest actual intentionalist argues that the correct interpretation is the one that takes the author's actual intention into consideration. Thus, while what is written constrains our interpretations, so authorial intention operates as a constraint on the interpretation of what has been written.

Modest actual intentionalism begins with the premise that, unless shown otherwise, we have no reason to suppose that our interpretation of artworks and literary texts differs in kind from our interpretation of everyday speaking and action. In everyday conversation, our interpretive goal is standardly to understand what our interlocutors intend to say. When, in a pacific tone of voice, we query, "What do you mean by that?" we are asking our interlocutor to clarify what he or she intends to say. The natural slide from "means" to "intends" here signals that our normal interpretive goal is to discover the meaning-intentions of other speakers. The modest actual intentionalist maintains that we have no grounds to presume that matters stand differently with respect to artworks and literary texts (though, as we shall see, this is perhaps the major bone of contention between modest actual intentionalists and hypothetical intentionalists).

According to the modest actual intentionalist, when we interpret an artwork or a literary text, we are attempting to discern the point the author intends, just as in a conversation we aim at determining what our informant intends/means to say. This, of course, does not entail that we ignore the relevant conventions, linguistic and otherwise, that obtain in the situation, but rather that we use them in order to interpret cospeakers.

The anti-intentionalist maintains that it is sufficient for the interpretation of artworks and literary texts that we attend to the pertinent linguistic and literary conventions, and that talk of authorial intentions is out of place. This intuition is strongly (though not decisively) encouraged if we take as our prototype of artistic interpretation (the interpretation of artworks) the words and sentences of literary texts. However, two things should be said here.

First, not all, and perhaps even not most, instances of artistic interpretation concern the meanings of words or sentences. Even if words and sentences in literature could be adequately interpreted solely in light of linguistic and literary conventions, much art is not linguistic and, therefore, lacks the kind of determinate meaning conventions that words and sentences might be thought to possess.

Dutch still lifes, for example, juxtapose commonplace objects, like articles of food and watches, in a single scene; the viewer must fill in the meaning of these juxtapositions interpretively. There is no conventional algorithm that will give us the meaning of these juxtapositions – that tells us in a rulelike fashion that the food stands for our appetitive nature and the watch symbolizes a call for moderation. Rather, the viewer needs to try to make sense out of these juxtapositions by speculating about what the painter intended to communicate by means of them.[7]

Knowledge of the history of iconography, of course, is relevant here. But interpretation in such a case, and in so many others, is not a matter of subsuming the items in a literally grammarless painting under meaning conventions, but rather of inferring the point of what the painter, in his historical context, intended to get across. Since so much of artistic interpretation is concerned with interpretation in circumstances where there are no determinate meaning conventions and disambiguating grammars, much artistic interpretation cannot be construed as merely tracking and applying conventions, but must be construed as something else – striving to recognize the intentions of artists in the way we try to locate the intentions of interlocutors in everyday speech. Thus, at the very least, the modest actual intentionalist seems to propose a more comprehensive model of our interpretive activities than does the anti-intentional conventionalist.[8]

Of course, anti-intentionalists not only fail to model comprehensively the interpretation of the nonliterary arts. They also lack a comprehensive model for literary interpretation. For a great deal of literary interpretation (maybe most?) concerns the meanings not merely of words and sentences but of larger literary structures, like recurring or echoing motifs, whose communicative structure is not governed by determinate, grammar-like or dictionary-like conventions or rules.

Consider the recurring, overlapping, and expanding motifs of cannibalism, of eating, and of being eaten in Melville's *Moby-Dick*.[9] There are no conventions or rules to tell us what these mean. Rather, we proceed by trying to figure out what Melville intended to say by means of these imagistic patterns. Thus, once again, the model of artistic interpretation that the anti-intentionalist advances is not even comprehensive for literature, even if it were always applicable to the interpretation of words and sentences. In this regard, modest actual intentionalism appears to be a superior account of artistic interpretation than anti-intentionalism, on the grounds that it is more comprehensive.

Second, there is also the question whether anti-intentionalism is even a comprehensive account of the way in which we interpret the words and sentences of literary texts. The problem of irony has already been mentioned. And similar issues arise over how to identify and interpret cases of allusion, since the attribution of an allusion will require, logically, that we have access to the author's knowledge stock (did the author really know the referent to which she is said to be alluding?) as well as to her ongoing artistic practice (is she the sort of artist for whom allusion is a likely option?).

In such cases, adverting to dictionary meanings and grammatical rules is not enough; one must go beyond the resources of the text and the pertinent linguistic and literary conventions and ask questions about the actual author – about what she knew or believed (or is likely to have known and believed) as well as what her inclinations, desires, and intentions were (or probably were). In order to interpret confidently many cases of irony and allusion, we need knowledge about who the author actually is, including knowledge about her mental states, including her intentions.

Moreover, the lessons illustrated by the cases of irony and allusion are applicable to the interpretation of literary words and sentences generally, since irony and allusion make evident that literary words and sentences are not just word sequences but utterances, and understanding utterances requires reference to authors and inferences about authorial or speaker's intentions. At this point, the anti-intentionalist may suggest that there is some special problem epistemologically about securing access to authorial intentions, since authorial intentions are nonobservable mental states. However, these reservations seem scarcely compelling, since in everyday life we are usually extremely successful in excavating the intentions behind the words and deeds of others.

With regard to linguistic and expressive behavior, we have little difficulty in inferring (typically accurately) the intentions of conspecifics. So why does the anti-intentionalist imagine that there should be some special difficulty with respect to artistic and literary behavior? If there is no problem with interpreting ordinary utterances by reference to speakers' intentions in everyday life, why fear that some unique difficulty erupts when it comes to the utterance meanings of literary works?

Interpreting literary texts or the historically situated point of nonlinguistic artworks – construed as utterances – involves us largely in inferring authorial intentions. Contra anti-intentionalism, this mobilizes information about the actual creator of the artwork in question – information about who he was, his culture, the genre he worked in, his oeuvre, and his ideological, religious, intellectual (etc.) convictions. The practice of artistic interpretation is, in great measure, a process of inference about the actual intentions of artists.

This, of course, is not to deny that the primary evidence for these inferences is generally the artwork itself. But as in ordinary conversation, when we closely scrutinize the artwork, we are doing so in order to uncover the best clues we have for authorial intent. We are reading, looking, and/or listening, guided by the aim of identifying the intentions of the creator of the artwork. Tracking authorial intent need not send us "outside" the artwork; typically, attending closely to the artwork is our best avenue for approaching authorial intent.

Nevertheless, since an artwork, such as a piece of literature, is not simply an abstract sequence of words but a particular, historically located utterance, our search for authorial intentions requires that we often supplement the reading of the text with information concerning the context of its production, including knowledge of who the author was, his historical circumstances, his entire oeuvre, and the genre in which he was working. Access to this information does not supplant our reading of the text, but gives us the background necessary to understand its semantic and structural choices – the choices that make it the particular utterance it is – contextually.

This is a point upon which both modest actual intentionalists and hypothetical intentionalists agree. Where they disagree is about the range of information about the artist that is interpretively permissible as well as about whether our legitimate access to actual authorial intention is *always* restricted to all and only well-warranted inferences.

III. Hypothetical intentionalism

For modest actual intentionalists and hypothetical intentionalists, the artwork is not an abstract concatenation of signs, symbols, and articulations whose meaning is decipherable solely in virtue of conventions. Each artwork is a situated, contextually concrete, and particular expression, the production of an individual artist with some point, and, therefore, best understood on the model of an utterance. But in order to understand an utterance, one requires a conception of the relevant historically located utterer.

A literary work, for example, is not simply a string of sentences; it is an organized whole, unified by a purpose, the source of which is the artist.[10] Thus, when we read, we read the text as a contextually situated utterance whose meaning must be connected to some definite speaker. We need to read this way in order to discover the specific point of the utterance in context. That is, literary works are concrete speech acts, not abstract word sequences, and, therefore, their meaning is, in part, relative to the speaker in question and his or her historical circumstances.

Modest actual intentionalists and hypothetical intentionalists share this starting point. They concur that, in treating artworks and literature as utterances, we are committed to essaying inferences about the actual author, including, notably, inferences about what she intended by her artwork. The inductive grounds for these inferences may include not only (though most importantly) the artwork itself but also public knowledge about the biography of the artist (her beliefs and experiences), historical knowledge about the conditions (both art-historical and social) in which the artwork was produced, knowledge about the genre to which the artwork belongs, and knowledge about other works by the same artist, up to and including knowledge of her entire oeuvre. From this, we form hypotheses about the actual intentions of the artist that both partially constitute and also further enable our interpretation of her concrete utterance contextually.

Because modest actual intentionalists and hypothetical intentionalists agree so extensively on the nature of interpretation, the two positions generally converge in their interpretations of artworks. However, the two positions are not equivalent, because, despite their broad consensus, they disagree over the range of "extratextual" information that is legitimately available to the interpreter, and, therefore, the two positions may, at times, render different interpretations.

The modest actual intentionalist allows the interpreter access to the private avowals of artists as found, say, in private notebooks, sketches, diaries, and interviews (both with the artist and his confidantes). According to the modest actual intentionalist, these may, when used cautiously, play a justifiable role in interpretation.

Contrariwise, the hypothetical intentionalist precludes invocations of authorial intention culled from such private sources, restricting the inductive grounds of interpretive inferences to authorial intention to the work itself, the author's publicly accessible biography, historical knowledge of the context in which the work was produced, the author's oeuvre, and the prevailing conventions of the genre of which the work is a member. For the hypothetical intentionalist, the best-warranted hypothesis indicated by these sources is the correct interpretation of the work, even if it diverges from the sincere assertions of authorial intention found in, for example, the artist's private papers, including his notes and letters about a specific work.

However, since the modest actual intentionalist allows access, albeit mindful, to private avowals of authorial intention, the modest actual intentionalist realizes that the best warranted hypothesis (concerning actual authorial intention as obtained by respecting the protocols of hypothetical intentionalism) may part company with the author's actual intention. And where this happens, if the author's actual intention is supportable by the artwork, the modest actual intentionalist will defend the interpretation consistent with the author's intention over the best-warranted inference derivable by the hypothetical intentionalist. For this is how we proceed in everyday interpretation, not only in our understanding of ordinary conversations but with respect to more formal discourse, like wills.

Though this difference between modest actual intentionalists and hypothetical intentionalists may not, in general, result in different interpretations, in certain circumstances it can. For example, as Paisley Livingston points out, we have evidence that Henry James intended *The Turn of the Screw* to be a ghost story.[11] That is what James said.[12] But, as is well known, there is also a popular interpretation of the novella that says that the story is purposefully ambiguous between being an example of a supernatural tale and being a psychological study of a disturbed governess who fantasizes the presence of ghosts.

Suppose that the latter interpretation is the best-warranted hypothesis available without consulting James's avowals about the story; then the hypothetical intentionalist will favor the ambiguity interpretation, whereas the modest actual intentionalist will favor the ghost interpretation.[13] Thus, though similar in many ways, modest actual intentionalism and hypothetical intentionalism are not the same, because in certain instances, they deliver different verdicts about the correct interpretation of given artworks.

Since modest actual intentionalists and hypothetical intentionalists agree that interpretive activity in large measure involves hypothesizing the actual intentions of authors, what accounts for their different attitudes toward the admissibility of private avowals of authorial intention? From the perspective of modest actual intentionalism, the hypothetical intentionalist seems satisfied with the warranted assertibility of the relevant authorial intentions, even where the truth about said intentions is accessible and diverges from the hypothetical intentionalist's best inference. But why settle for the warranted assertibility of an interpretation where the truth of the matter diverges from our best hypothesis and, in addition, is available to us? We do not usually prefer warranted assertibility over truth where the difference is evident to us.[14] So, why should this be so when it comes to the interpretation of artworks?

The hypothetical intentionalist's answer to this query is straightforward: the interpretation of artworks and literature is a different form of inquiry from other sorts, so talk about what we "usually prefer" in other domains of acquiring knowledge is not germane to this debate. Jerrold Levinson, perhaps the leading hypothetical intentionalist of the moment, writes, for example:

> [I]t is arguably one of the ground rules of the game of literary decipherment that literary works are not supposed to require authors to explain what they mean, and thus that direct authorial pronouncements of meaning can be set aside by the reader devoted to the central job of interpretation. The task of intuiting our way to an optimal construal of authorial intention for a text emerging from a rich author-specific public context is simply different from that of arriving at the truth about the author's intention with respect to a given text, from all the available evidence no matter what sort – diaristic, journalistic, electroencephalographic. Though as appreciators of literature we are entitled and expected to construe an author's offering against the background of the author's earlier work and the author's public identity as a writer, and in light of the author's explicit intentions for how a work is to be approached on the categorical plane (e.g., as a historical novel), we are, I think, implicitly enjoined from allowing an author's proclamations of meaning achieved to have an *evidential* role in the construction of a picture of what the author is most reasonably thought to have been trying to convey through that text offered in context.[15]

That is, according to Levinson, the language game of literary interpretation excludes interpretive reliance on direct avowals of authorial intention. It is true that our interpretive activities revolve around formulating the best hypotheses of authorial intent, but this is not the goal of the game; it is, again according to Levinson, merely a "heuristic."[16] What we are really after – when all is said and done – is the best-warranted hypothesis concerning authorial intention within the inductive parameters described by hypothetical intentionalism. This is what the interpretation game asks of audiences.

The interpretation game does not require or even permit reference to actual authorial intentions that are derived from nonpublic authorial pronouncements and that diverge from our best-warranted inferences à la hypothetical intentionalism. This constraint is, allegedly, in the service of the special interests of our interpretive institutions and practices. In this regard, hypothetical intentionalism, rather than modest actual intentionalism, putatively best reflects the special rules and purposes of the institution of literary interpretation narrowly and the institution of artistic interpretation more broadly.[17] Adherence to the rules of interpretive practice, then, is the hypothetical intentionalist's bottom line.

But does hypothetical intentionalism really better reflect our prevailing interpretive practices than modest actual intentionalism? What is the evidence?[18] It cannot be that hypothetical intentionalism, but not modest actual intentionalism, describes interpretation primarily as concerned with framing well-warranted hypotheses about actual authorial intentions, since both approaches endorse this description of interpretation. Nor can hypothetical intentionalism claim as evidence in its behalf that, in general, audiences are satisfied with interpretations arrived at inferentially through the avenues enumerated by hypothetical intentionalism. For in most cases audiences are so satisfied because they presume that our best hypotheses of this sort coincide with actual authorial intention.

That is, they are reading, listening, or viewing for actual intention, and their natural default assumption is that, unless other pertinent evidence surfaces on the horizon, our best hypotheses – based on the work, its genre, and the author's public biography and oeuvre – probably zero in on the author's actual intention. However, that audiences usually embrace this rather natural default assumption hardly entails that they would not revise it should evidence – such as contrary authorial avowals of intention – appear that is at variance with the default assumption. For a provisional default assumption, no matter how natural, does not constitute an unbreachable rule of our interpretive practices.

And yet, the hypothetical intentionalist claims that it is a steadfast rule of our interpretive practices – such as the literary language game – that we forswear resort to authorial avowals of intention. To the modest actual intentionalist, of course, this sounds like an instance of begging the question that elevates, through little more than confident assertion, hypothetical intentionalism as a deep rule that governs all our interpretive practices. Indeed, the modest actual intentionalist may ask why, if there is such a settled rule with respect to the institution of interpretation, there is nevertheless such a heated and protracted debate between modest actual intentionalism and hypothetical intentionalism.

After all, the participants in this debate are all competent interpreters. So, if there is a clear-cut rule here, then how can so many otherwise informed practitioners (i.e., the actual intentionalists) be so utterly unaware of its existence? What kind of *rule* escapes the notice of so many?

Needless to say, what might turn out to be the sheer ignorance of modest actual intentionalists about the rules of the interpretation game is not a conclusive argument against hypothetical intentionalism. However, inasmuch as the hypothetical intentionalist is invoking a supposed rule of our actual interpretive practices – a rule that allegedly says that reference to authorial intentions as evidence of interpretive correctness is *always* out-of-bounds – we are entitled to question whether such a rule does really seem to govern our interpretive practices.

And to adjudicate that question, it is fair to consider an illustrative counter-example that indicates that there is no ironclad rule here that, with regard to our actual interpretive practices, mandates that the best-warranted inference of authorial intent à la hypothetical intentionalism is, in fact, always to be preferred to the invocation of "private" authorial intentions. That is, if the hypothetical intentionalist is postulating a rule of our interpretive practices on the basis of a rational reconstruction of what we actually do, then it pays to consider empirical case studies.

IV. The case of Andy Kaufman

The release of Milos Forman's film *Man on the Moon* (1999) has rekindled a great deal of interest in the work and career of the late comic Andy Kaufman (1949–84).[19] Kaufman, who called himself a "song-and-dance man" rather than a "comic," was perhaps best known for his role as Latka Gravas on the television series *Taxi*. Kaufman also often appeared on *Saturday Night Live* and other variety formats, such as *Fridays;* was a frequent guest on Carson and Letterman; played the comedy-club circuit, the college circuit, and night clubs; and made two ill-fated feature motion pictures. He was particularly respected by other comics, including, notably, Robin Williams, Lily Tomlin, Steve Martin, and Michael Richards.

One of Kaufman's recurrent strategies was to make the audience think that they were witnessing a truly awful performance by an inept comic, only to reveal, on the turn of a dime, that they were in the hands of a master.

For example, he would begin a series of seemingly incompetent imitations of Nixon and Archie Bunker in a "foreign" accent so thick and so ill-timed that the audience would begin to become embarrassed for the performer: they had never seen anything so wretched. Then he would announce, still in character, that he was about to do an impersonation of Elvis Presley; the groans would be audible. But the imitation of Presley would be so gloriously on the money that the audience would not only be overwhelmed by its precision but also come to realize that they had been had by the earlier parts of the performance. The incompetence had been staged by a performer who could imitate anything – including an execrable stand-up routine. Laughter and applause would greet Kaufman's exit from the stage, not only for a perfectly observed rendition of the King but also in appreciation of the "practical joke" Kaufman had played on the audience.

Similarly, in his first performance on *Saturday Night Live*, Kaufman appeared nervous and fidgety. Silence loomed for what seemed an inordinate amount of time. It appeared that Kaufman either had forgotten his routine or was too frozen with fear to begin it. Then he fiddled with the record player beside him. It blared out the theme song from the old TV show *Mighty Mouse*. This garnered some titters, part nostalgia, part camp. But still the performer seemed lost – until we heard the refrain "Here I come to save the day," which Kaufman lip-synched with such perfection and bravura, transforming himself, in a single beat, from a vulnerable schlemiel to a matinee idol, that the audience exploded in laughter.

In both of these performances, and many others, Kaufman was exploring the boundary between theater and reality by first convincing (or nearly convincing) the audience that they really might be watching the most pathetic attempt at comedy ever, and then revealing that it was all an act. In this way, Kaufman's concerns correlated with those of contemporary performance artists – except that Kaufman was practicing his version of deconstruction on mainstream television far away from the lofts of Soho. Kaufman's use of pastiche and his preferred pop-culture iconography – especially the imagery of fifties' TV and music – also aligned Kaufman's sensibility with that of emerging postmodern performance art. But in some ways, Kaufman's investigation of the line between theater and reality was more effective than that of performance artists because, due to his adagio pacing, he often got people to believe or at least to take seriously the proposition that they were actually watching disasters of such embarrassing proportions that they would squirm in their seats. Kaufman would not begin these performances with a "wink" – or any other marker of comic framing that might cue the audience – and he unflinchingly stayed in his inept character for so long that viewers would start to worry that something was wrong, until he turned the tables.

Kaufman provoked a fight on the set of *Fridays* that left the newspapers speculating that it was real, while also developing a character, named Tony Clifton, who was the epitome of the crude, rude, conceited lounge singer. Clifton appeared in a number of shows, but Kaufman himself would deny that he was Tony Clifton, as would "Tony Clifton" when he (Clifton) was interviewed, though it became known eventually that Clifton and Kaufman were one (Clifton perhaps being the dark doppelgänger of Kaufman's Latka Gravas character, a naif of saccharine innocence). Through inventions like these, Kaufman was able to satirize the conventions of popular performance while also interrogating their conditions of credibility and the unwritten terms of the audience/performer contract.

Perhaps Kaufman's most ambitious experiment along these lines was his wrestling career. It began with his challenging women from the audiences at comedy clubs and colleges to come on stage and wrestle with him. And Kaufman and his wrestling partners really grappled – at least in the sense that they tried to pin each other. Kaufman brought this act to television, where he stoked the audiences' passions by making inflammatory, derogatory remarks about women and their abilities that would outrage both feminists and Daughters of the American Revolution. These wrestling matches were not popular, eventually getting Kaufman voted off *Saturday Night Live*, but he persisted.

Not able to find a home for his "Intergender Wrestling Championship" at Madison Square Garden, he traveled south to Memphis to challenge women.

Here he ran into Jerry Lawler, a professional wrestler and beloved figure on the scene. Lawler taunted Kaufman into meeting him in the ring. Before their bout, Kaufman made a series of highly insulting videos of Lawler, Memphis, and the South in general. Claiming that he was from Hollywood and had brains, Kaufman demeaned the intelligence and cleanliness of Southerners. At the time of the scheduled bout, the population of Memphis crowded into the amphitheater, screaming for Kaufman's head. Jerry Lawler complied, dealing Kaufman a series of pile drivers that resulted in Kaufman's removal from the ring on a stretcher.

Yet the debacle did not end there. Kaufman and Lawler appeared on the Letterman show, ostensibly to reconcile, but instead Lawler decked Kaufman, and Kaufman retaliated by throwing hot coffee at Lawler. Various rematches, grudge fights, and shouting exchanges ensued, often before cameras. Kaufman seemed out of control, gripped by an incomprehensible, obsessional fantasy that he really was a professional wrestler. His popularity suffered, but he persevered. The whole spectacle looked like a sorry mess, a descent into madness. After Kaufman's death, the 1989 "documentary" *I'm from Hollywood*, written and directed by Joe Orr and Lynne Margulies (Kaufman's former lover), reviewed the entire episode, leaving the strong impression that the affair was nothing short of pathological. Robin Williams and Tony D'Anza say as much on the videotape, and there is nothing else in the program to contradict them.

However, recently, several of Kaufman's close associates, including Bob Zmuda and Jerry Lawler, have come forward to bear testimony about Kaufman's actual intentions concerning what we might call his "wrestling project." As a result of this insider information, we can now say that, though the women Kaufman wrestled were genuinely committed to defeating him (and he them), thereby making that aspect of the project authentic, most of the rest of it (the matches with Lawler, the Letterman show, and possibly even *I'm from Hollywood*) was pure theater. The wrestling project was an opportunity for Kaufman to explore, reflexively and often parodically, the features of professional wrestling that fascinated him, such as the fact that, though "everyone knows" that professional wrestling is fake (theatrical), it is nevertheless able to move fans emotionally to the point of screaming seriously for blood. Through his wrestling conceit, Kaufman discovered a vantage position from which to survey, albeit comically, some of the rhetorical levers that make the engine of professional wrestling run.

It makes a big difference whether one watches tapes of Kaufman's wrestling career under the influence of the madness interpretation or the reflexivity interpretation. When I first saw Lawler smash Kaufman into the mat, it saddened and sickened me. Unaware of Kaufman's true intentions, Lawler struck me as a bully meting out excessive punishment to a weakling – admittedly an obnoxious weakling, but still a weakling, and probably a crazed one. It seemed wrong to crush such a demented wimp so mercilessly, though, of course, the wimp himself too bore some of the responsibility for the sordid event. How, one wondered, could anyone have allowed this situation to spiral as uncontrollably as this? Decency, it seemed to me, bade us to avert our eyes from the whole absurd, unhappy predicament in favor of remembering Kaufman's better days as a performer.

However, once apprized by insiders of Kaufman's actual intentions, I no longer avert my eyes. I pay close attention to Kaufman's stylistic choices and savor their comic resonances – his outlandish costume, for example, composed of thermal underwear and swimming trunks, and his "natural" fright wig, recalling some silent clown. Rather than turn away, I reflect on his brazen, subversive foregrounding of some of the deepest conventions of professional wrestling. Posing himself as the villain (what is called a Tar Heel), by extravagantly belittling women and the South, against the hero ("good guy") Jerry Lawler, Kaufman bared the données of professional wrestling by deploying them hyperbolically. Each one of Kaufman's choices, including his gestures and behavior ringside, once grasped with the comic-reflexive distance Kaufman intended (at least for his coterie), appears as an insight, telegraphed through exaggeration, into the practice of professional wrestling. Thus, like a work of what is often called high art, Kaufman's wrestling project and parts thereof sustain and reward repeated viewing and contemplation.

By now the relevance of Kaufman's wrestling project to the debate between modest actual intentionalism and hypothetical intentionalism should be evident. Without insider information with regard to private avowals of Kaufman's actual intentions, the madness interpretation is the best-warranted hypothesis concerning Kaufman's wrestling career. This is so because Kaufman planned it that way. He controlled the information about what he was doing and even planted disinformation about it so the interpretation that would most recommend itself to appropriately backgrounded viewers (those fully informed of all the contextually relevant information surrounding the wrestling project *except for* information about private avowals of authorial intent) would be the madness interpretation. That is, the madness interpretation is the one that the hypothetical intentionalist would proffer for acceptance.

On the other hand, if we are modest actual intentionalists, we may help ourselves to the insider information about Kaufman's authorial intentions, and this will incline us far more in the direction of the reflexivity interpretation.

But which interpretation is correct? The madness interpretation or the reflexivity interpretation? Without begging the question in this debate, I think we can say this much: the reflexivity interpretation is now at least the canonical interpretation of Kaufman's wrestling project.

Moreover, if the reflexivity interpretation is the canonical interpretation here, that may tell us something about the debate between hypothetical intentionalism and actual intentionalism. It may tell us this much: our interpretive practices have no rules that prohibit us from using insider information about private avowals of authorial intention in determining the outcome of our interpretive quandaries.

The hypothetical intentionalist primarily rests his case against weak forms of intentionalism on the claim that, given the nature of our interpretive practices, we *always* prefer well-warranted (à la hypothetical intentionalism) hypotheses about authorial intent over private avowals of authorial intent. This is a rule of the language game of interpretation. This premise of hypothetical intentionalism is, however, undermined if at least sometimes it is evident that in our actual interpretive practices we go with private avowals of authorial intent that are at odds with our otherwise best-warranted hypotheses about authorial intent. Furthermore, the example of Andy Kaufman's wrestling project, inasmuch as the reflexivity interpretation is presently canonical, shows that our actual interpretive practices are open to incorporating avowals of authorial intention in acceptable interpretations. There is no such rule as the one hypothetical intentionalists invoke against modest actual intentionalism. Andy Kaufman represents one counterexample to the hypothetical intentionalist's putative rule, though there are others.[20]

The hypothetical intentionalist may make the fair observation that usually artists will abide by the standard communicative conventions of their art forms just because this will enhance the probability that they will be understood, and that typically artists have an interest in being understood. Artists behave in this way because they presume that the audience expects them abide by said conventions. Thus, it is advisable – inasmuch as the artist desires uptake – for the artist to play within the conventions. But however *advisable*, there is no necessity here. An artist may eschew conventional approaches. The risk is his, and it is up to him whether he takes it or not.[21]

A poet may decide to proceed in a manner that is not usual, because his agenda diverges from the norm. And the results may fascinate readers so much that they will avail themselves of whatever resources they can locate, including private avowals of authorial intention, even if discovered in unpublished notebooks or through confidences bestowed by the artist on acquaintances.[22] This surely describes our actual interpretive practices better than the supposed rule recommended by the hypothetical intentionalist. And, with respect to comedic performance, something like this is the best description of what has happened with regard to Andy Kaufman's wrestling project.

Andy Kaufman's wrestling project, involving the comic-reflexive exploration of the nexus of theater, reality, and emotion, was an unusual one – one that for full effectiveness required that he draw spectators into his subterfuge (much in the way that an experimental psychologist misdirects his subjects). Because his aims were unusual, he broke, or at least waived, the so-called rules, denying his audience a knowing "wink." We may marvel that he was willing to risk so much in terms of popularity by continuing his wrestling project, though we probably would not think it quite so strange if he were categorized as an avant-gardist or conceptual artist addressing a small inner circle. And, in any case, we do not know how Kaufman would have continued the project had he lived. Perhaps somewhere down the line there might have been a "wink," and then everyone would have "gotten it." But what remains of the project is curious and intriguing enough that we want to understand it interpretively. And to do so, we take advantage of the kinds of information about authorial intention that the hypothetical intentionalist rules "out of bounds." We do so because, in fact, there are no rules here. Only fascination with Kaufman and his art drives our interpretive enterprise.

V. Hypothetical intentionalism again: the second round

The hypothetical intentionalist maintains that his position respects an implicit rule of the language game of interpretation that modest actual intentionalism forgets. Supposedly that rule enjoins us to refrain from relying on private avowals of authorial intention when interpreting artworks, literature, and the like. The modest actual intentionalist responds that if there is such an implicit rule, then we would expect it to be reflected in our actual interpretive practices. But this does not appear to be the case. Elsewhere I have cited a number of reasons to question the existence of the hypothetical intentionalist's alleged rule.[23] Herein I have dwelt at length on the case of Andy Kaufman. However, insofar as the hypothetical intentionalist primarily advances the superiority of his view over that of modest actual intentionalism in virtue of the existence of this putative universal prohibition, one counterexample should suffice.

But, of course, it is hard to imagine that the hypothetical intentionalist will take this objection lying down. So let us spend some time proleptically speculating on how he might attempt to deal with the case of Andy Kaufman. Supposing that the hypothetical intentionalist agrees that the reflexivity interpretation is the canonical interpretation of Kaufman's wrestling project, he may argue that this is perfectly consistent with the terms of hypothetical intentionalism. So, can the hypothetical intentionalist take the reflexivity interpretation on board, and, if so, how?

First, for example, he might contend that the relevant insider information about Kaufman's intentions really is public. After all, it is now obtainable in published biographies. But, of course, it was not publicly accessible knowledge at the time of the wrestling matches. The madness interpretation was the best hypothesis back then. So what will the hypothetical intentionalist do here? Go relativist – claiming that the madness interpretation is the best-warranted interpretation relative to one time period and the reflexivity interpretation for another?

Furthermore, if the hypothetical intentionalist regards private avowals of authorial intention (and confidential information thereof) to be public simply so long as it is published, one wonders whether there is an issue of principle here, since the boundary between private avowals and public ones will become so unstable. One would have thought that diaries stand as the epitome of the sort of private avowals that the hypothetical intentionalist aspires to bracket. But diaries can be published. Does that make them public? Does the publication of a diary suddenly make the authorial intentions legitimately available for interpretation, whereas just previously they had been "out of bounds"? That seems arbitrary. Publication seems too slender a criterion to support the kind of distinction between *private* and *public* the hypothetical intentionalist desires. It makes it just too easy to move private authorial pronouncements into the public realm.

Or consider the case of a critic who goes into the archive, uncovers an author's private-meaning intentions, and incorporates them into an interpretation that is then published. Are we to say that the critic's interpretation is illegitimate from the perspective of hypothetical intentionalism (since he adverts to unpublished authorial avowals), though references to the author's intentions by readers of the critic's article are acceptable, since said intentions have been published in the critic's very own essay? But that is certainly paradoxical.[24]

Another line of response that the hypothetical intentionalist may raise with respect to Andy Kaufman is to remind us of a distinction he draws between categorical and semantic intentions. Semantic intentions concern the meaning of an utterance and parts thereof, while categorical intentions pertain to the genre or class to which the utterance belongs. Hypothetical intentionalists allow reference to private avowals of authorial intentions when it is a matter of fixing the category of the work, but disallow it with respect to authorial semantic intentions. In this light, the hypothetical intentionalist might claim that the intentions of Kaufman that concern us are categorical ones and, therefore, no threat to the hypothetical intentionalist position.

There are several problems with this tack. First, it is not clear what category Kaufman's wrestling career falls into. Whatever it is, it is pretty unprecedented. But the hypothetical intentionalist can say that it is irrelevant whether there is a preexisting category here, since what a categorical intention amounts to is the author's conception of how the work is to be approached. But the case of Kaufman complicates this tidy formula. It prompts us to ask, "Intended to be approached *by whom*?" The general audience or insiders? Clearly, if we are talking about the approach available to the general audience, as one supposes the hypothetical intentionalist would be, then the authorial intention was that the events be approached as typical wrestling matches and typical talk shows. But wouldn't that make the madness hypothesis more probable than the reflexivity interpretation?

Moreover, it is questionable whether the distinction between categorical intentions and semantic intentions, and the hypothetical intentionalist's divergent attitudes toward them, are genuinely defensible. What justifies the different attitudes? If it is merely the assertion that such difference in attitudes is one of the rules of the interpretation game, then that seems to beg the question.

Furthermore, categorical intentions and semantic intentions do not always seem to be distinct. Suppose the hypothetical intentionalist claims that the category to which Kaufman's wrestling project belongs is that of irony. Isn't irony typically treated as a semantic intention in debates about intentionalism? And, in any event, even if Kaufman had the categorical intention that the whole project be ironic, he also had the semantic intention that his various inflammatory remarks about women and the South be exaggerations of the competitive, confrontational braggadocio of professional wrestling. These semantic intentions must be taken to be relevant if the reflexivity interpretation is to be found comprehensive. Without them, the hypothetical intentionalist cannot fully embrace the reflexivity interpretation.

Finally, the hypothetical intentionalist may point out that, on his view, aesthetic considerations can enter into the determination of an interpretation. Where two epistemically well-warranted interpretations are in balance but one makes the work in question aesthetically better, the hypothetical intentionalist argues that the aesthetically more enhancing one is better. Why this should be so, the hypothetical intentionalist never says. But applied to the case of Andy Kaufman, the principle might work this way: given the madness interpretation and the reflexivity interpretation, the latter makes the work aesthetically better. Therefore the reflexivity interpretation is to be preferred.

Epistemically, it might be said that the reflexivity interpretation fits smoothly with other parts of Kaufman's oeuvre. Like his imitations, the wrestling project puts his audience in a quandary about the real status of what they are seeing. The only difference is that the wrestling project never broke frame – never let the viewers in on the gag – though the imitation routines did. Moreover, once one adopts the reflexivity hypothesis, it does a very comprehensive job of explaining the wrestling project. That is, the work supports the interpretation. So, inasmuch as the reflexivity interpretation can be motivated epistemically by the hypothetical intentionalist, he can invoke aesthetic considerations to argue in its behalf against the madness interpretation.

The modest actual intentionalist, of course, counts as significant the correspondence of the wrestling project with other parts of Kaufman's oeuvre, while also regarding it as imperative that the work support the reflexivity interpretation. And yet we question whether, using simply the resources of hypothetical intentionalism, this is enough to ground the reflexivity interpretation. For if we really believe that the madness hypothesis is compelling at all, then there is something morally and intellectually wrong with favoring the reflexivity interpretation solely on aesthetic grounds.

That is, if there are real grounds for regarding the wrestling project as pathological, then it seems morally callous and cruel toward the previously mentally disabled, now late Andy Kaufman, and dishonest to ourselves, to pretend that it is a brilliant feat of reflexivity. Nor do I think that most interpreters would feel comfortable doing so if they held reasonable suspicions that the work was really some kind of psychotic fugue or schizophrenic rampage. It would be like making believe the helpless spasms of a madman constituted jitterbugging.

We would, as I said earlier, prefer to turn away from the whole sorry mess. The only way to overcome this reluctance and to opt for the reflexivity interpretation is to satisfy ourselves about Kaufman's actual intentions, which, of course, are only available through the kind of insider information that hypothetical intentionalism precludes.[25]

For related reasons, the hypothetical intentionalist cannot absorb insider information about Kaufman's intentions by regarding that information as merely suggestive of an interpretation rather than as evidence for an interpretation, because, as I have argued, unless we are really satisfied (unless we take the insider information to be *evidentially sound*), we will not feel disposed to approach the wrestling project from an aesthetic or an artistic point of view. Perhaps we will agree that it is worthy of a medical or psychiatric interpretation/diagnosis. But that will not be stated in terms of reflexivity.

Thus, hypothetical intentionalism cannot – in comparison with modest actual intentionalism – lay equal claim to the reflexivity interpretation of Andy Kaufman's wrestling project. So, if the reflexivity interpretation is canonical in this case, hypothetical intentionalism does not afford an adequate model of the interpretive practices that gave rise to it.

VI. Conclusion

This paper has been narrowly concerned with the debate between modest actual intentionalism and hypothetical intentionalism. These two approaches share many points of tangency. Both, for example, conceive of interpretation as, in large measure, occupied with searching for the best-warranted hypotheses of authorial intent. However, they disagree about the range of data that may be consulted in the process of constructing these hypotheses. Specifically, the modest actual intentionalist permits information about the authorial intention to play a role in interpretation even if that information hails from insider or private sources. The hypothetical intentionalist rejects usage of such information about authorial intention, arguing that this would violate an implicit rule of our interpretive practices.

In order to assess the hypothetical intentionalist's argument against modest actual intentionalism, I have taken a long look at the comedy of Andy Kaufman. If the hypothetical intentionalist is correct about the implicit rules of our interpretive practices, then we would expect interpreters uniformly to abstain from relying upon insider information about Kaufman's intentions. Therefore, insofar as this appears unlikely, modest actual intentionalism is not endangered by the hypothetical intentionalist's invocation of his implicit rules of interpretation. If the hypothetical intentionalist wishes to argue that interpreters should not rely on Kaufman's avowals of intent, then he needs to do more than merely assert the existence of a prohibition.[26]

Notes

1 Examples of actual intentionalists' arguments include E. D. Hirsch, *Validity in Interpretation* (New Haven: Yale University Press, 1967); E. D. Hirsch, *The Aims of Interpretation* (Chicago: University of Chicago Press, 1976); Gary Iseminger, "An Intentional Demonstration," in Gary Iseminger (ed.), *Intention and Interpretation* (Philadelphia: Temple University Press, 1992); Gary Iseminger, "Actual Intentionalism vs. Hypothetical Intentionalism," *Journal of Aesthetics and Art Criticism* 54 (1996); Gary Iseminger, "Interpretive Relevance, Contradiction and Compatibility with the Text," *Journal of Aesthetics and Art Criticism* 56 (1998); Noël Carroll, "Art, Intention, and Conversation," in Iseminger (ed.), *Intention and Interpretation*; Noël Carroll, "Anglo-American Aesthetics and Contemporary Criticism," *Journal of Aesthetics and Art Criticism* 51 (1993); Noël Carroll, "The Intentional Fallacy: Defending Myself," *Journal of Aesthetics and Art Criticism* 55 (1997); Noël Carroll, "Interpretation and Intention: The Debate between Hypothetical and Actual Intentionalism," *Metaphilosophy* 31 (2000); Paisley Livingston, "Intentionalism in Aesthetics," *New Literary History* 29 (1998); William Irwin, *Intentionalist Interpretation: A Philosophical Explanation and Defense* (Westport, CT: Greenwood, 2000). The hypothetical intentionalist who will concern us in this essay is Jerrold Levinson; his position is set forth in "Intention and Interpretation in Literature," in *The Pleasures of Aesthetics* (Ithaca, NY: Cornell University Press, 1996).

2 Statements of anti-intentionalism can be found in W. K. Wimsatt and Monroe C. Beardsley, "The Intentional Fallacy," in *The Verbal Icon* (Lexington: University of Kentucky Press, 1954); Monroe C. Beardsley, *Aesthetics* (Indianapolis: Hackett, 1981); Monroe C. Beardsley, *The Possibility of Criticism* (Detroit: Wayne State University Press, 1970); Monroe C. Beardsley, "Intentions and Interpretations: A Fallacy Revived," in Michael Wreen and Donald Callen (eds.), *The Aesthetic Point of View* (Ithaca, NY: Cornell University Press, 1982); George Dickie and W. Kent Wilson, "The Intentional Fallacy: Defending Beardsley," *Journal of Aesthetics and Art Criticism* 53 (1995).

3 An overview of the debates about artistic meaning and intention can be found in Robert Stecker's *Artworks: Definition, Meaning, Value* (University Park, PA: Penn State University Press, 1997).

4 This version of actual intentionalism is suggested by E. D. Hirsch, who says: "Verbal meaning is whatever someone has willed to convey by a particular sequence of linguistic signs *and* which can be conveyed (shared) by means of

those signs" (*Validity in Interpretation*, 31, emphasis added). See also Irwin, *Intentionalist Interpretation*, 4. Above, I say "compatible with and/or *supportable by*" in order to accommodate the case of irony.

5   In my own writings, I have tried to characterize this notion of relevance by saying that our best hypotheses about the author's actual intentions should constrain our interpretive activities. In his "Can Novel Critical Interpretations Create Art Objects Distinct from Themselves?" in Michael Krausz (ed.), *Is There a Single Right Interpretation?* (University Park, PA: Penn State University Press, 2002), 181–208., Philip Percival, however, alleges that my contention that, given our conversational interests, hypotheses about actual authorial intention should constrain our interpretations is muddled. His argument is that it does not follow from my demonstration that aesthetic interests do not trump our conversational interests that conversational interests trump other values we might seek in interpretations. Percival's observation is true, but I never claimed the entailment he suggests. I only claimed that conversational interests constrain other interests. Nor does Percival bother to consider the sorts of reasons that I advance in favor of the constraint – some of which are ethical reasons, including mutual respect and self-integrity.

Another muddle that Percival attributes to me is this: if we have conversational interests in artworks, why should that stop the critic from introducing his own original line of thought? Percival notes: "He [the critic] might be so bold as to suppose he has something to say through the canvas of *The Potato Eaters* more interesting than what Van Gogh had to say."

This example is woefully underdescribed. Is it that the critic utterly disregards Van Gogh's intentions here, or does he work with them? If he works with them, then doesn't that satisfy my notion of constraint? But if what the critic says is completely irrelevant to Van Gogh's intentions, would we still consider the concept of a conversation to be applicable?

Moreover, if a critic uses an artwork to make his own point, in the way that a preacher in a sermon uses some news item as a parable of faith, why call that an interpretation rather than, as some say, an application?

6   Extreme actual intentionalism is represented in Steven Knapp and Walter Benn Michaels, "Against Theory," *Critical Inquiry* 8 (1982); Steven Knapp and Walter Benn Michaels, "Against Theory 2: Hermeneutics and Deconstruction," *Critical Inquiry* 14 (1987).

7   This example comes from Carolyn Korsmeyer, *Making Sense of Taste: Food and Philosophy* (Ithaca, NY: Cornell University Press, 1999), 162.

8   One anti-intentionalist, Kent Wilson, has suggested that where there are no determinate meaning conventions of the sort found in language, we should not speak of interpreting the meaning of artworks at all. But this seems to be a very *ad hoc* way of settling the debate over intentionalism, since that debate has always been thought to be relevant to the interpretation of artworks in general. Standardly, nonlinguistic artworks are thought to possess meaning (e.g., montage in film and television). From the perspective of the philosophy of art, stipulatively to restrict the notion of meaning to linguistic matters not only seems arbitrary but, as well, fails to take seriously our interpretive practices. One does not explain the phenomenon by denying its existence. This is to give up the philosophical project of

discovering the presiding conditions of possibility of our interpretive practices. Thus, Wilson's suggestion not only involves exiting the debate but also implies that Wilson himself, by effectively attempting to regiment our actual interpretive practices unrealistically, shirks the philosophical responsibility of reconstructing them. To declare, by fiat, that all nonlinguistic artworks lack meaning because they are not linguistic appears at root to beg the question. See W. Kent Wilson, "Confession of a Weak Anti-Intentionalist: Exposing Myself," *Journal of Aesthetics and Art Criticism* 55 (1997).

9   The example comes again from Korsmeyer, *Making Sense of Taste*, 194–200.

10 Even the apparent strings of sentences explored by surrealists are not merely strings of sentences; their seeming randomness is purposively driven by the desire to make a philosophical point.

11 Livingston, "Intentionalism in Aesthetics," 841–4.

12 It is true that James indicated this intention in the preface to *The Turn of the Screw* and that the hypothetical intentionalist might claim that publication of this authorial avowal renders it public rather than private and grants the hypothetical intentionalist legitimate access to it. On the one hand, it seems to me rather arbitrary to attempt to draw the line between admissible authorial avowals and inadmissible ones this way; suppose that James's preface was accidentally lost by the printer and never published in the text, surfacing only much later in James's private papers. Would that change the meaning of the text?

On the other hand, for purposes of explicating the difference between modest actual intentionalism and hypothetical intentionalism, let us just imagine that James never published the preface. It would still be the case that the modest actual intentionalist would be willing to weigh James's explicit intentions, once discovered, in this case, whereas the hypothetical intentionalist would not.

13 It is not strained to conjecture that the hypothetical intentionalist might think that the ambiguity interpretation is the best-warranted hypothesis on his grounds, since, where an inference is well supported epistemically, the hypothetical intentionalist allows to come into play aesthetic considerations concerning which rival interpretation makes the relevant work better aesthetically. Thus, if the hypothetical intentionalist takes the ambiguity interpretation to be well warranted and also believes it makes *The Turn of the Screw* aesthetically better (more interesting) than the ghost interpretation, he will favor the ambiguity interpretation. See Levinson, "Intention and Interpretation in Literature," 179.

14 This observation is pursued at greater length in Carroll, "Interpretation and Intention," 82–4.

15 Levinson, "Intention and Interpretation in Literature," 208. Moreover, Levinson's invocation of a literary language game in this quotation is not a wayward aside. He also adverts to this language game on pp. 177, 178, 184, 194, 196, and 198, generally to iterate the point made above.

16 Ibid., 200.

17 Though the title of Levinson's article refers to literature and though he speaks of the special interests of literature, his hypothetical intentionalism can be taken to apply across the arts, since he discusses not only examples from literature but ones from music and film as well.

18   It should be noted that the interpretative-language-game argument is not the only objection that the hypothetical intentionalist may raise against actual intentionalism. Another may be that in countenancing authorial pronouncements of authorial intention, the actual intentionalist is unable to acknowledge and to account for failures of authorial intention – cases where the author fails to realize his or her intention in the text.

But this does not seem to be an apt objection to modest actual intentionalism, since, for interpretive correctness, modest actual intentionalism requires that the authorial intentions we take seriously for hermeneutical purposes square with the text. Thus, the modest actual intentionalist explains cases of failed authorial intention in terms of the distance between the author's avowed intention and what we find in the text or artwork. Unlike the extreme actual intentionalist, the modest actual intentionalist does not accept authorial pronouncements as always and exclusively decisive, but can admit and explain cases of failed intention. That is, failed intentions are not impossible within the purview of modest actual intentionalism.

Furthermore, because the preceding argument seems more appropriately aimed at extreme actual intentionalism rather than at modest actual intentionalism, in what follows I will concentrate primarily upon challenging the interpretive-language-game objection rehearsed above.

However, before leaving this issue, another point must be broached. Perhaps the hypothetical intentionalist has in mind this objection: the actual intentionalist has no way of accounting for the meaning of a text where the actual authorial intention fails.

Suppose that the author's intended meaning does not correspond with what is written on the page. Does this entail that the modest actual intentionalist must say that what the author has written is meaningless, despite the fact that it is written in plain and intelligible English?

The modest actual intentionalist, however, is not driven to this counterintuitive conclusion. For the modest actual intentionalist here does acknowledge that there is such a thing as utterance meaning. In the case envisioned, the passage of writing in question has utterance meaning. Nevertheless, it does not follow from the likelihood that we will acknowledge that such a passage possesses utterance meaning that it is only utterance meaning that we ever do or should seek in literary texts. Where texts do possess authorial meaning, we do pursue it, and the literary institution, as I will argue, appears to license this as permissible. Moreover, as argued above, the search for authorial meaning is, by default, our operating assumption. Settling for utterance meaning is, I contend, a secondary and not altogether satisfying result.

Nor does it follow from the fact that sometimes we may just have to do with utterance meaning that utterance meaning is always what we are or should be after. The maxim that underwrites such a conclusion could not be generalized to other forms of life.

19   At least two biographies have appeared recently: Bill Zehme, *Lost in the Funhouse: The Life and Mind of Andy Kaufman* (New York: Delacorte Press, 1999); Bob Zmuda (with Matthew Scott Hansen), *Andy Kaufman Revealed!* (Boston: Little, Brown & Co., 1999). Scholarly comment on Andy Kaufman's

work includes Philip Auslander, *Presence and Resistance: Postmodernism and Cultural Politics in Contemporary American Performance* (Ann Arbor: University of Michigan Press, 1992), chs. 7 and esp. 8.

20   Other cases are discussed in Carroll, "Interpretation and Intention," 87–94. In that article, I also point out that many feminist literary critics, taken pretheoretically as exemplars of our actual interpretive practices, very frequently employ biographical information, including avowals of authorial intention, derived from "nonpublic" sources. Is one to suppose that feminist critics are ignorant of the rules of the game in this regard? But one would have thought that the practice of these feminist critics is, in part, constitutive of our interpretive practices and their implicit rules. In his *Intentionalist Interpretation*, 27, William Irwin also cites tendencies in feminist criticism that favor actual intentionalism. He mentions, as an example, Paula Bennett's *My Life a Loaded Gun: Female Creativity and Feminist Poetics* (Boston: Beacon Press, 1986).

21   The same point is made by William Irwin in *Intentionalist Interpretation*, 57, 59.

22   The above is offered merely as an argument against one of the central premises of hypothetical intentionalism's case against modest actual intentionalism. It is intended to show that, since sometimes interpreters will quite naturally heed private avowals of authorial intention, there cannot be an implicit rule governing our interpretive practices to the contrary. This argument does not show that authorial intentions always constrain our interpretations. In order to reach that conclusion, one must take into consideration the conversational and ethical issues discussed in Carroll, "Art, Intention, and Conversation," and Irwin, *Intentionalist Interpretation*.

23   Carroll, "Interpretation and Intention."

24   In "Intention and Interpretation in Literature," Jerrold Levinson, a hypothetical intentionalist, offers an interpretation of Kafka's "Country Doctor." He notes that the substance of this interpretation derives from Walter Sokel's *Franz Kafka* (New York: Columbia University Press, 1966). Part of that "substance" includes references concerning Kafka's beliefs about writing. Interestingly, Sokel's information about Kafka's beliefs come from Kafka's personal documents, including his diaries and letters. How is it that the hypothetical intentionalist allows access to private avowals of belief, but not intentions? The question should be especially vexing, since a leading component of intention is belief. The distinction the hypothetical intentionalist is striving to sustain here seems remarkably thin, and perhaps porous. See Levinson, "Intention and Interpretation in Literature," 185; Sokel, *Franz Kafka*, 3–8.

25   Nor is it open to the hypothetical intentionalist to say that he can base his attribution of the reflexivity interpretation on the supposition that Kaufman's intentions were likely to have been the same as other comics working in this genre, since there were no other comics like Kaufman (though some other comics did appreciate what he was doing) and there is not (yet) a genre hereabouts.

26   Although this article uses the concept of utterance meaning, I have come to be suspicious of the idea. For my present thinking, see Noël Carroll (2011) "Art Interpretation" in *The British Journal of Aesthetics* 51(2), 117–135.

Index

Minerva's Night Out: Philosophy, Pop Culture, and Moving Pictures, First Edition. Noël Carroll.
© 2013 Blackwell Publishing Ltd. Published 2013 by Blackwell Publishing Ltd.